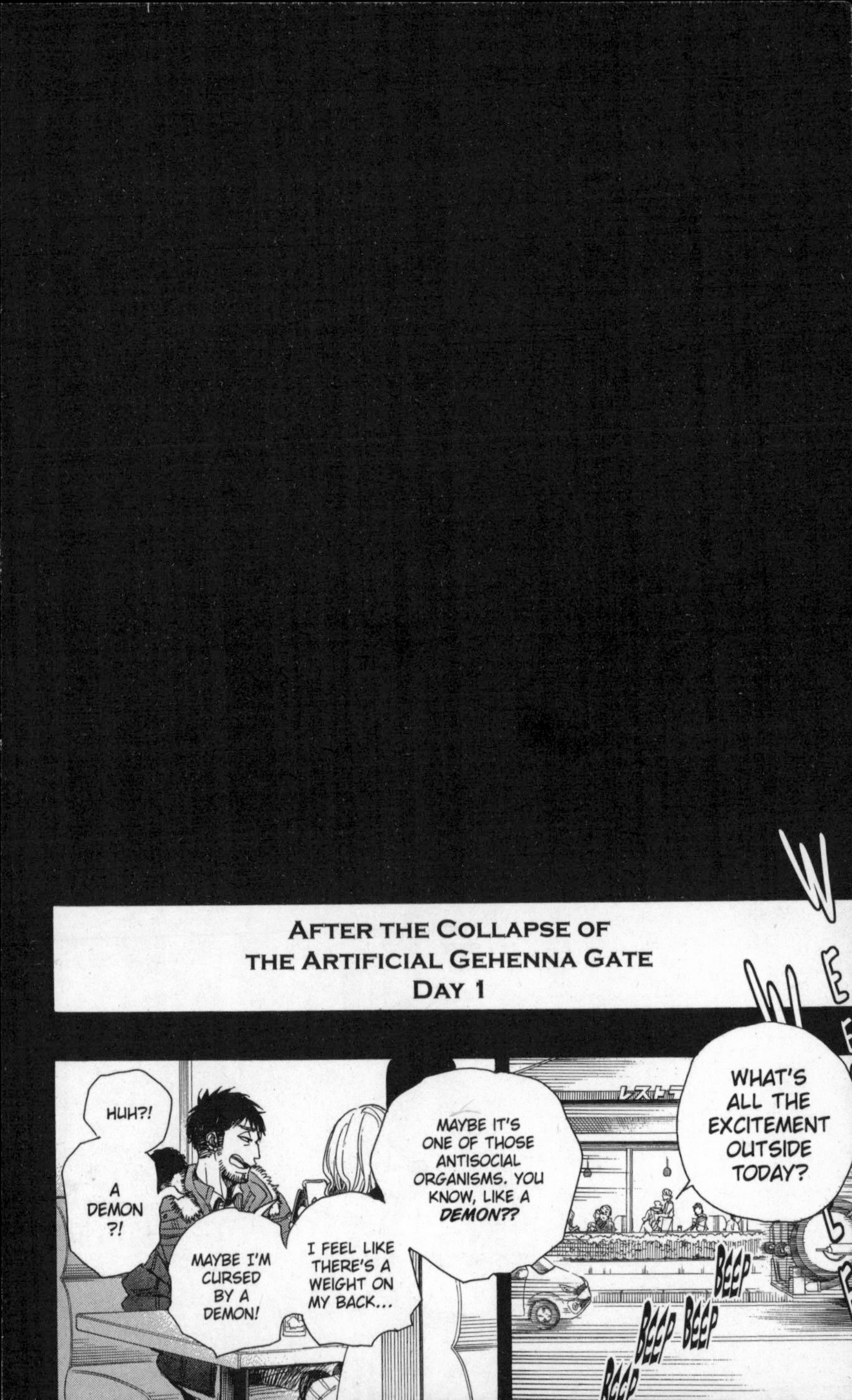
AFTER THE COLLAPSE OF THE ARTIFICIAL GEHENNA GATE DAY 1
WHAT'S ALL THE EXCITEMENT OUTSIDE TODAY?
BEEP BEEP BEEP BEEP
MAYBE IT'S ONE OF THOSE ANTISOCIAL ORGANISMS. YOU KNOW, LIKE A *DEMON??*
HUH?!
A DEMON ?!
I FEEL LIKE THERE'S A WEIGHT ON MY BACK...
MAYBE I'M CURSED BY A DEMON!

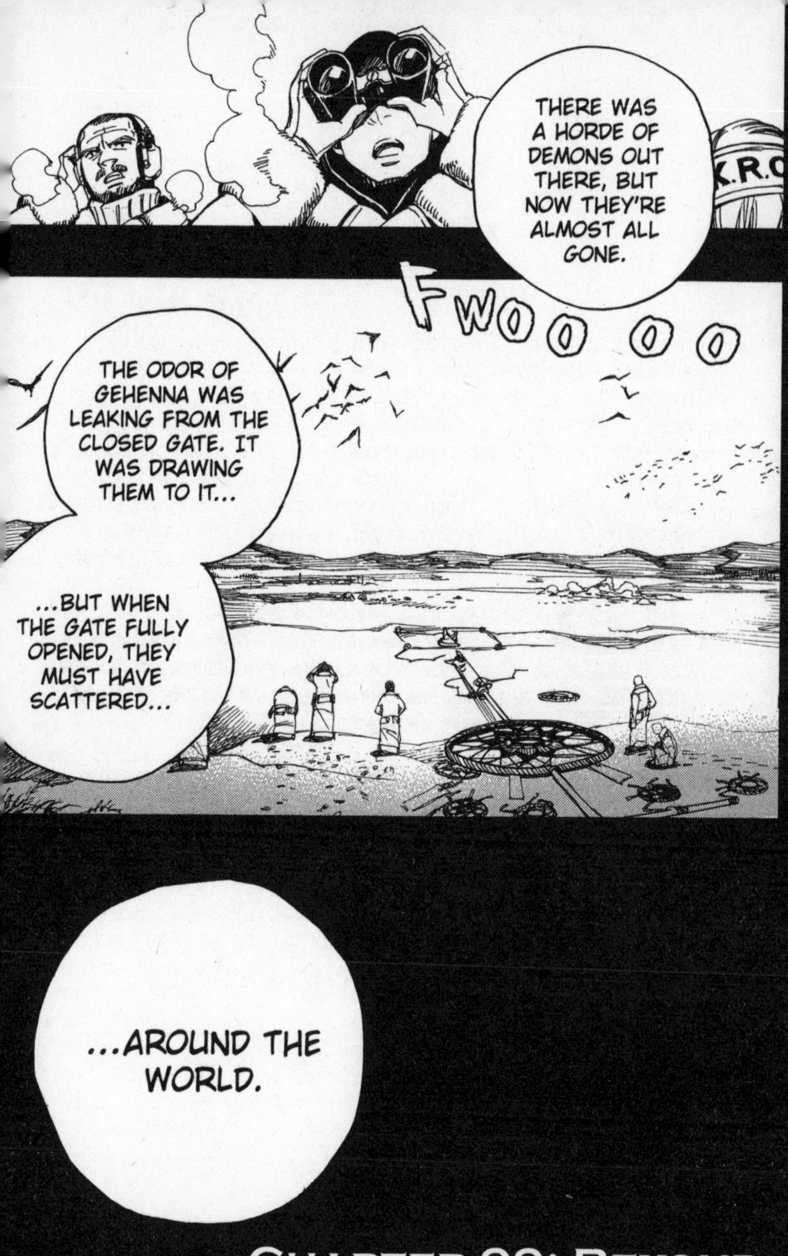
K.R.O
THERE WAS A HORDE OF DEMONS OUT THERE, BUT NOW THEY'RE ALMOST ALL GONE.
FWOOOOO
THE ODOR OF GEHENNA WAS LEAKING FROM THE CLOSED GATE. IT WAS DRAWING THEM TO IT...
...BUT WHEN THE GATE FULLY OPENED, THEY MUST HAVE SCATTERED...
...AROUND THE WORLD.

Chapter 99: Beyond the Snow, Part 8

◉ THE STORY SO FAR ◉

UNKNOWN TO RIN OKUMURA, BOTH HUMAN AND DEMON BLOOD RUNS IN HIS VEINS. IN AN ARGUMENT WITH HIS FOSTER FATHER, FATHER FUJIMOTO, RIN LEARNS THAT SATAN IS HIS TRUE FATHER. SATAN SUDDENLY APPEARS AND TRIES TO DRAG RIN DOWN TO GEHENNA BECAUSE RIN HAS INHERITED HIS POWER. FATHER FUJIMOTO FIGHTS TO DEFEND RIN, BUT DIES IN THE PROCESS. RIN DECIDES TO BECOME AN EXORCIST SO HE CAN SOMEDAY DEFEAT SATAN AND BEGINS STUDYING AT THE EXORCISM CRAM SCHOOL UNDER THE INSTRUCTION OF HIS TWIN BROTHER YUKIO, WHO IS ALREADY AN EXORCIST.

RIN AND THE OTHERS SUCCEED IN DEFEATING THE IMPURE KING, AWAKENED BY THE FORMER EXORCIST, TODO. MEANWHILE, YUKIO FIGHTS TODO, AND AS THE BATTLE RAGES, HE SENSES THE SAME FLAME IN HIS OWN EYES AS HIS BROTHER. AFRAID, HE KEEPS IT A SECRET.

LATER, MYSTERIOUS EVENTS BEGIN OCCURRING AROUND THE GLOBE ORCHESTRATED BY A SECRET SOCIETY KNOWN AS THE ILLUMINATI. FINALLY, THE JAPANESE GOVERNMENT PUBLICLY RECOGNIZES THE EXISTENCE OF DEMONS.

WANTING TO LEARN MORE ABOUT THE FLAME OF SATAN IN HIS LEFT EYE, YUKIO GOES TO CONFRONT MEPHISTO. HOWEVER, AFTER AN ATTEMPT ON MEPHISTO'S LIFE, THE ORDER ARRESTS YUKIO AS A SUSPECT. RIN GOES TO BREAK YUKIO OUT OF CONFINEMENT, BUT YUKIO TELLS HIM GOODBYE. RIN ATTACKS IN A RAGE, BUT THE KOMA SWORD BREAKS WHEN HE STRIKES, CAUSING RIN'S FLAME TO BLAZE OUT OF CONTROL. SHIEMI MANAGES TO BRING RIN BACK TO HIMSELF. REALIZING HE NEEDS TO LEARN THE TRUTH ABOUT HIS AND HIS BROTHER'S BIRTH, RIN CONFRONTS MEPHISTO AND DEMANDS THE TRUTH...

BLUE EXORCIST

OSCEOLA REDARM

Another Arch Knight, he is an inspector at the Mexico Branch. He arrests Lightning for assaulting K.R.C. Laboratory Director Drac Dragulescu.

DRAC DRAGULESCU

An Arch Knight at the Romania Branch, director of K.R.C. Laboratory and former director of Section 13. Lightning has accused him of being connected to the Illuminati.

LUCIFER

Commander-in-chief of the Illuminati. Known as the King of Light, he is the highest power in Gehenna. He plans to resurrect Satan and merge Assiah and Gehenna into one.

SHIRO FUJIMOTO

The man who raised Rin and Yukio. He held the rank of Paladin, but Satan possessed him and he gave his life defending Rin. There is a possibility that he was a clone of Azazel created by Section 13.

YURI EGIN

Rin and Yukio's mother. She conceived with Satan and died soon after giving birth. The Knights of the True Cross Keep all information about her classified.

KURO

A Cat Sidhe who was once Shiro's familiar. After Shiro's death, he began turning back into a demon. Rin saved him, and now the two are practically inseparable. His favorite drink is the catnip wine Shiro used to make.

KONEKOMARU MIWA

He was once a pupil of Suguro's father and is now Suguro's friend. He's an Exwire who hopes to become an Exorcist someday. He is small in size and has a quiet and composed personality.

IZUMO KAMIKI

An Exwire with the blood of shrine maidens. She has the ability to become a Tamer and can summon two white foxes. The Illuminati had taken her captive, but with help from Rin and the others, she escaped and settled her grudge against the insane professor Gedoin.

NORIKO PAKU

An old friend of Kamiki. The two girls joined the Exorcism Cram School together, but Paku dropped out when she couldn't keep up. Now she takes classes in the general curriculum at True Cross Academy Private High School.

SHURA KIRIGAKURE

A Senior Exorcist First Class who holds the titles of Knight, Tamer, Doctor and Aria. Rin and Yukio helped free her from a contract entered by her ancestor.

MEPHISTO PHELES

President of True Cross Academy and head of the Exorcism Cram School. He was Father Fujimoto's friend, and now he is Rin and Yukio's guardian. The number two power in Gehenna and known as Samael, King of Time.

LEWIN LIGHT

An Arch Knight, he is Arthur's right-hand man as well as number two in the Order. An expert in Arias and summoning, he goes by the nickname "Lightning." He is performing an independent investigation into the Illuminati.

CAST OF CHARACTERS

RIN OKUMURA

Born of a human mother and Satan, the God of Demons, Rin Okumura has powers he can barely control. After Satan kills Father Fujimoto, Rin's foster father, Rin decides to become an Exorcist so he can someday defeat Satan. Now a first-year student at True Cross Academy and an Exwire at the Exorcism Cram School, he hopes to someday become a Knight. When Yukio broke his Koma Sword, the power of Satan swallowed him, but Shiemi called him back to himself.

YUKIO OKUMURA

Rin's brother. Hoping to become a doctor, he's a genius who is the youngest student ever to become an instructor at the Exorcism Cram School. However, the flame of Satan lies in his left eye. He has begun to question the righteousness of the Knights of the True Cross and has gone to meet the Illuminati.

SHIEMI MORIYAMA

Daughter of the owner of Futsumaya, an Exorcist supply shop. She possesses the ability to become a Tamer and can summon a baby Greenman named Nee. She decided to quit the Exorcism Cram School, but she hasn't revealed the reason why.

RYUJI SUGURO

Heir to the venerable Buddhist sect known as Myodha in Kyoto. He wants to achieve the titles of Dragoon and Aria. He is Lightning's apprentice and they are conducting an investigation together.

RENZO SHIMA

Once a pupil of Suguro's father and now Suguro's friend. Currently, he is a double agent providing information to both the Illuminati and the Knights of the True Cross.

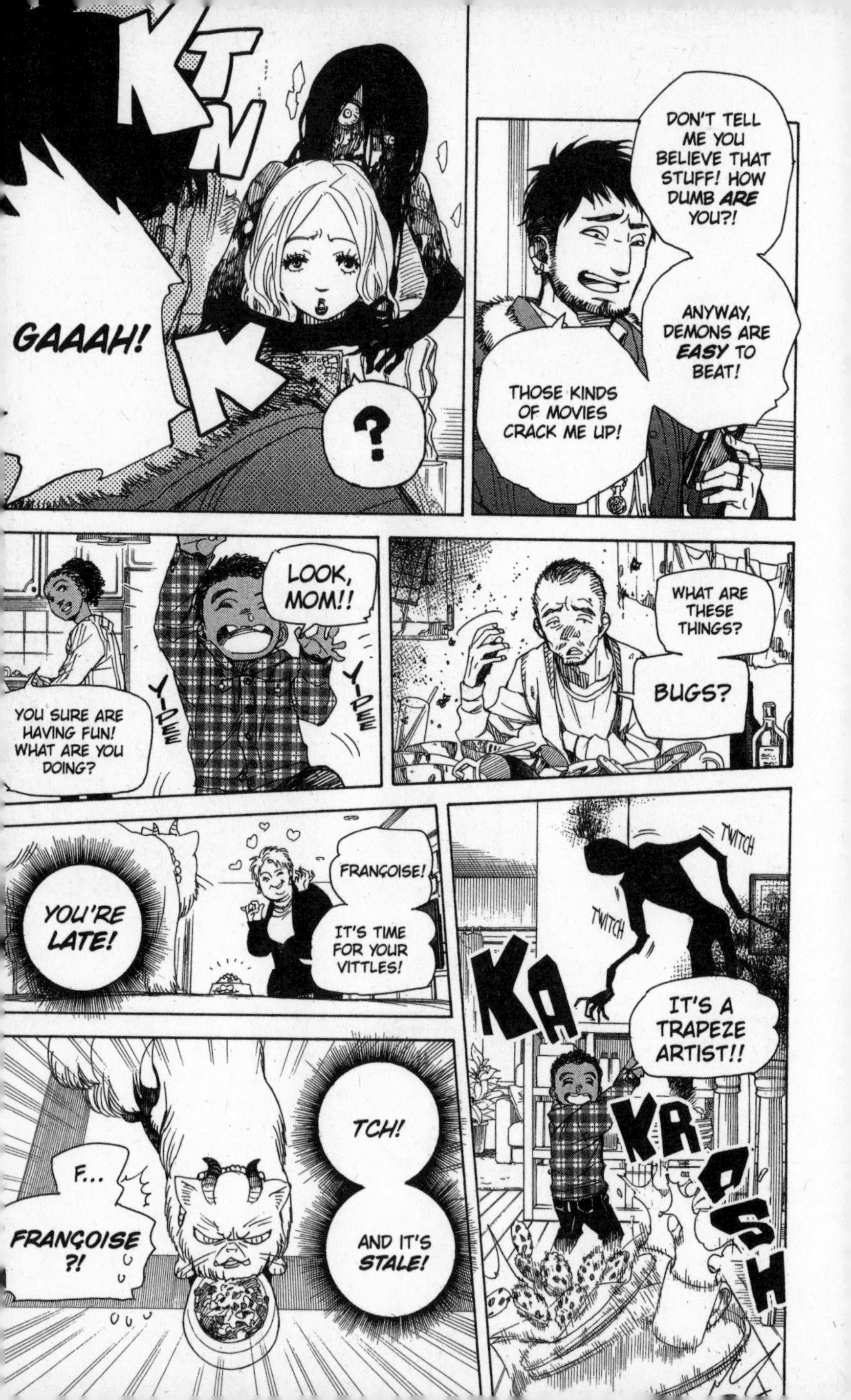
DON'T TELL ME YOU BELIEVE THAT STUFF! HOW DUMB **ARE** YOU?!
ANYWAY, DEMONS ARE **EASY** TO BEAT!
THOSE KINDS OF MOVIES CRACK ME UP!
KTN
GAAAH!
K
?
WHAT ARE THESE THINGS?
BUGS?
LOOK, MOM!!
YIPEE
YIPEE
YOU SURE ARE HAVING FUN! WHAT ARE YOU DOING?
TWITCH
TWITCH
KA
IT'S A TRAPEZE ARTIST!!
KRASH
FRANÇOISE!
IT'S TIME FOR YOUR VITTLES!
YOU'RE LATE!
TCH!
AND IT'S *STALE!*
F...
FRANÇOISE ?!

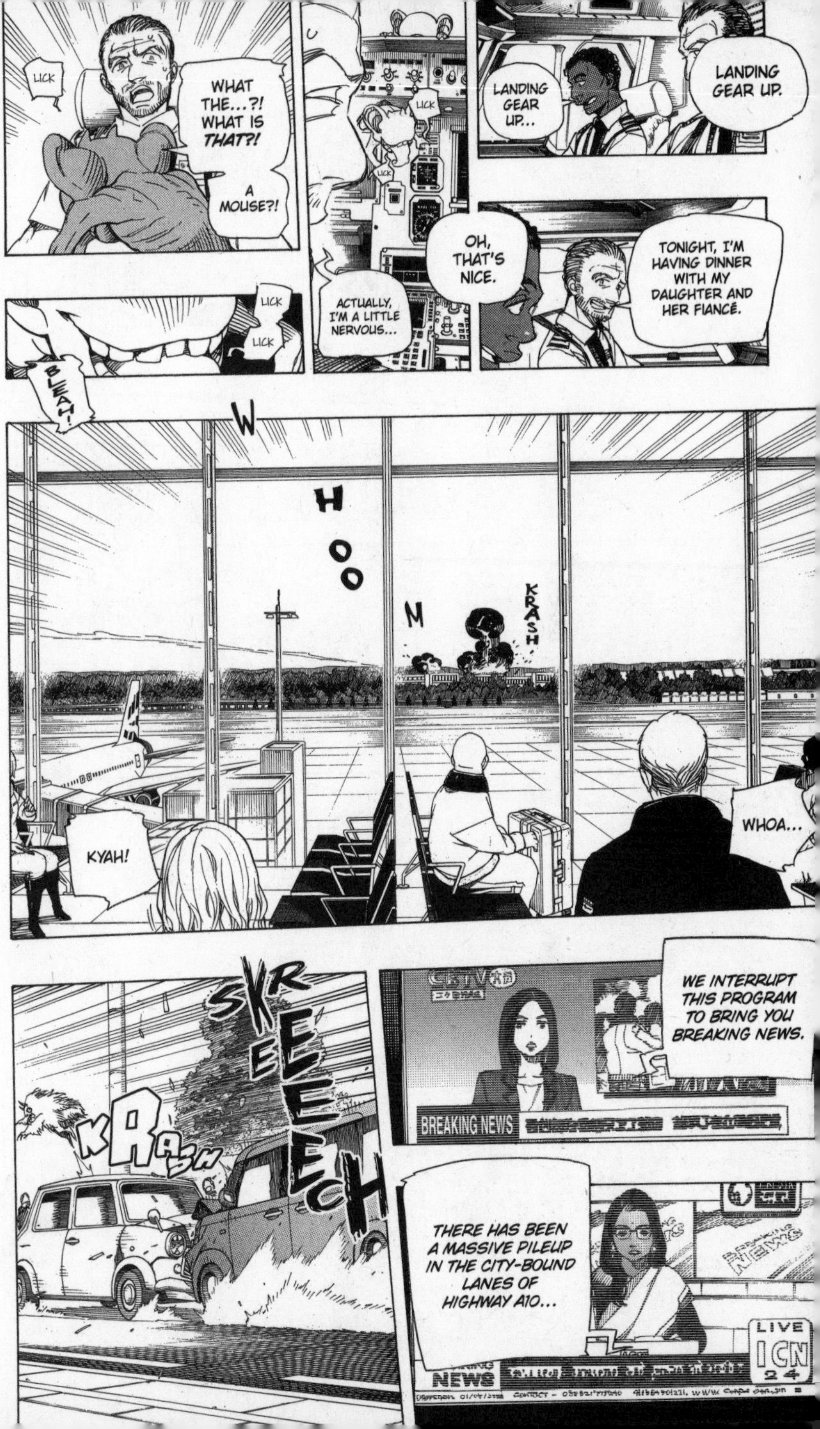

LANDING GEAR UP.
LANDING GEAR UP...
TONIGHT, I'M HAVING DINNER WITH MY DAUGHTER AND HER FIANCÉ.
OH, THAT'S NICE.
LICK
LICK
ACTUALLY, I'M A LITTLE NERVOUS...
LICK
WHAT THE...?! WHAT IS *THAT?!*
A MOUSE?!
LICK
LICK
BLEAH!
WHOOM
KRASH
WHOA...
KYAH!
BREAKING NEWS
WE INTERRUPT THIS PROGRAM TO BRING YOU BREAKING NEWS.
THERE HAS BEEN A MASSIVE PILEUP IN THE CITY-BOUND LANES OF HIGHWAY A10...
NEWS
LIVE
ICN 24
SKREEEEECH
KRASH

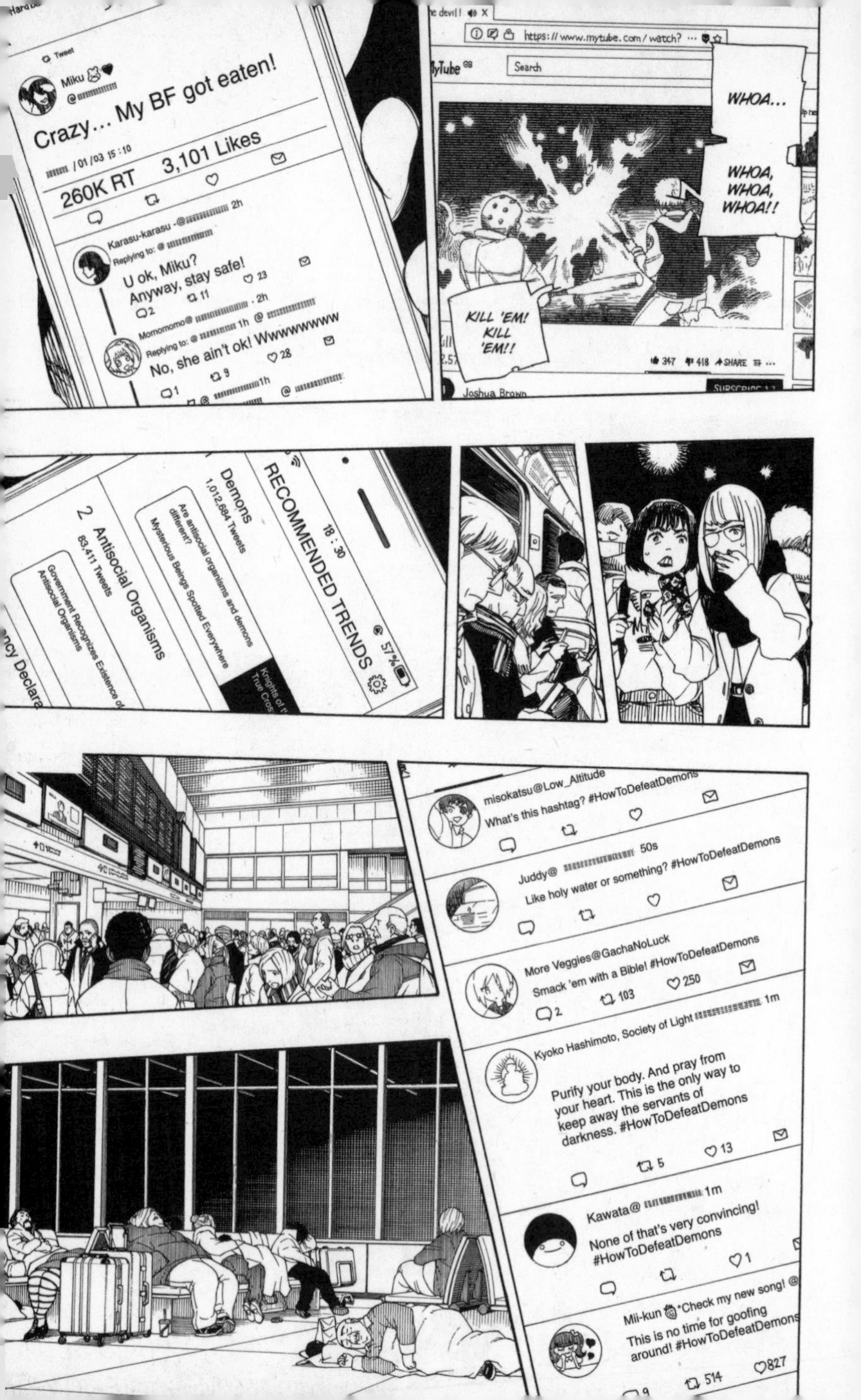

https://www.mytube.com/watch?
MyTube
Search
WHOA...
WHOA, WHOA, WHOA!!
KILL 'EM! KILL 'EM!!
347
418
SHARE
Joshua Brown
Tweet
Miku
Crazy... My BF got eaten!
/01/03 15:10
260K RT
3,101 Likes
Karasu-karasu
2h
Replying to: @
U ok, Miku?
Anyway, stay safe!
2
11
23
Momomomo@
1h
2h
Replying to: @
No, she ain't ok! Wwwwwww
9
28
1
1h
18 : 30
57%
RECOMMENDED TRENDS
Demons
1,012,684 Tweets
Are antisocial organisms and demons different?
Mysterious Beings Spotted Everywhere
2
Antisocial Organisms
83,411 Tweets
Government Recognizes Existence of Antisocial Organisms
misokatsu@Low_Altitude
What's this hashtag? #HowToDefeatDemons
Judy@
50s
Like holy water or something? #HowToDefeatDemons
More Veggies@GachaNoLuck
Smack 'em with a Bible! #HowToDefeatDemons
2
103
250
Kyoko Hashimoto, Society of Light
1m
Purify your body. And pray from your heart. This is the only way to keep away the servants of darkness. #HowToDefeatDemons
5
13
Kawata@
1m
None of that's very convincing! #HowToDefeatDemons
1
Mii-kun *Check my new song!
This is no time for goofing around! #HowToDefeatDemons
9
514
827

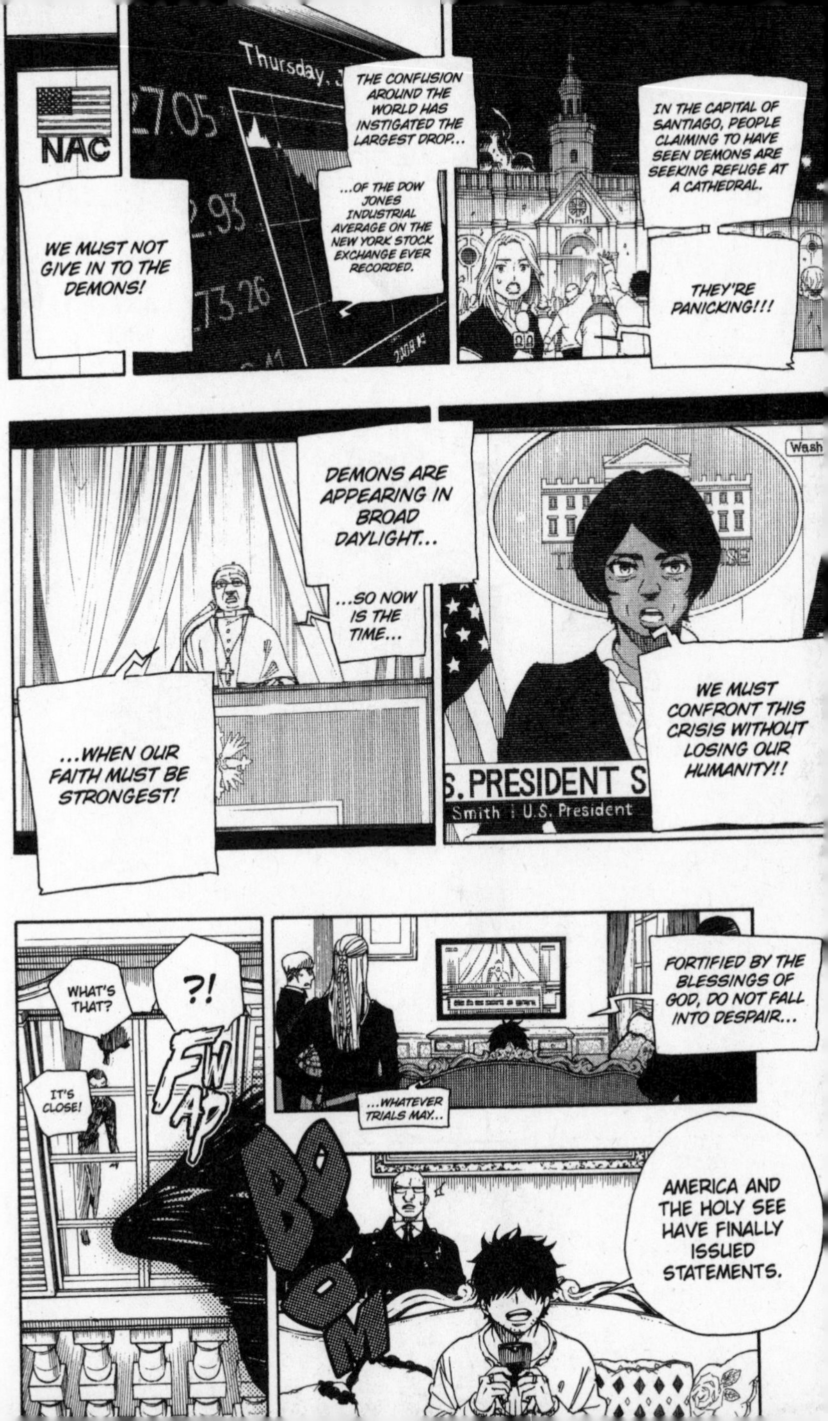
IN THE CAPITAL OF SANTIAGO, PEOPLE CLAIMING TO HAVE SEEN DEMONS ARE SEEKING REFUGE AT A CATHEDRAL.
THEY'RE PANICKING!!!
Thursday, J
THE CONFUSION AROUND THE WORLD HAS INSTIGATED THE LARGEST DROP...
...OF THE DOW JONES INDUSTRIAL AVERAGE ON THE NEW YORK STOCK EXCHANGE EVER RECORDED.
NAC
WE MUST NOT GIVE IN TO THE DEMONS!
Wash
WE MUST CONFRONT THIS CRISIS WITHOUT LOSING OUR HUMANITY!!
S. PRESIDENT S
Smith | U.S. President
DEMONS ARE APPEARING IN BROAD DAYLIGHT...
...SO NOW IS THE TIME...
...WHEN OUR FAITH MUST BE STRONGEST!
FORTIFIED BY THE BLESSINGS OF GOD, DO NOT FALL INTO DESPAIR...
...WHATEVER TRIALS MAY...
AMERICA AND THE HOLY SEE HAVE FINALLY ISSUED STATEMENTS.
?!
WHAT'S THAT?
IT'S CLOSE!
FWAP
BOOM

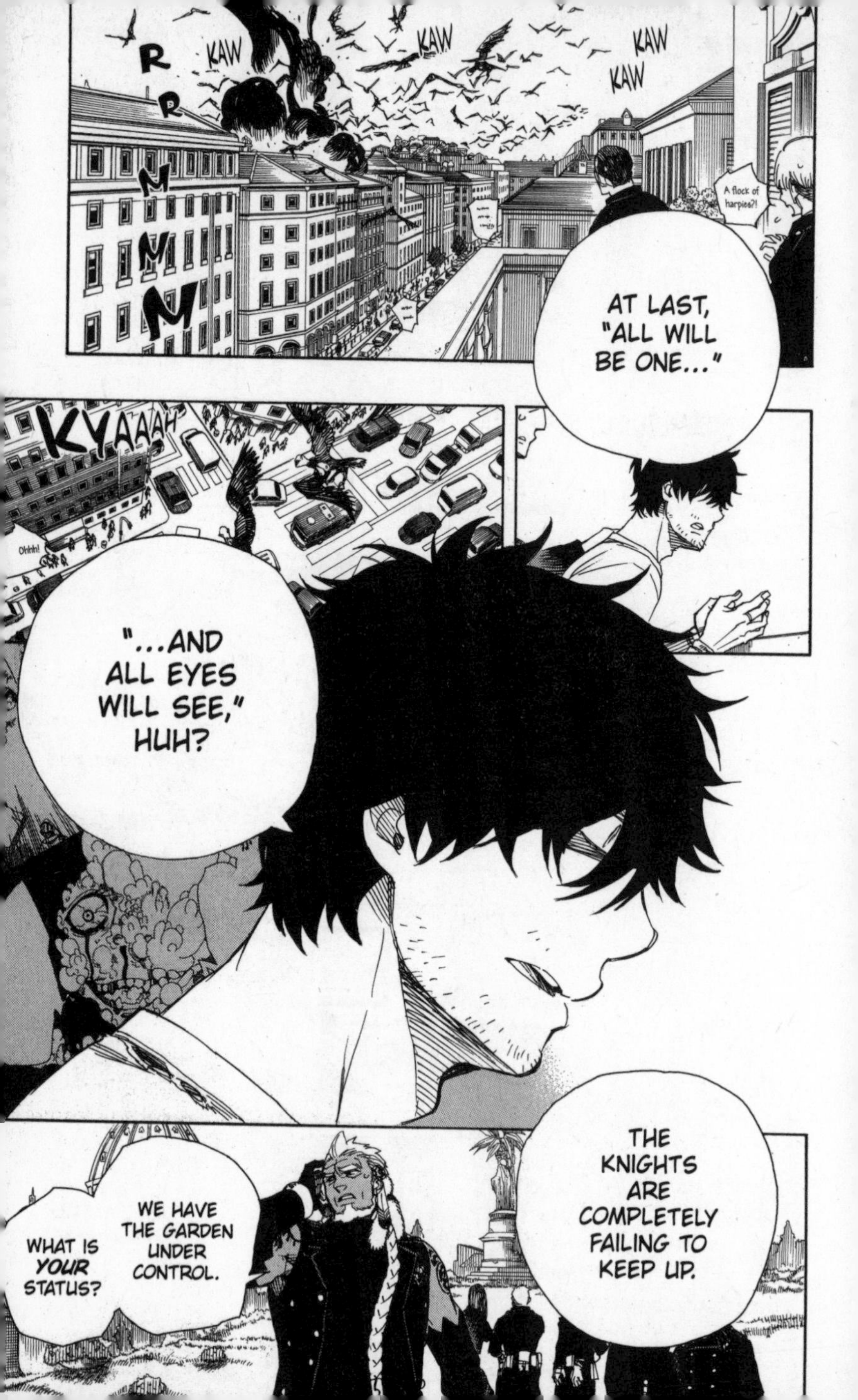
KAW
KAW
A flock of harpies?!
KAW
KAW
RRMMM
AT LAST, "ALL WILL BE ONE..."
KYAAAH
Ohhh!
"...AND ALL EYES WILL SEE," HUH?
THE KNIGHTS ARE COMPLETELY FAILING TO KEEP UP.
WE HAVE THE GARDEN UNDER CONTROL.
WHAT IS *YOUR* STATUS?

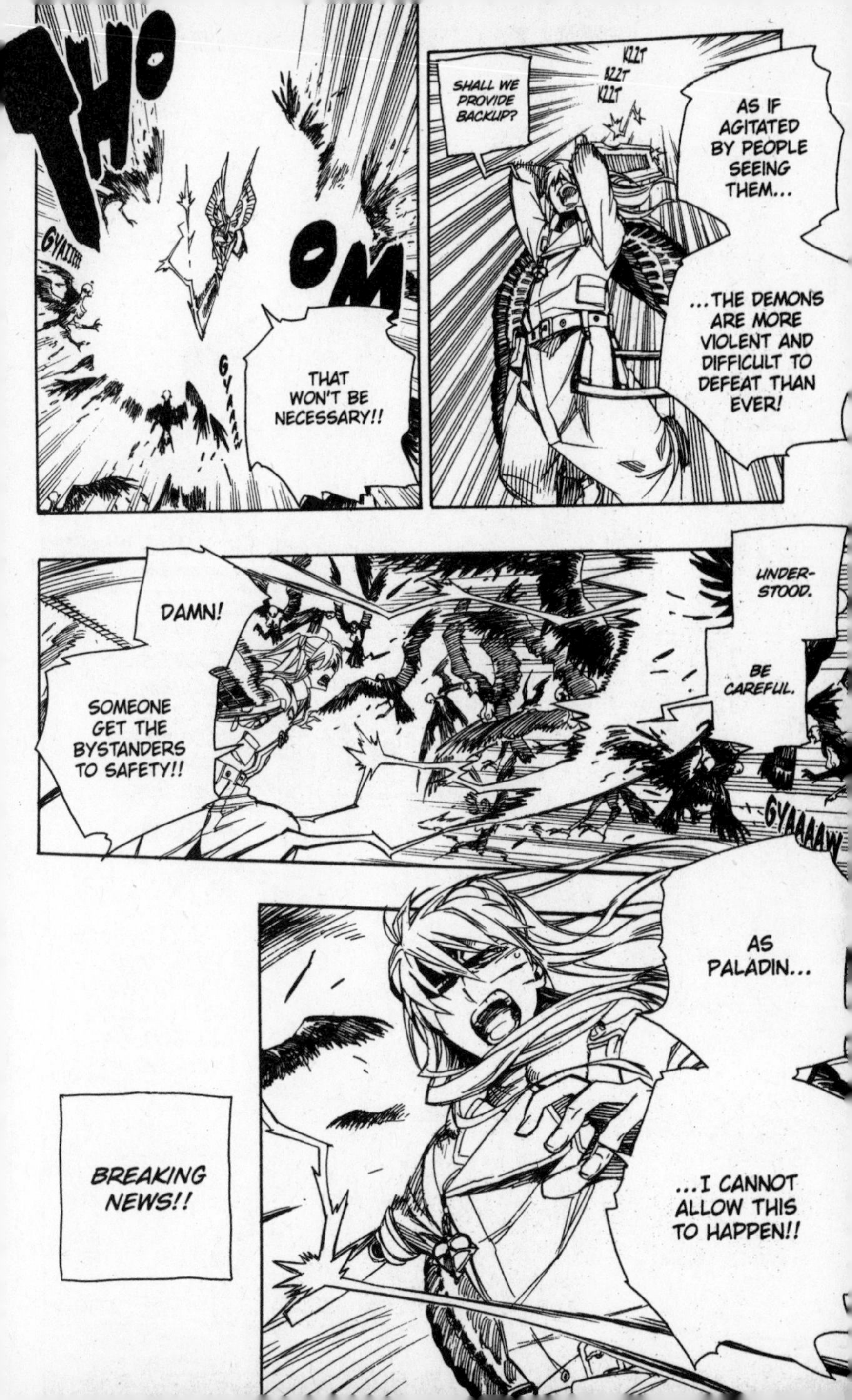
AS IF AGITATED BY PEOPLE SEEING THEM...
SHALL WE PROVIDE BACKUP?
KZZT
BZZT
KZZT
...THE DEMONS ARE MORE VIOLENT AND DIFFICULT TO DEFEAT THAN EVER!
THOOM
THAT WON'T BE NECESSARY!!
UNDERSTOOD.
BE CAREFUL.
DAMN!
SOMEONE GET THE BYSTANDERS TO SAFETY!!
GYAAAAW
AS PALADIN...
...I CANNOT ALLOW THIS TO HAPPEN!!
BREAKING NEWS!!

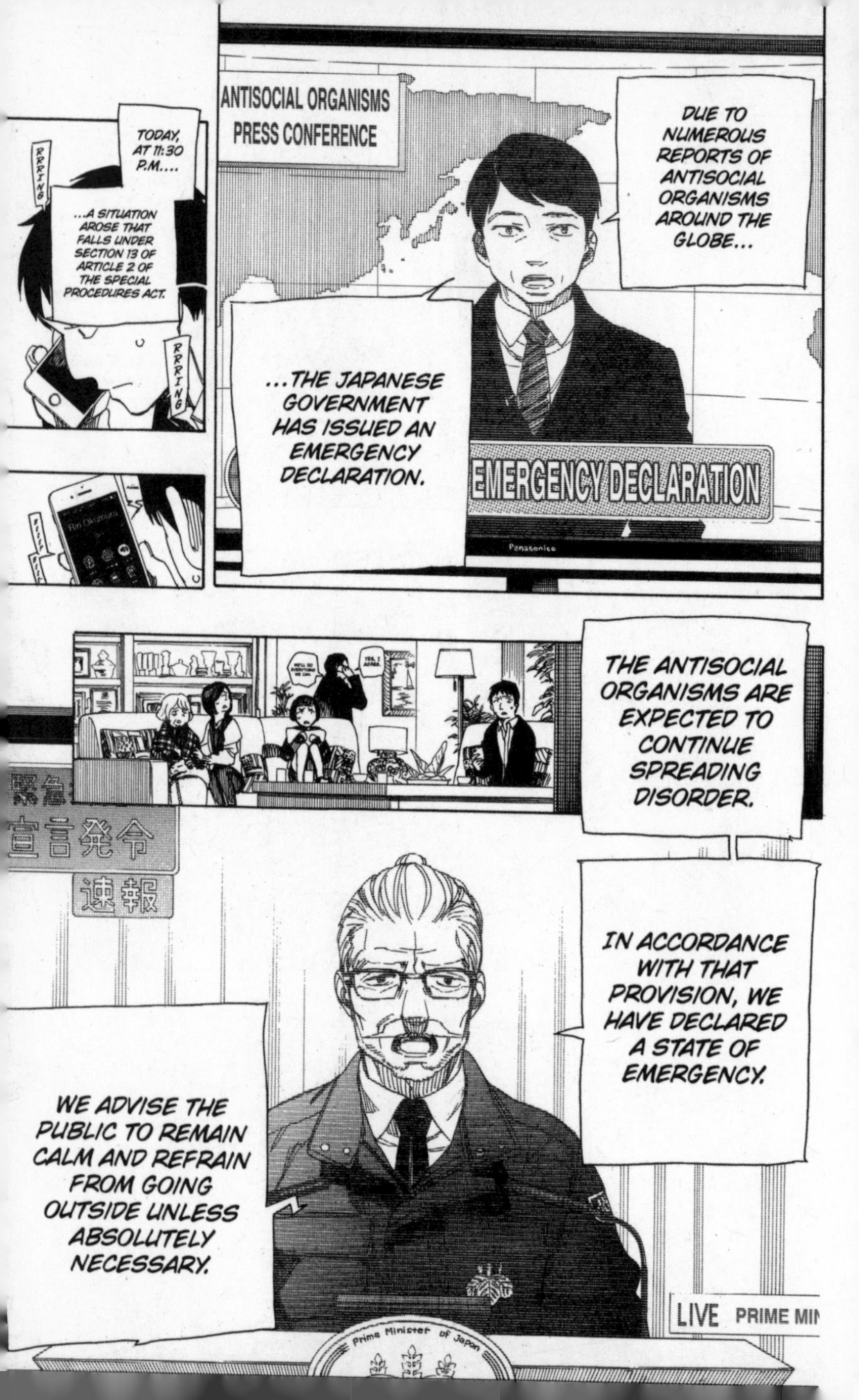
ANTISOCIAL ORGANISMS PRESS CONFERENCE
DUE TO NUMEROUS REPORTS OF ANTISOCIAL ORGANISMS AROUND THE GLOBE...
...THE JAPANESE GOVERNMENT HAS ISSUED AN EMERGENCY DECLARATION.
EMERGENCY DECLARATION
Panasonic
TODAY, AT 11:30 P.M....
RRRING
...A SITUATION AROSE THAT FALLS UNDER SECTION 13 OF ARTICLE 2 OF THE SPECIAL PROCEDURES ACT.
RRRING
Rin Okumura
THE ANTISOCIAL ORGANISMS ARE EXPECTED TO CONTINUE SPREADING DISORDER.
YES, I AGREE.
WE'LL DO EVERYTHING WE CAN.
緊急
宣言発令
速報
IN ACCORDANCE WITH THAT PROVISION, WE HAVE DECLARED A STATE OF EMERGENCY.
WE ADVISE THE PUBLIC TO REMAIN CALM AND REFRAIN FROM GOING OUTSIDE UNLESS ABSOLUTELY NECESSARY.
LIVE PRIME MIN
Prime Minister of Japan

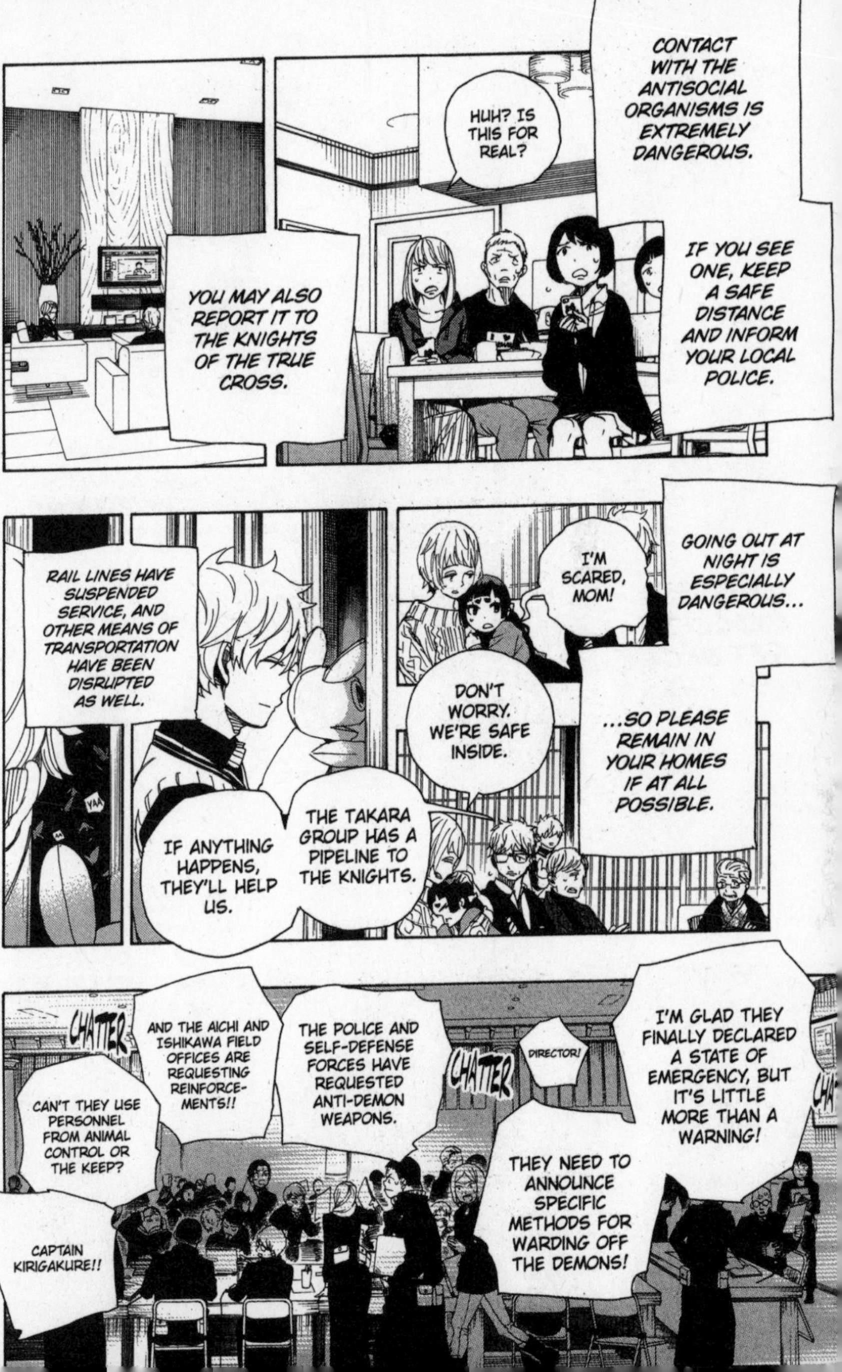
CONTACT WITH THE ANTISOCIAL ORGANISMS IS EXTREMELY DANGEROUS.
HUH? IS THIS FOR REAL?
IF YOU SEE ONE, KEEP A SAFE DISTANCE AND INFORM YOUR LOCAL POLICE.
YOU MAY ALSO REPORT IT TO THE KNIGHTS OF THE TRUE CROSS.
GOING OUT AT NIGHT IS ESPECIALLY DANGEROUS...
I'M SCARED, MOM!
...SO PLEASE REMAIN IN YOUR HOMES IF AT ALL POSSIBLE.
DON'T WORRY. WE'RE SAFE INSIDE.
THE TAKARA GROUP HAS A PIPELINE TO THE KNIGHTS.
IF ANYTHING HAPPENS, THEY'LL HELP US.
RAIL LINES HAVE SUSPENDED SERVICE, AND OTHER MEANS OF TRANSPORTATION HAVE BEEN DISRUPTED AS WELL.
YAA
I'M GLAD THEY FINALLY DECLARED A STATE OF EMERGENCY, BUT IT'S LITTLE MORE THAN A WARNING!
DIRECTOR!
THE POLICE AND SELF-DEFENSE FORCES HAVE REQUESTED ANTI-DEMON WEAPONS.
CHATTER
AND THE AICHI AND ISHIKAWA FIELD OFFICES ARE REQUESTING REINFORCE-MENTS!!
CHATTER
THEY NEED TO ANNOUNCE SPECIFIC METHODS FOR WARDING OFF THE DEMONS!
CAN'T THEY USE PERSONNEL FROM ANIMAL CONTROL OR THE KEEP?
CAPTAIN KIRIGAKURE!!

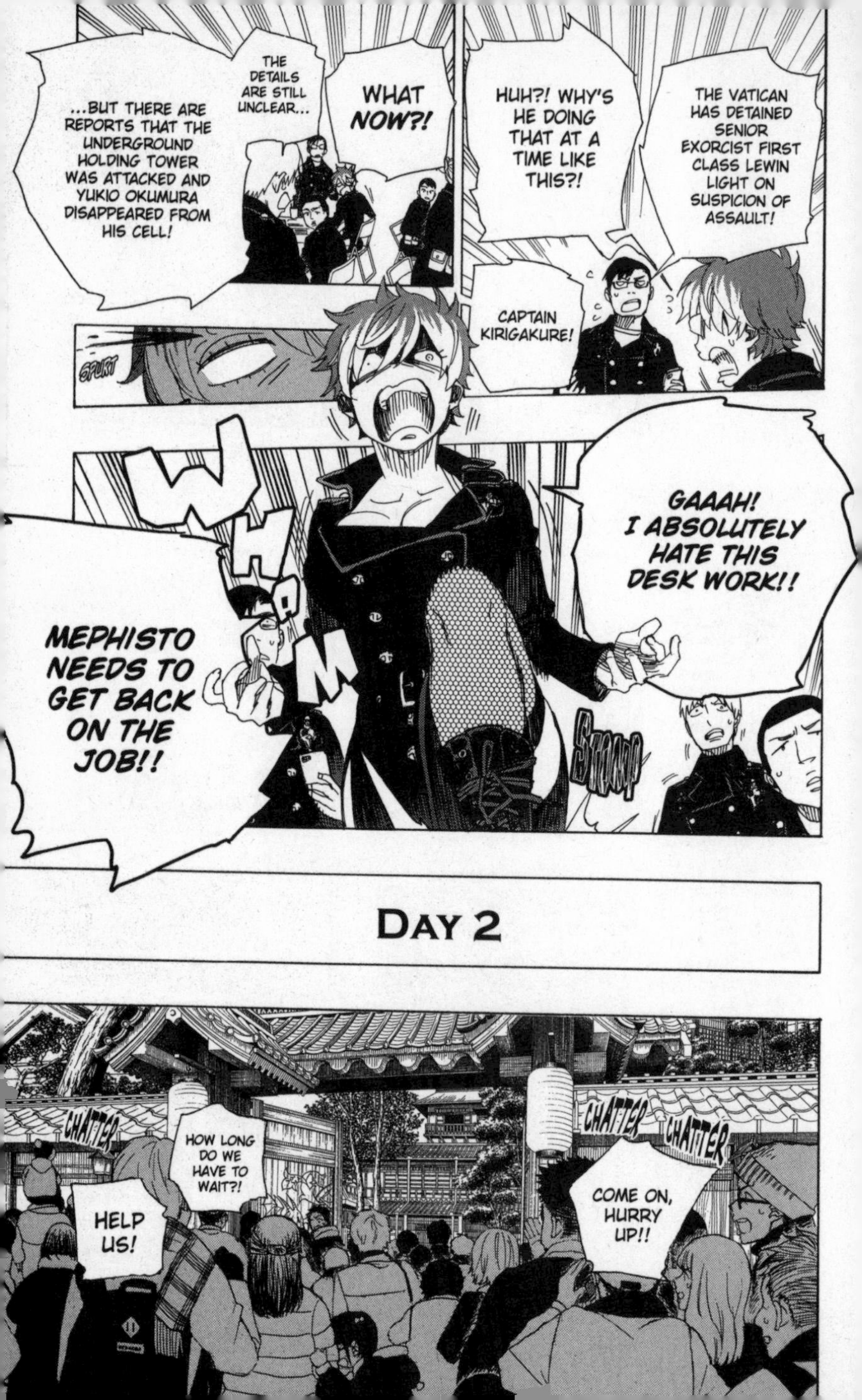
THE VATICAN HAS DETAINED SENIOR EXORCIST FIRST CLASS LEWIN LIGHT ON SUSPICION OF ASSAULT!
HUH?! WHY'S HE DOING THAT AT A TIME LIKE THIS?!
WHAT NOW?!
THE DETAILS ARE STILL UNCLEAR...
...BUT THERE ARE REPORTS THAT THE UNDERGROUND HOLDING TOWER WAS ATTACKED AND YUKIO OKUMURA DISAPPEARED FROM HIS CELL!
CAPTAIN KIRIGAKURE!
SPURT
GAAAH! I ABSOLUTELY HATE THIS DESK WORK!!
WHAM
MEPHISTO NEEDS TO GET BACK ON THE JOB!!
DAY 2
CHATTER
CHATTER
COME ON, HURRY UP!!
HOW LONG DO WE HAVE TO WAIT?!
CHATTER
HELP US!

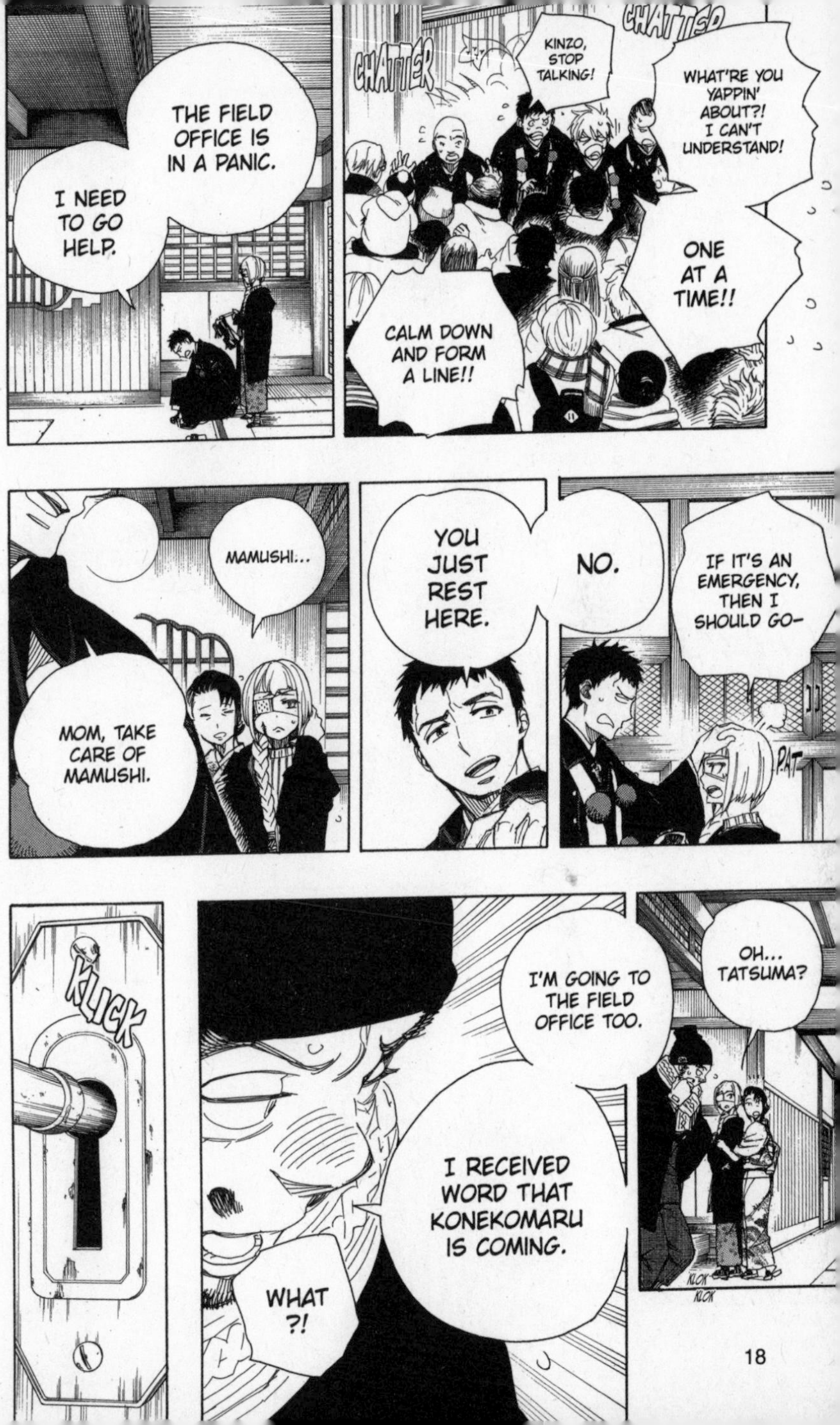
CHATTER
WHAT'RE YOU YAPPIN' ABOUT?! I CAN'T UNDERSTAND!
KINZO, STOP TALKING!
CHATTER
ONE AT A TIME!!
CALM DOWN AND FORM A LINE!!
THE FIELD OFFICE IS IN A PANIC.
I NEED TO GO HELP.
IF IT'S AN EMERGENCY, THEN I SHOULD GO-
PAT
NO.
YOU JUST REST HERE.
MAMUSHI...
MOM, TAKE CARE OF MAMUSHI.
OH... TATSUMA?
KLOK KLOK
I'M GOING TO THE FIELD OFFICE TOO.
I RECEIVED WORD THAT KONEKOMARU IS COMING.
WHAT?!
KLICK

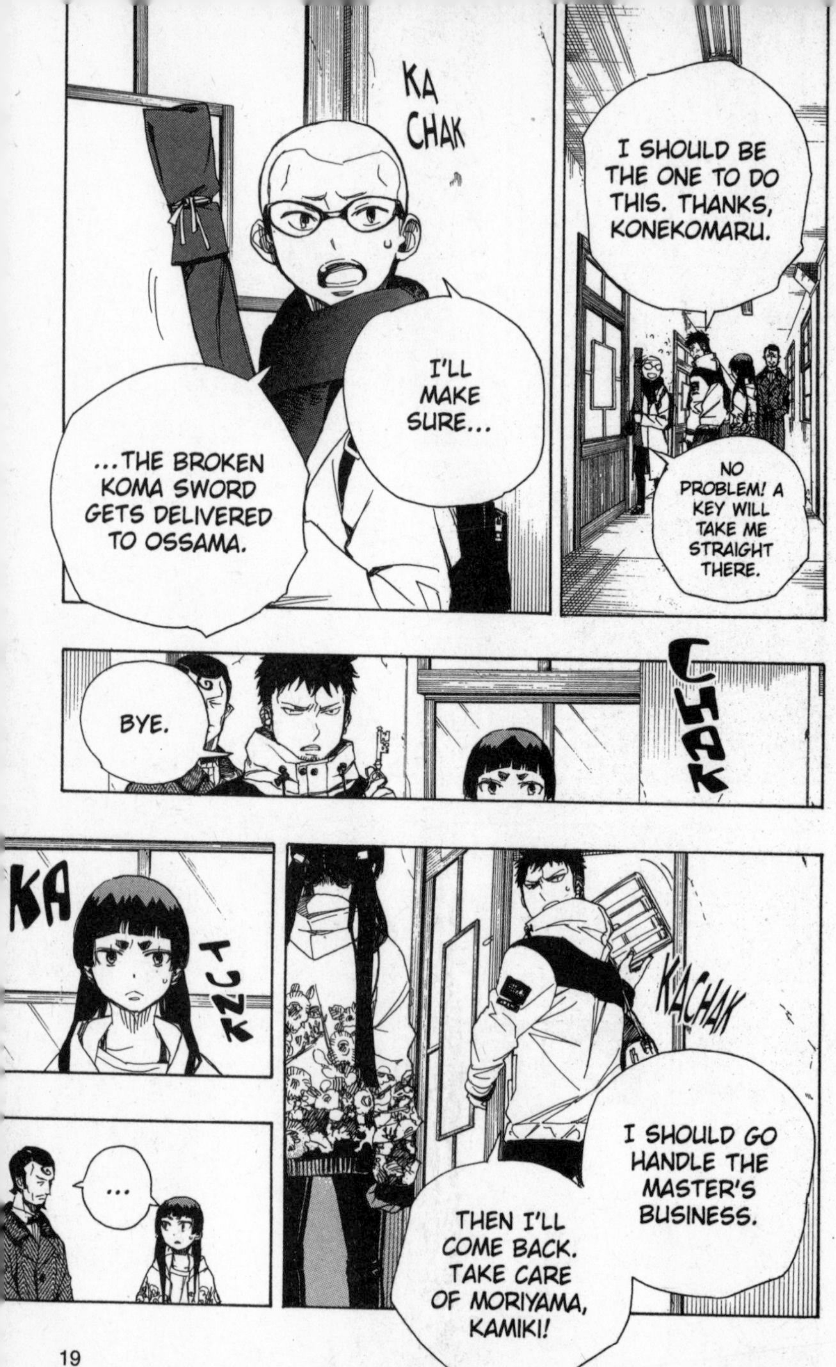
I SHOULD BE THE ONE TO DO THIS. THANKS, KONEKOMARU.
NO PROBLEM! A KEY WILL TAKE ME STRAIGHT THERE.
KA CHAK
I'LL MAKE SURE...
...THE BROKEN KOMA SWORD GETS DELIVERED TO OSSAMA.
CHAK
BYE.
KACHAK
I SHOULD GO HANDLE THE MASTER'S BUSINESS.
THEN I'LL COME BACK. TAKE CARE OF MORIYAMA, KAMIKI!
KA
TUNK
...

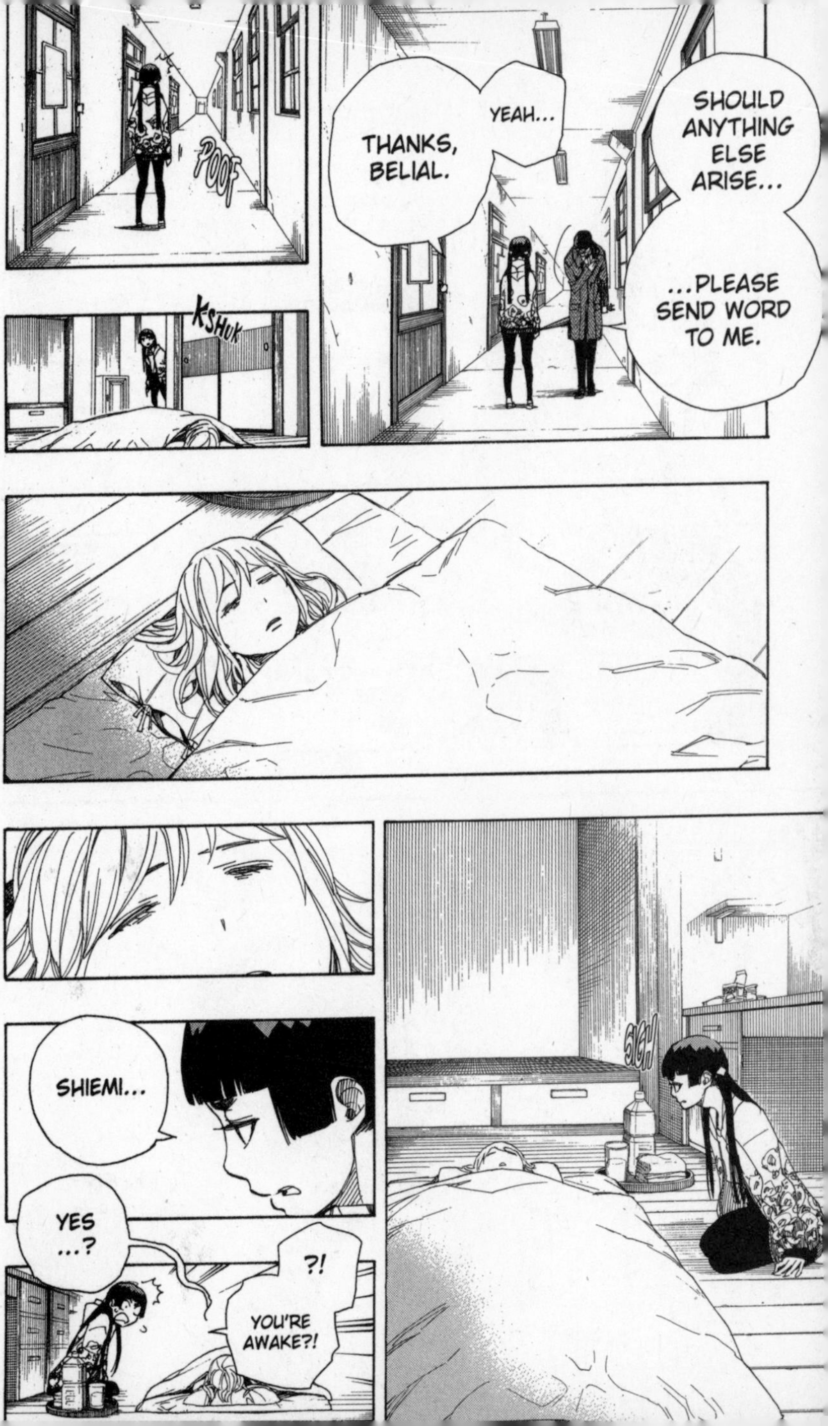
SHOULD ANYTHING ELSE ARISE...
...PLEASE SEND WORD TO ME.
YEAH...
THANKS, BELIAL.
POOF
K-SHUK
SIGH
SHIEMI...
YES ...?
?!
YOU'RE AWAKE?!

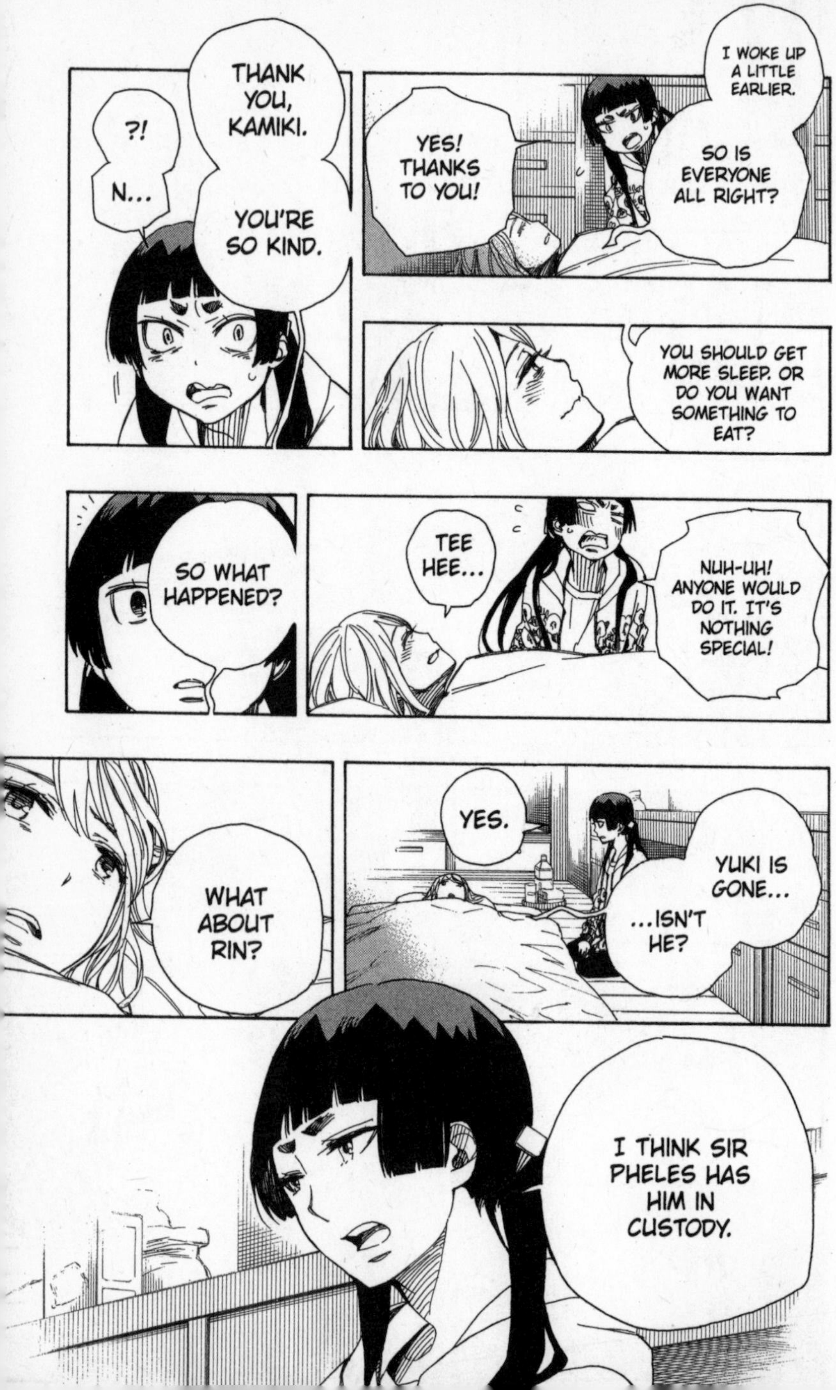

I WOKE UP A LITTLE EARLIER.
SO IS EVERYONE ALL RIGHT?
YES! THANKS TO YOU!
YOU SHOULD GET MORE SLEEP. OR DO YOU WANT SOMETHING TO EAT?
THANK YOU, KAMIKI.
YOU'RE SO KIND.
?!
N...
NUH-UH! ANYONE WOULD DO IT. IT'S NOTHING SPECIAL!
TEE HEE...
SO WHAT HAPPENED?
YUKI IS GONE...
...ISN'T HE?
YES.
WHAT ABOUT RIN?
I THINK SIR PHELES HAS HIM IN CUSTODY.

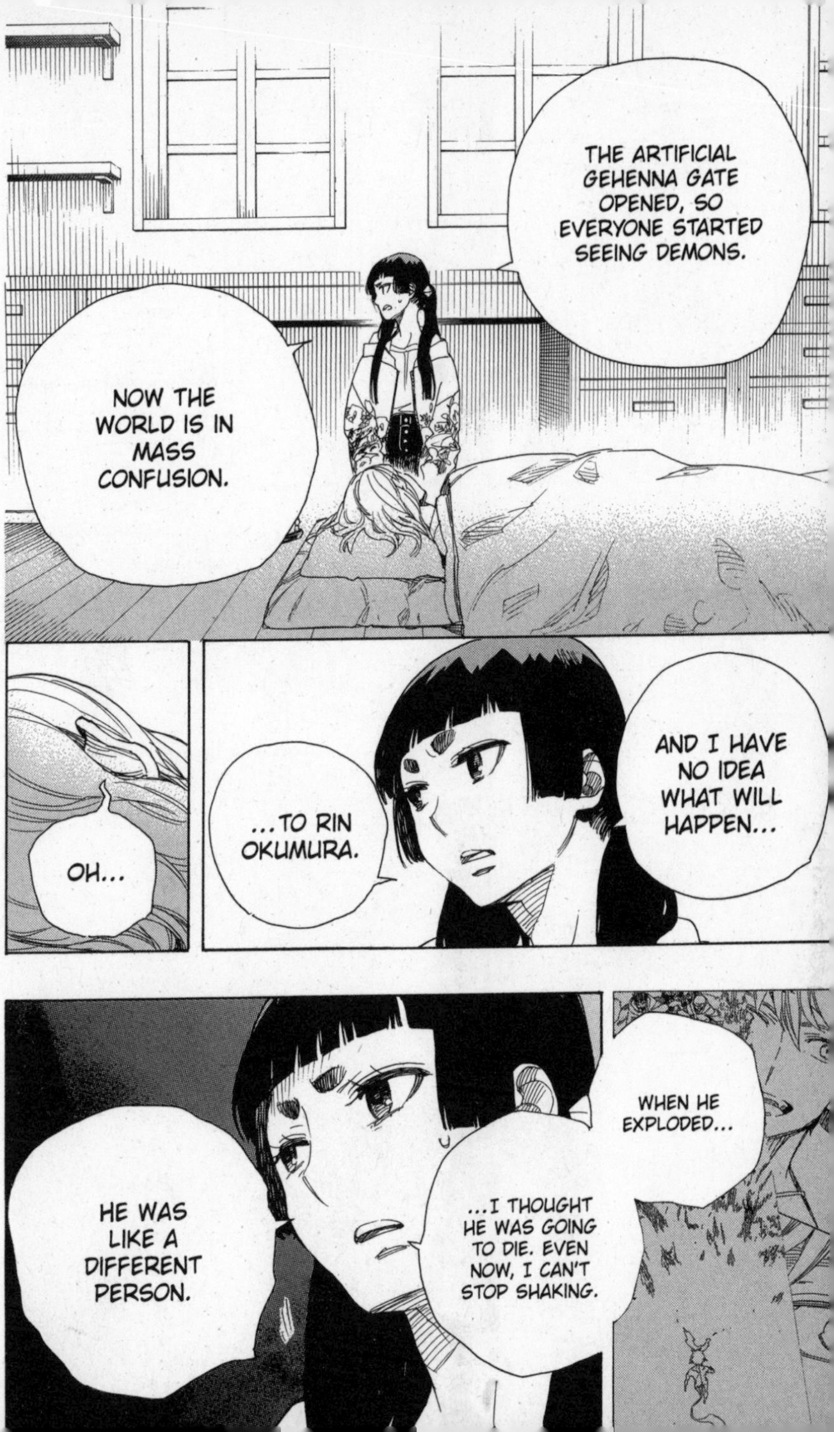
THE ARTIFICIAL GEHENNA GATE OPENED, SO EVERYONE STARTED SEEING DEMONS.
NOW THE WORLD IS IN MASS CONFUSION.
AND I HAVE NO IDEA WHAT WILL HAPPEN...
...TO RIN OKUMURA.
OH...
WHEN HE EXPLODED...
...I THOUGHT HE WAS GOING TO DIE. EVEN NOW, I CAN'T STOP SHAKING.
HE WAS LIKE A DIFFERENT PERSON.

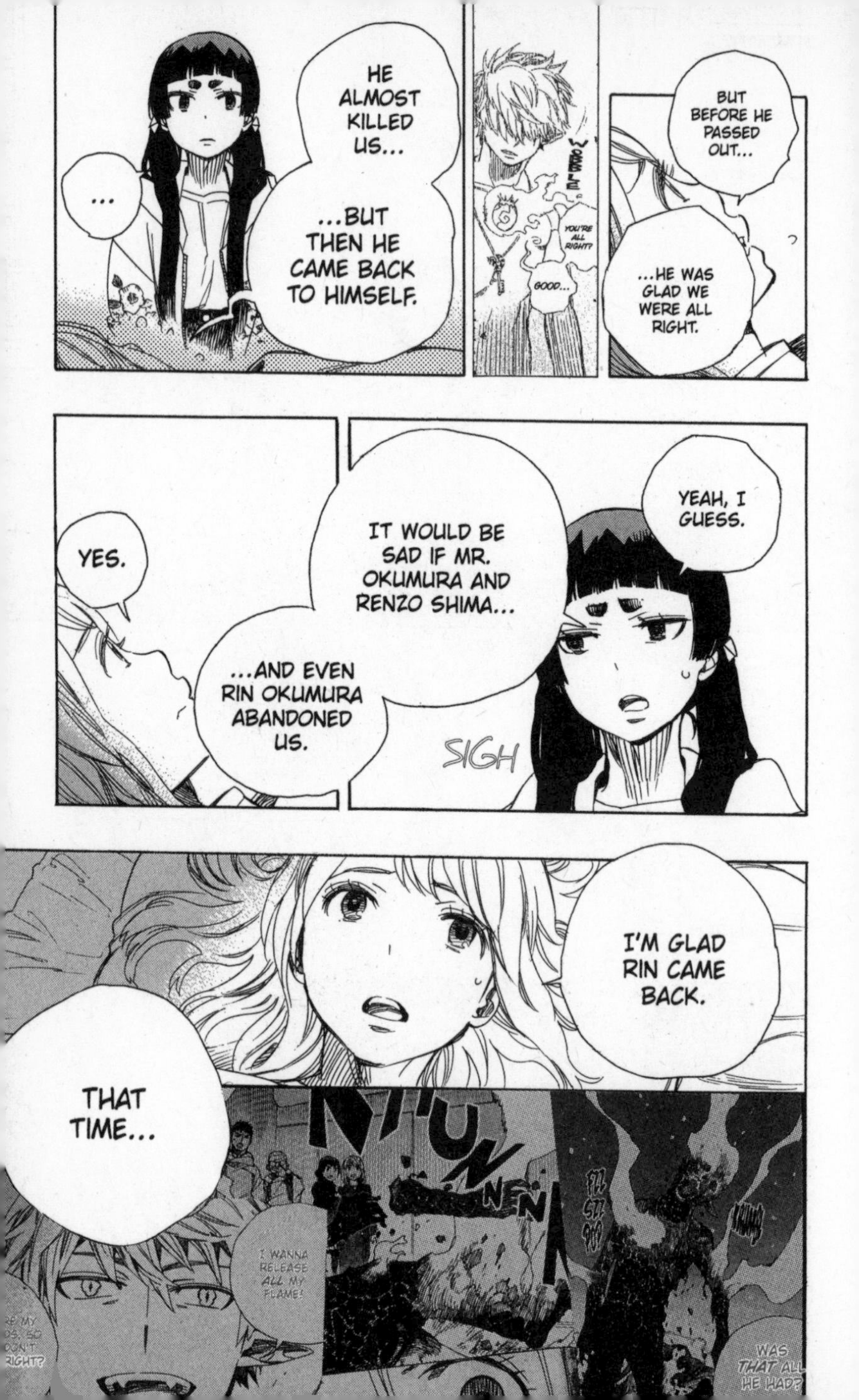
BUT BEFORE HE PASSED OUT...
...HE WAS GLAD WE WERE ALL RIGHT.
WOBBLE
YOU'RE ALL RIGHT?
GOOD...
HE ALMOST KILLED US...
...BUT THEN HE CAME BACK TO HIMSELF.
...
YEAH, I GUESS.
IT WOULD BE SAD IF MR. OKUMURA AND RENZO SHIMA...
...AND EVEN RIN OKUMURA ABANDONED US.
SIGH
YES.
I'M GLAD RIN CAME BACK.
THAT TIME...
WAS THAT ALL HE HAD?
I WANNA RELEASE ALL MY FLAME!

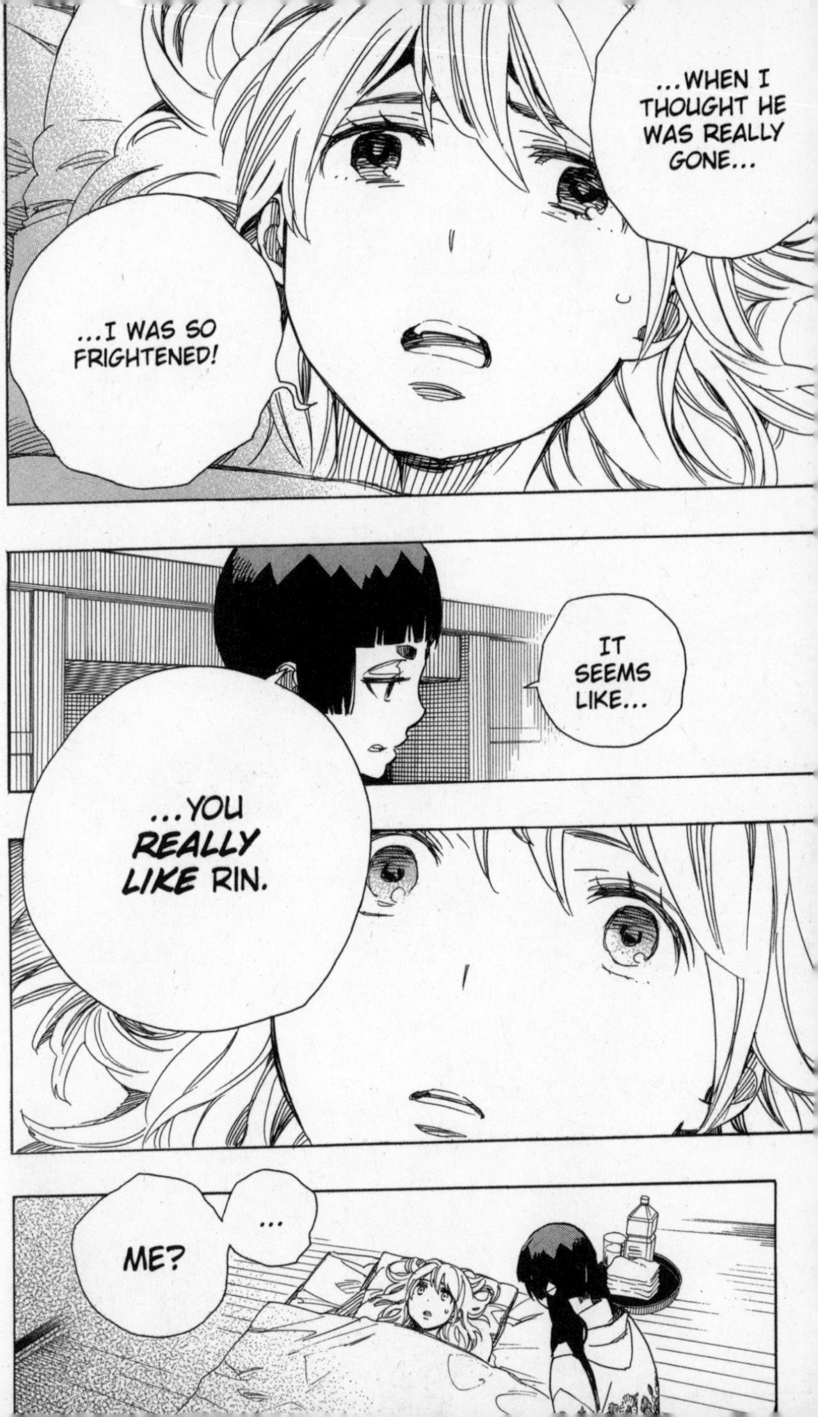
...WHEN I THOUGHT HE WAS REALLY GONE...
...I WAS SO FRIGHTENED!
IT SEEMS LIKE...
...YOU *REALLY LIKE* RIN.
...
ME?

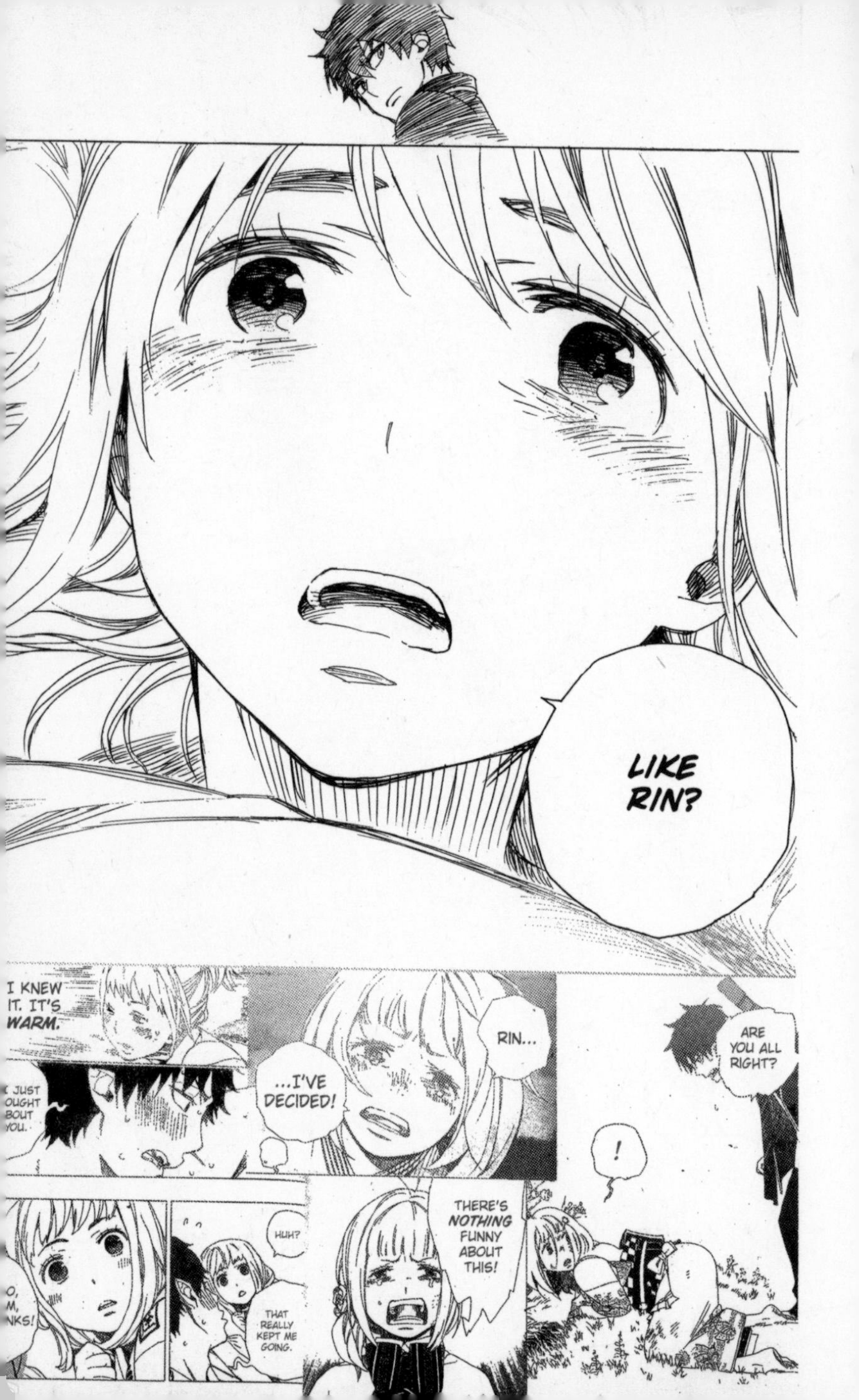
LIKE RIN?
ARE YOU ALL RIGHT?
!
RIN...
...I'VE DECIDED!
I KNEW IT. IT'S **WARM.**
JUST OUGHT BOUT YOU.
THERE'S **NOTHING** FUNNY ABOUT THIS!
HUH?
THAT REALLY KEPT ME GOING.
O, M, NKS!

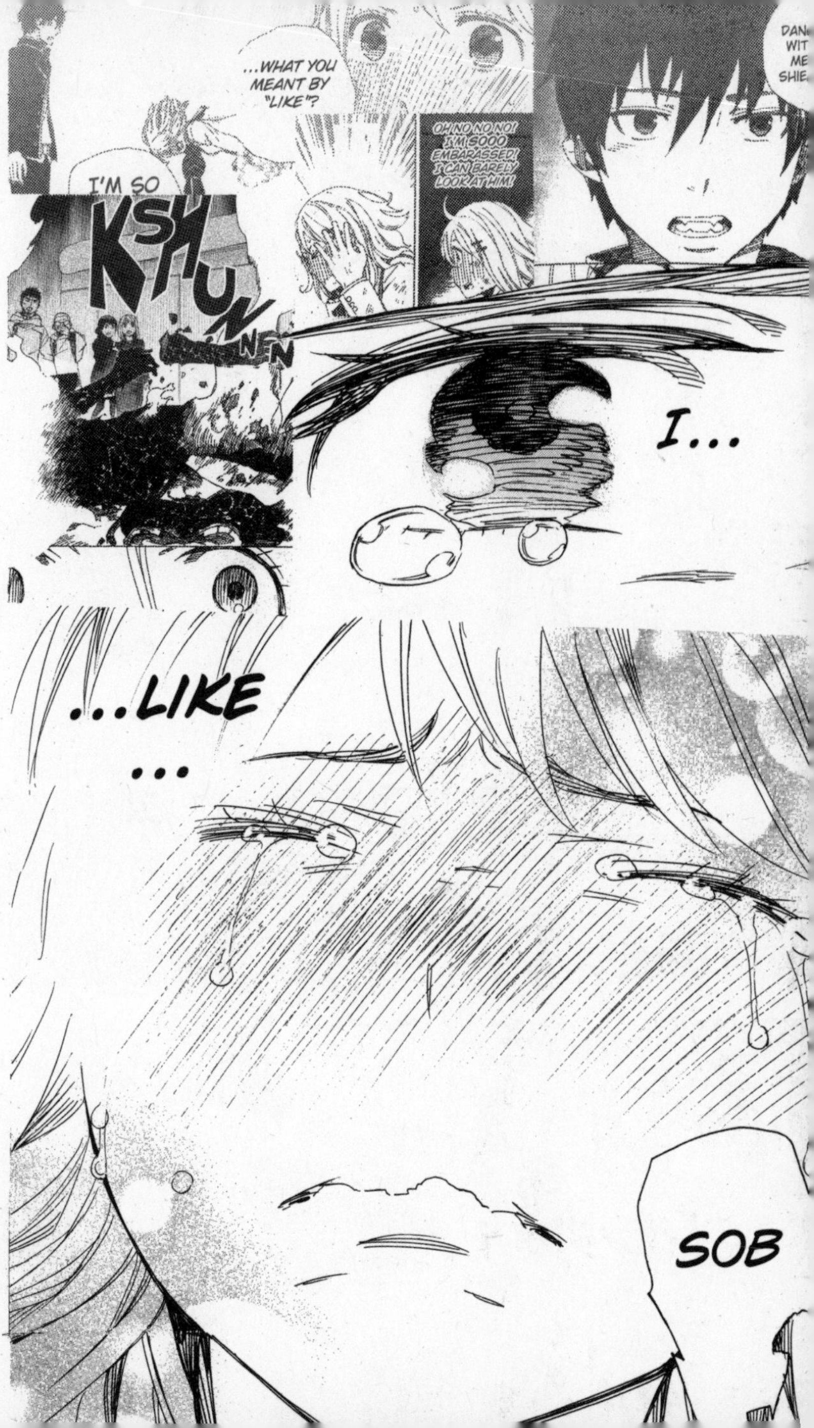
OH NO NO NO! I'M SOOO EMBARASSED! I CAN BARELY LOOK AT HIM!
...WHAT YOU MEANT BY "LIKE"?
I'M SO
KSHUNNEN
I...
...LIKE
...
SOB

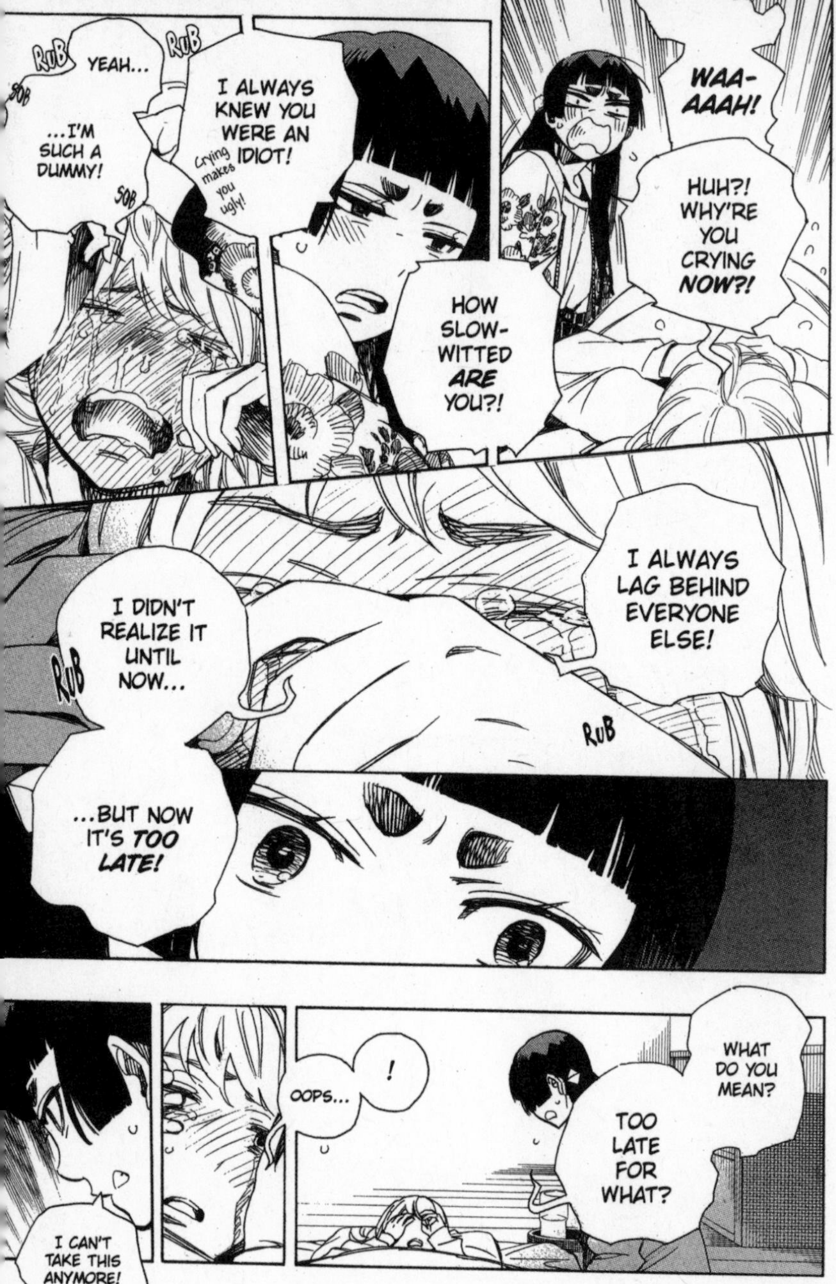
WAA-AAAH!
HUH?! WHY'RE YOU CRYING NOW?!
HOW SLOW-WITTED ARE YOU?!
I ALWAYS KNEW YOU WERE AN IDIOT!
Crying makes you ugly!
RUB
RUB
YEAH...
SOB
...I'M SUCH A DUMMY!
SOB
I ALWAYS LAG BEHIND EVERYONE ELSE!
RUB
I DIDN'T REALIZE IT UNTIL NOW...
RUB
...BUT NOW IT'S TOO LATE!
WHAT DO YOU MEAN?
TOO LATE FOR WHAT?
!
OOPS...
I CAN'T TAKE THIS ANYMORE!

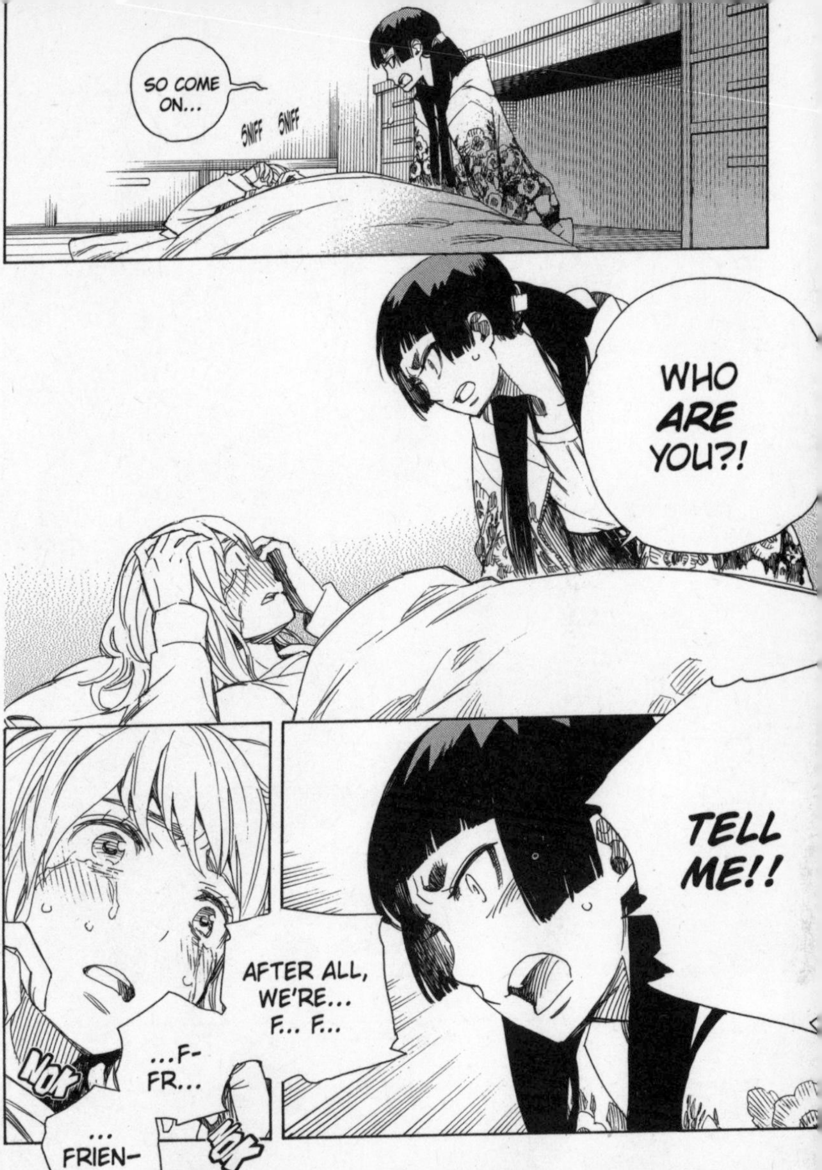
SO COME ON...
SNIFF SNIFF
WHO ARE YOU?!
TELL ME!!
AFTER ALL, WE'RE... F... F...
NOK
...F- FR...
... FRIEN-
NOK
NOK NOK
?!

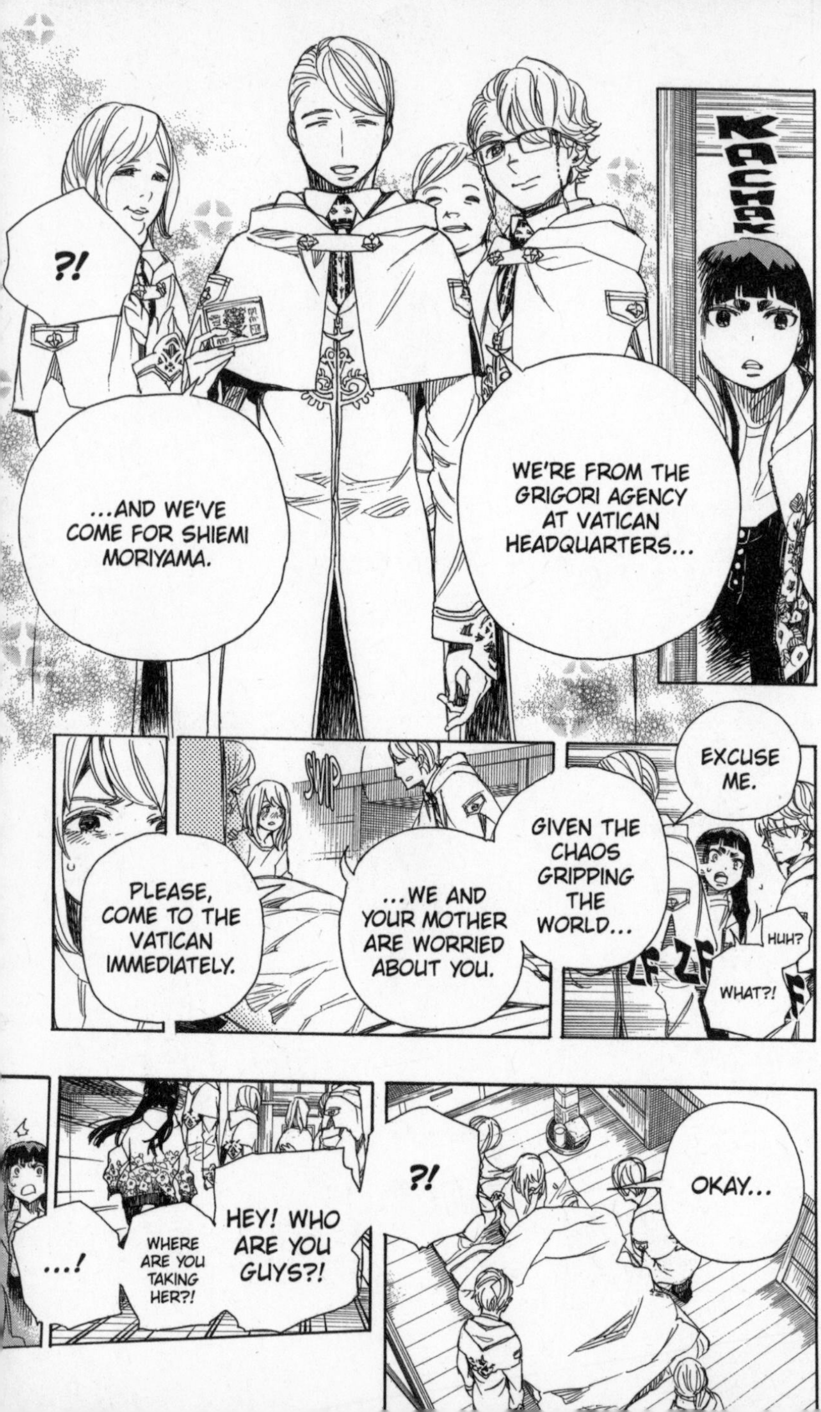
KACHAK
WE'RE FROM THE GRIGORI AGENCY AT VATICAN HEADQUARTERS...
...AND WE'VE COME FOR SHIEMI MORIYAMA.
?!
EXCUSE ME.
GIVEN THE CHAOS GRIPPING THE WORLD...
HUH?
WHAT?!
...WE AND YOUR MOTHER ARE WORRIED ABOUT YOU.
PLEASE, COME TO THE VATICAN IMMEDIATELY.
OKAY...
?!
HEY! WHO ARE YOU GUYS?!
WHERE ARE YOU TAKING HER?!
...!

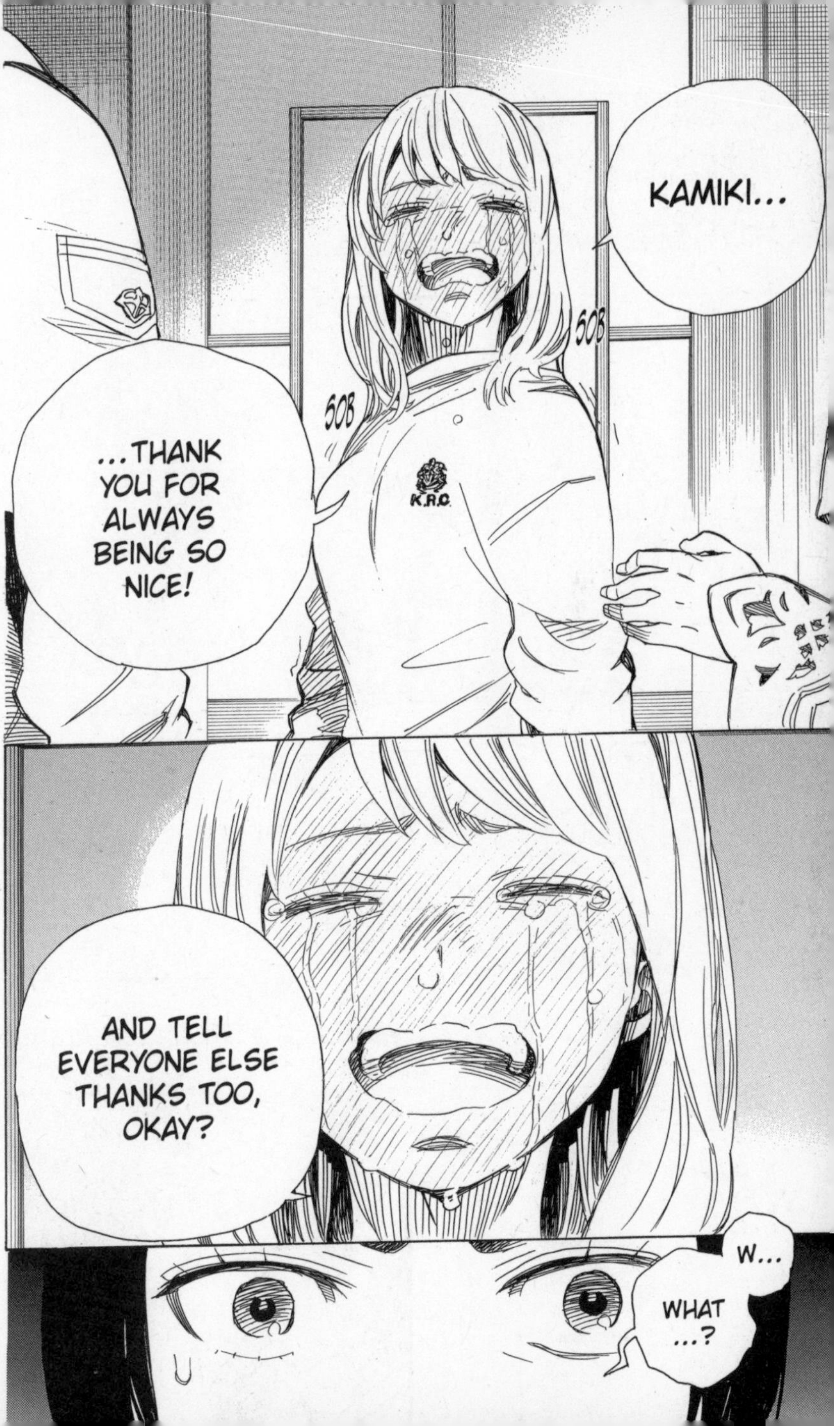
KAMIKI...
SOB
SOB
...THANK YOU FOR ALWAYS BEING SO NICE!
AND TELL EVERYONE ELSE THANKS TOO, OKAY?
W... WHAT ...?

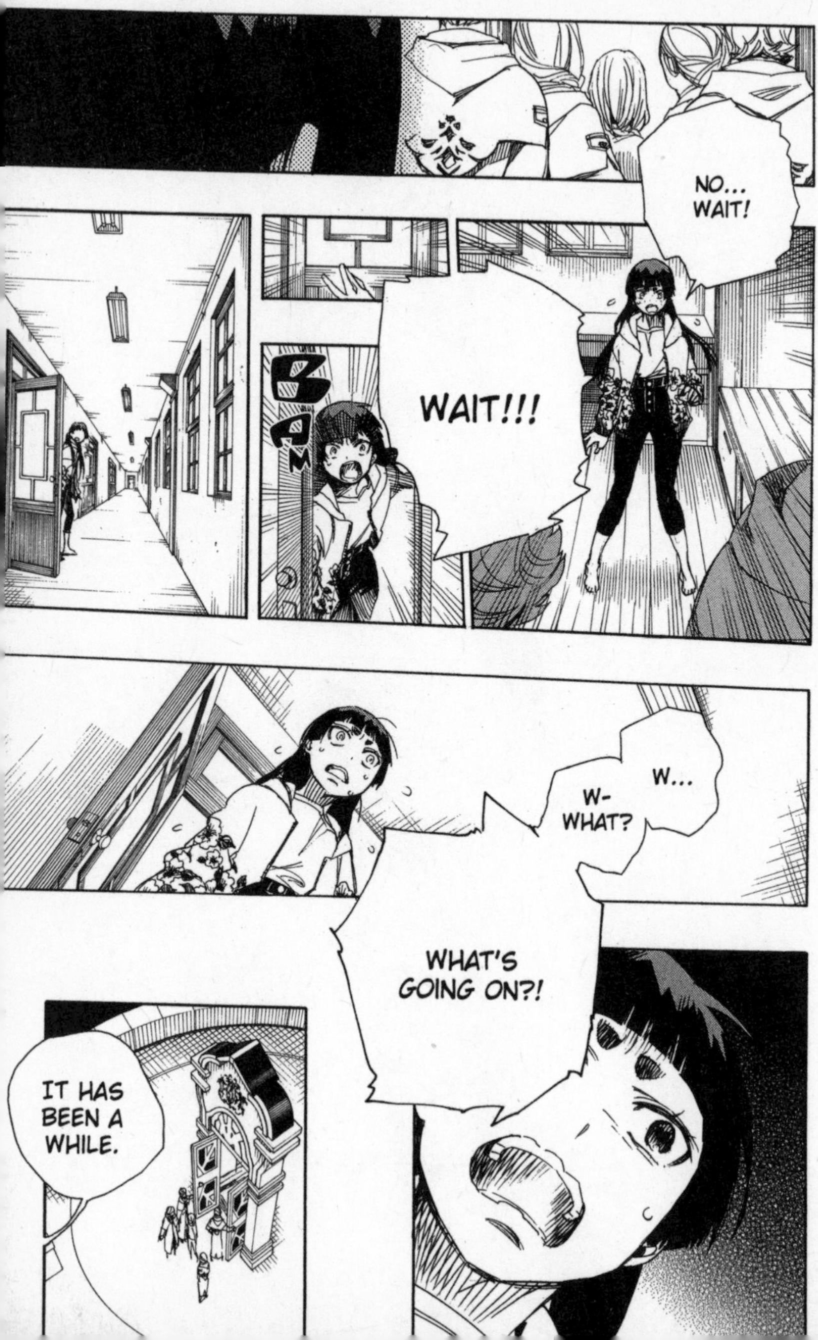
NO... WAIT!
WAIT!!!
BAM
W...
W- WHAT?
WHAT'S GOING ON?!
IT HAS BEEN A WHILE.

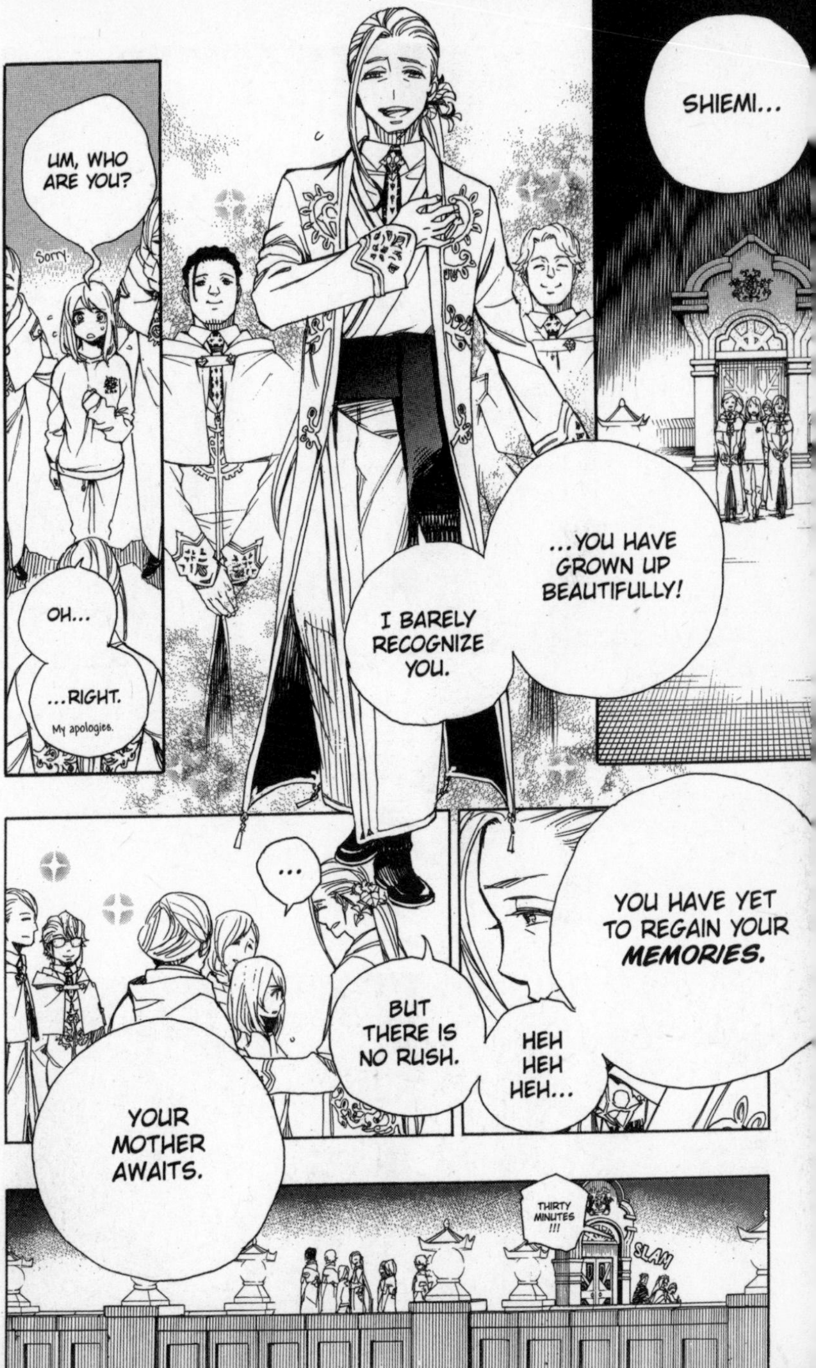
SHIEMI...
...YOU HAVE GROWN UP BEAUTIFULLY!
I BARELY RECOGNIZE YOU.
UM, WHO ARE YOU?
Sorry.
OH...
...RIGHT.
My apologies.
YOU HAVE YET TO REGAIN YOUR *MEMORIES.*
HEH HEH HEH...
BUT THERE IS NO RUSH.
...
YOUR MOTHER AWAITS.
THIRTY MINUTES !!!
SLAM

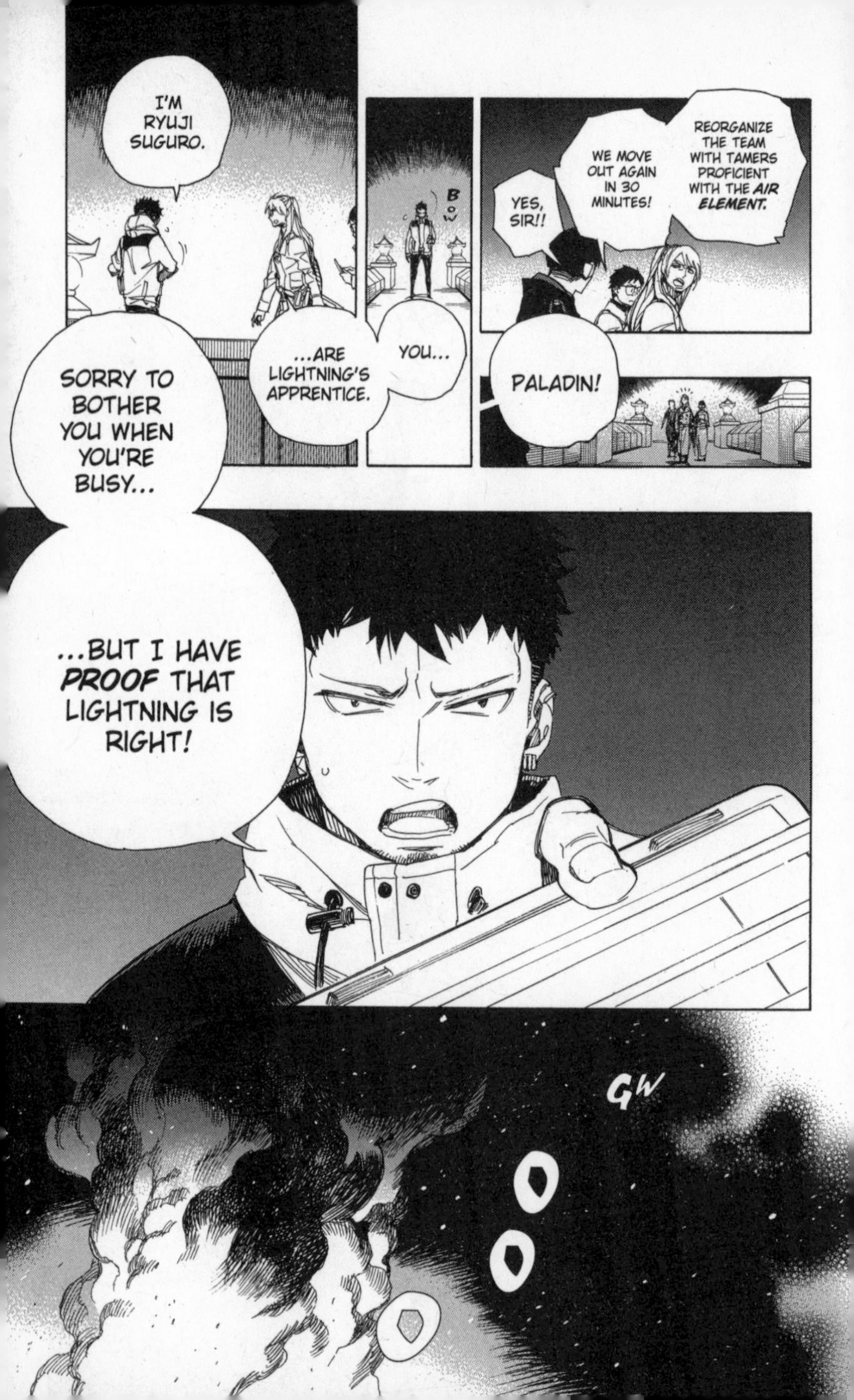
REORGANIZE THE TEAM WITH TAMERS PROFICIENT WITH THE *AIR ELEMENT.*
WE MOVE OUT AGAIN IN 30 MINUTES!
YES, SIR!!
PALADIN!
BOW
YOU...
I'M RYUJI SUGURO.
...ARE LIGHTNING'S APPRENTICE.
SORRY TO BOTHER YOU WHEN YOU'RE BUSY...
...BUT I HAVE *PROOF* THAT LIGHTNING IS RIGHT!
GWOOO

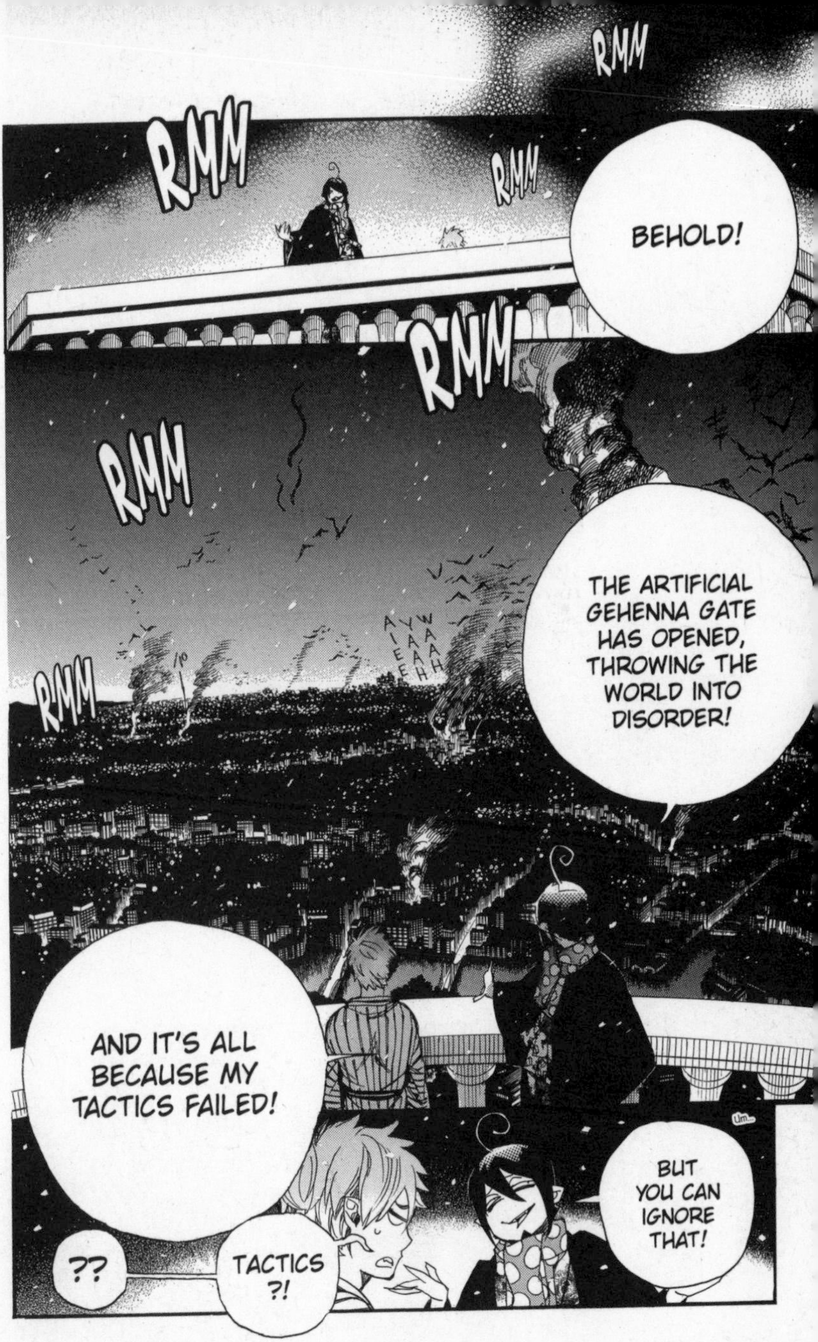
RMM
RMM
RMM
BEHOLD!
RMM
RMM
THE ARTIFICIAL GEHENNA GATE HAS OPENED, THROWING THE WORLD INTO DISORDER!
WAAAH
YAAAH
AIEEE
RMM
AND IT'S ALL BECAUSE MY TACTICS FAILED!
Um...
BUT YOU CAN IGNORE THAT!
TACTICS ?!
??

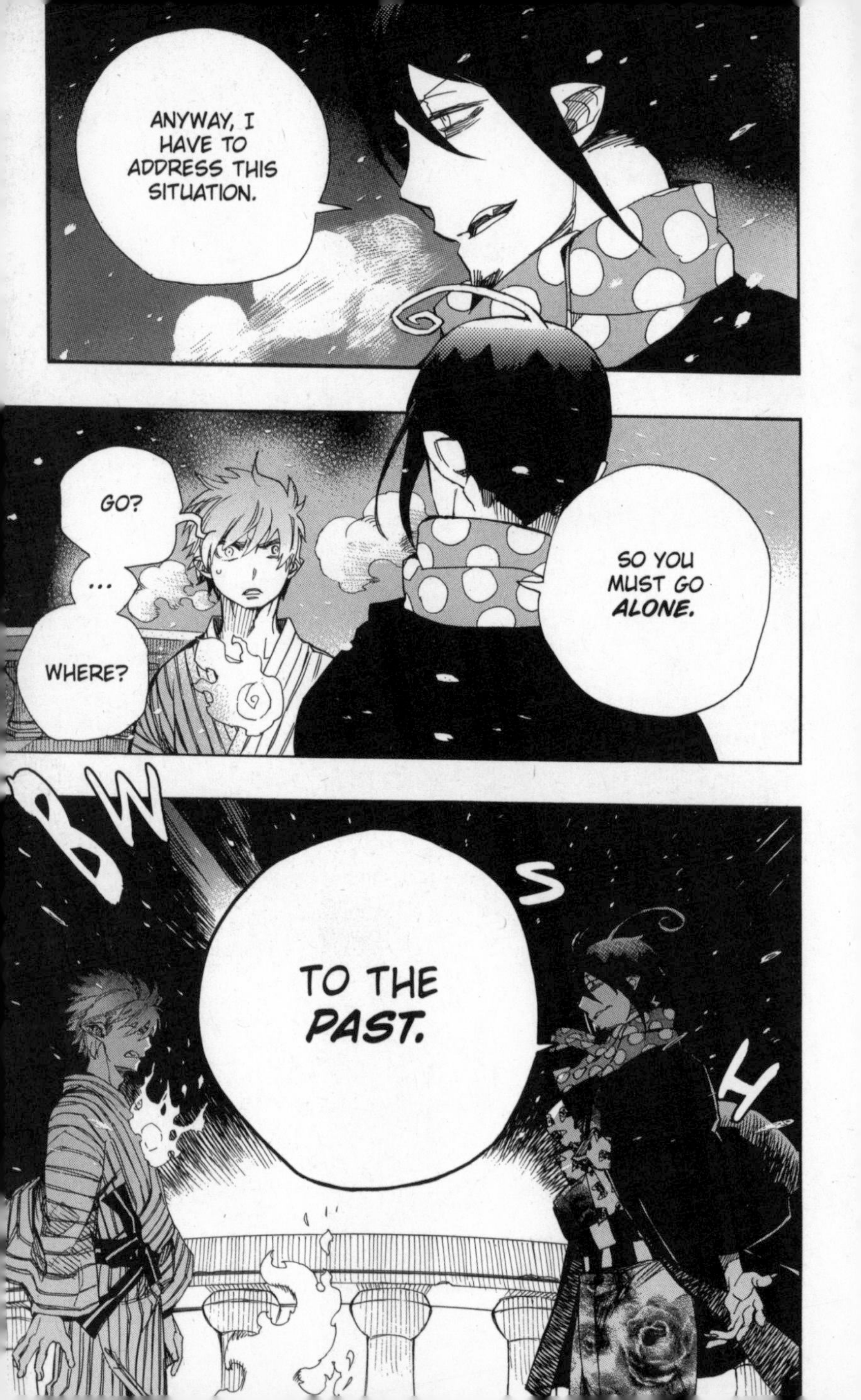
ANYWAY, I HAVE TO ADDRESS THIS SITUATION.
SO YOU MUST GO ALONE.
GO?
...
WHERE?
TO THE PAST.
BWSH

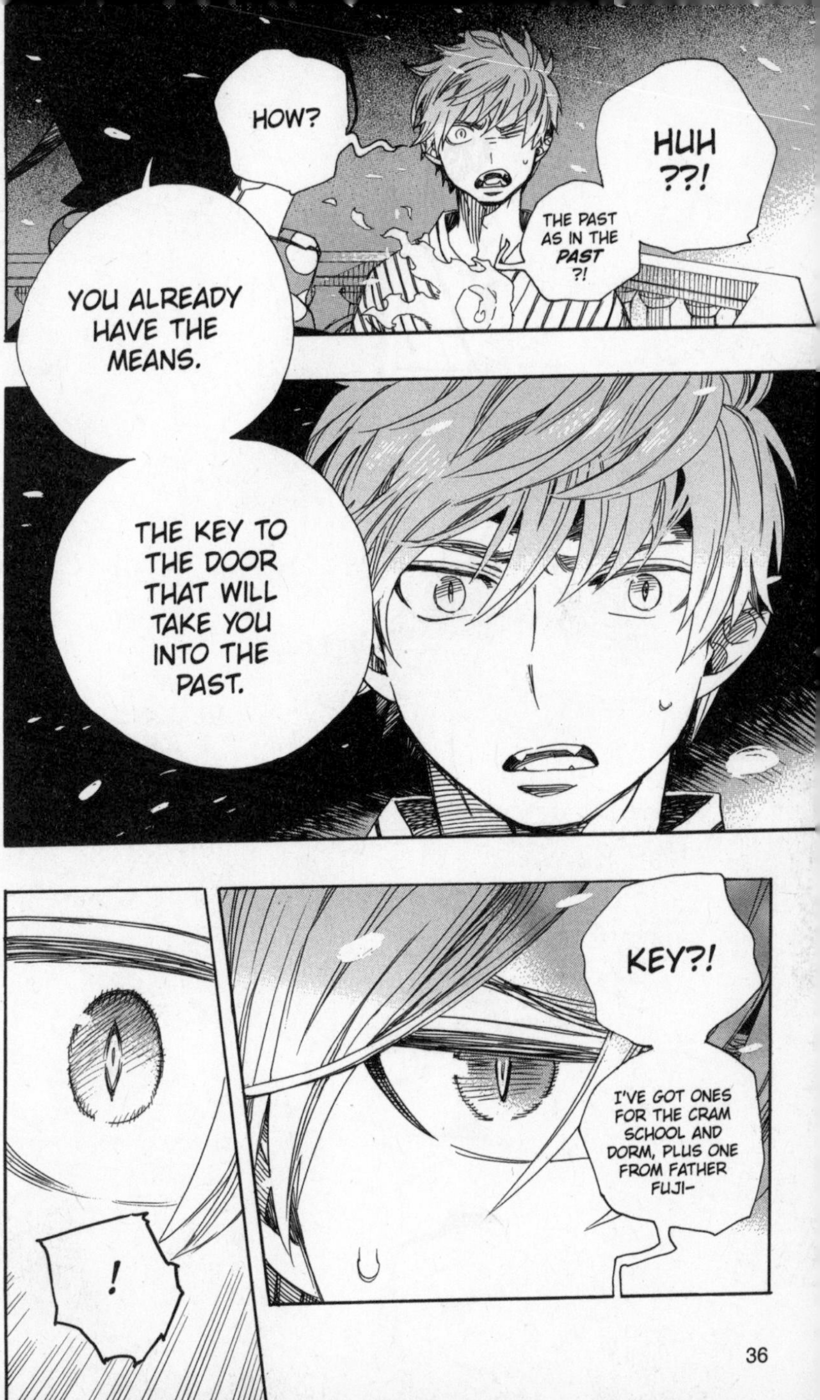
HUH ??!
THE PAST AS IN THE PAST ?!
HOW?
YOU ALREADY HAVE THE MEANS.
THE KEY TO THE DOOR THAT WILL TAKE YOU INTO THE PAST.
KEY?!
I'VE GOT ONES FOR THE CRAM SCHOOL AND DORM, PLUS ONE FROM FATHER FUJI-
!

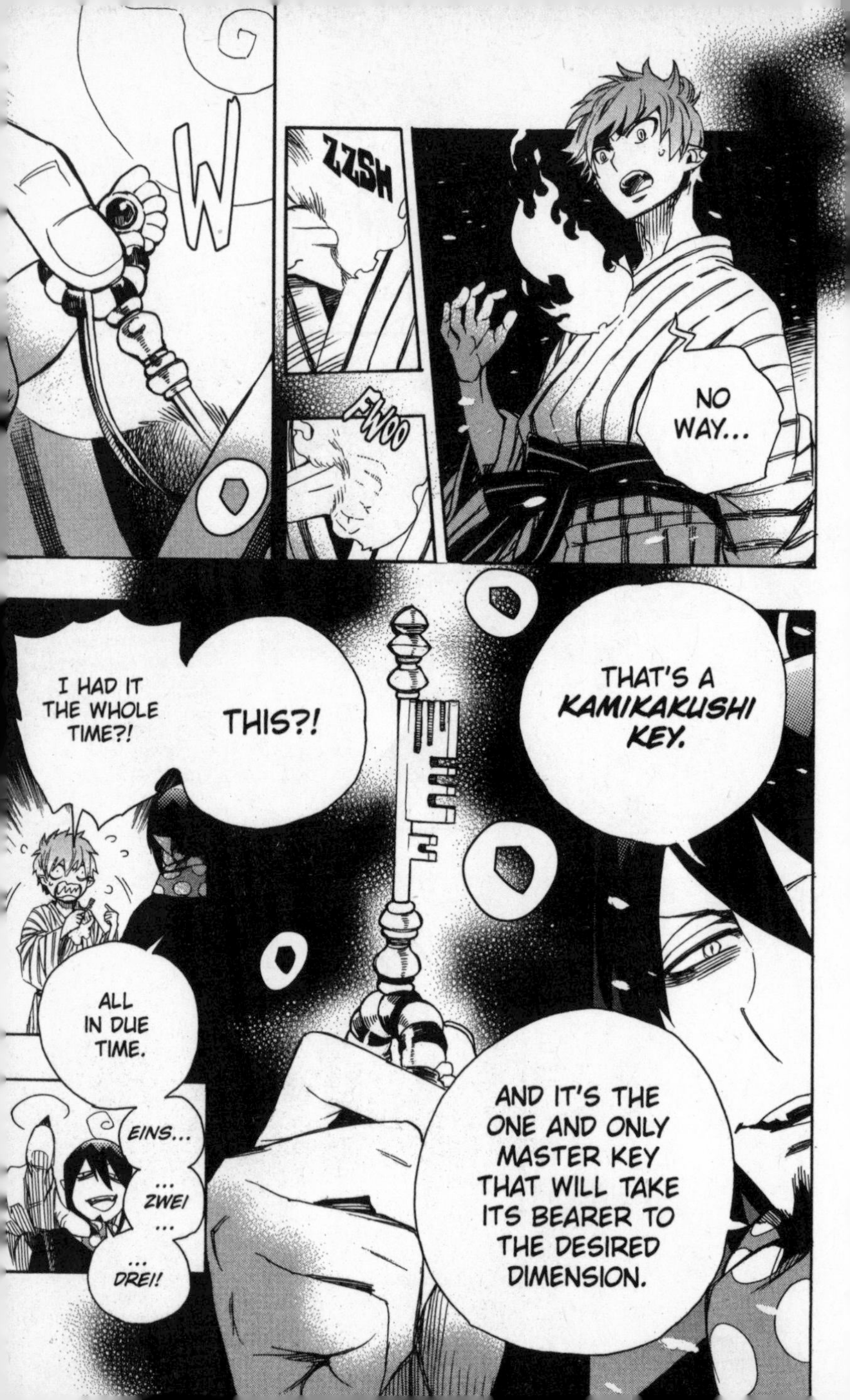
NO WAY...
ZZSH
FWOO
W
THAT'S A *KAMIKAKUSHI* KEY.
THIS?!
I HAD IT THE WHOLE TIME?!
AND IT'S THE ONE AND ONLY MASTER KEY THAT WILL TAKE ITS BEARER TO THE DESIRED DIMENSION.
ALL IN DUE TIME.
EINS...
...ZWEI...
...DREI!

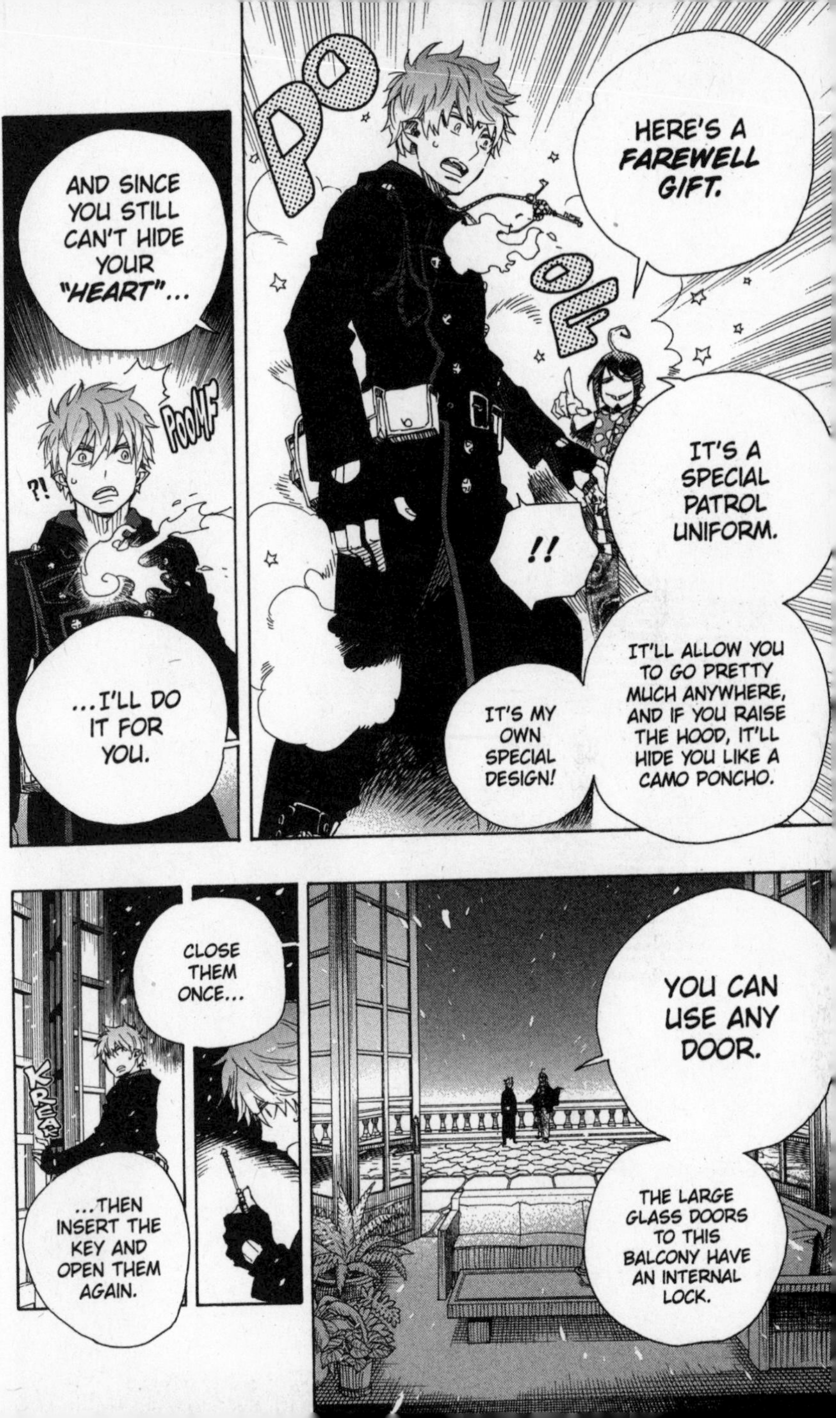
HERE'S A *FAREWELL GIFT.*
POOF
IT'S A SPECIAL PATROL UNIFORM.
!!
IT'LL ALLOW YOU TO GO PRETTY MUCH ANYWHERE, AND IF YOU RAISE THE HOOD, IT'LL HIDE YOU LIKE A CAMO PONCHO.
IT'S MY OWN SPECIAL DESIGN!
AND SINCE YOU STILL CAN'T HIDE YOUR *"HEART"*...
POOMF
?!
...I'LL DO IT FOR YOU.
YOU CAN USE ANY DOOR.
THE LARGE GLASS DOORS TO THIS BALCONY HAVE AN INTERNAL LOCK.
CLOSE THEM ONCE...
KREAK
...THEN INSERT THE KEY AND OPEN THEM AGAIN.

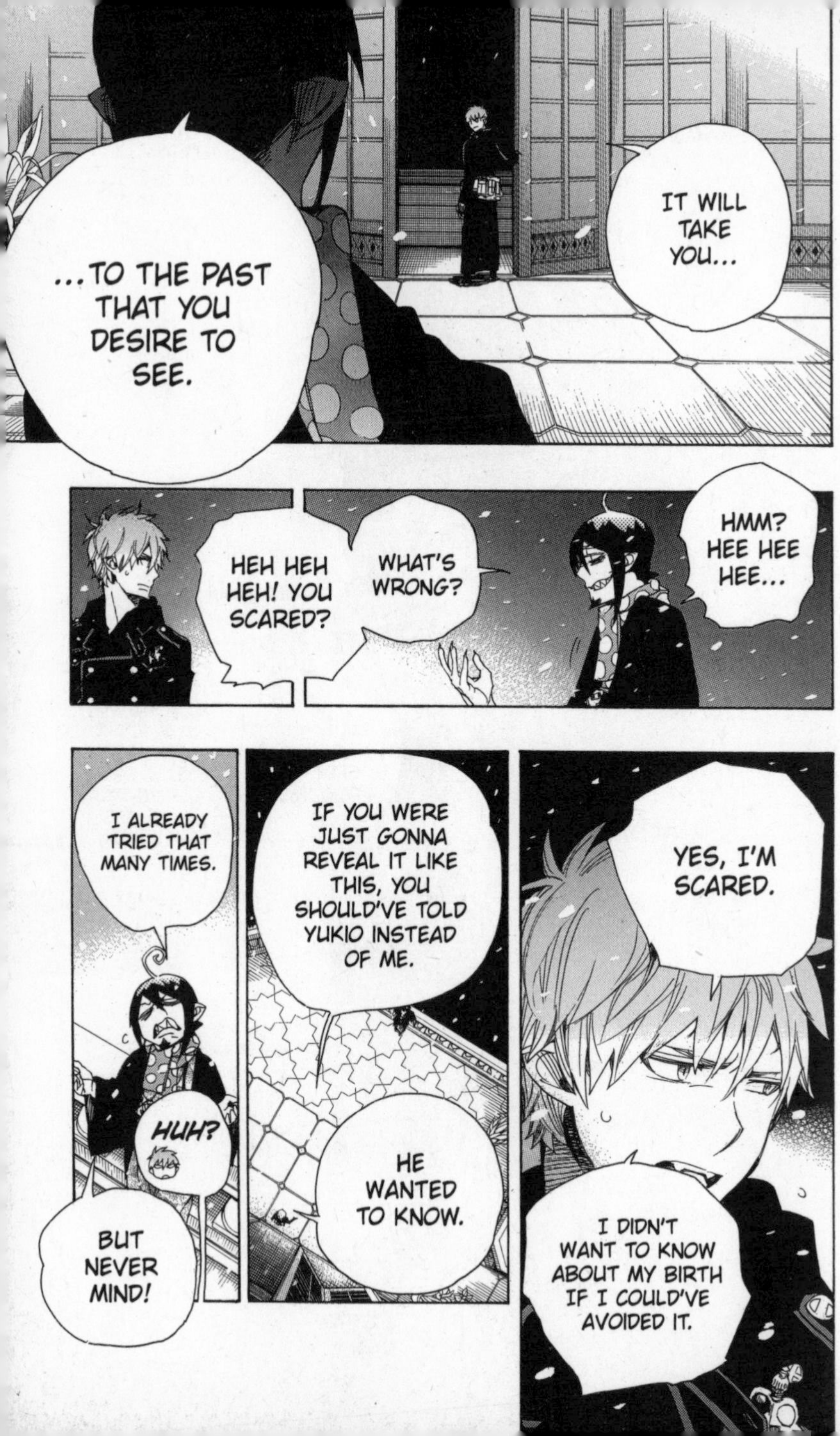
IT WILL TAKE YOU...
...TO THE PAST THAT YOU DESIRE TO SEE.
HMM? HEE HEE HEE...
WHAT'S WRONG?
HEH HEH HEH! YOU SCARED?
YES, I'M SCARED.
I DIDN'T WANT TO KNOW ABOUT MY BIRTH IF I COULD'VE AVOIDED IT.
IF YOU WERE JUST GONNA REVEAL IT LIKE THIS, YOU SHOULD'VE TOLD YUKIO INSTEAD OF ME.
HE WANTED TO KNOW.
I ALREADY TRIED THAT MANY TIMES.
HUH?
BUT NEVER MIND!

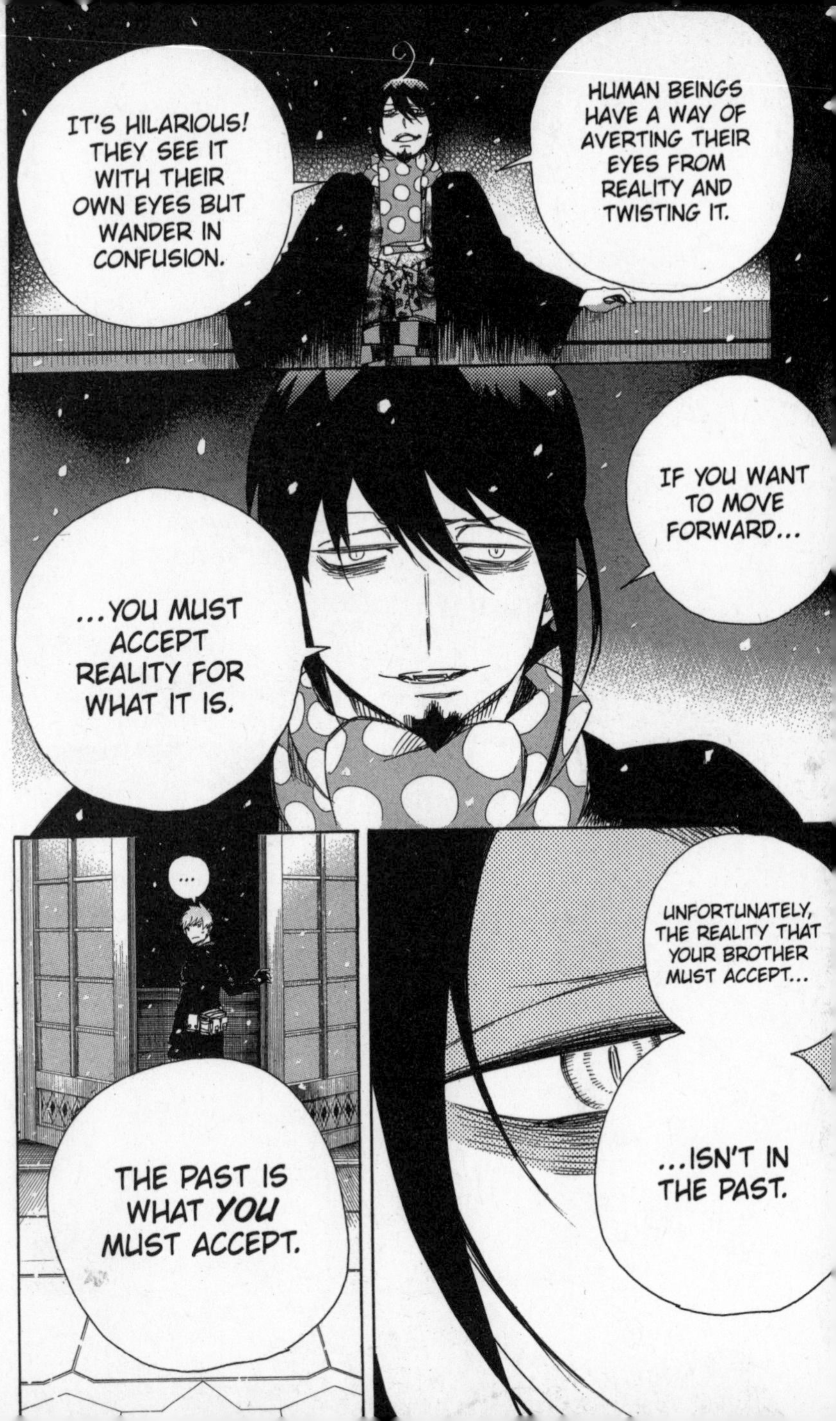
HUMAN BEINGS HAVE A WAY OF AVERTING THEIR EYES FROM REALITY AND TWISTING IT.
IT'S HILARIOUS! THEY SEE IT WITH THEIR OWN EYES BUT WANDER IN CONFUSION.
IF YOU WANT TO MOVE FORWARD...
...YOU MUST ACCEPT REALITY FOR WHAT IT IS.
UNFORTUNATELY, THE REALITY THAT YOUR BROTHER MUST ACCEPT...
...ISN'T IN THE PAST.
...
THE PAST IS WHAT *YOU* MUST ACCEPT.

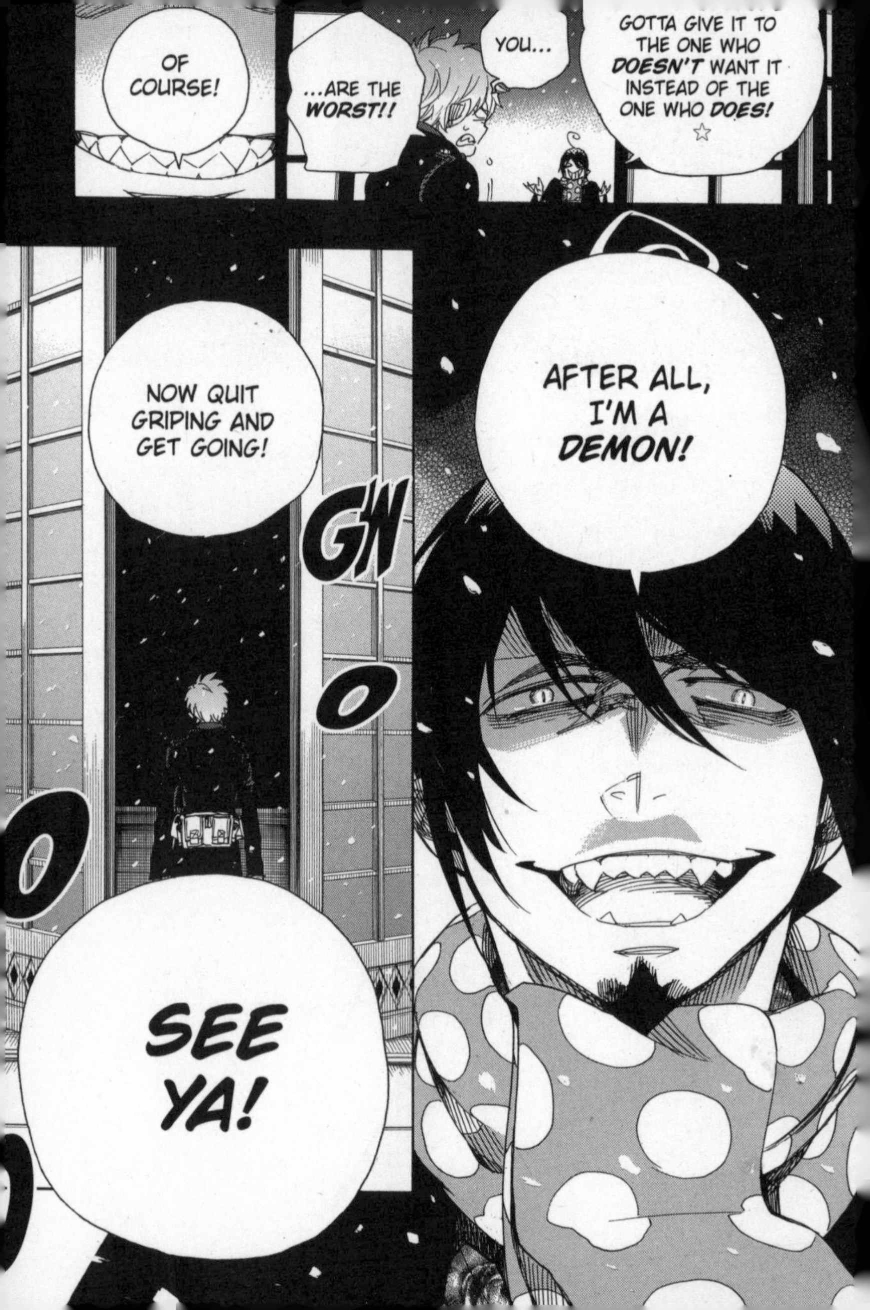
GOTTA GIVE IT TO THE ONE WHO **DOESN'T** WANT IT INSTEAD OF THE ONE WHO **DOES!** ☆
YOU...
...ARE THE **WORST!!**
OF COURSE!
AFTER ALL, I'M A **DEMON!**
NOW QUIT GRIPING AND GET GOING!
GWOO
SEE YA!

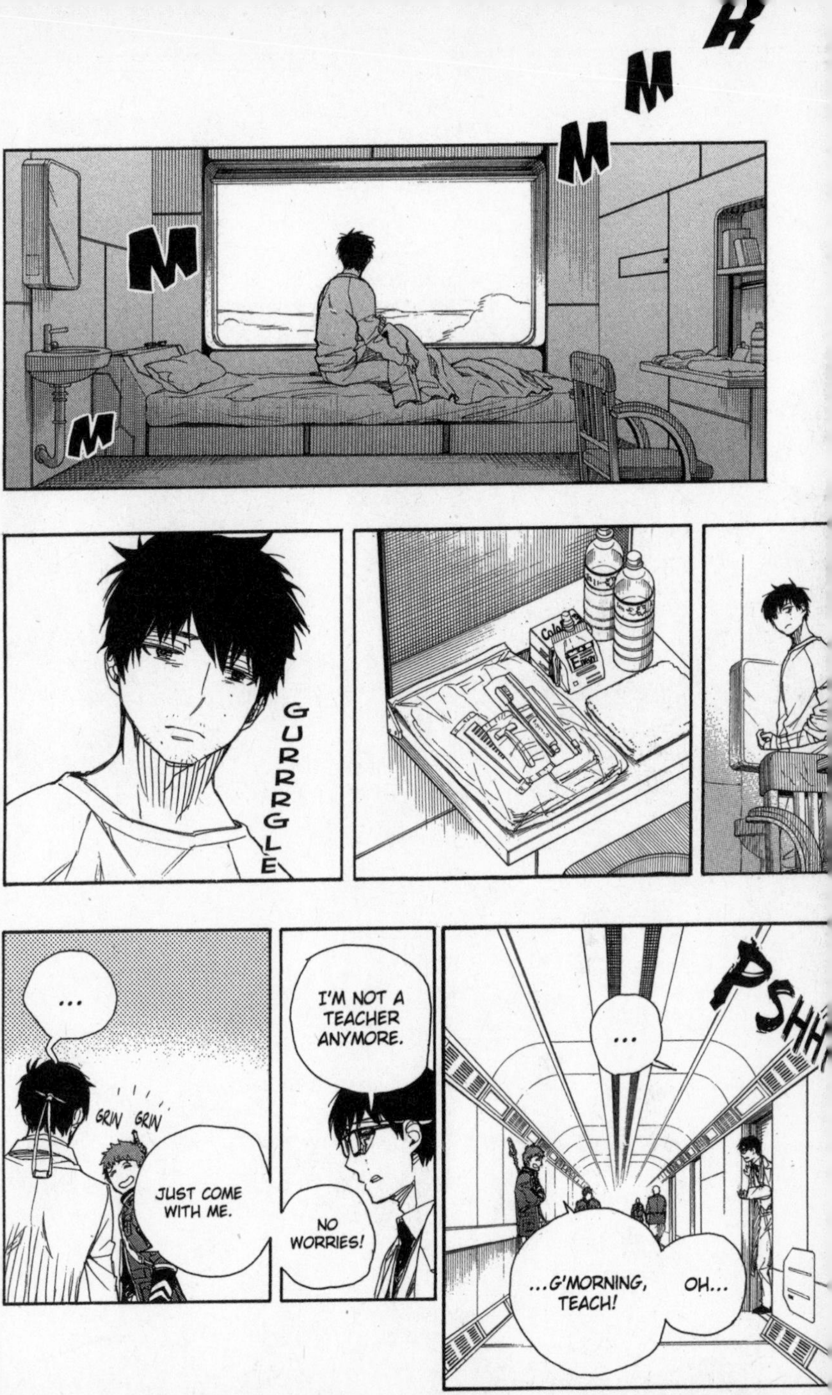
MMMMMR
GURRRGLE
PSHH
...
OH...
...G'MORNING, TEACH!
I'M NOT A TEACHER ANYMORE.
NO WORRIES!
...
GRIN GRIN
JUST COME WITH ME.

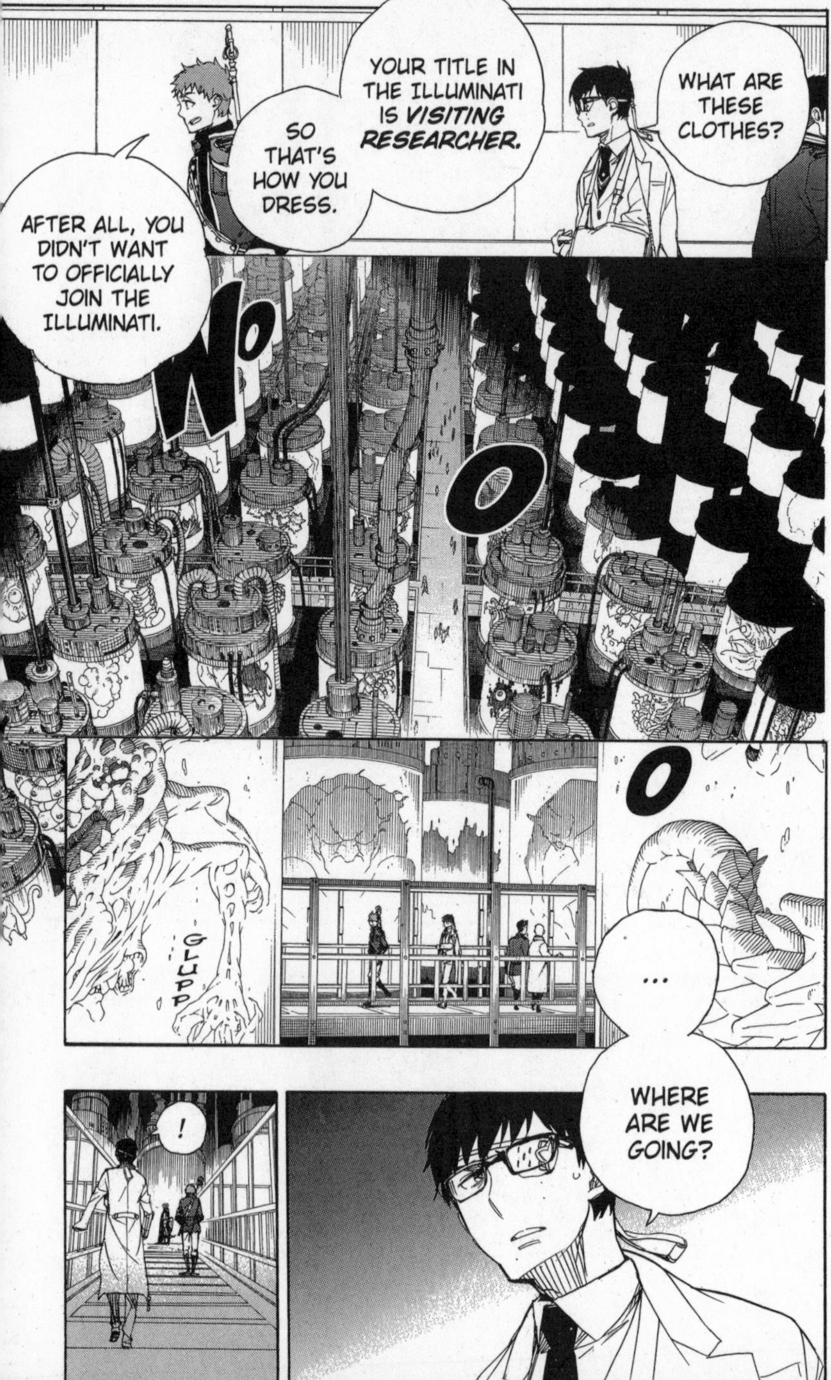
WHAT ARE THESE CLOTHES?
YOUR TITLE IN THE ILLUMINATI IS *VISITING RESEARCHER.*
SO THAT'S HOW YOU DRESS.
AFTER ALL, YOU DIDN'T WANT TO OFFICIALLY JOIN THE ILLUMINATI.
Wo
O
O
...
GLUPP
WHERE ARE WE GOING?
!

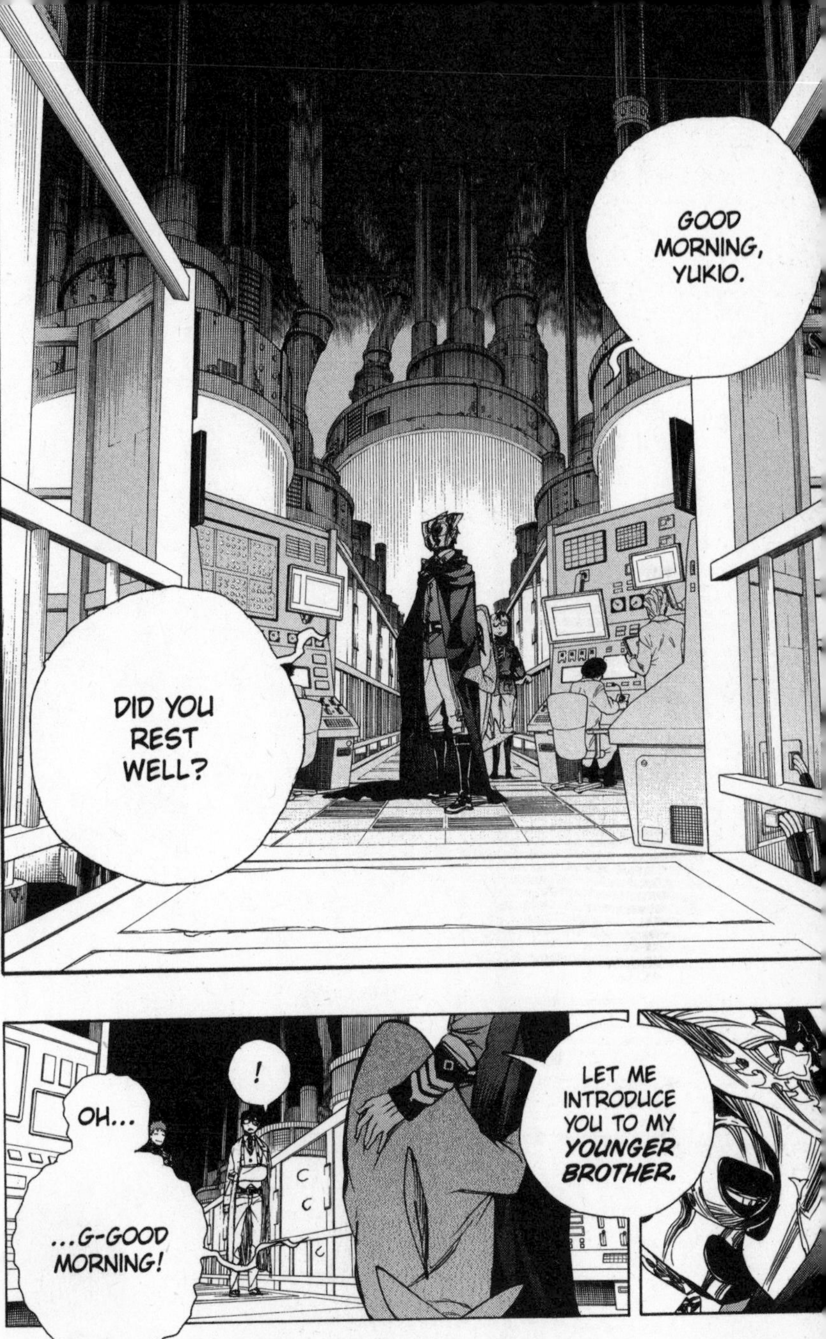
GOOD MORNING, YUKIO.
DID YOU REST WELL?
LET ME INTRODUCE YOU TO MY *YOUNGER BROTHER.*
!
OH...
...G-GOOD MORNING!

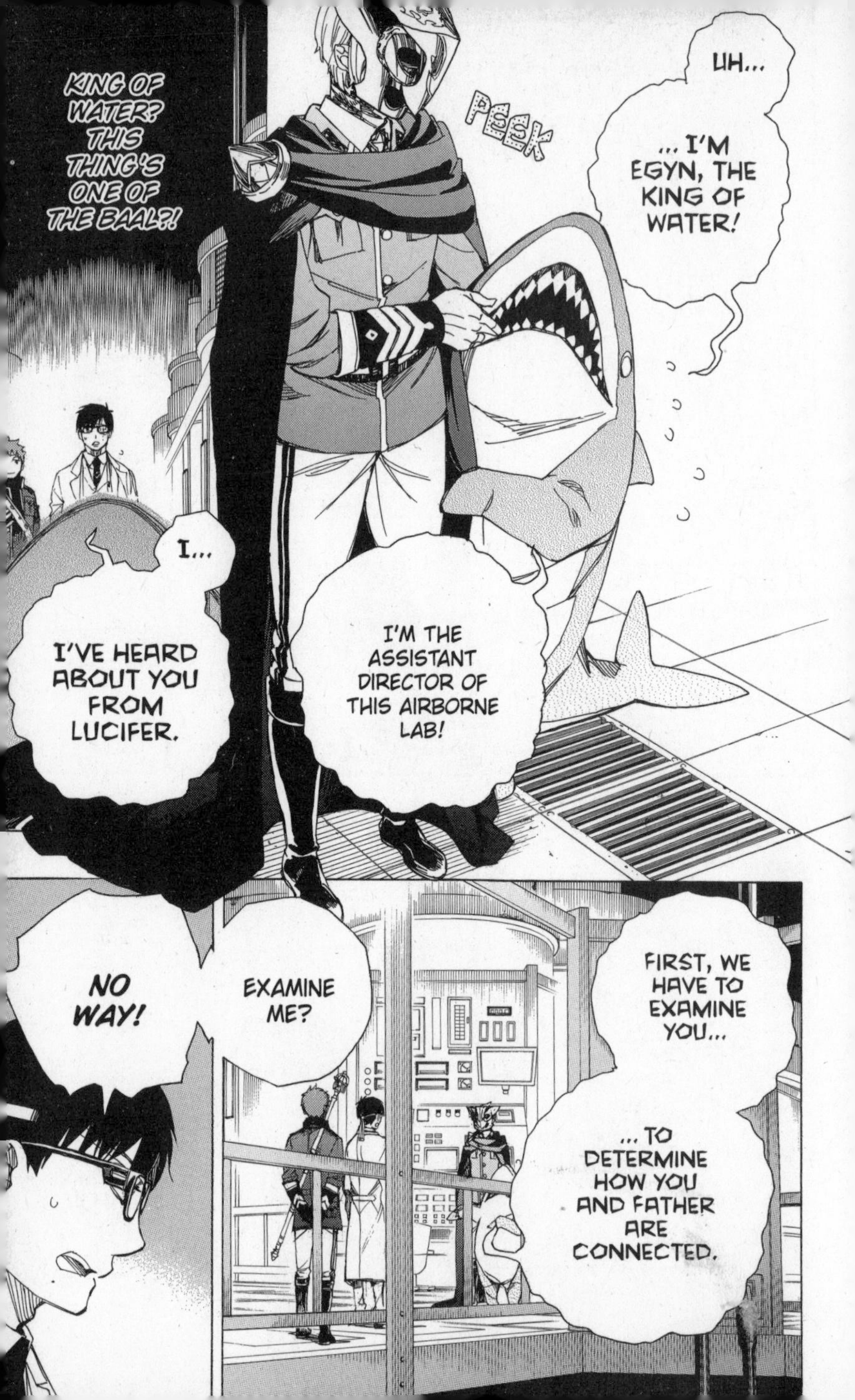
UH...
... I'M EGYN, THE KING OF WATER!
PEEK
KING OF WATER? THIS THING'S ONE OF THE BAAL?!
I'M THE ASSISTANT DIRECTOR OF THIS AIRBORNE LAB!
I...
I'VE HEARD ABOUT YOU FROM LUCIFER.
FIRST, WE HAVE TO EXAMINE YOU...
... TO DETERMINE HOW YOU AND FATHER ARE CONNECTED.
EXAMINE ME?
NO WAY!

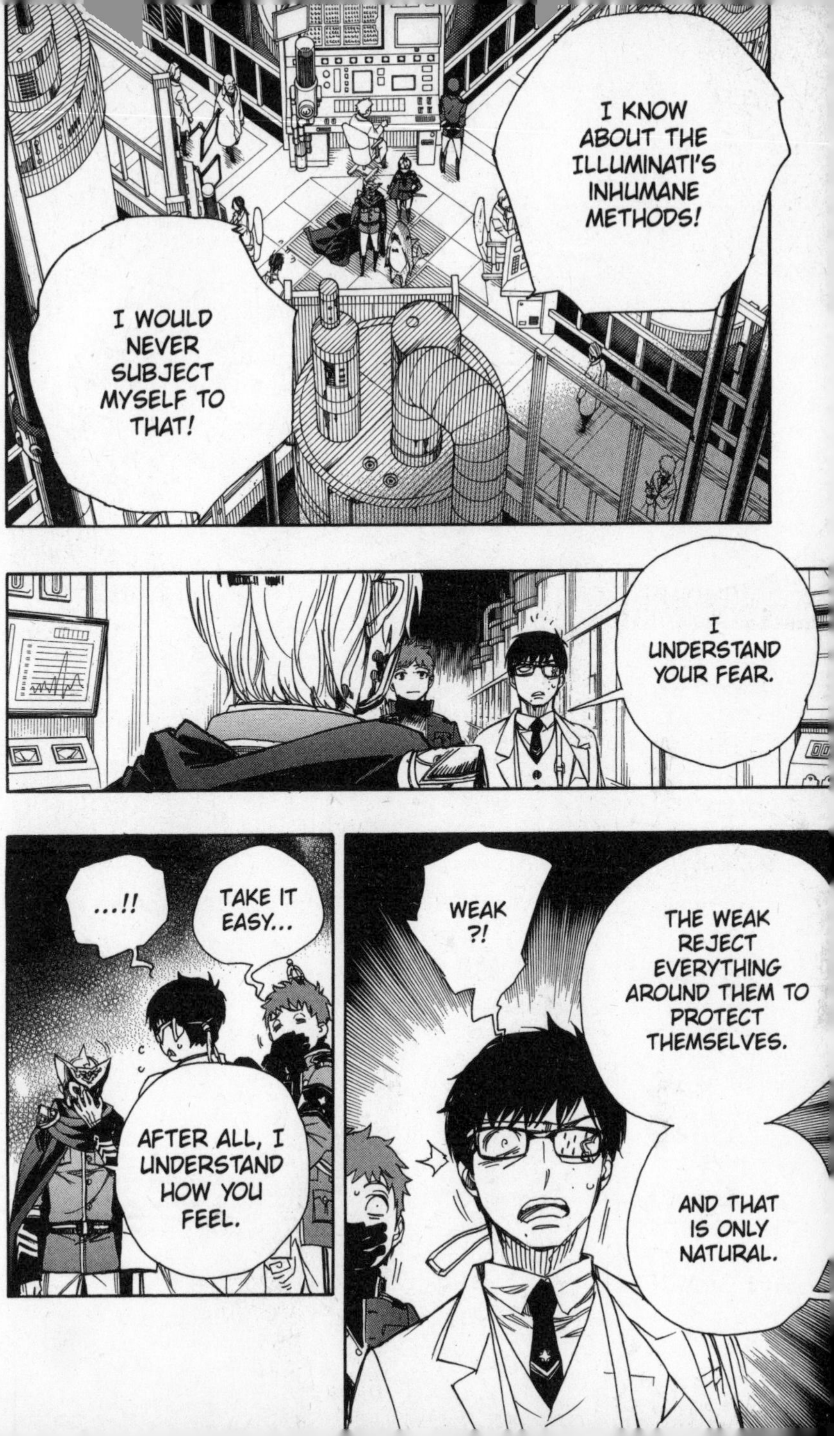
I KNOW ABOUT THE ILLUMINATI'S INHUMANE METHODS!
I WOULD NEVER SUBJECT MYSELF TO THAT!
I UNDERSTAND YOUR FEAR.
THE WEAK REJECT EVERYTHING AROUND THEM TO PROTECT THEMSELVES.
WEAK ?!
AND THAT IS ONLY NATURAL.
TAKE IT EASY...
...!!
AFTER ALL, I UNDERSTAND HOW YOU FEEL.

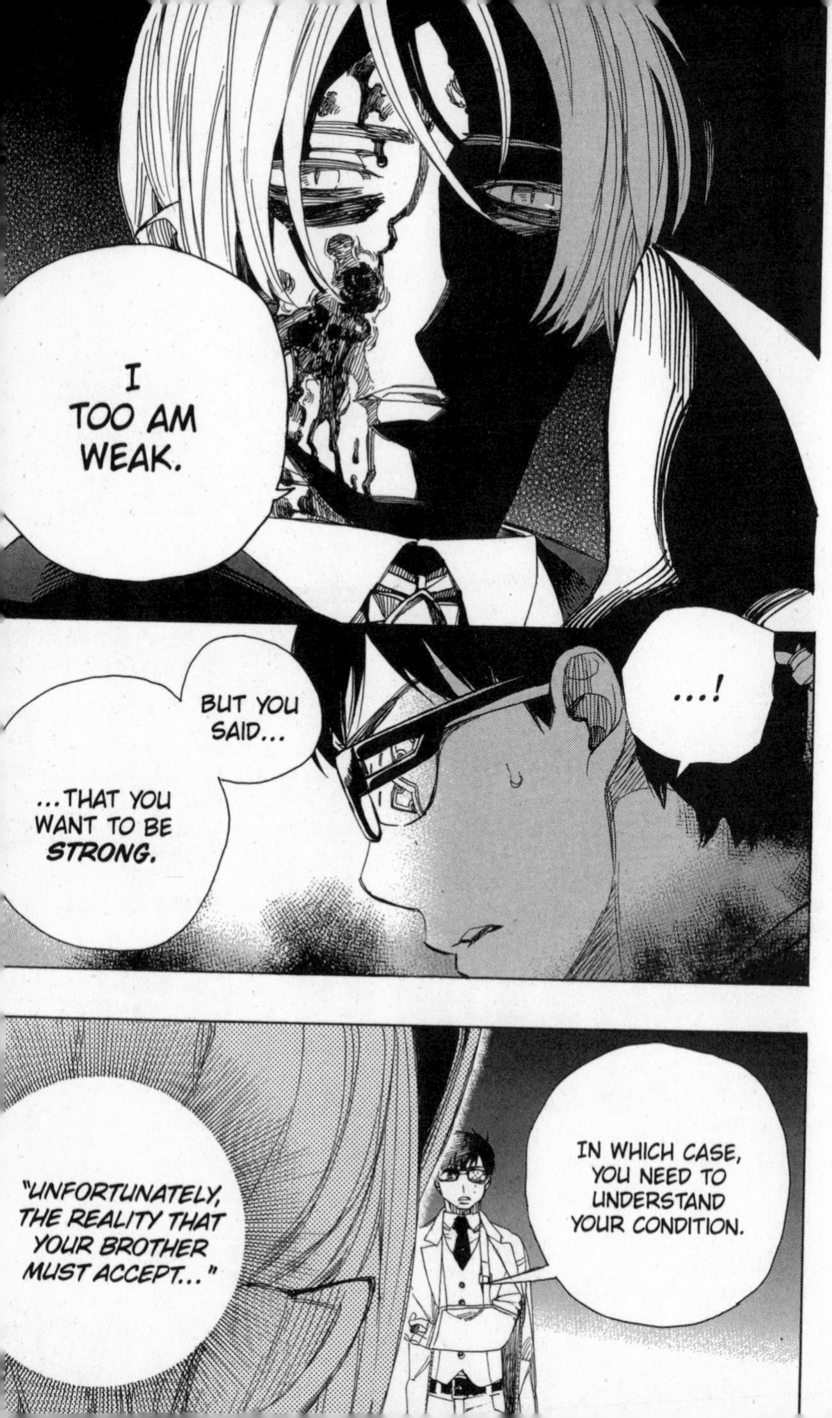
I TOO AM WEAK.
...!
BUT YOU SAID...
...THAT YOU WANT TO BE *STRONG*.
IN WHICH CASE, YOU NEED TO UNDERSTAND YOUR CONDITION.
"UNFORTUNATELY, THE REALITY THAT YOUR BROTHER MUST ACCEPT..."

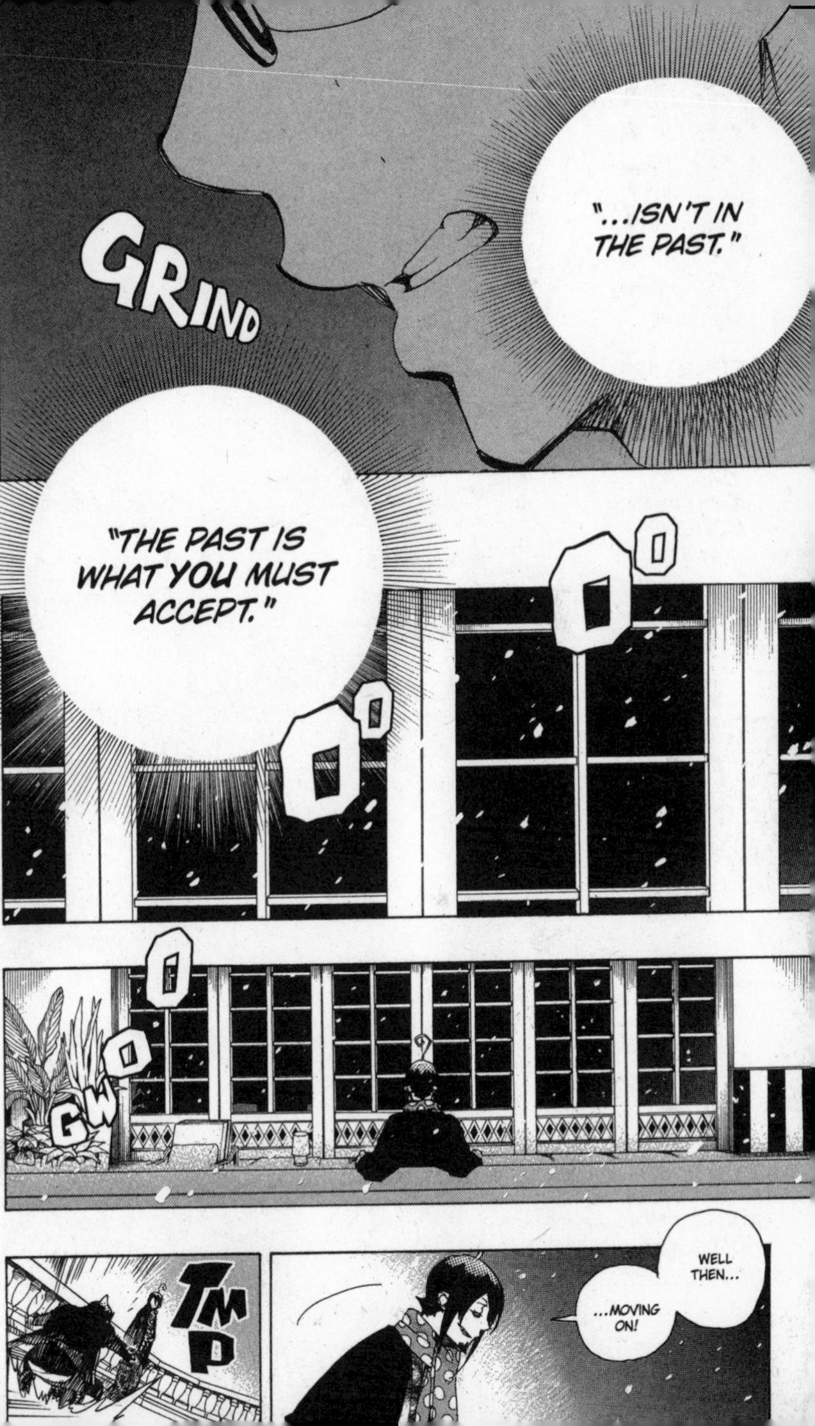
"...ISN'T IN THE PAST."
GRIND
"THE PAST IS WHAT YOU MUST ACCEPT."
GWOOOOOO
WELL THEN...
...MOVING ON!
TMP

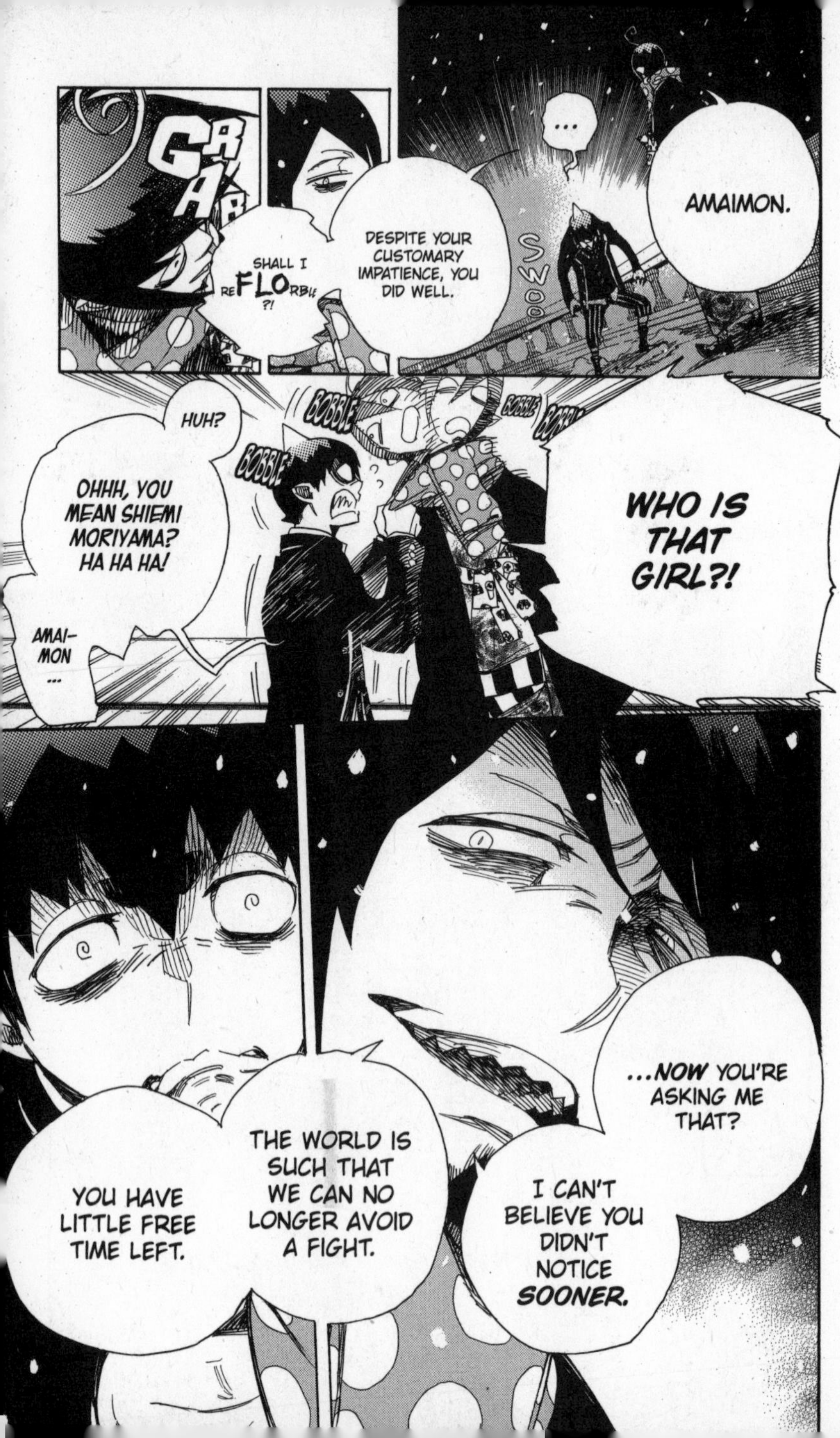
...
AMAIMON.
DESPITE YOUR CUSTOMARY IMPATIENCE, YOU DID WELL.
SWOO
GRAB
SHALL I REFLORBLE?!
WHO IS THAT GIRL?!
BOBBLE BOBBLE BOBBLE BOBBLE
HUH?
OHHH, YOU MEAN SHIEMI MORIYAMA? HA HA HA!
AMAI-MON...
...NOW YOU'RE ASKING ME THAT?
I CAN'T BELIEVE YOU DIDN'T NOTICE SOONER.
THE WORLD IS SUCH THAT WE CAN NO LONGER AVOID A FIGHT.
YOU HAVE LITTLE FREE TIME LEFT.

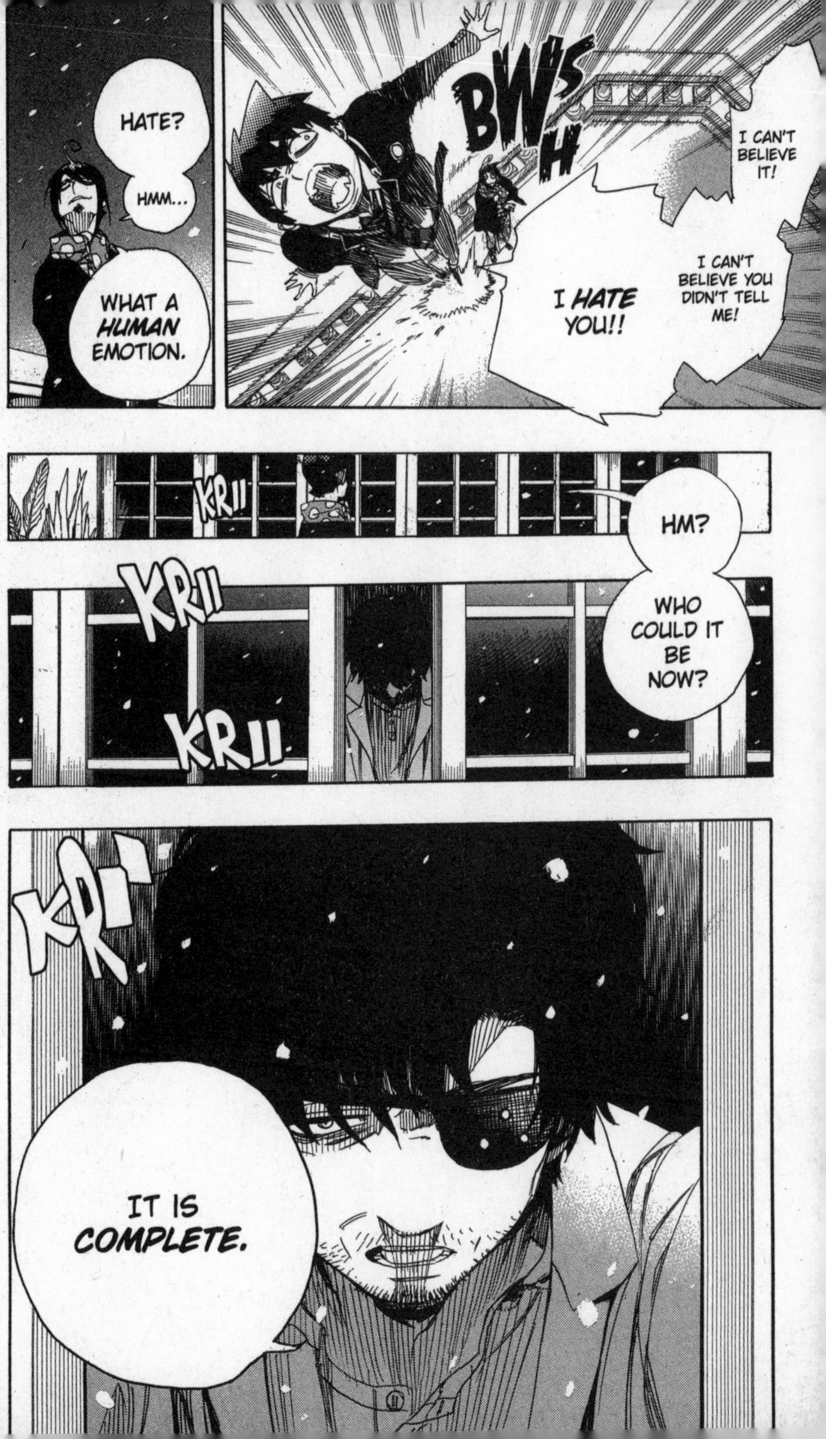
I CAN'T BELIEVE IT!
I CAN'T BELIEVE YOU DIDN'T TELL ME!
BWSH
I HATE YOU!!
HATE?
HMM...
WHAT A HUMAN EMOTION.
HM?
KRII
WHO COULD IT BE NOW?
KRII
KRII
KRI
IT IS COMPLETE.

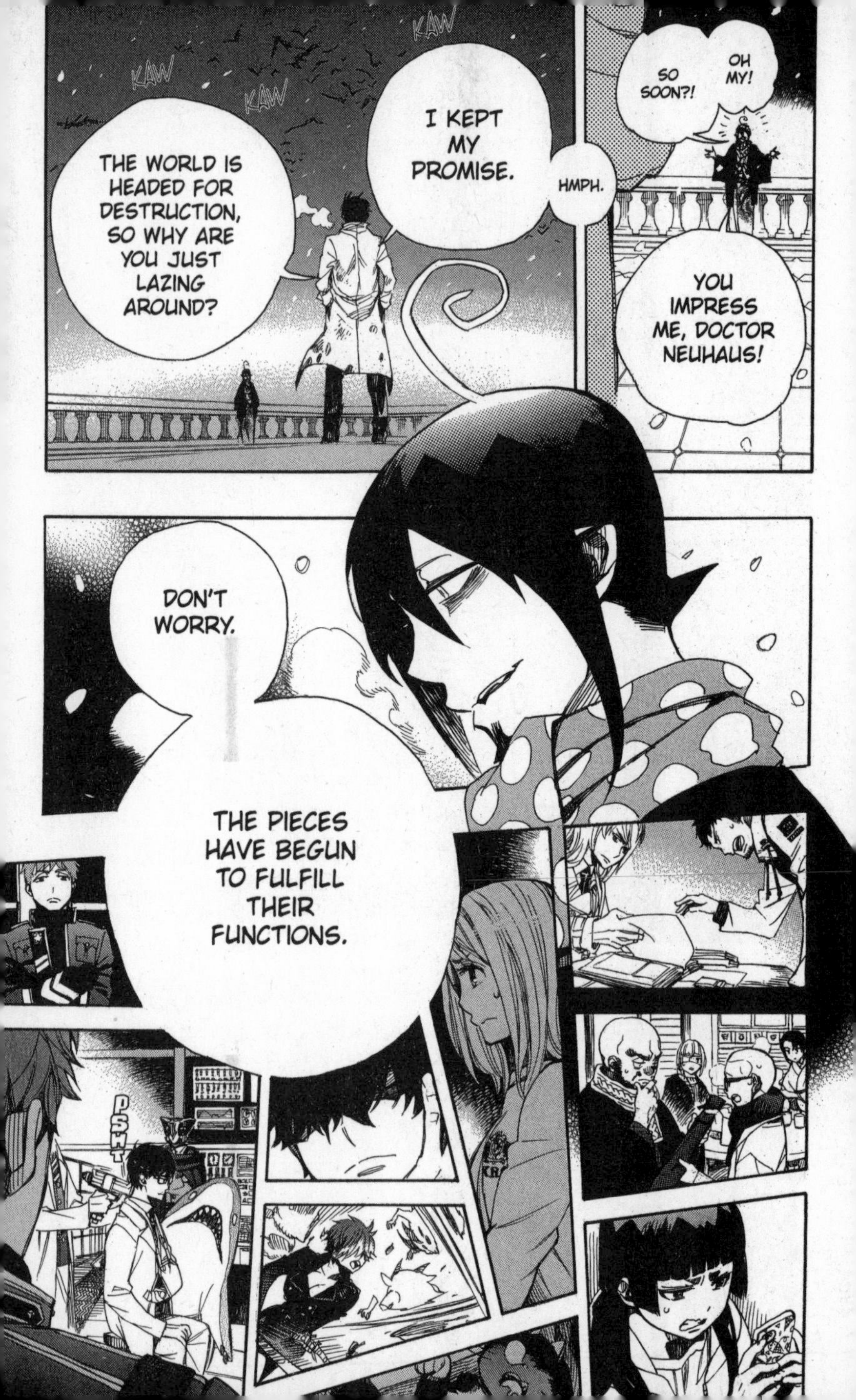
OH MY!
SO SOON?!
YOU IMPRESS ME, DOCTOR NEUHAUS!
HMPH.
I KEPT MY PROMISE.
KAW
KAW
KAW
THE WORLD IS HEADED FOR DESTRUCTION, SO WHY ARE YOU JUST LAZING AROUND?
DON'T WORRY.
THE PIECES HAVE BEGUN TO FULFILL THEIR FUNCTIONS.
PSHT

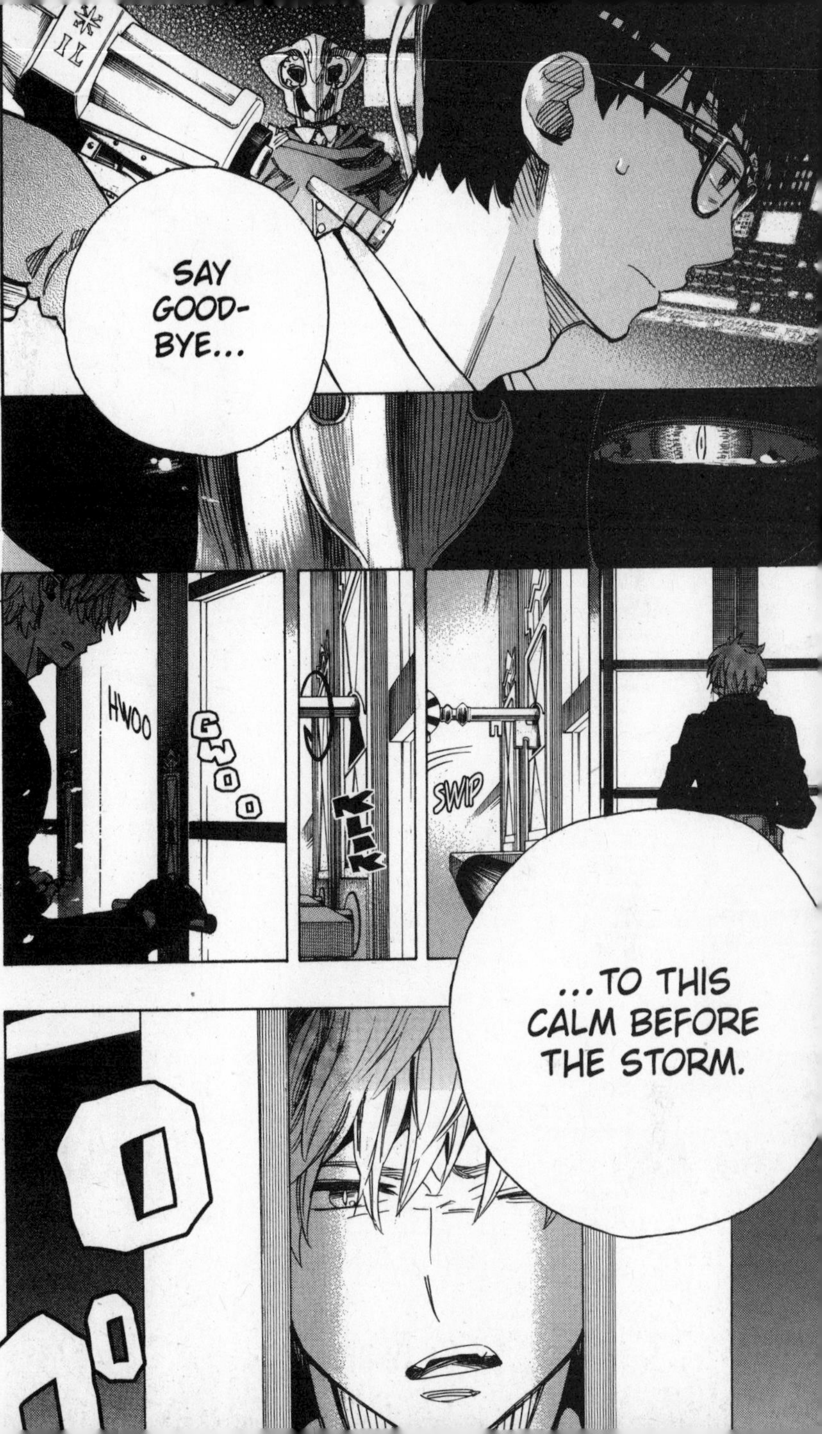
SAY GOOD-BYE...
SWIP
KLIK
GWOOO
HWOO
...TO THIS CALM BEFORE THE STORM.

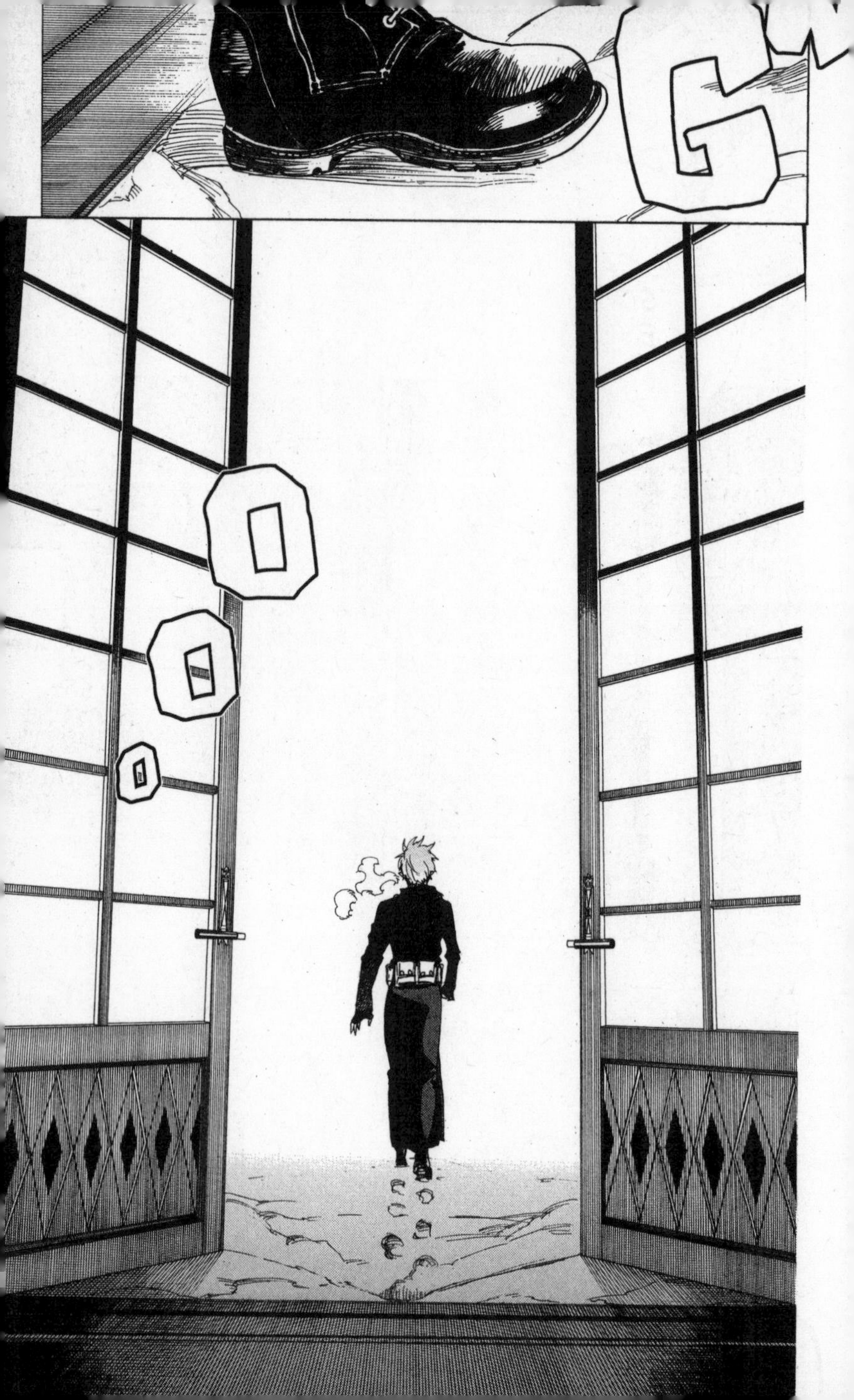
GW

Blue Exorcist Chapter 99: Beyond the Snow, Part 8

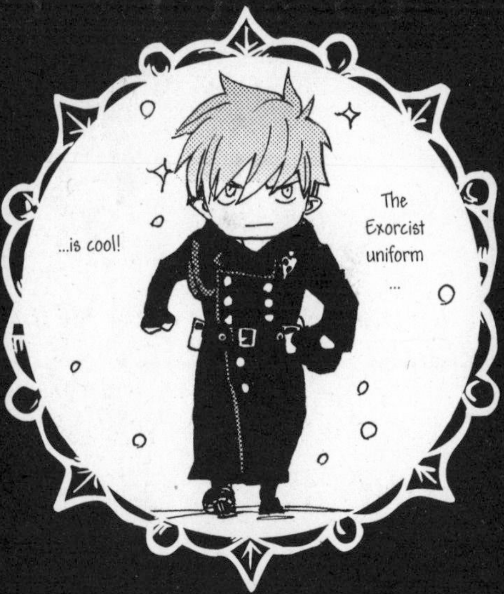
The Exorcist uniform ...
...is cool!

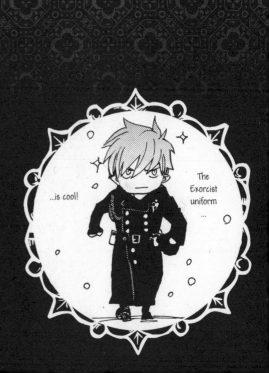

CHAPTER 100: SsC00:40

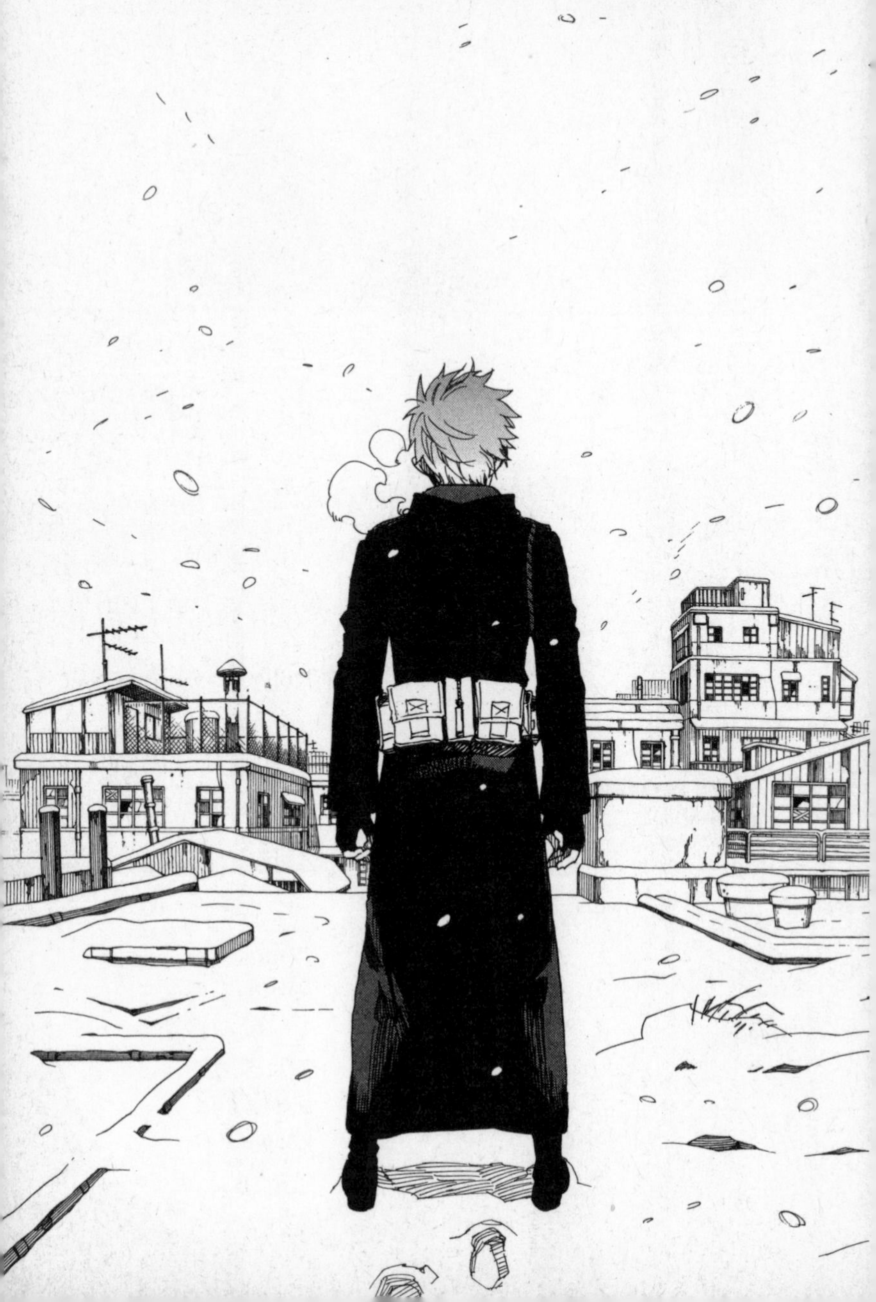

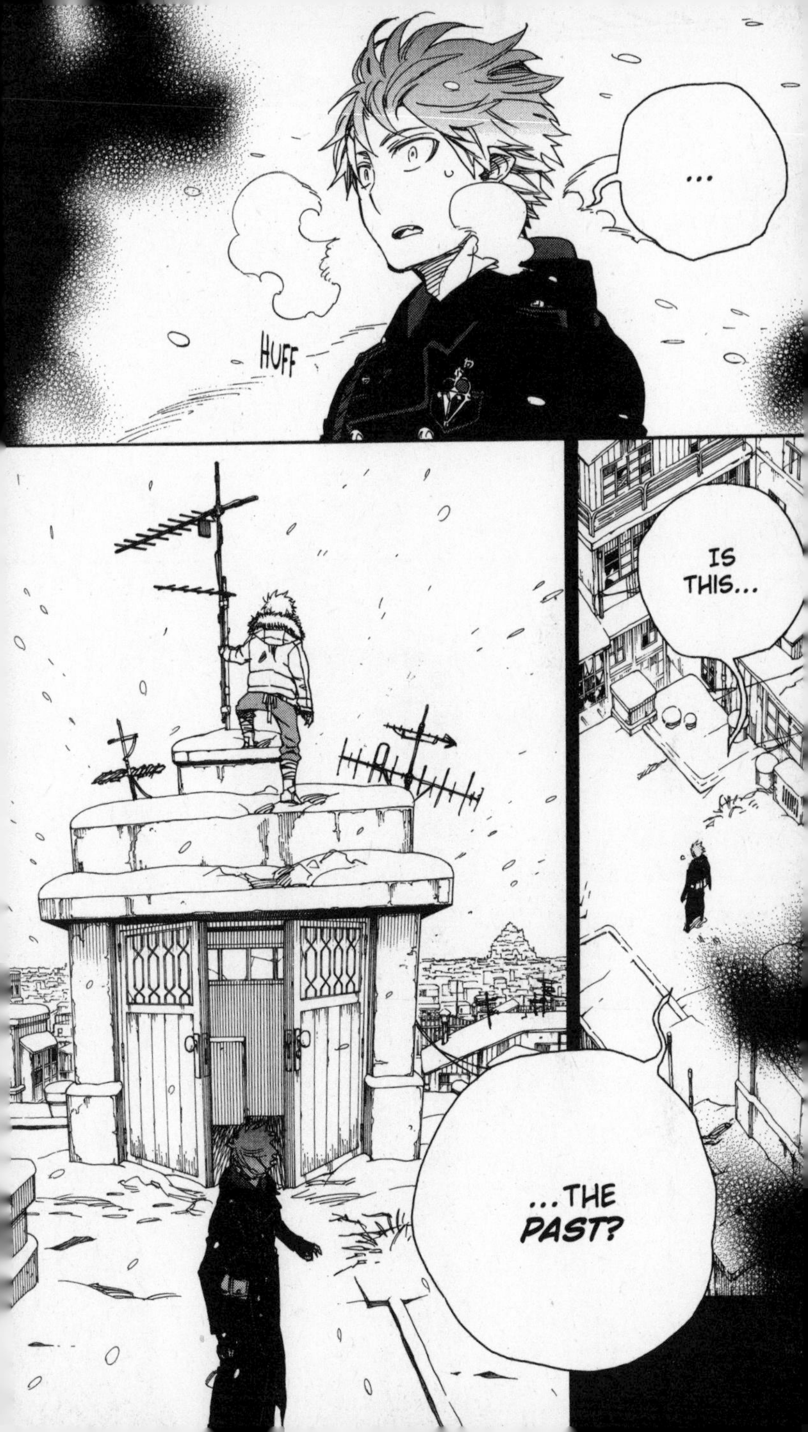
...
HUFF
IS THIS...
...THE PAST?

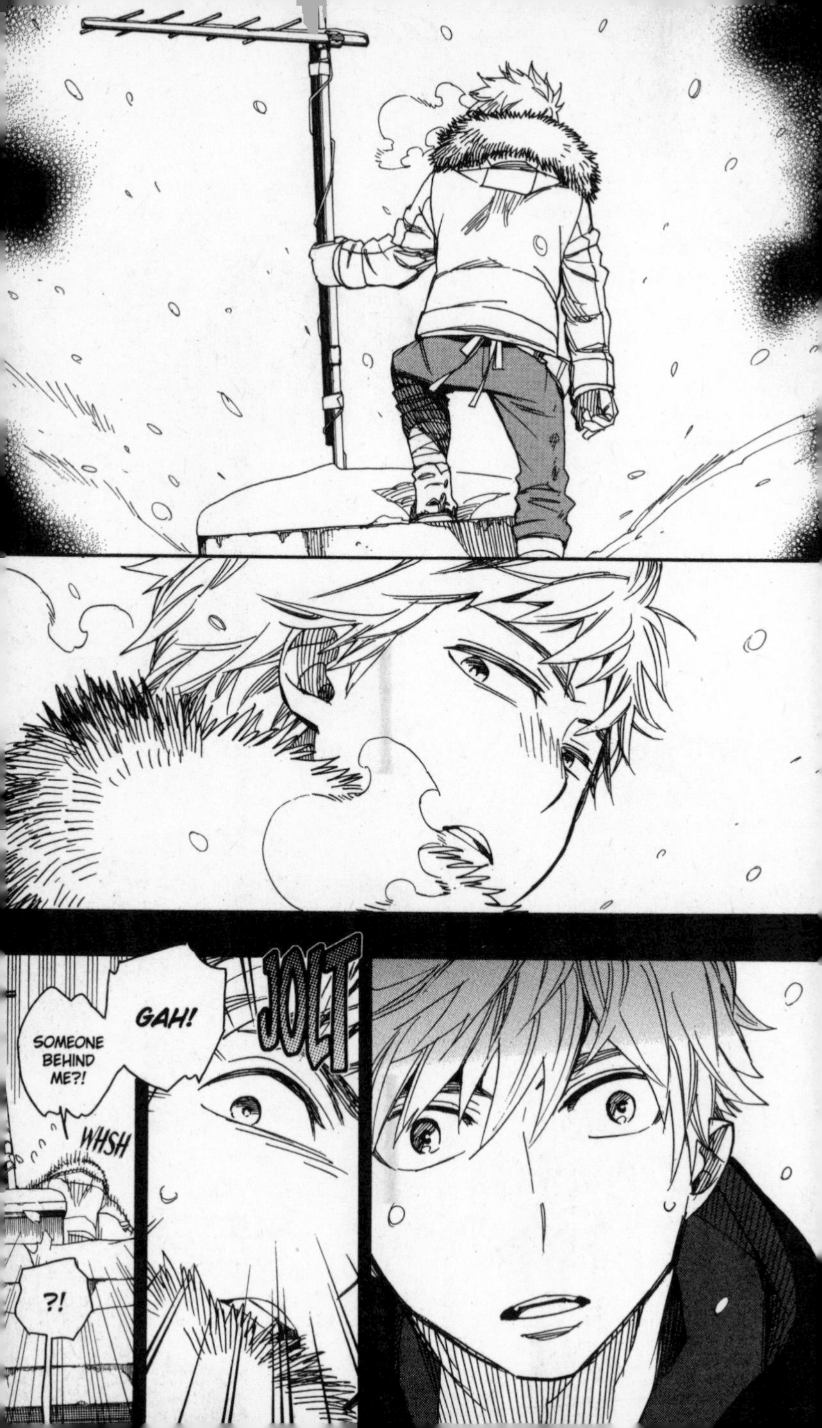
JOLT
GAH!
SOMEONE BEHIND ME?!
WHSH
?!

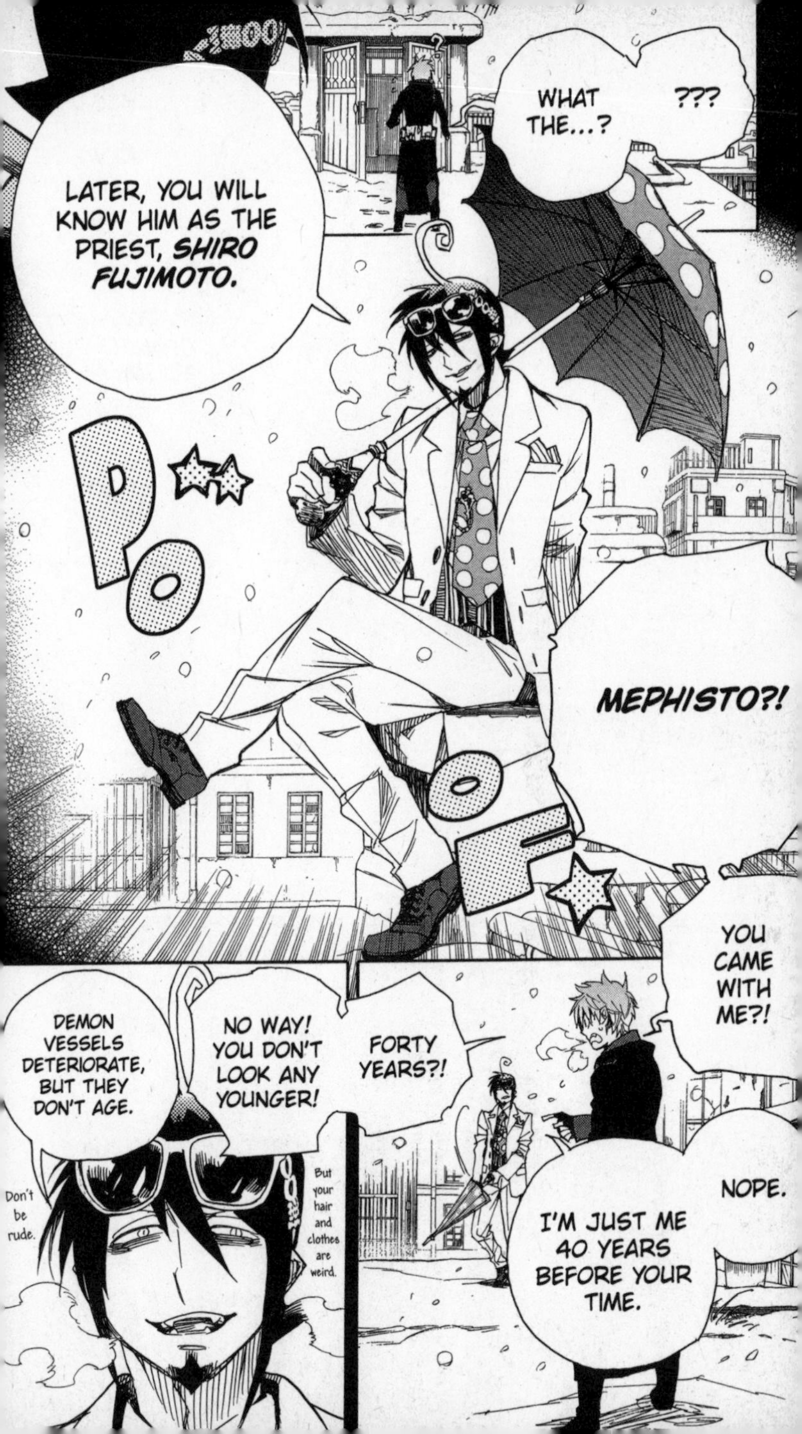
WHAT THE...?
???
LATER, YOU WILL KNOW HIM AS THE PRIEST, SHIRO FUJIMOTO.
POOF
MEPHISTO?!
YOU CAME WITH ME?!
NOPE.
I'M JUST ME 40 YEARS BEFORE YOUR TIME.
FORTY YEARS?!
NO WAY! YOU DON'T LOOK ANY YOUNGER!
But your hair and clothes are weird.
DEMON VESSELS DETERIORATE, BUT THEY DON'T AGE.
Don't be rude.

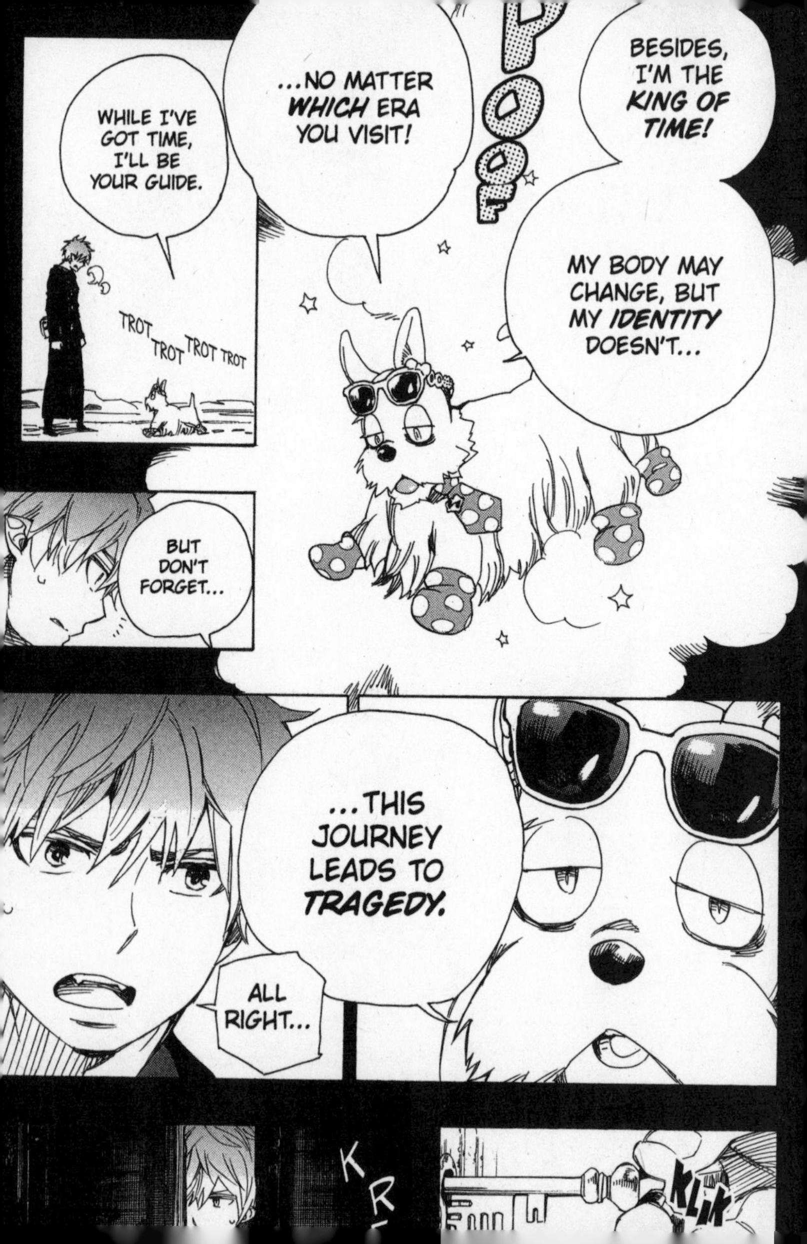
BESIDES, I'M THE KING OF TIME!
POOF
MY BODY MAY CHANGE, BUT MY IDENTITY DOESN'T...
...NO MATTER WHICH ERA YOU VISIT!
WHILE I'VE GOT TIME, I'LL BE YOUR GUIDE.
TROT TROT TROT TROT
BUT DON'T FORGET...
...THIS JOURNEY LEADS TO TRAGEDY.
ALL RIGHT...
KLIK
KR

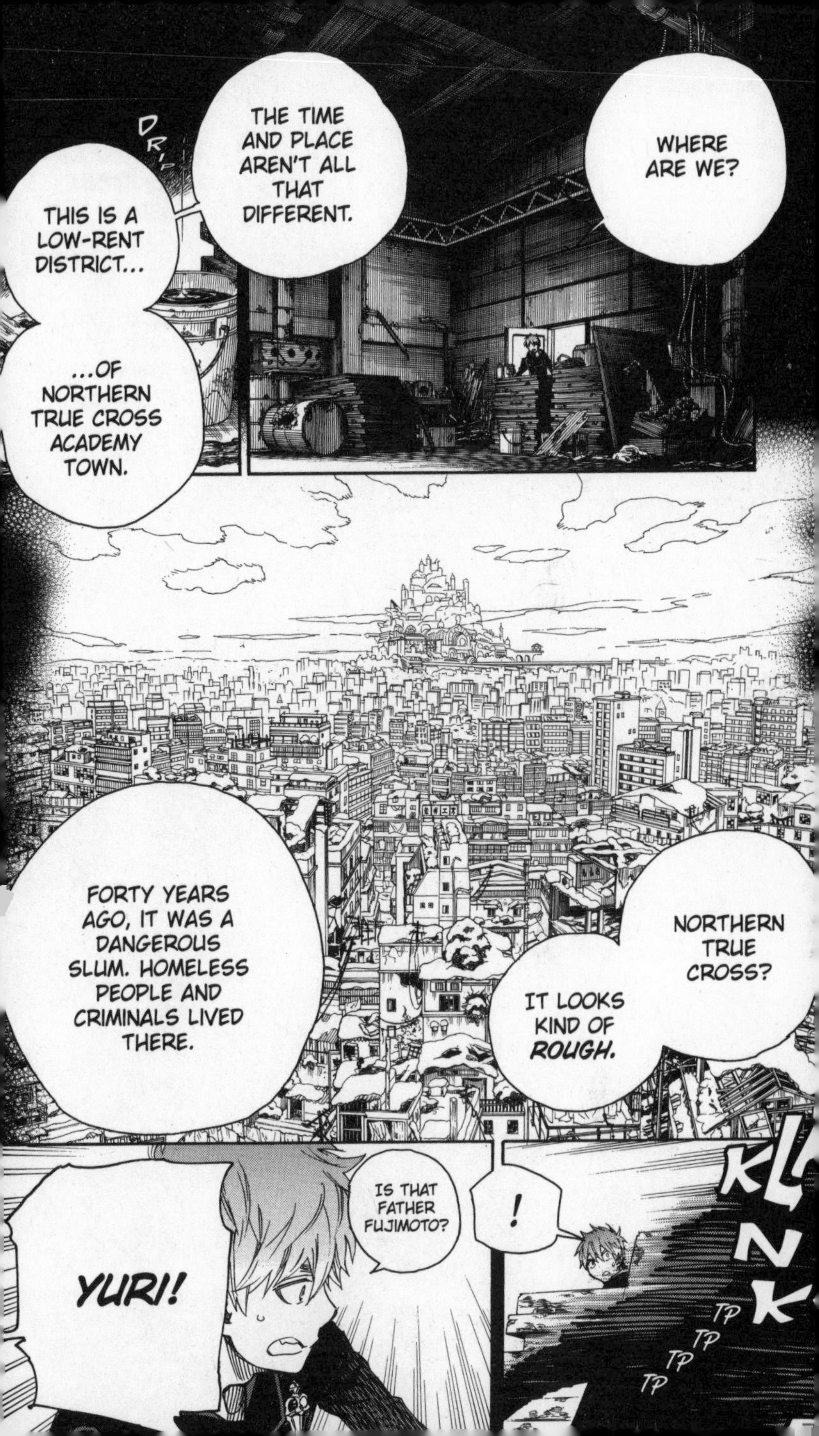
WHERE ARE WE?
THE TIME AND PLACE AREN'T ALL THAT DIFFERENT.
DRIP
THIS IS A LOW-RENT DISTRICT...
...OF NORTHERN TRUE CROSS ACADEMY TOWN.
NORTHERN TRUE CROSS?
IT LOOKS KIND OF ROUGH.
FORTY YEARS AGO, IT WAS A DANGEROUS SLUM. HOMELESS PEOPLE AND CRIMINALS LIVED THERE.
KLUNK
TP TP TP TP
!
IS THAT FATHER FUJIMOTO?
YURI!

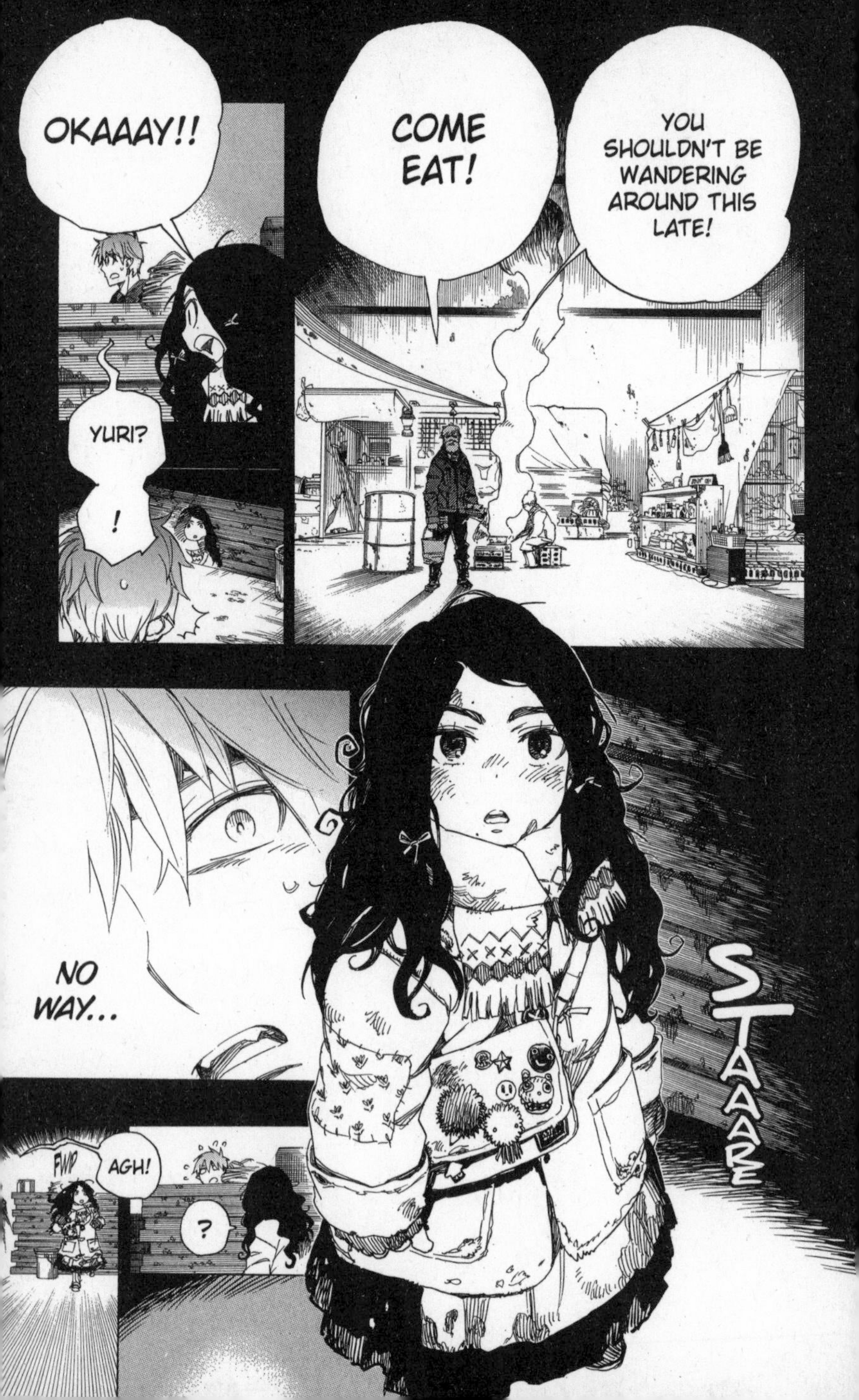
YOU SHOULDN'T BE WANDERING AROUND THIS LATE!
COME EAT!
OKAAAY!!
YURI?
!
STAAARE
NO WAY...
AGH!
FWIP
?

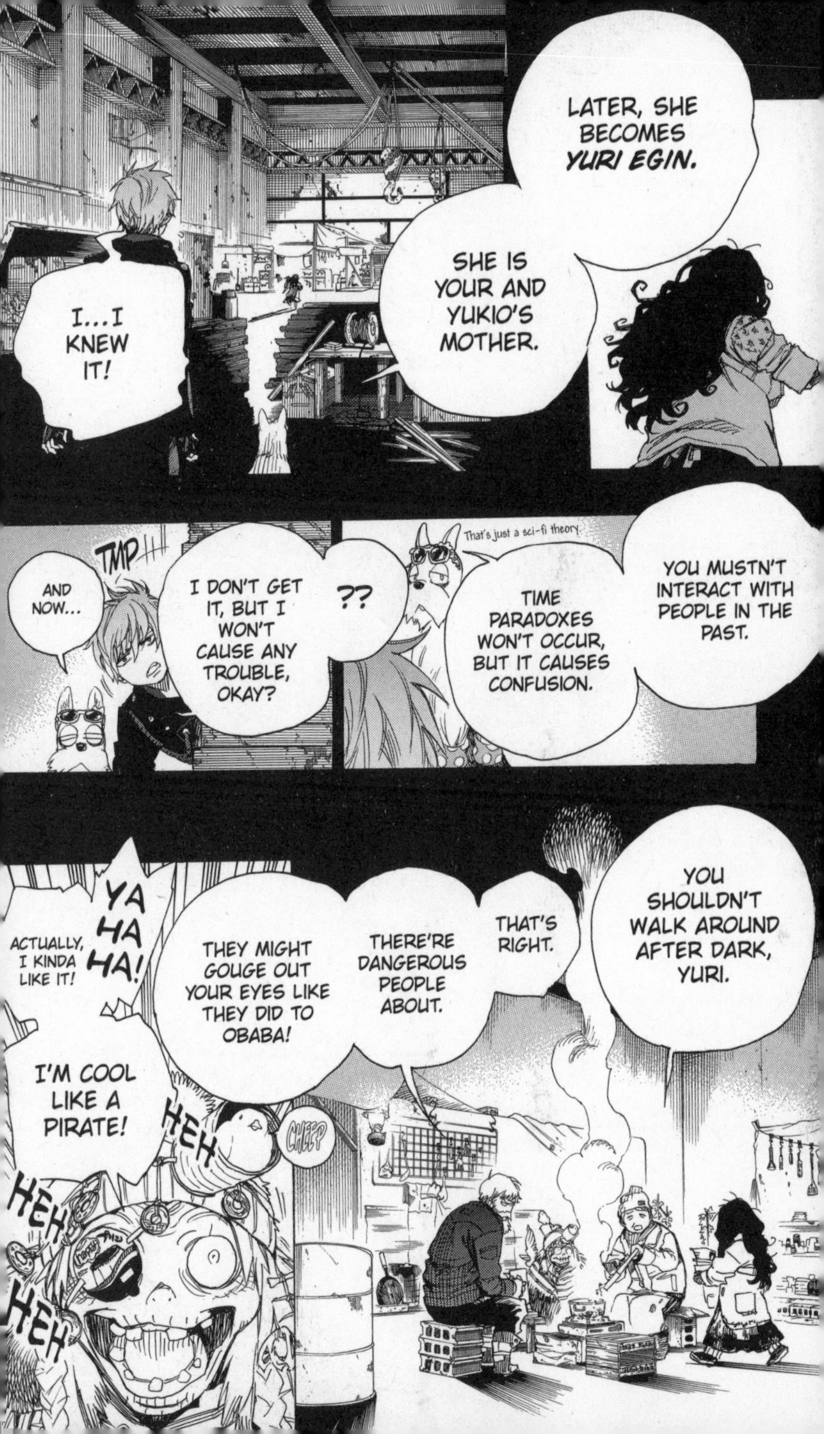
LATER, SHE BECOMES YURI EGIN.
SHE IS YOUR AND YUKIO'S MOTHER.
I...I KNEW IT!
YOU MUSTN'T INTERACT WITH PEOPLE IN THE PAST.
That's just a sci-fi theory.
TIME PARADOXES WON'T OCCUR, BUT IT CAUSES CONFUSION.
??
TMP
I DON'T GET IT, BUT I WON'T CAUSE ANY TROUBLE, OKAY?
AND NOW...
YOU SHOULDN'T WALK AROUND AFTER DARK, YURI.
THAT'S RIGHT.
THERE'RE DANGEROUS PEOPLE ABOUT.
THEY MIGHT GOUGE OUT YOUR EYES LIKE THEY DID TO OBABA!
YA HA HA!
ACTUALLY, I KINDA LIKE IT!
I'M COOL LIKE A PIRATE!
CHEEP
HEH
HEH
HEH
HEH

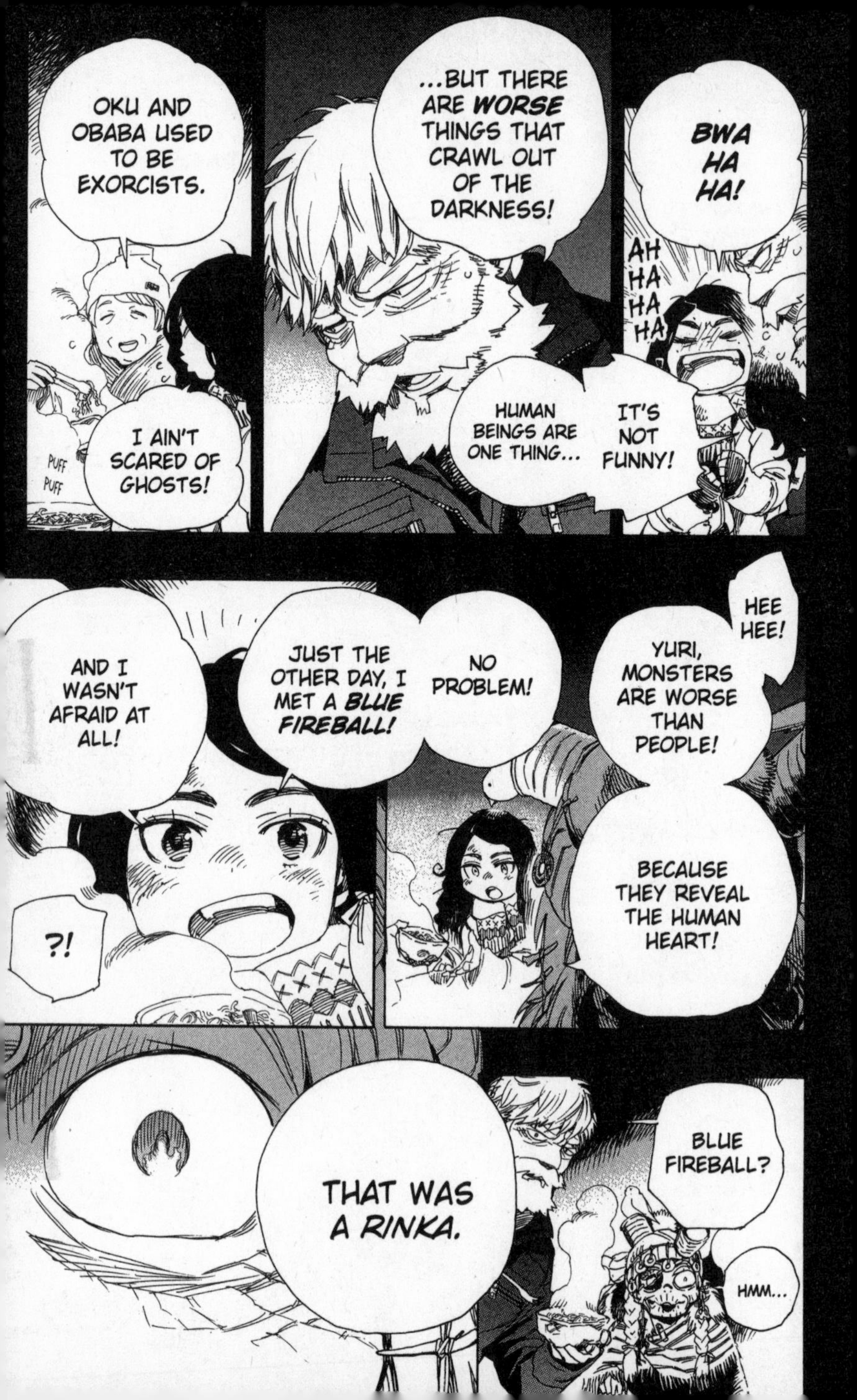
BWA HA HA!
AH HA HA HA HA
IT'S NOT FUNNY!
...BUT THERE ARE WORSE THINGS THAT CRAWL OUT OF THE DARKNESS!
HUMAN BEINGS ARE ONE THING...
OKU AND OBABA USED TO BE EXORCISTS.
I AIN'T SCARED OF GHOSTS!
PUFF PUFF
HEE HEE!
YURI, MONSTERS ARE WORSE THAN PEOPLE!
BECAUSE THEY REVEAL THE HUMAN HEART!
NO PROBLEM!
JUST THE OTHER DAY, I MET A BLUE FIREBALL!
AND I WASN'T AFRAID AT ALL!
?!
BLUE FIREBALL?
HMM...
THAT WAS A RINKA.

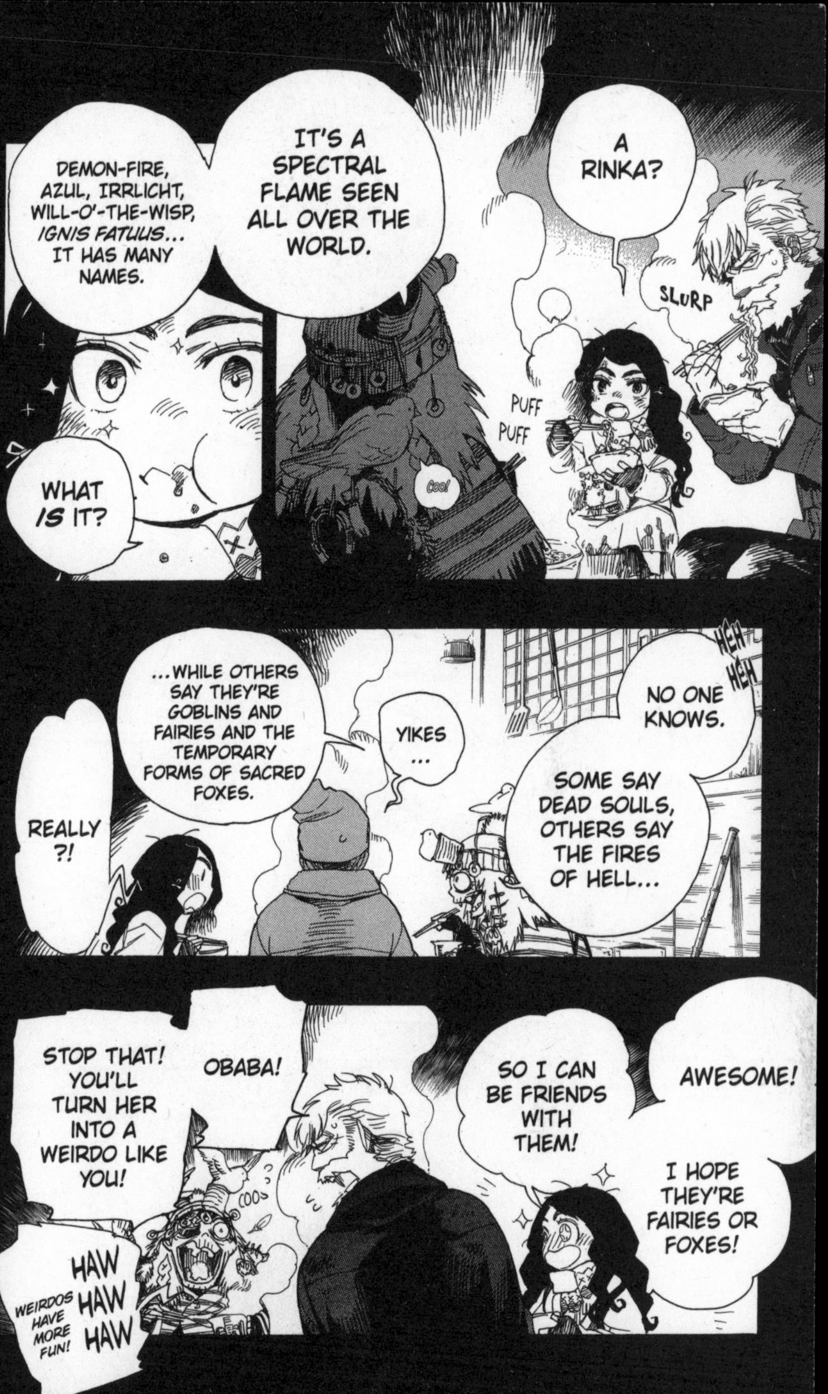
A RINKA?
SLURP
PUFF PUFF
COO!
WHAT *IS* IT?
IT'S A SPECTRAL FLAME SEEN ALL OVER THE WORLD.
DEMON-FIRE, AZUL, IRRLICHT, WILL-O'-THE-WISP, *IGNIS FATUUS*... IT HAS MANY NAMES.
NO ONE KNOWS.
HEH HEH
SOME SAY DEAD SOULS, OTHERS SAY THE FIRES OF HELL...
YIKES ...
...WHILE OTHERS SAY THEY'RE GOBLINS AND FAIRIES AND THE TEMPORARY FORMS OF SACRED FOXES.
REALLY ?!
AWESOME!
I HOPE THEY'RE FAIRIES OR FOXES!
SO I CAN BE FRIENDS WITH THEM!
OBABA!
STOP THAT! YOU'LL TURN HER INTO A WEIRDO LIKE YOU!
COOS
HAW HAW HAW
WEIRDOS HAVE MORE FUN!

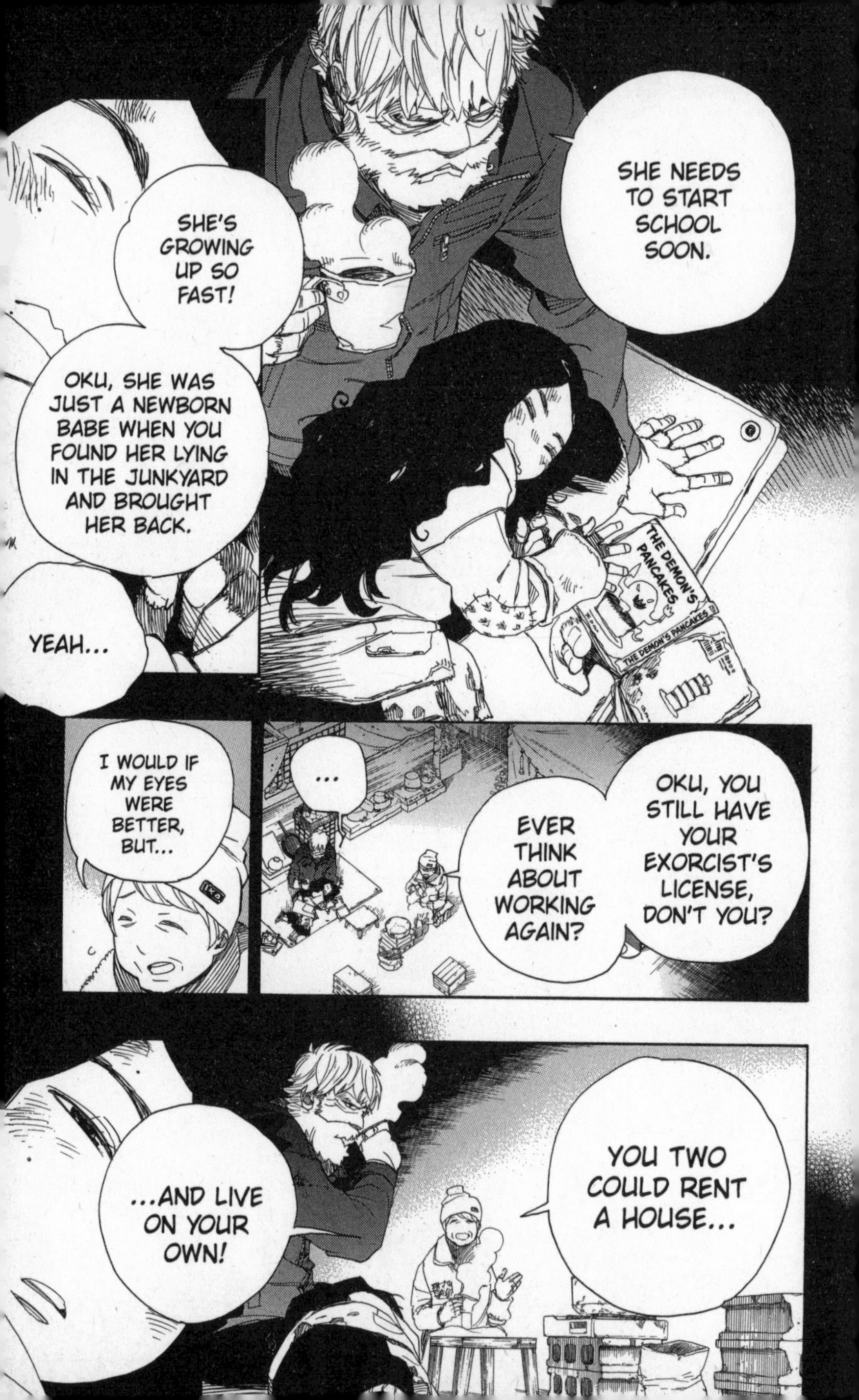
SHE NEEDS TO START SCHOOL SOON.
SHE'S GROWING UP SO FAST!
OKU, SHE WAS JUST A NEWBORN BABE WHEN YOU FOUND HER LYING IN THE JUNKYARD AND BROUGHT HER BACK.
YEAH...
THE DEMON'S PANCAKES
THE DEMON'S PANCAKES
OKU, YOU STILL HAVE YOUR EXORCIST'S LICENSE, DON'T YOU?
EVER THINK ABOUT WORKING AGAIN?
...
I WOULD IF MY EYES WERE BETTER, BUT...
YOU TWO COULD RENT A HOUSE...
...AND LIVE ON YOUR OWN!

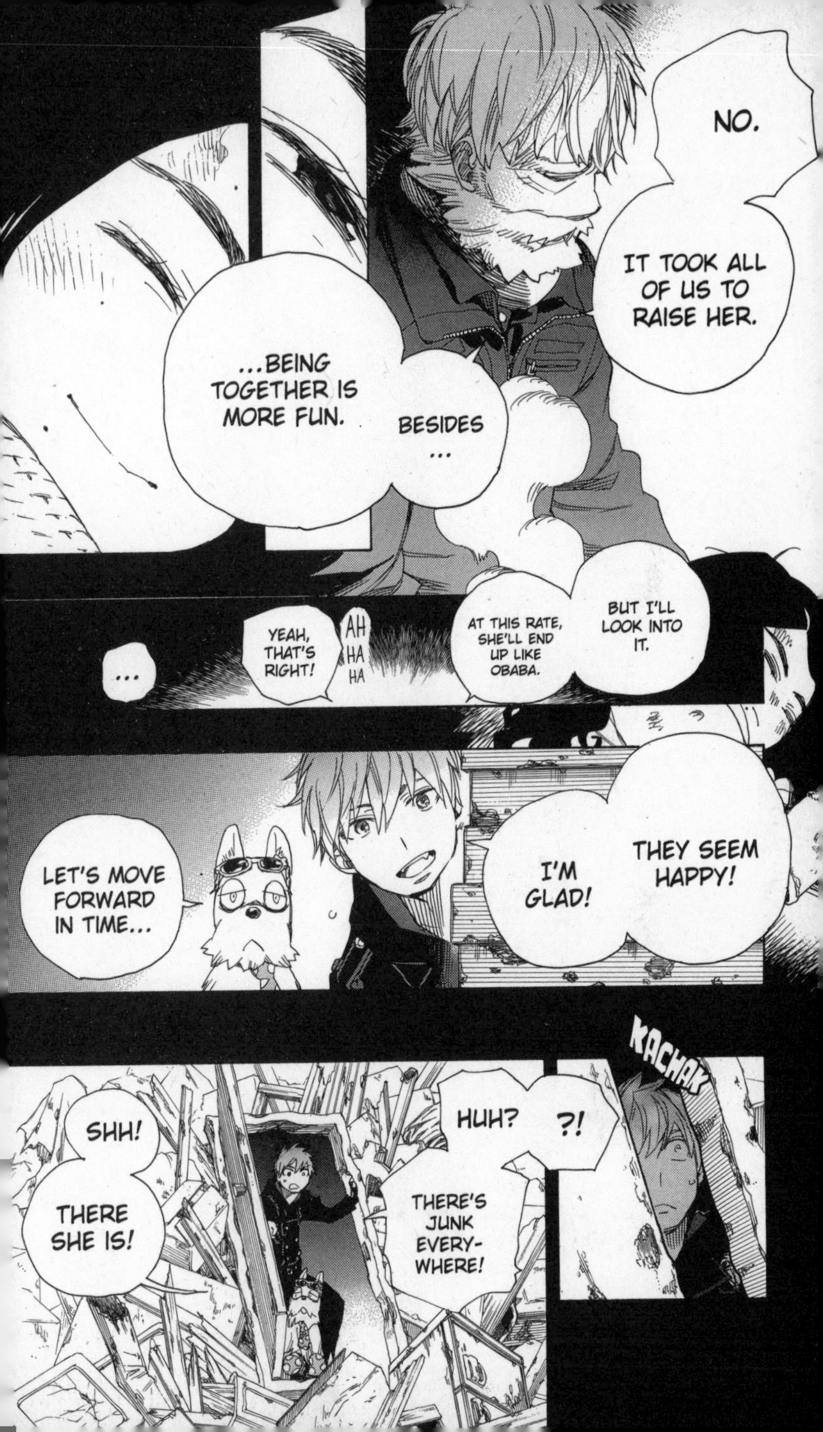
NO.
IT TOOK ALL OF US TO RAISE HER.
BESIDES...
...BEING TOGETHER IS MORE FUN.
BUT I'LL LOOK INTO IT.
AT THIS RATE, SHE'LL END UP LIKE OBABA.
AH HA HA
YEAH, THAT'S RIGHT!
...
THEY SEEM HAPPY!
I'M GLAD!
LET'S MOVE FORWARD IN TIME...
KACHAK
?!
HUH?
THERE'S JUNK EVERY-WHERE!
SHH!
THERE SHE IS!

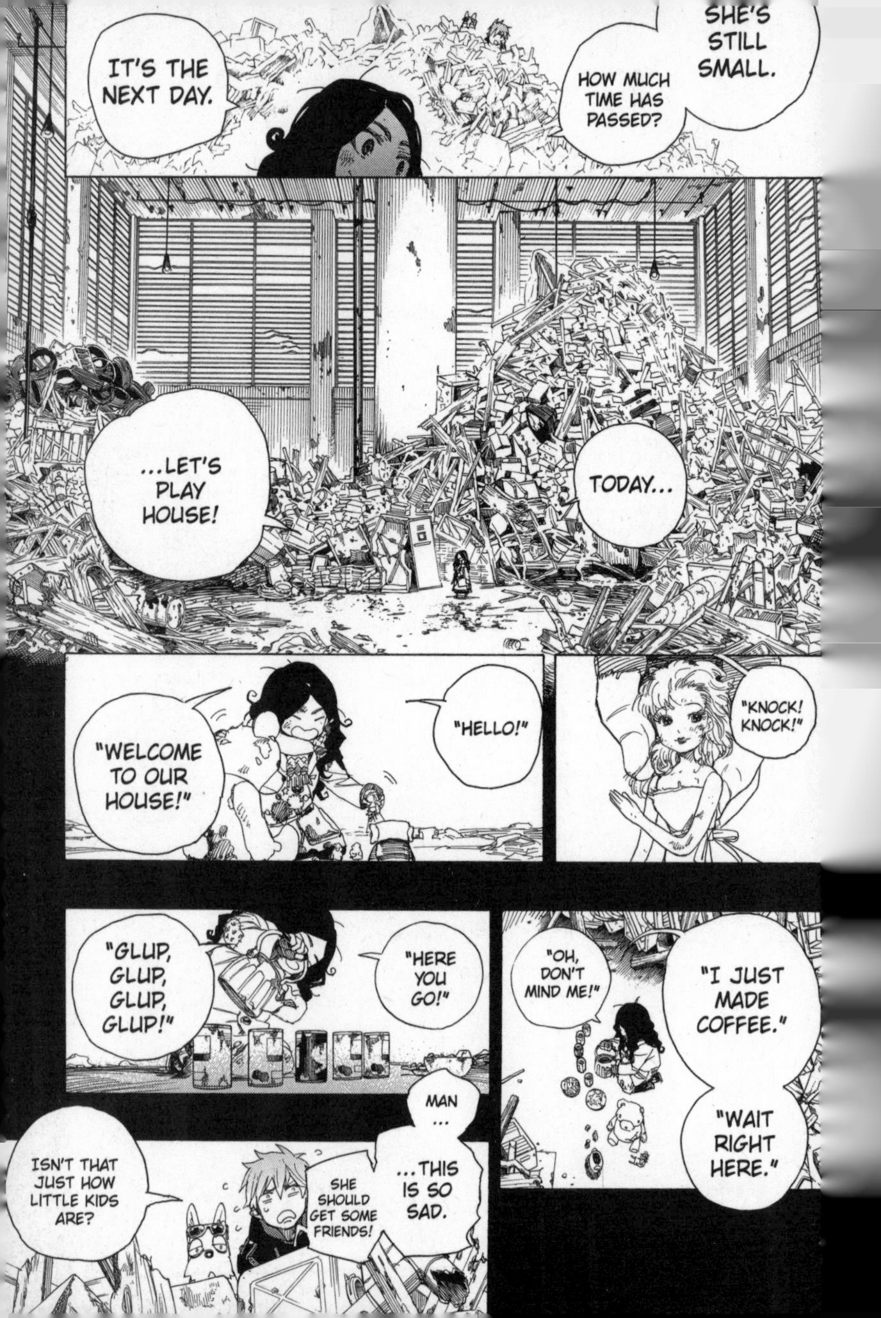
SHE'S STILL SMALL.
HOW MUCH TIME HAS PASSED?
IT'S THE NEXT DAY.
TODAY...
...LET'S PLAY HOUSE!
"KNOCK! KNOCK!"
"HELLO!"
"WELCOME TO OUR HOUSE!"
"I JUST MADE COFFEE."
"WAIT RIGHT HERE."
"OH, DON'T MIND ME!"
"HERE YOU GO!"
"GLUP, GLUP, GLUP, GLUP!"
MAN ...
...THIS IS SO SAD.
SHE SHOULD GET SOME FRIENDS!
ISN'T THAT JUST HOW LITTLE KIDS ARE?

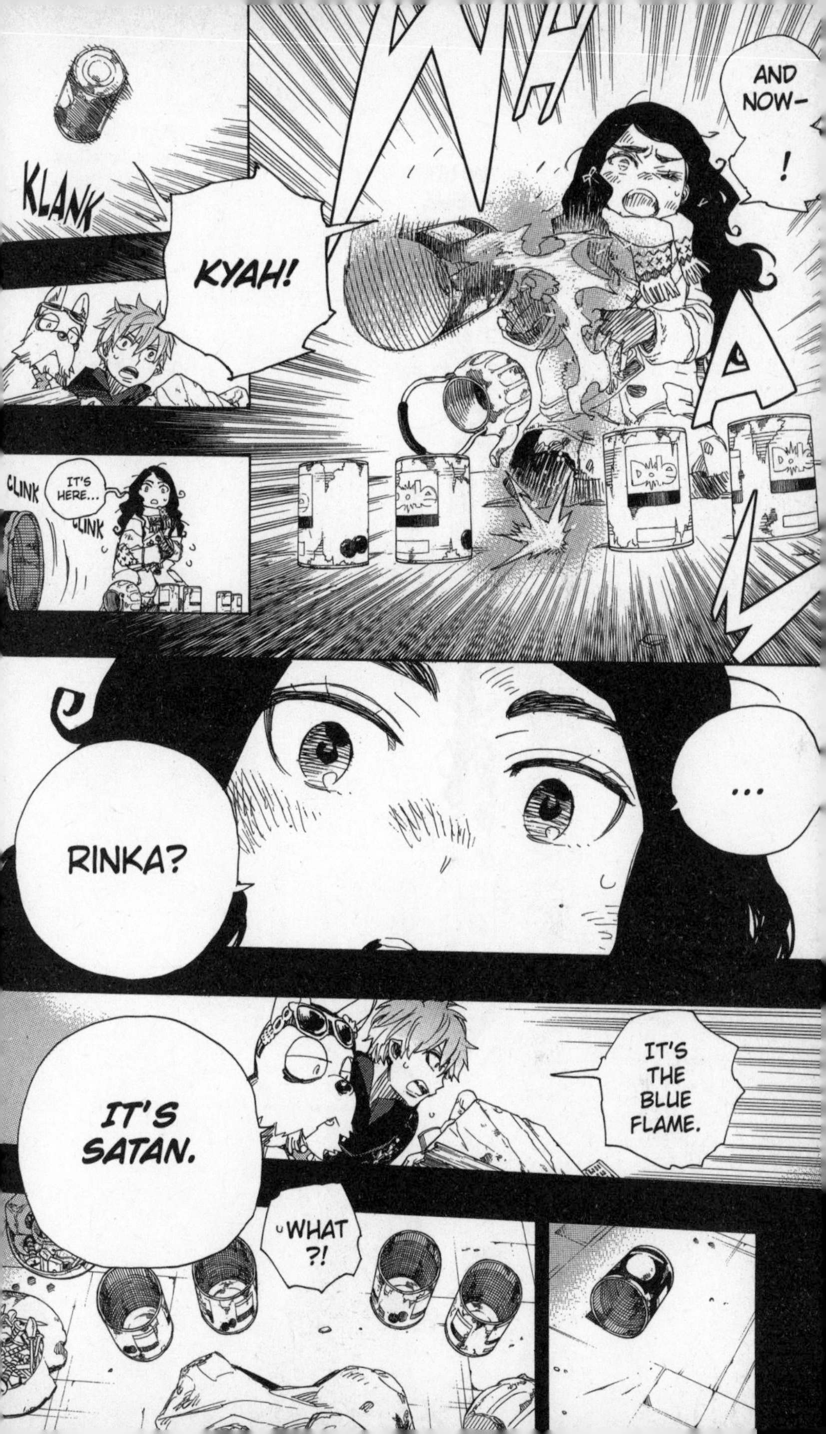
AND NOW–
!
KLANK
KYAH!
CLINK
IT'S HERE...
CLINK
...
RINKA?
IT'S THE BLUE FLAME.
IT'S SATAN.
WHAT ?!

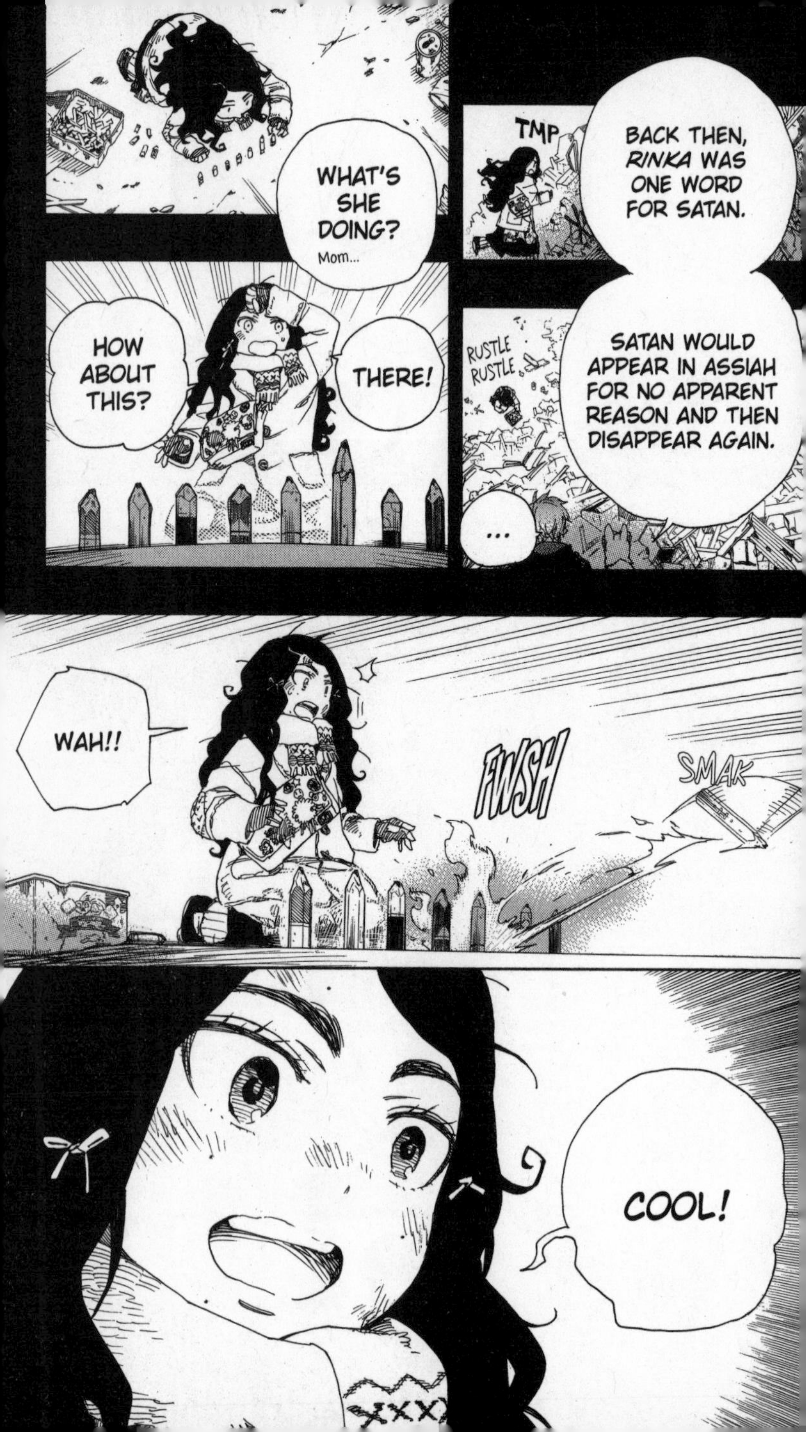
TMP
BACK THEN, *RINKA* WAS ONE WORD FOR SATAN.
RUSTLE RUSTLE
SATAN WOULD APPEAR IN ASSIAH FOR NO APPARENT REASON AND THEN DISAPPEAR AGAIN.
...
WHAT'S SHE DOING?
Mom...
THERE!
HOW ABOUT THIS?
SMAK
FWSH
WAH!!
COOL!

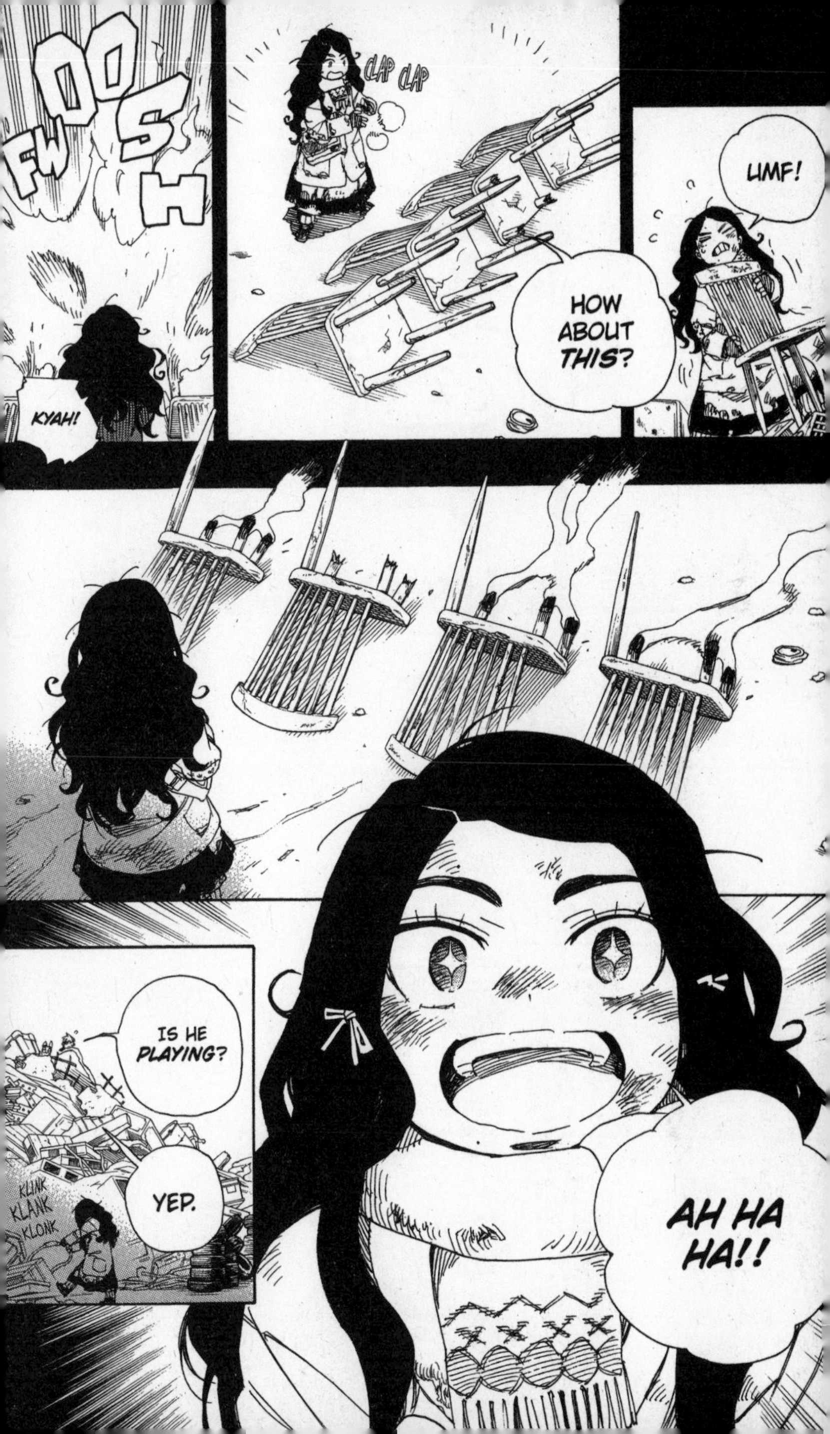
UMF!
CLAP CLAP
HOW ABOUT THIS?
FWOOSH
KYAH!
AH HA HA!!
IS HE PLAYING?
KLINK KLANK KLONK
YEP.

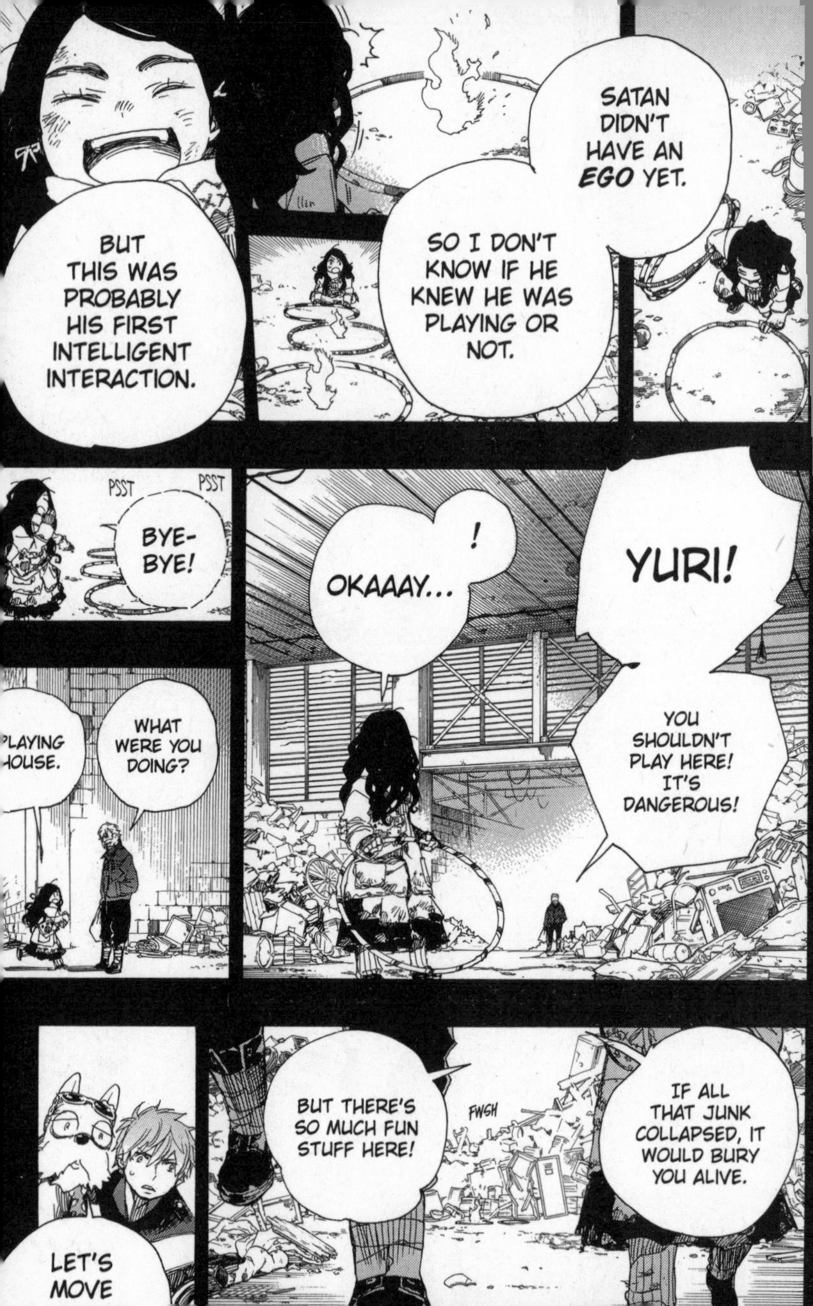
SATAN DIDN'T HAVE AN EGO YET.
SO I DON'T KNOW IF HE KNEW HE WAS PLAYING OR NOT.
BUT THIS WAS PROBABLY HIS FIRST INTELLIGENT INTERACTION.
YURI!
YOU SHOULDN'T PLAY HERE! IT'S DANGEROUS!
!
OKAAAY...
PSST
PSST
BYE-BYE!
WHAT WERE YOU DOING?
PLAYING HOUSE.
IF ALL THAT JUNK COLLAPSED, IT WOULD BURY YOU ALIVE.
FWSH
BUT THERE'S SO MUCH FUN STUFF HERE!
LET'S MOVE

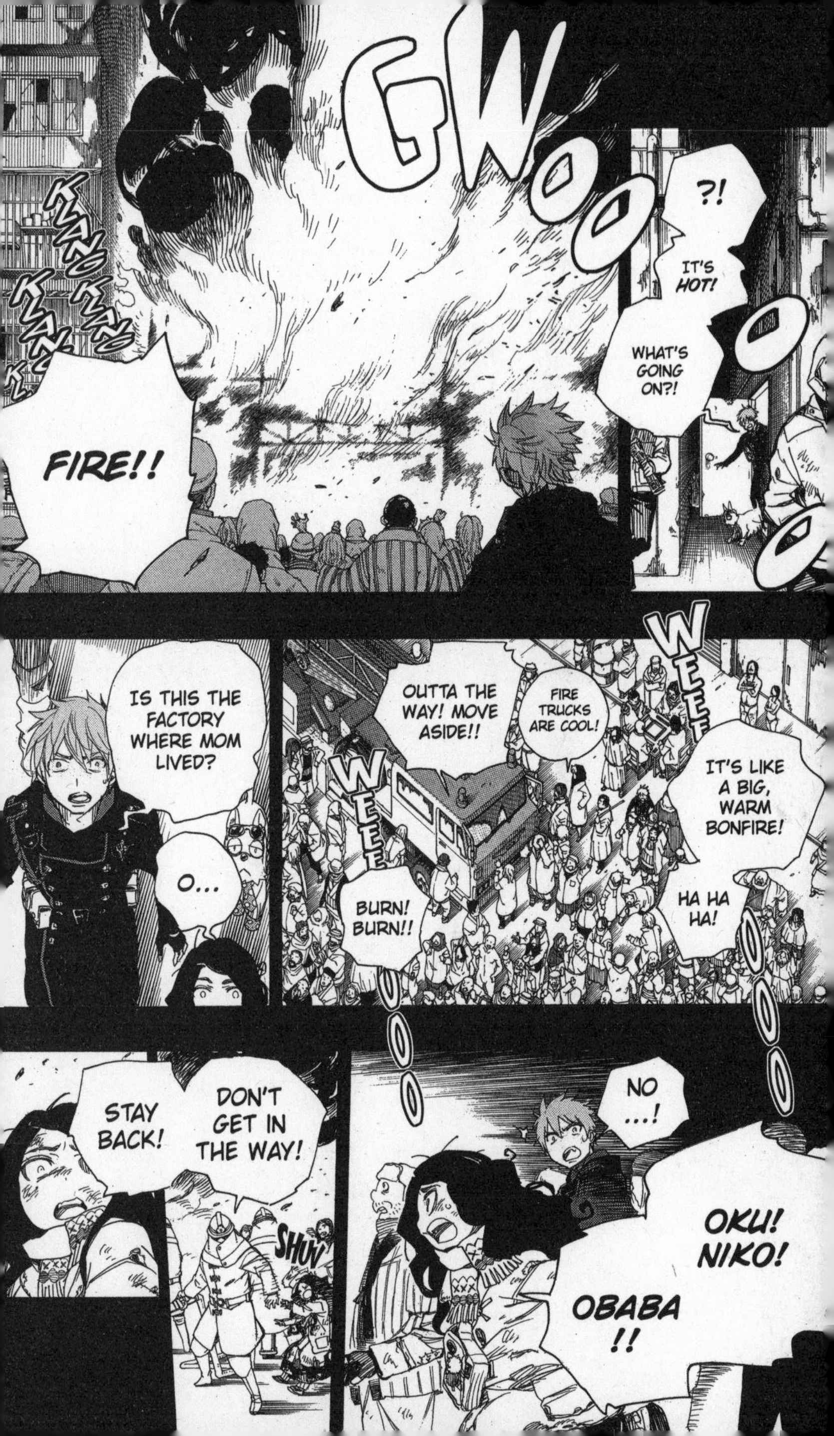
GWOOOO
?!
IT'S HOT!
WHAT'S GOING ON?!
KLANG KLANG KLANG
FIRE!!
WEEE
OUTTA THE WAY! MOVE ASIDE!!
FIRE TRUCKS ARE COOL!
IT'S LIKE A BIG, WARM BONFIRE!
WEEE
BURN! BURN!!
HA HA HA!
IS THIS THE FACTORY WHERE MOM LIVED?
O...
OOOO
NO ...!
OKU! NIKO!
OBABA !!
DON'T GET IN THE WAY!
STAY BACK!
SHUV

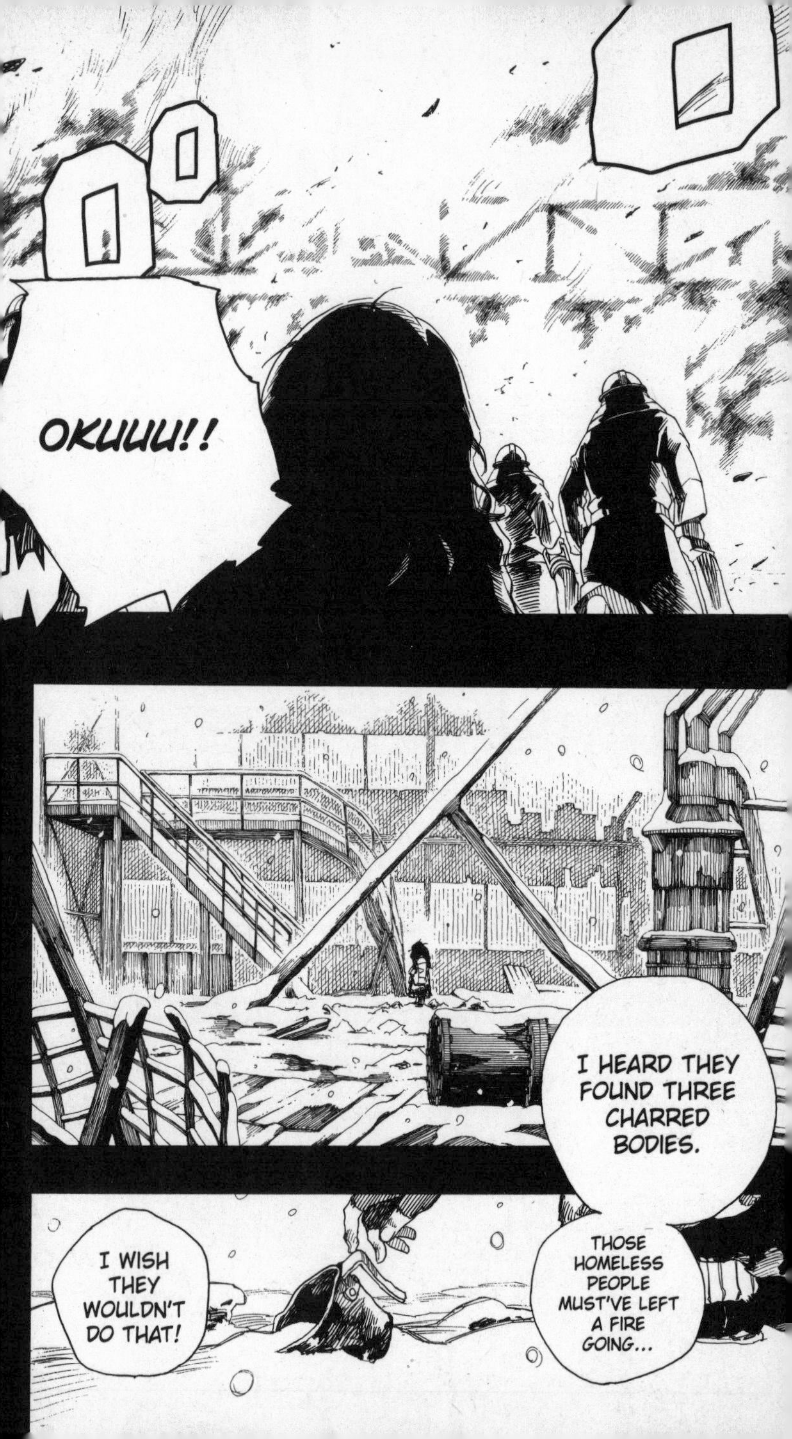
OKUUU!!
I HEARD THEY FOUND THREE CHARRED BODIES.
THOSE HOMELESS PEOPLE MUST'VE LEFT A FIRE GOING...
I WISH THEY WOULDN'T DO THAT!

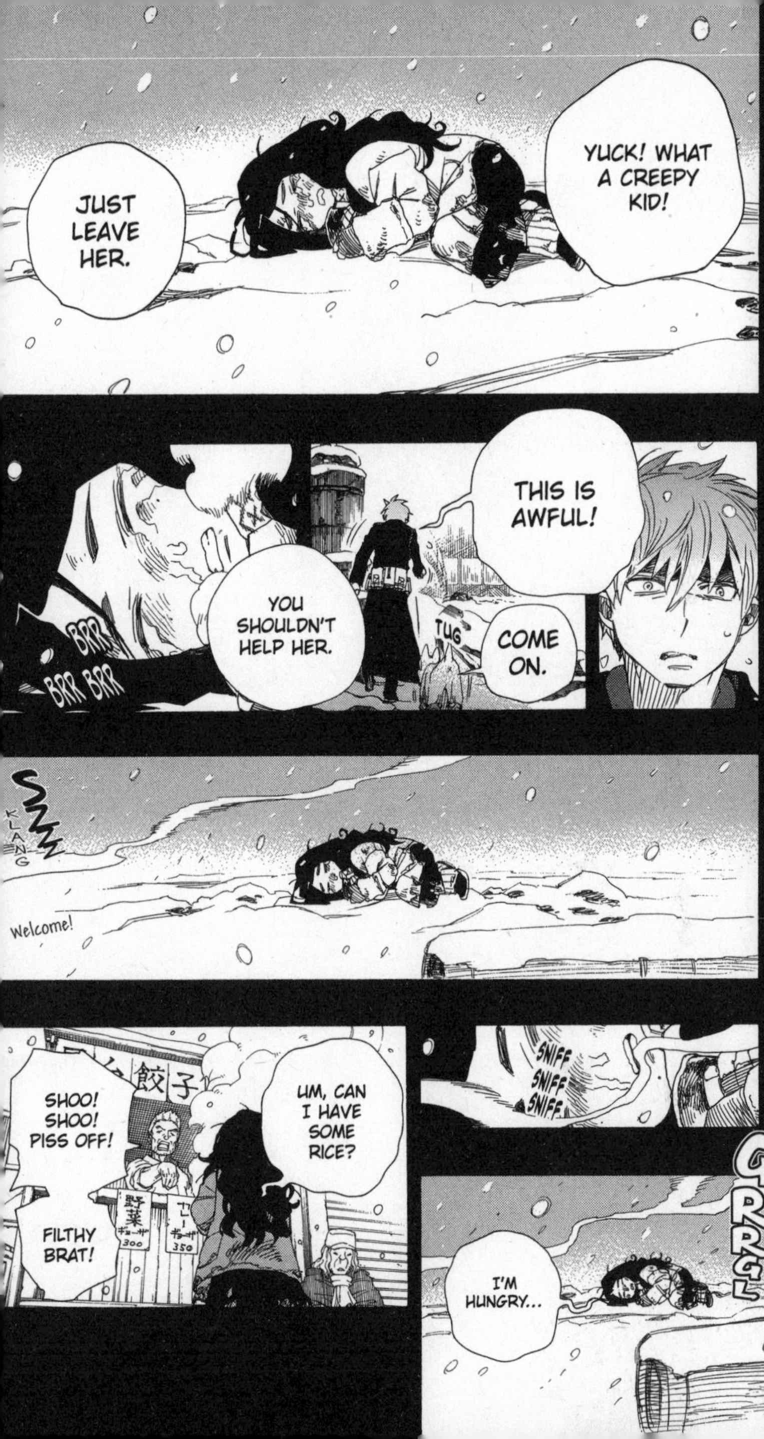
YUCK! WHAT A CREEPY KID!
JUST LEAVE HER.
THIS IS AWFUL!
COME ON.
TUG
YOU SHOULDN'T HELP HER.
BRR
BRR BRR
KLANG
Welcome!
SNIFF
SNIFF
SNIFF
GRRGL
I'M HUNGRY...
UM, CAN I HAVE SOME RICE?
餃子
SHOO! SHOO! PISS OFF!
FILTHY BRAT!
野菜 ギョーザ 300
カレー ギョーザ 350

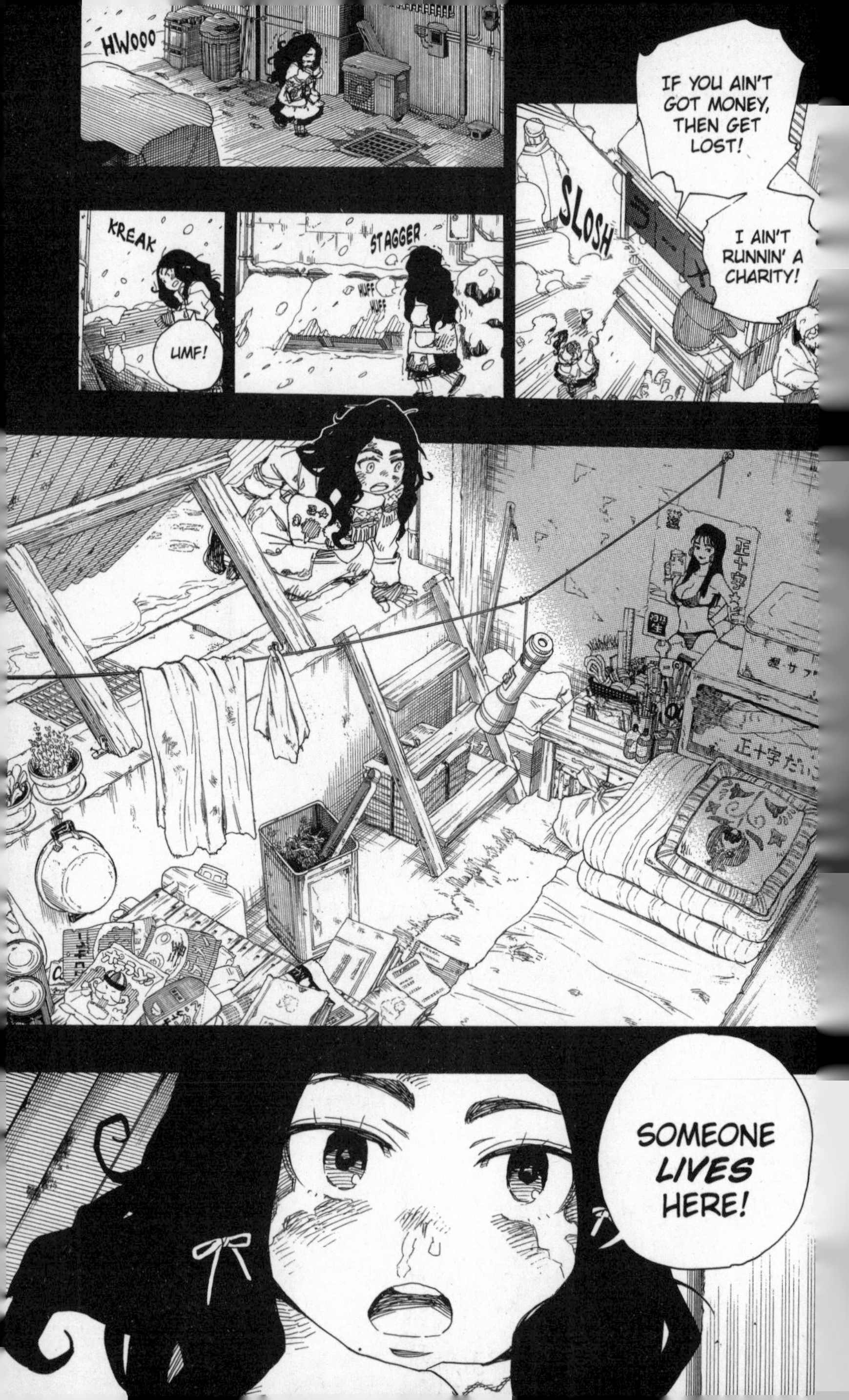
IF YOU AIN'T GOT MONEY, THEN GET LOST!
SLOSH
I AIN'T RUNNIN' A CHARITY!
HWOOO
STAGGER
HUFF HUFF
KREAK
UMF!
SOMEONE *LIVES* HERE!

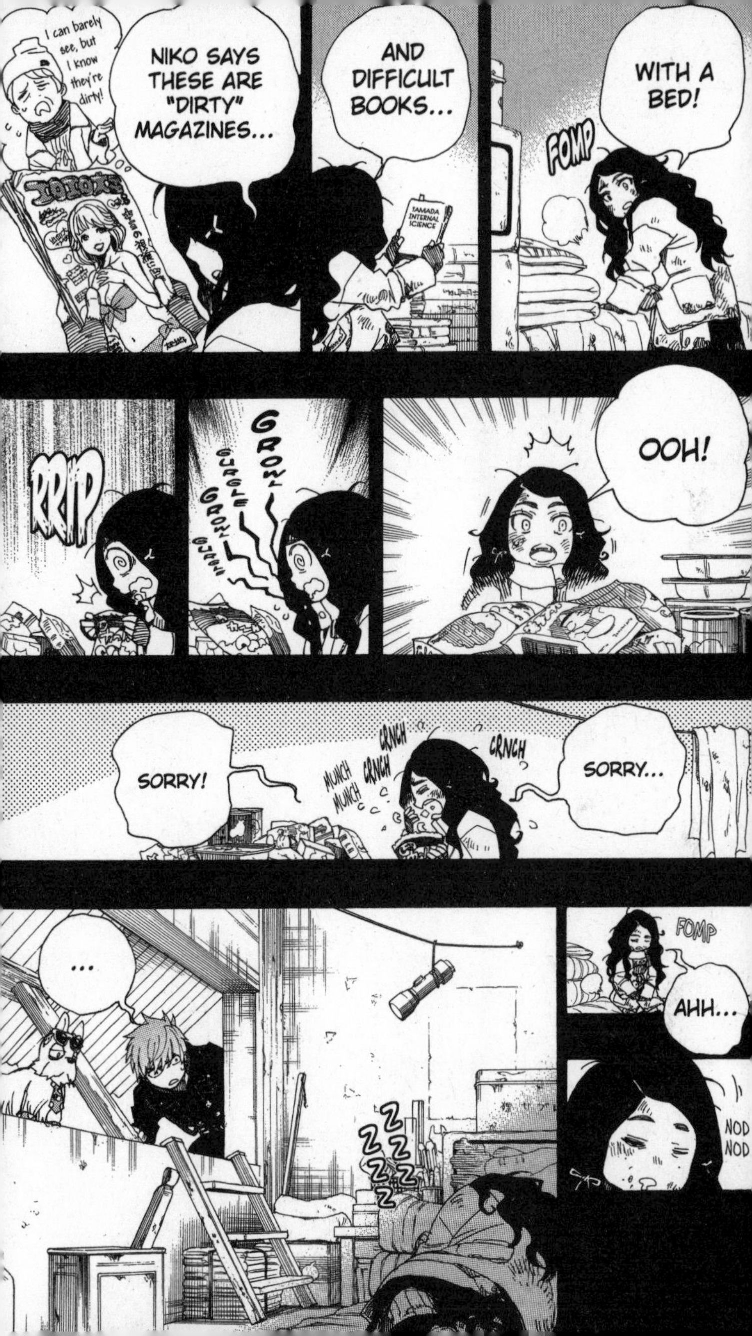
FOMP
WITH A BED!
AND DIFFICULT BOOKS...
YAMADA INTERNAL SCIENCE
NIKO SAYS THESE ARE "DIRTY" MAGAZINES...
I can barely see, but I know they're dirty!
OOH!
GROWL
GURGLE
GROWL
GURGLE
RRIP
SORRY...
CRNCH
CRNCH
CRNCH
MUNCH
MUNCH
SORRY!
FOMP
AHH...
NOD NOD
...
ZZZZZ

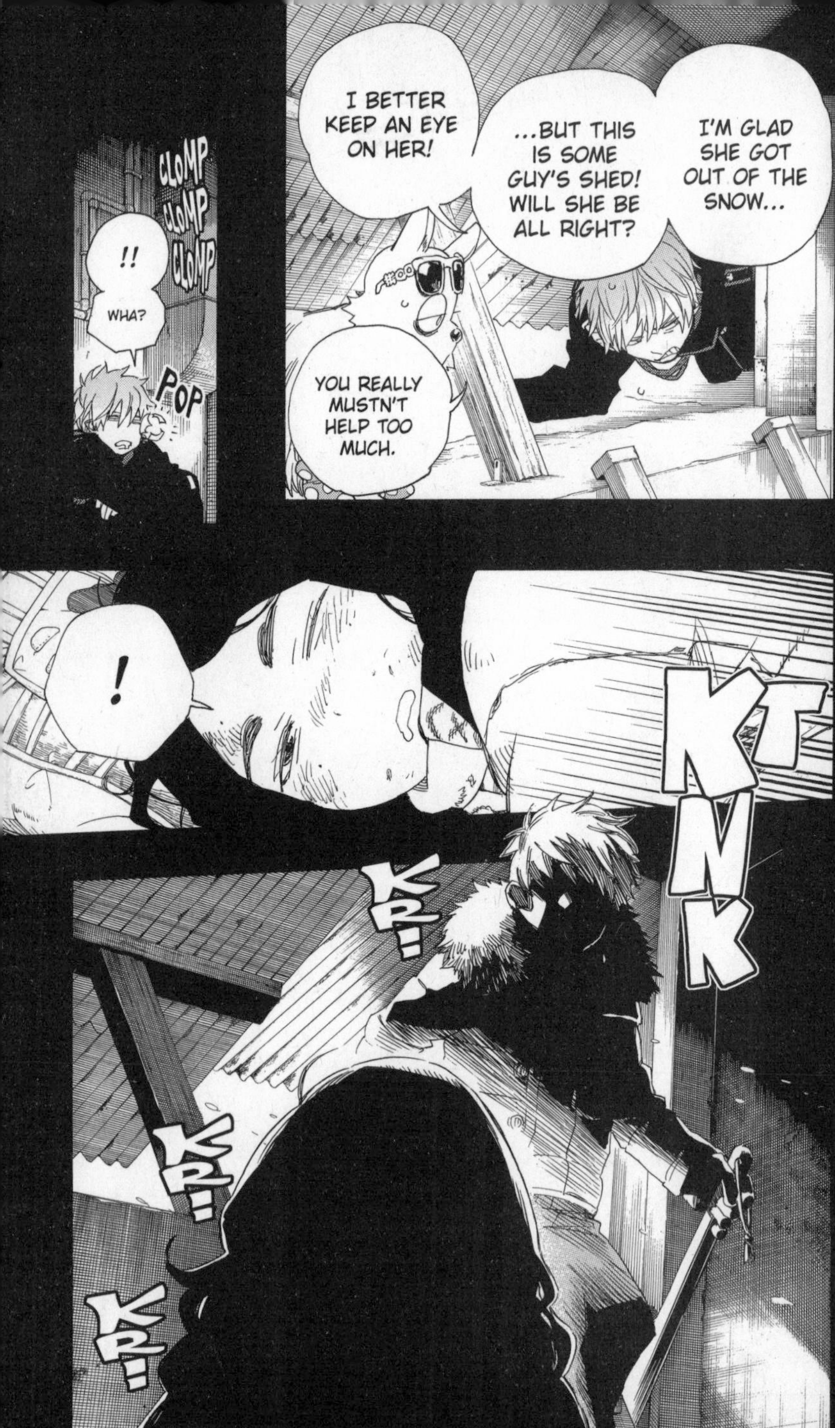
I'M GLAD SHE GOT OUT OF THE SNOW...
...BUT THIS IS SOME GUY'S SHED! WILL SHE BE ALL RIGHT?
I BETTER KEEP AN EYE ON HER!
YOU REALLY MUSTN'T HELP TOO MUCH.
CLOMP CLOMP CLOMP
!!
WHA?
POP
!
KTNK
KR!
KR!
KR!

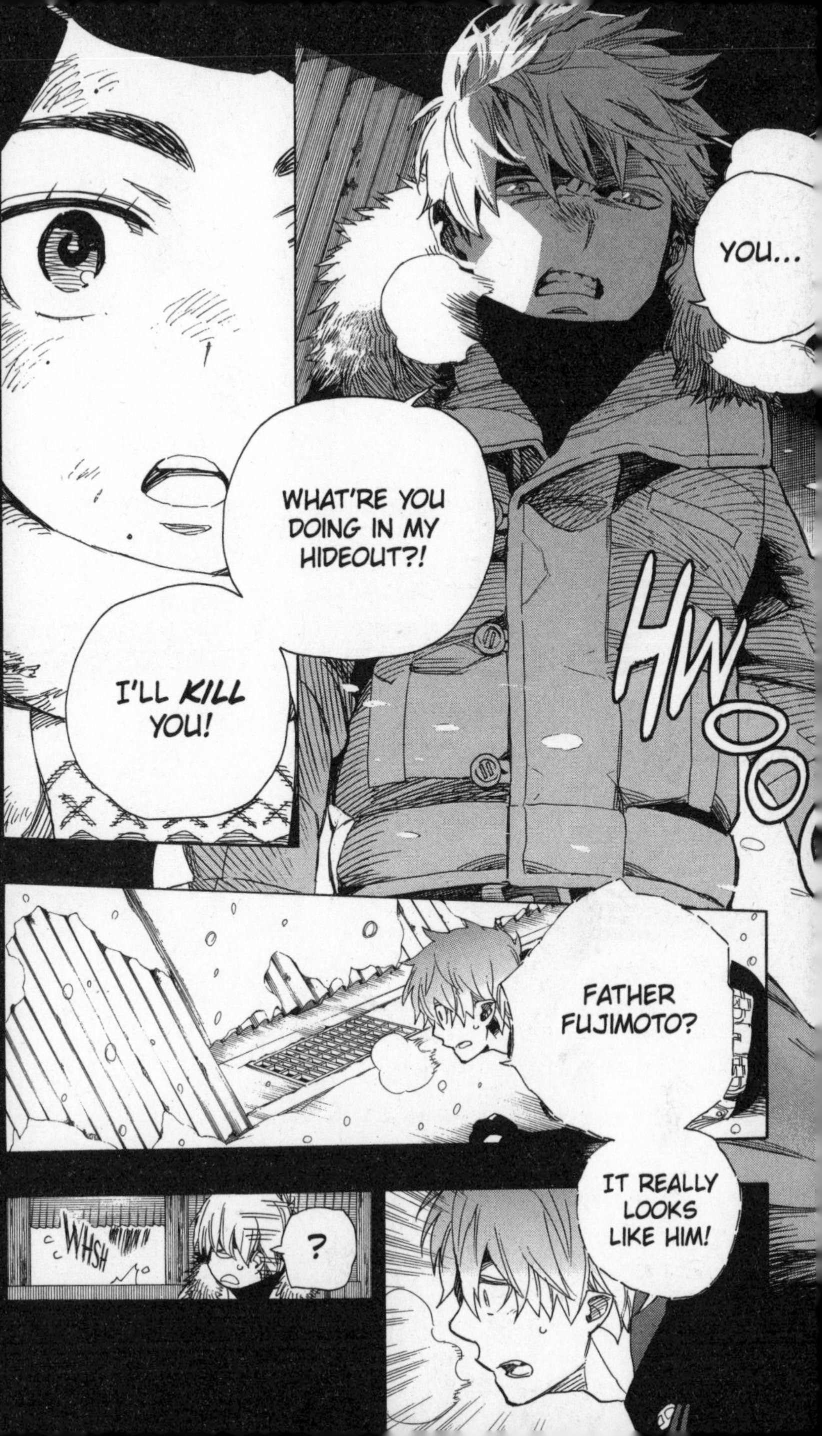
YOU...
WHAT'RE YOU DOING IN MY HIDEOUT?!
I'LL KILL YOU!
HWOOO
FATHER FUJIMOTO?
IT REALLY LOOKS LIKE HIM!
WHSH
?

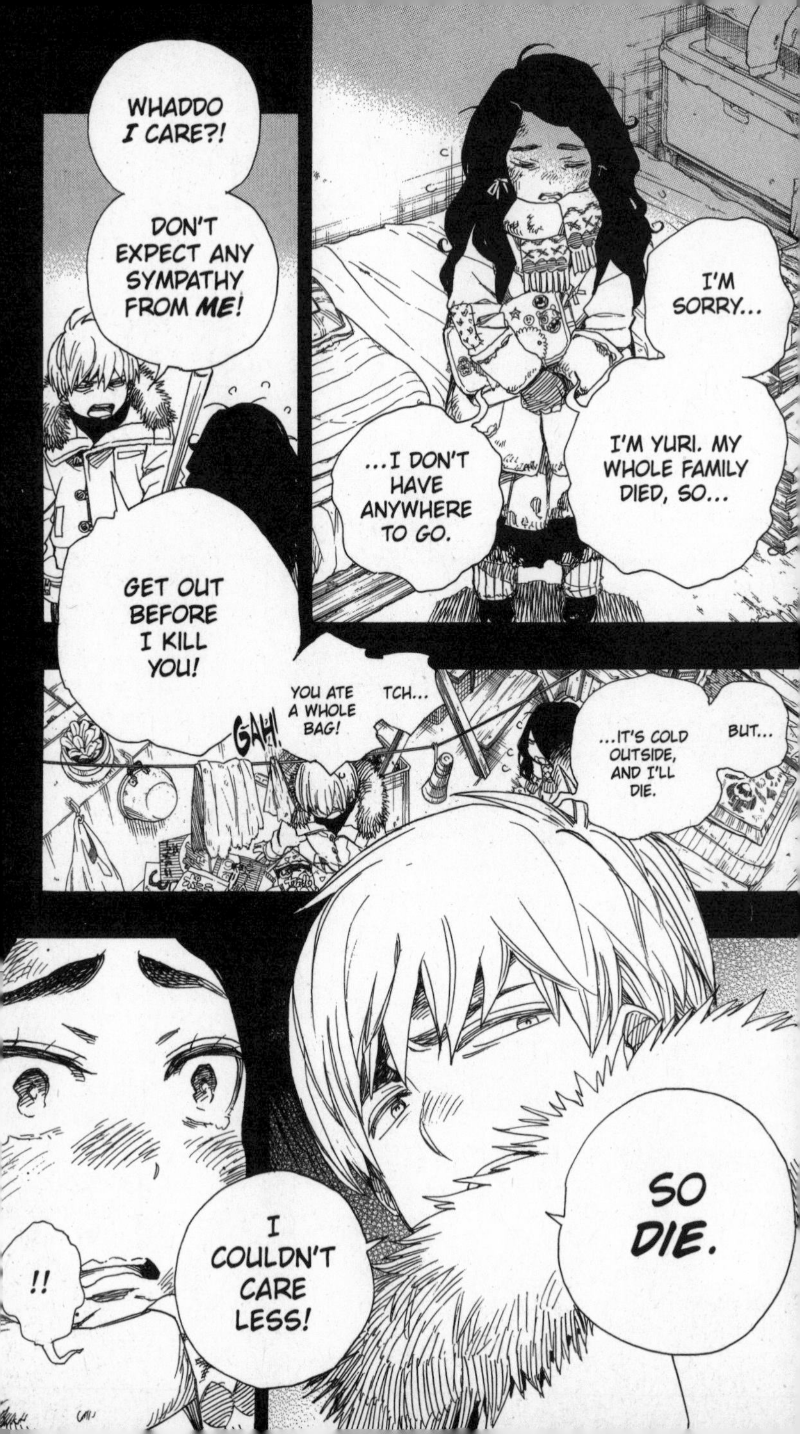
I'M SORRY...
I'M YURI. MY WHOLE FAMILY DIED, SO...
...I DON'T HAVE ANYWHERE TO GO.
WHADDO I CARE?!
DON'T EXPECT ANY SYMPATHY FROM ME!
GET OUT BEFORE I KILL YOU!
BUT...
...IT'S COLD OUTSIDE, AND I'LL DIE.
TCH...
YOU ATE A WHOLE BAG!
GAH!
SO DIE.
I COULDN'T CARE LESS!
!!

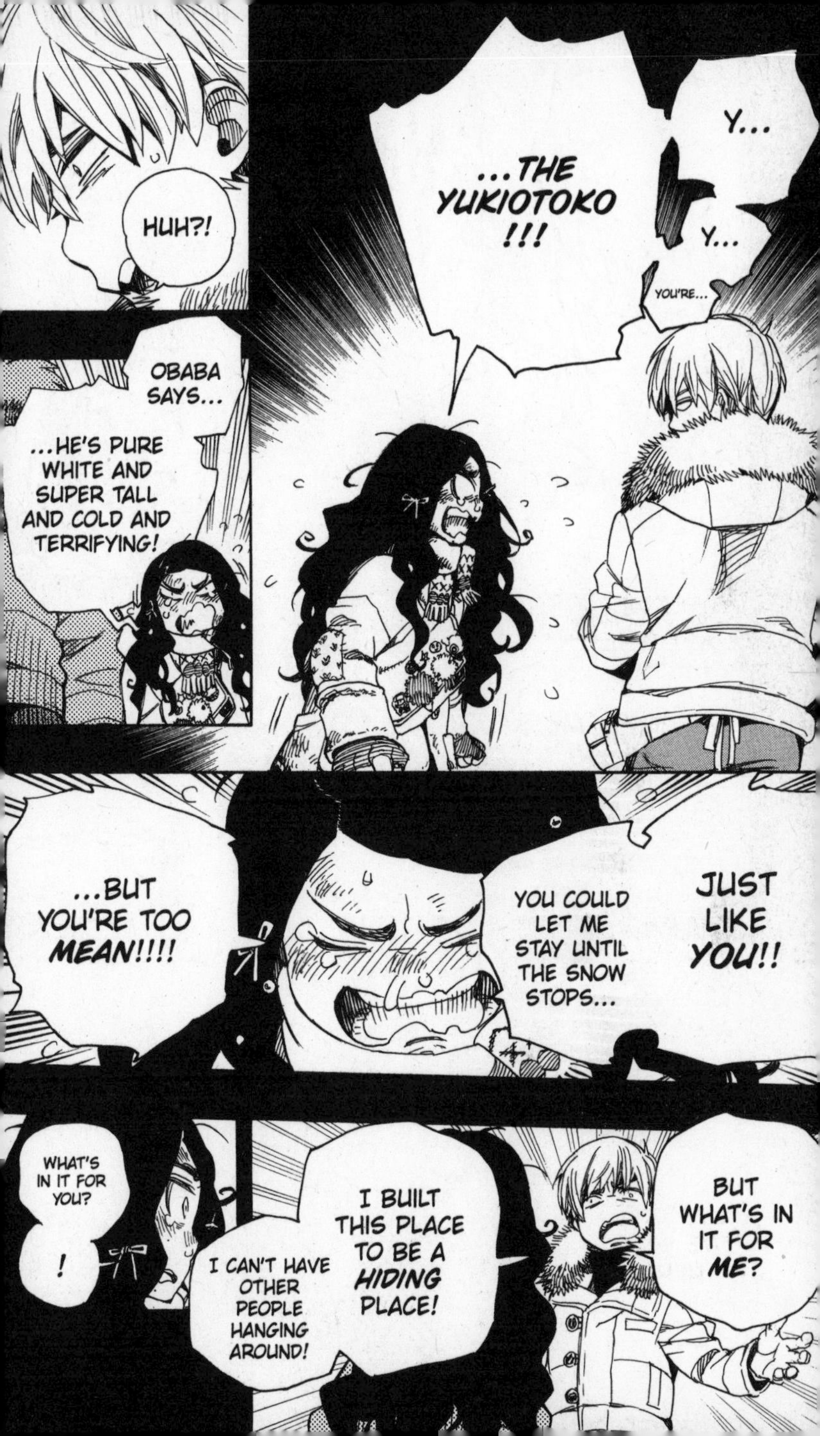
Y...
Y...
YOU'RE...
...THE YUKIOTOKO!!!
HUH?!
OBABA SAYS...
...HE'S PURE WHITE AND SUPER TALL AND COLD AND TERRIFYING!
JUST LIKE YOU!!
YOU COULD LET ME STAY UNTIL THE SNOW STOPS...
...BUT YOU'RE TOO MEAN!!!!
BUT WHAT'S IN IT FOR ME?
I BUILT THIS PLACE TO BE A HIDING PLACE!
I CAN'T HAVE OTHER PEOPLE HANGING AROUND!
WHAT'S IN IT FOR YOU?
!

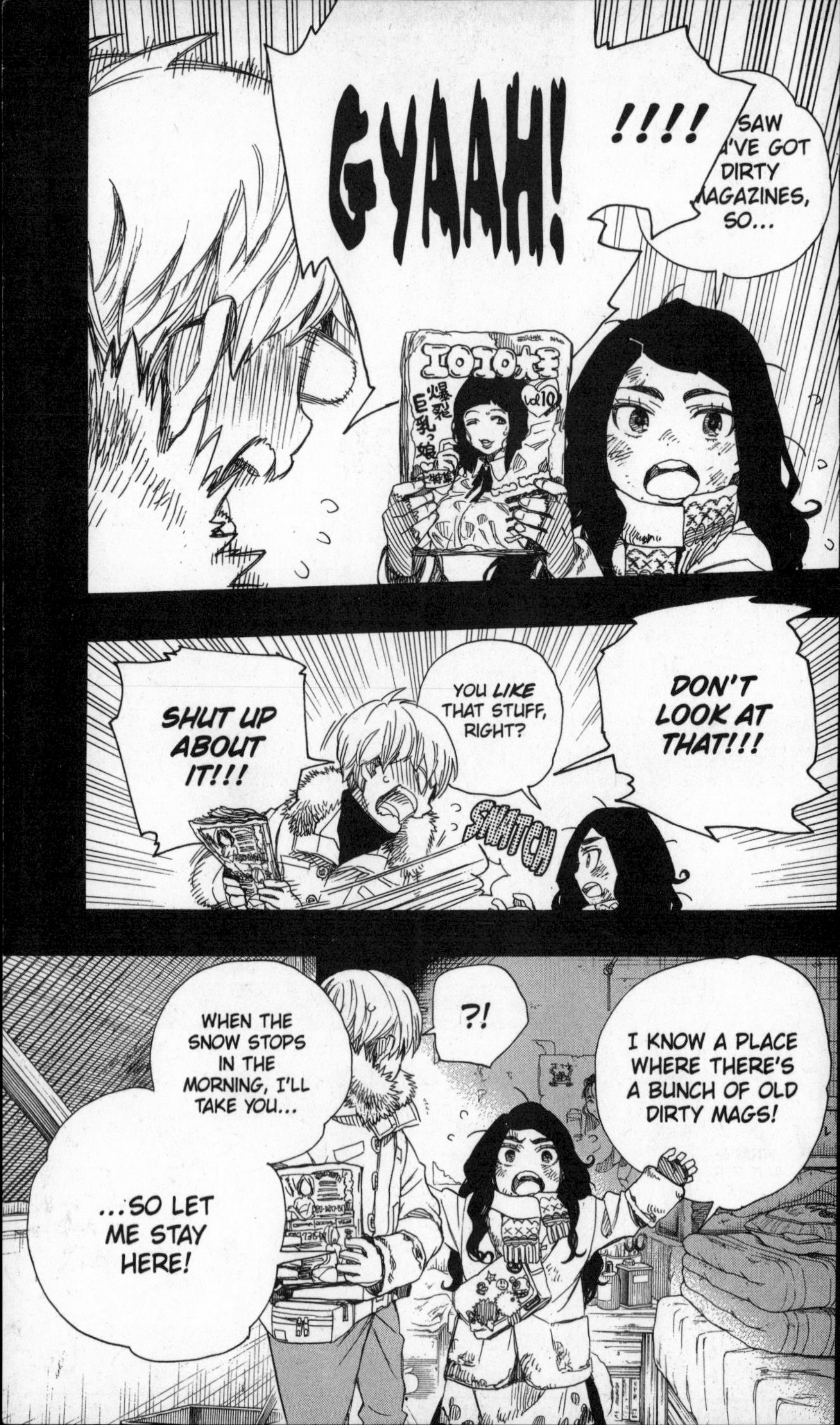
SAW 'VE GOT DIRTY AGAZINES, SO...
!!!!
GYAAH!
DON'T LOOK AT THAT!!!
YOU LIKE THAT STUFF, RIGHT?
SNATCH
SHUT UP ABOUT IT!!!
I KNOW A PLACE WHERE THERE'S A BUNCH OF OLD DIRTY MAGS!
?!
WHEN THE SNOW STOPS IN THE MORNING, I'LL TAKE YOU...
...SO LET ME STAY HERE!

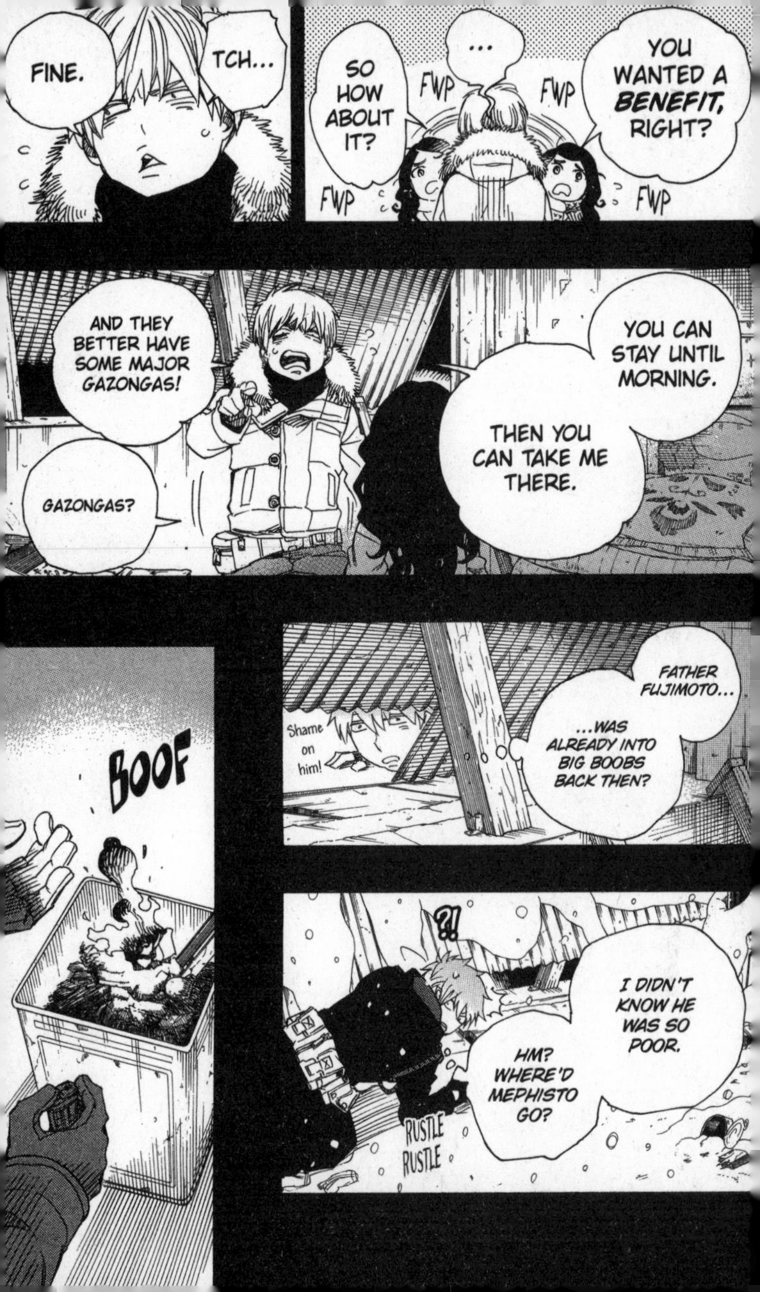
YOU WANTED A BENEFIT, RIGHT?
FWP
...
FWP
SO HOW ABOUT IT?
FWP
FWP
TCH...
FINE.
YOU CAN STAY UNTIL MORNING.
THEN YOU CAN TAKE ME THERE.
AND THEY BETTER HAVE SOME MAJOR GAZONGAS!
GAZONGAS?
FATHER FUJIMOTO...
...WAS ALREADY INTO BIG BOOBS BACK THEN?
Shame on him!
?!
I DIDN'T KNOW HE WAS SO POOR.
HM? WHERE'D MEPHISTO GO?
RUSTLE RUSTLE
BOOF

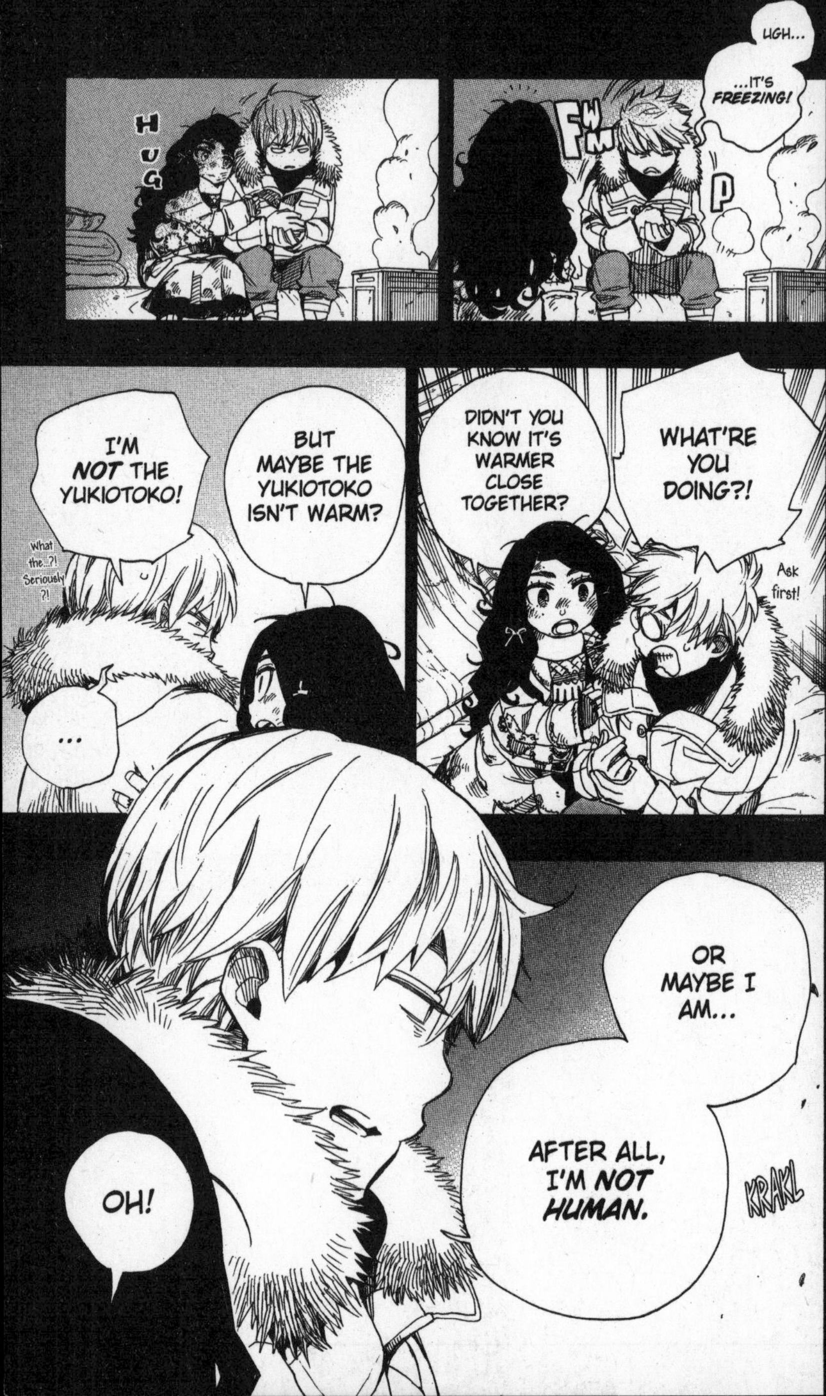
UGH...
...IT'S *FREEZING!*
FWM
P
HUG
WHAT'RE YOU DOING?!
DIDN'T YOU KNOW IT'S WARMER CLOSE TOGETHER?
Ask first!
BUT MAYBE THE YUKIOTOKO ISN'T WARM?
I'M *NOT* THE YUKIOTOKO!
What the...?! Seriously?!
...
OR MAYBE I AM...
AFTER ALL, I'M *NOT HUMAN.*
KRAKL
OH!

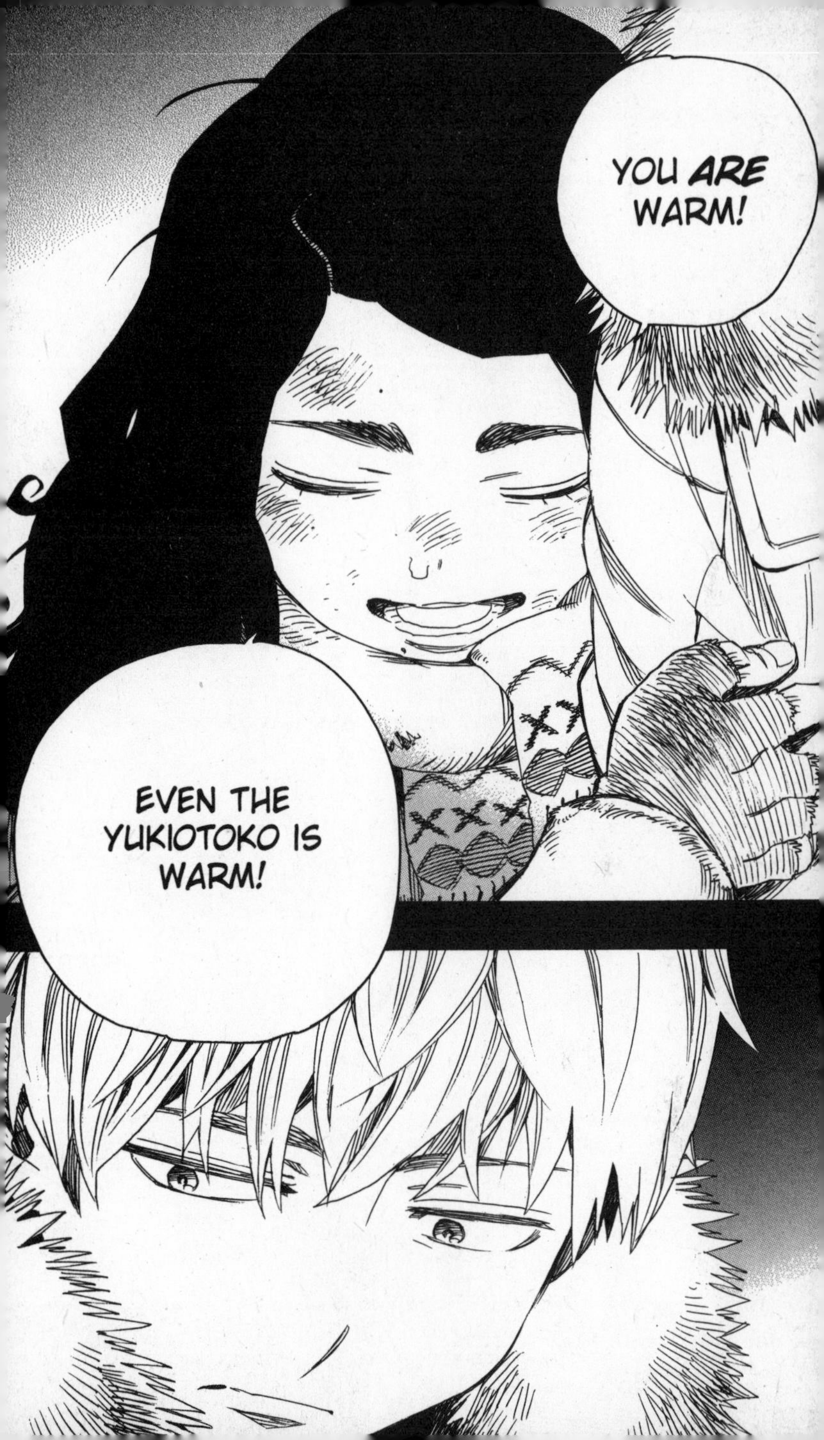
YOU *ARE* WARM!
EVEN THE YUKIOTOKO IS WARM!

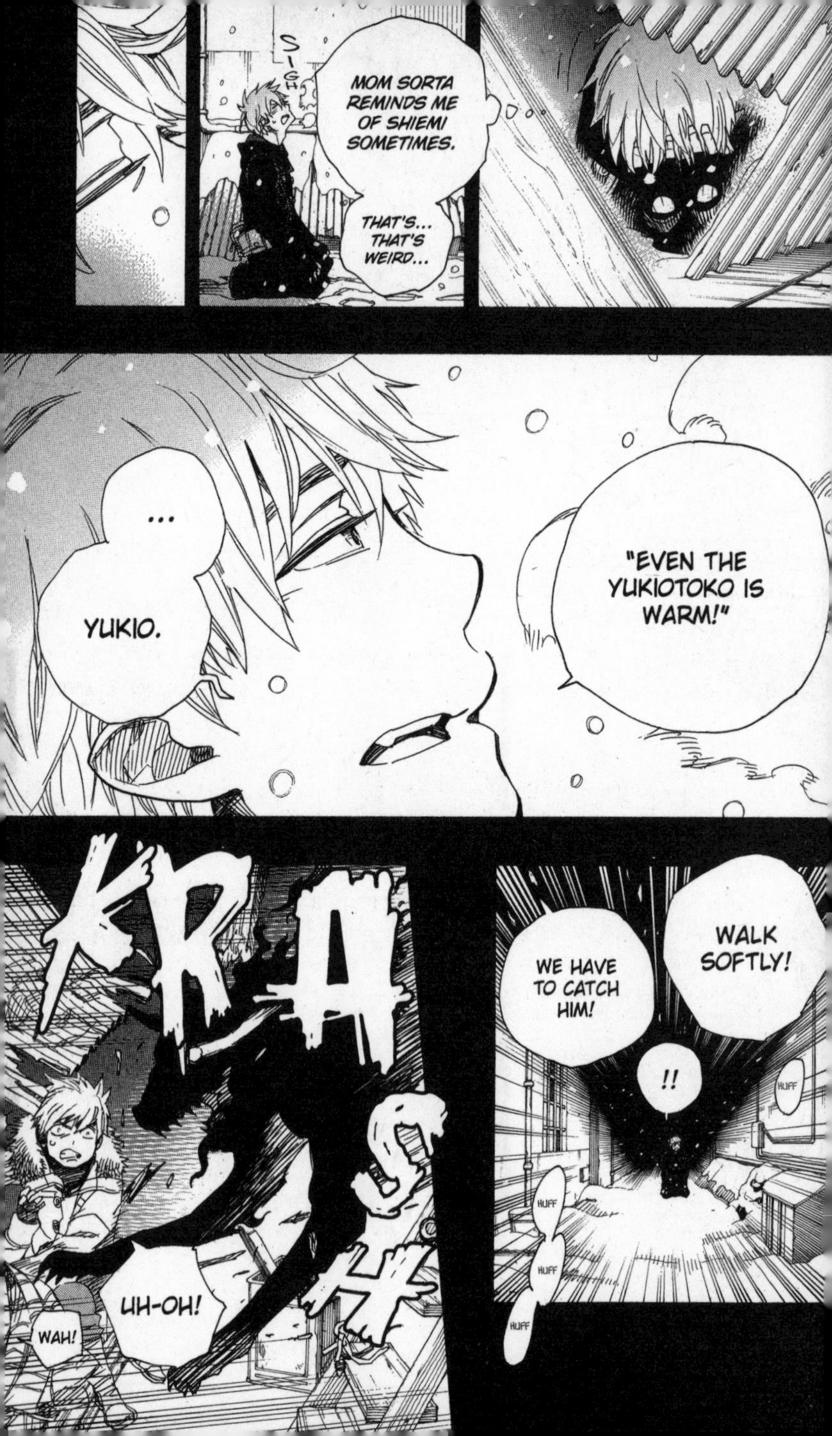
SIGH
MOM SORTA REMINDS ME OF SHIEMI SOMETIMES.
THAT'S... THAT'S WEIRD...
"EVEN THE YUKIOTOKO IS WARM!"
...
YUKIO.
WALK SOFTLY!
WE HAVE TO CATCH HIM!
!!
HUFF
HUFF
HUFF
HUFF
KRASH
UH-OH!
WAH!

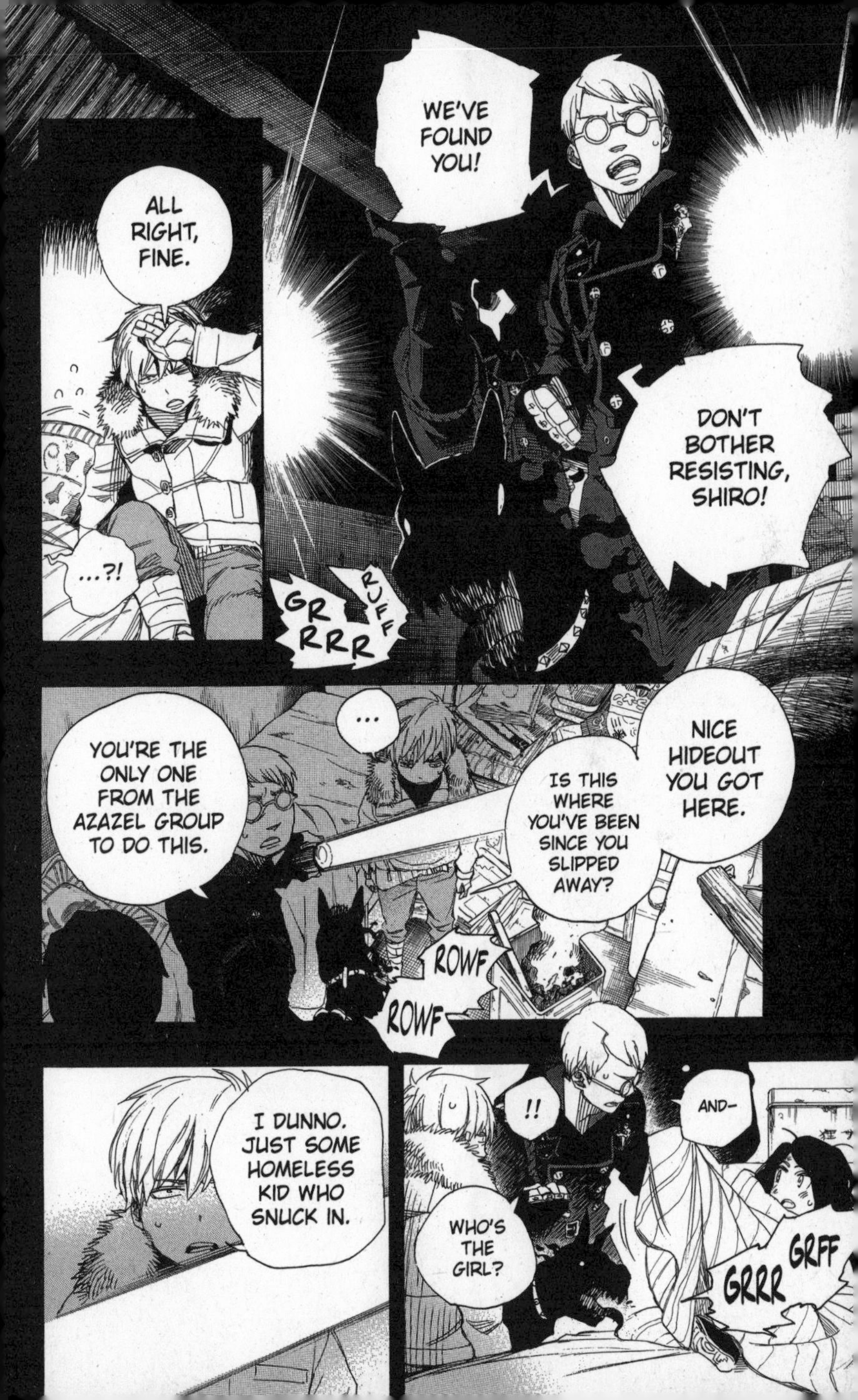
WE'VE FOUND YOU!
DON'T BOTHER RESISTING, SHIRO!
GRRRR
RUFF
ALL RIGHT, FINE.
...?!
NICE HIDEOUT YOU GOT HERE.
IS THIS WHERE YOU'VE BEEN SINCE YOU SLIPPED AWAY?
...
YOU'RE THE ONLY ONE FROM THE AZAZEL GROUP TO DO THIS.
ROWF
ROWF
AND-
!!
WHO'S THE GIRL?
GRFF
GRRR
I DUNNO. JUST SOME HOMELESS KID WHO SNUCK IN.

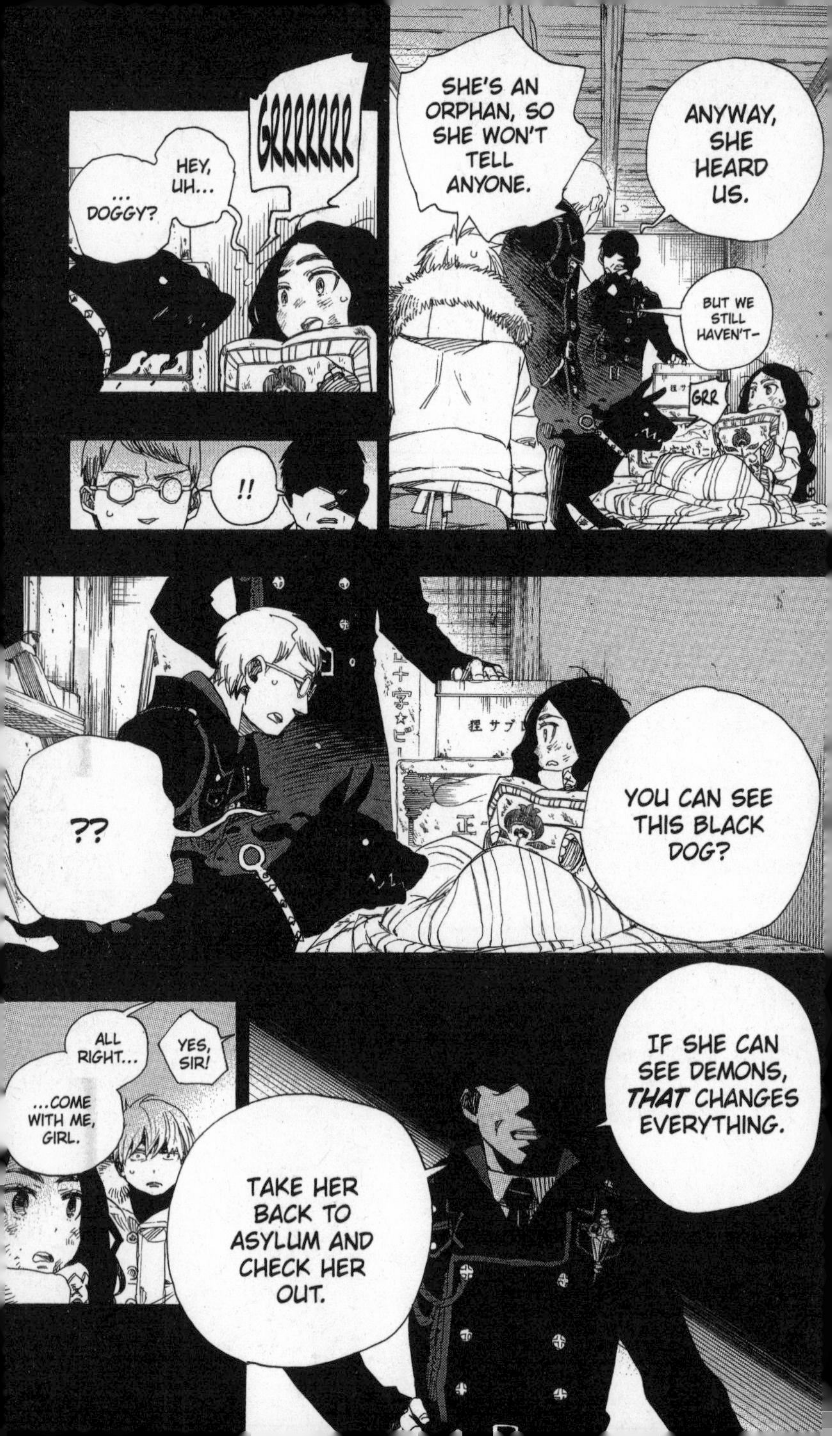
ANYWAY, SHE HEARD US.
SHE'S AN ORPHAN, SO SHE WON'T TELL ANYONE.
BUT WE STILL HAVEN'T-
GRR
GRRRRRRR
HEY, UH... ...DOGGY?
!!
YOU CAN SEE THIS BLACK DOG?
??
IF SHE CAN SEE DEMONS, *THAT* CHANGES EVERYTHING.
TAKE HER BACK TO ASYLUM AND CHECK HER OUT.
YES, SIR!
ALL RIGHT... ...COME WITH ME, GIRL.

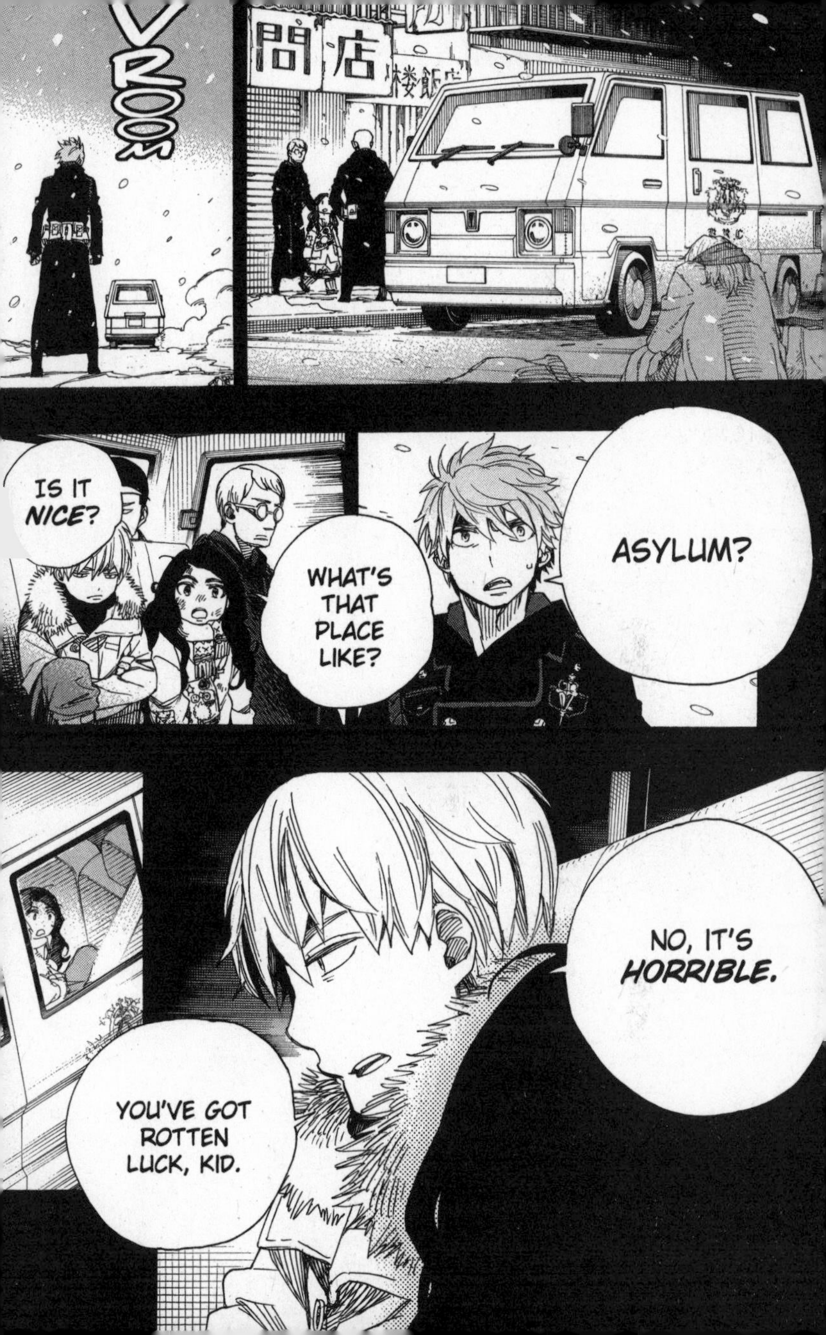
VROOM
ASYLUM?
WHAT'S THAT PLACE LIKE?
IS IT NICE?
NO, IT'S HORRIBLE.
YOU'VE GOT ROTTEN LUCK, KID.

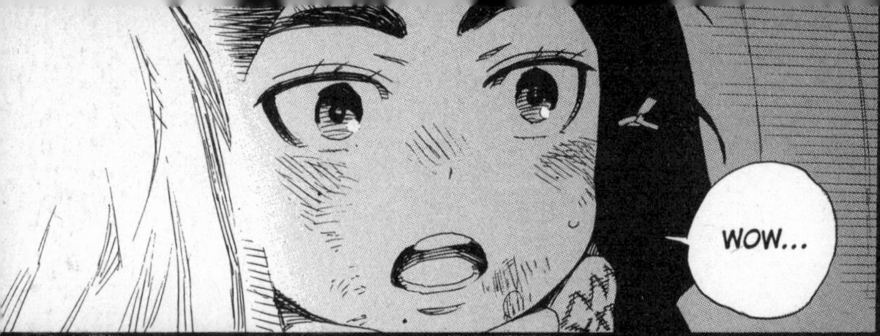
WOW...
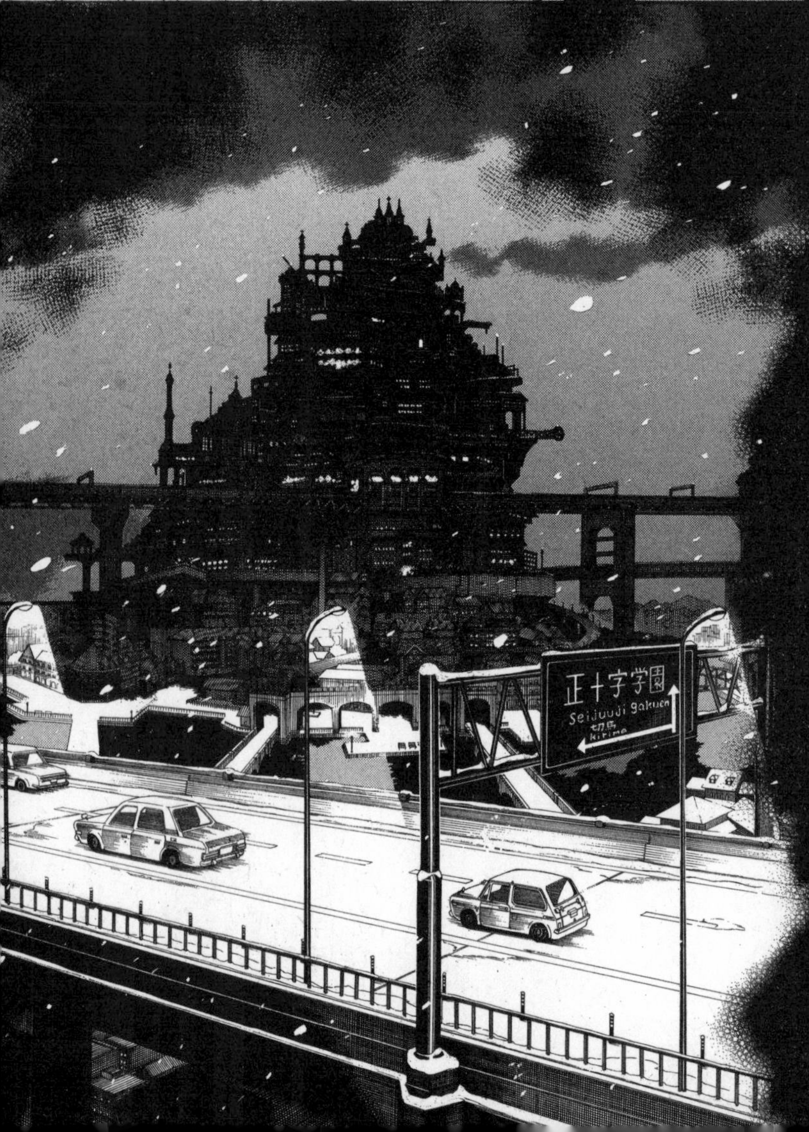
正十字学園
Seijuuji gakuen
切島
kirima

BLUE EXORCIST CHAPTER 100: SSC00:40

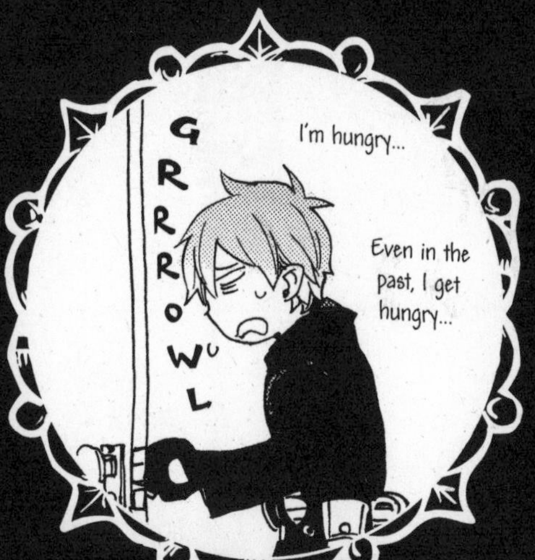
I'm hungry...
Even in the past, I get hungry...
GRRROWL

Chapter 101: SsC04:36

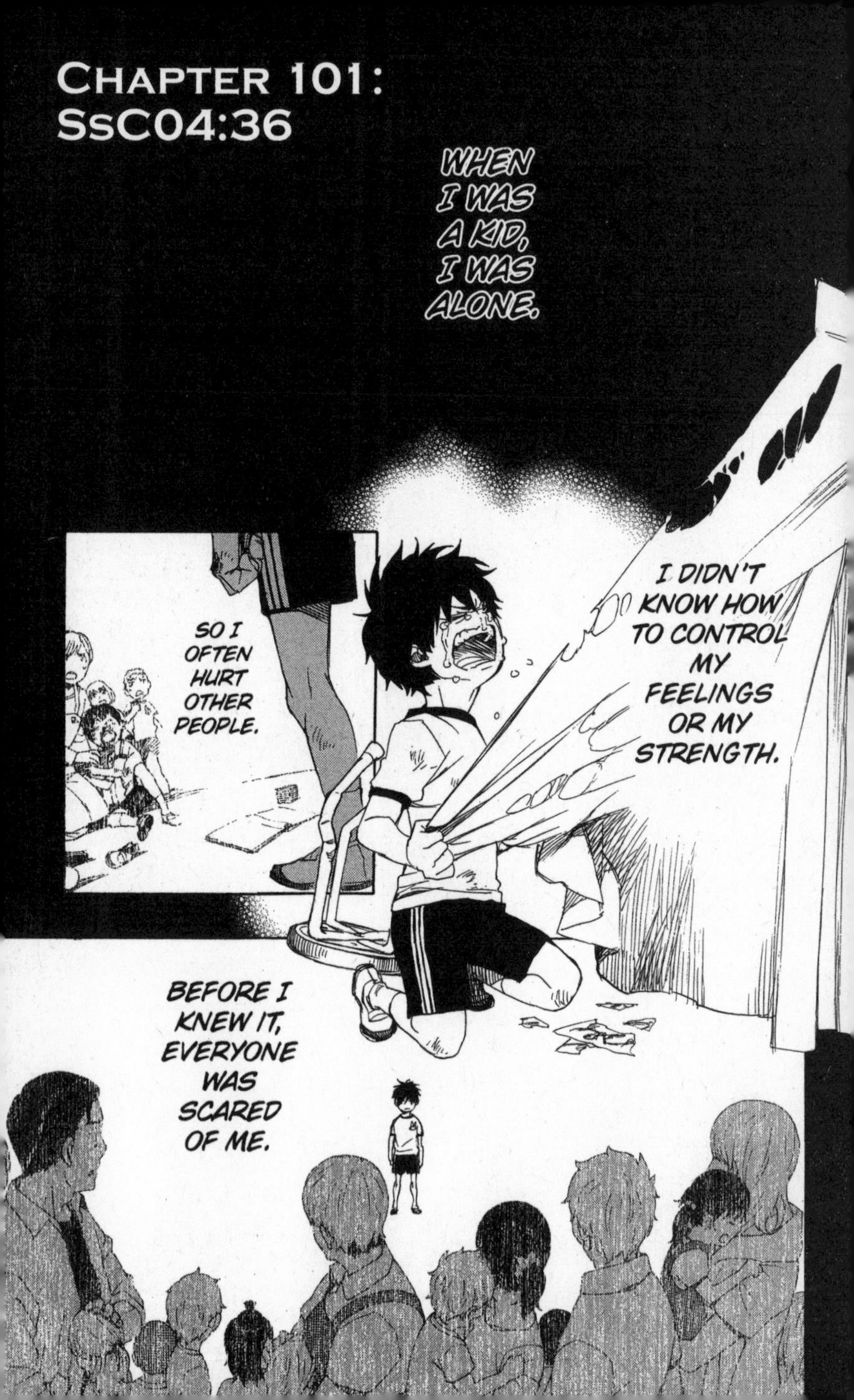
WHEN I WAS A KID, I WAS ALONE.
I DIDN'T KNOW HOW TO CONTROL MY FEELINGS OR MY STRENGTH.
SO I OFTEN HURT OTHER PEOPLE.
BEFORE I KNEW IT, EVERYONE WAS SCARED OF ME.

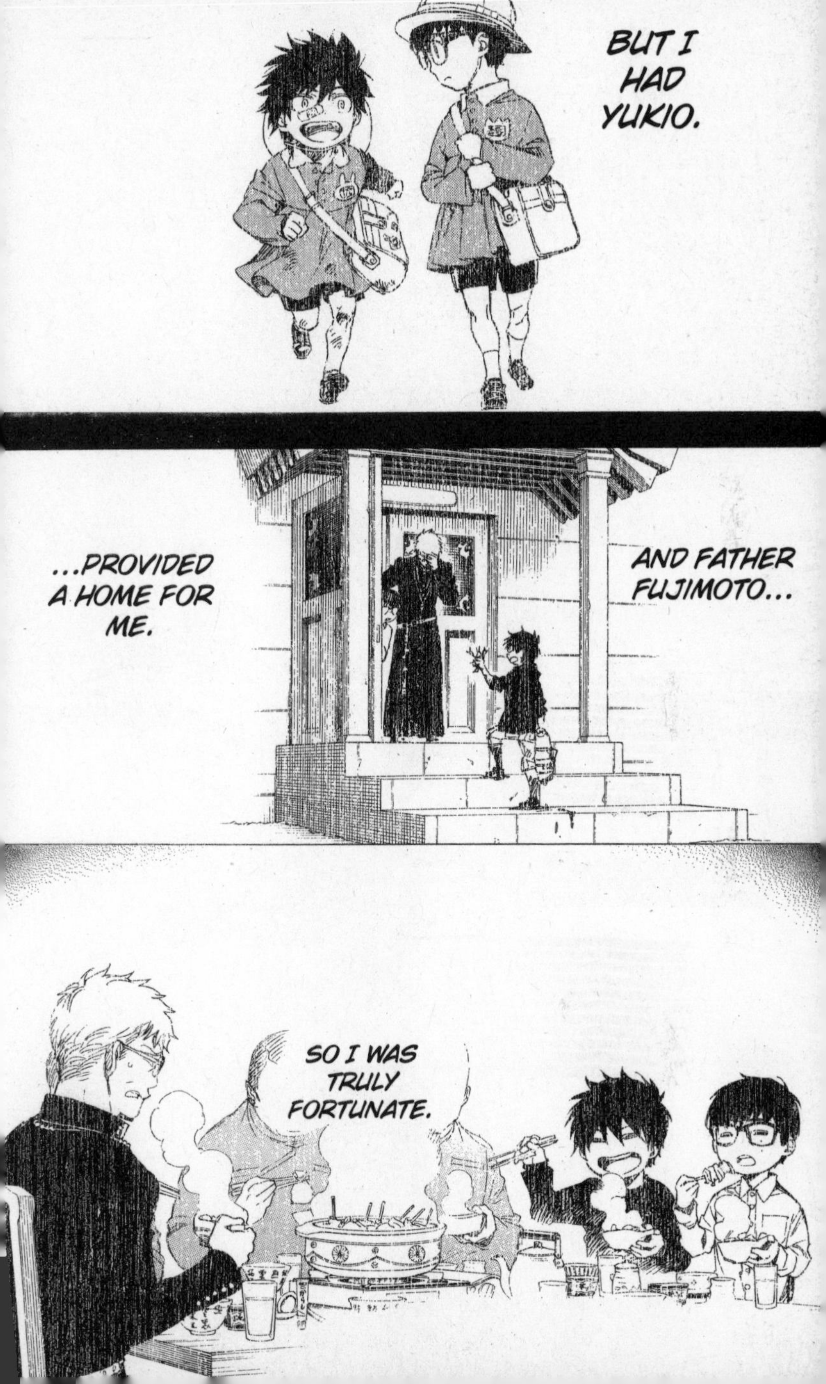
BUT I HAD YUKIO.
AND FATHER FUJIMOTO...
...PROVIDED A HOME FOR ME.
SO I WAS TRULY FORTUNATE.

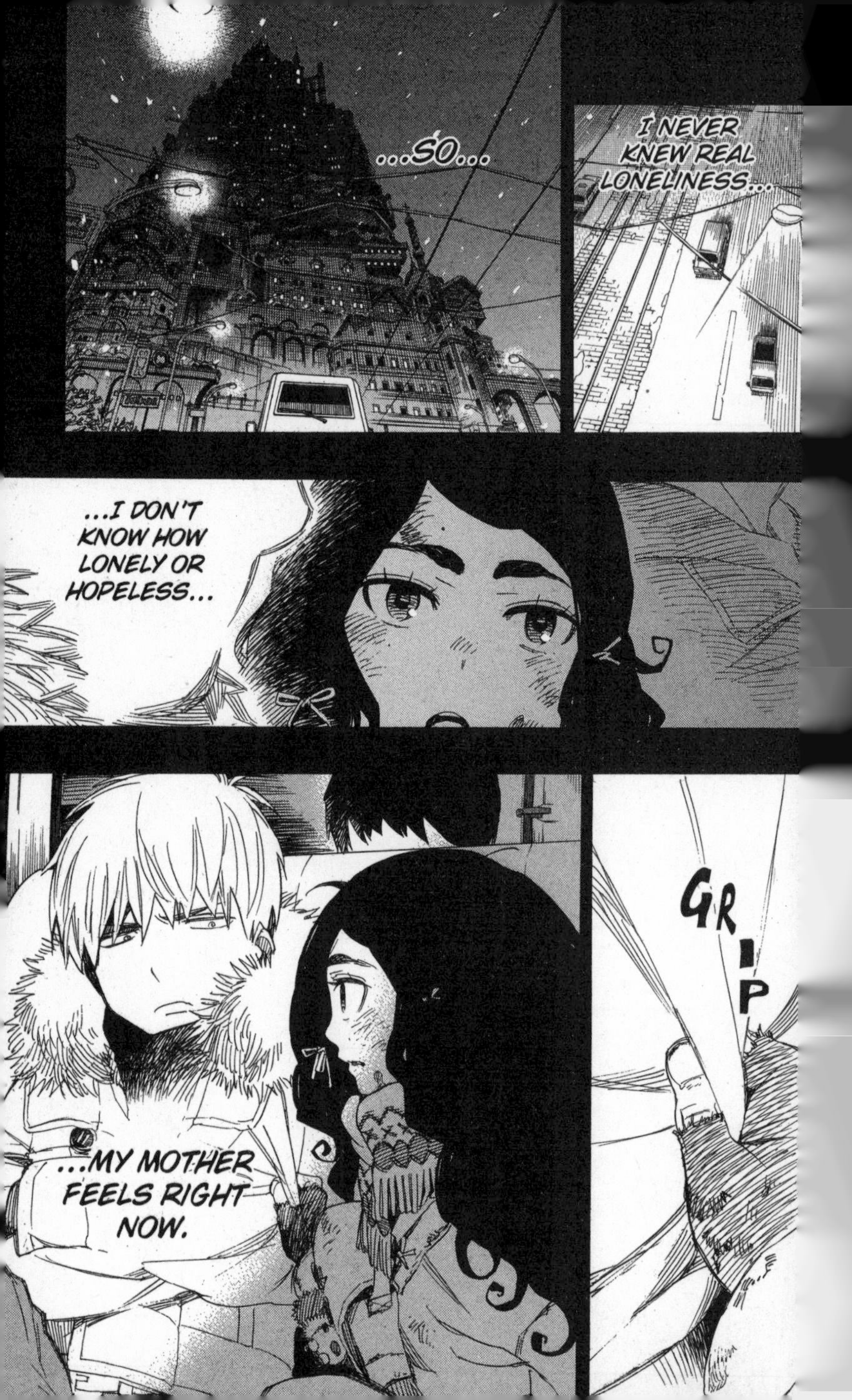
I NEVER KNEW REAL LONELINESS...
...SO...
...I DON'T KNOW HOW LONELY OR HOPELESS...
GRIP
...MY MOTHER FEELS RIGHT NOW.

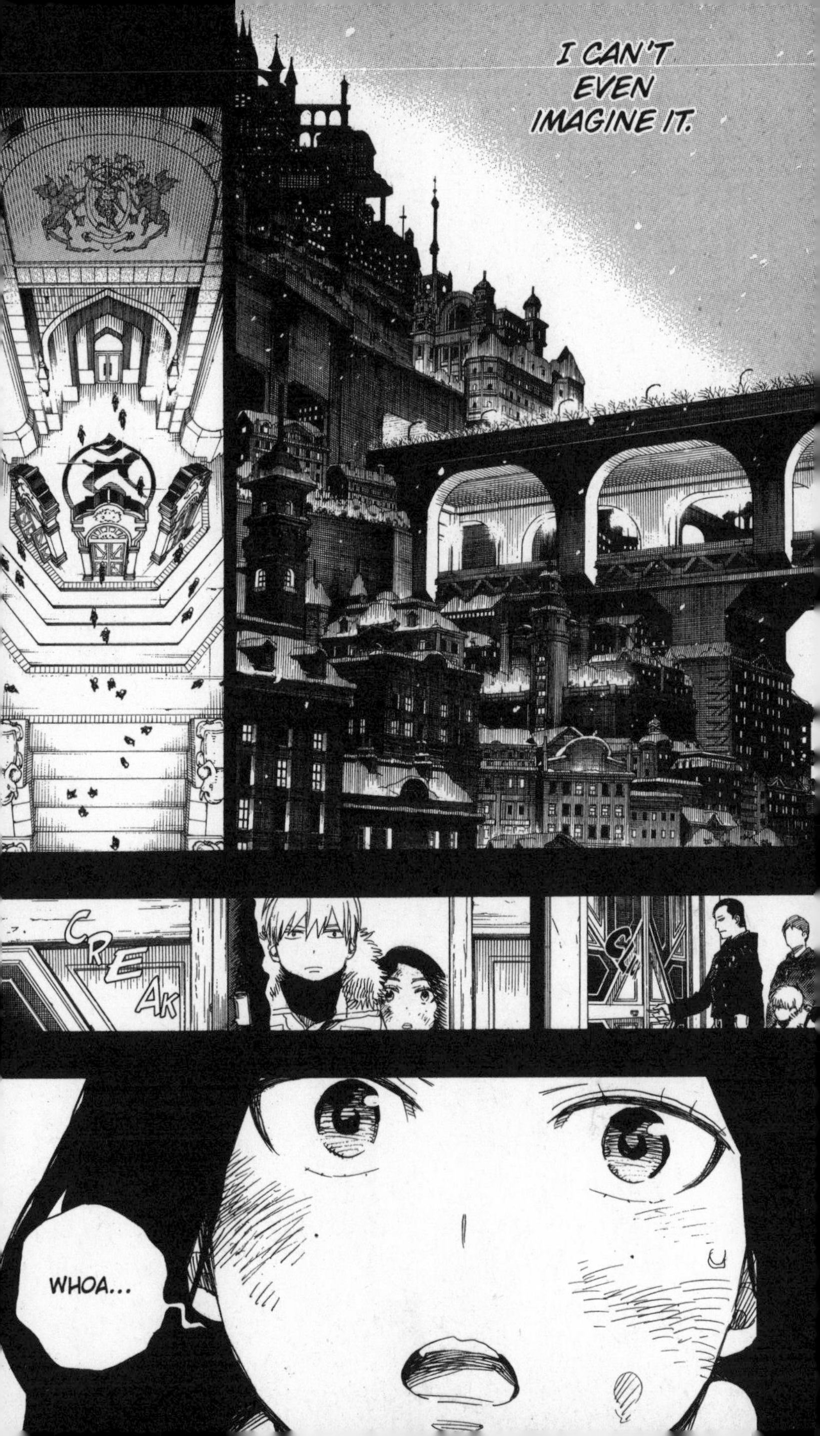
I CAN'T EVEN IMAGINE IT.
CREAK
WHOA...

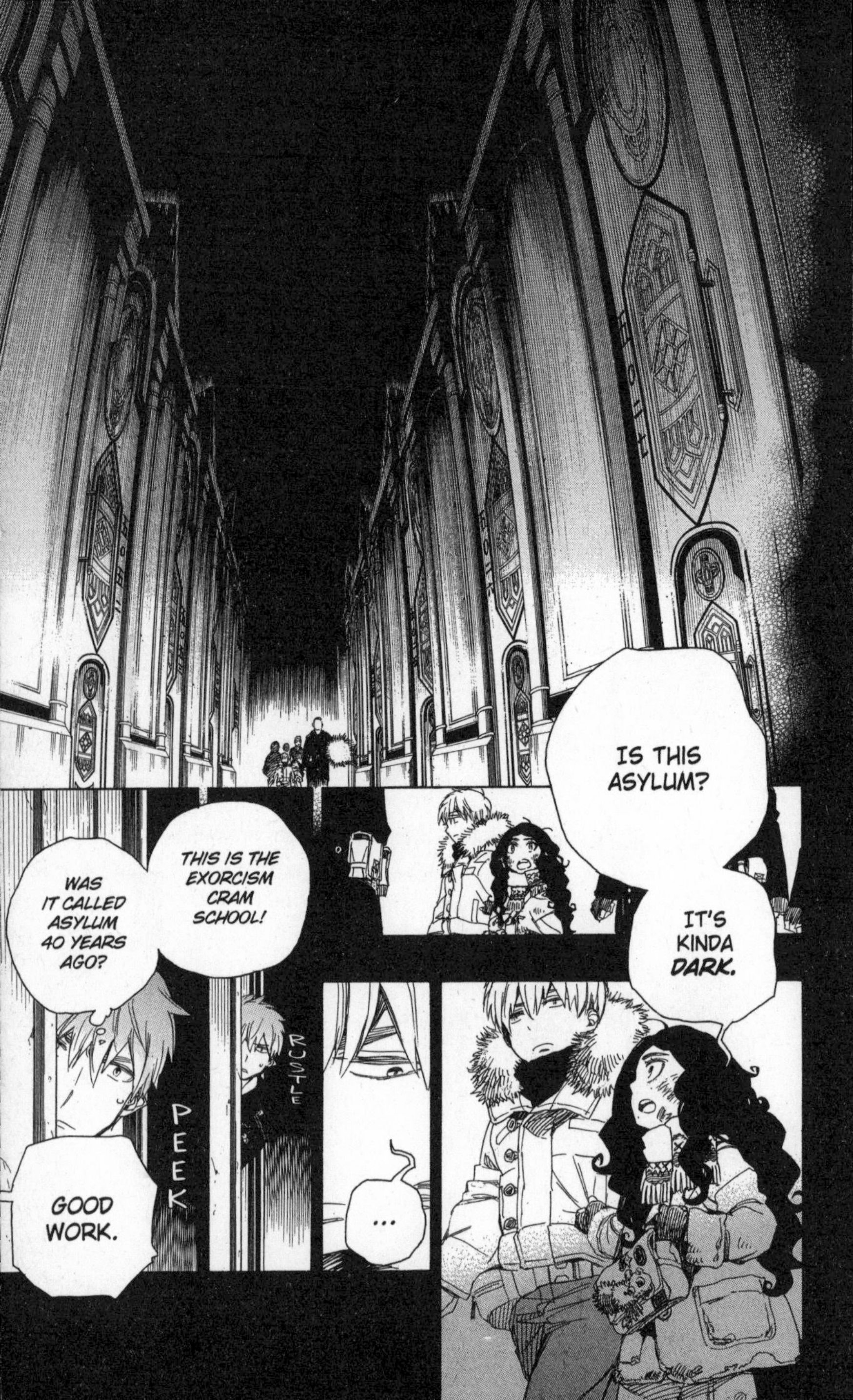
IS THIS ASYLUM?
IT'S KINDA DARK.
THIS IS THE EXORCISM CRAM SCHOOL!
WAS IT CALLED ASYLUM 40 YEARS AGO?
...
RUSTLE
PEEK
GOOD WORK.

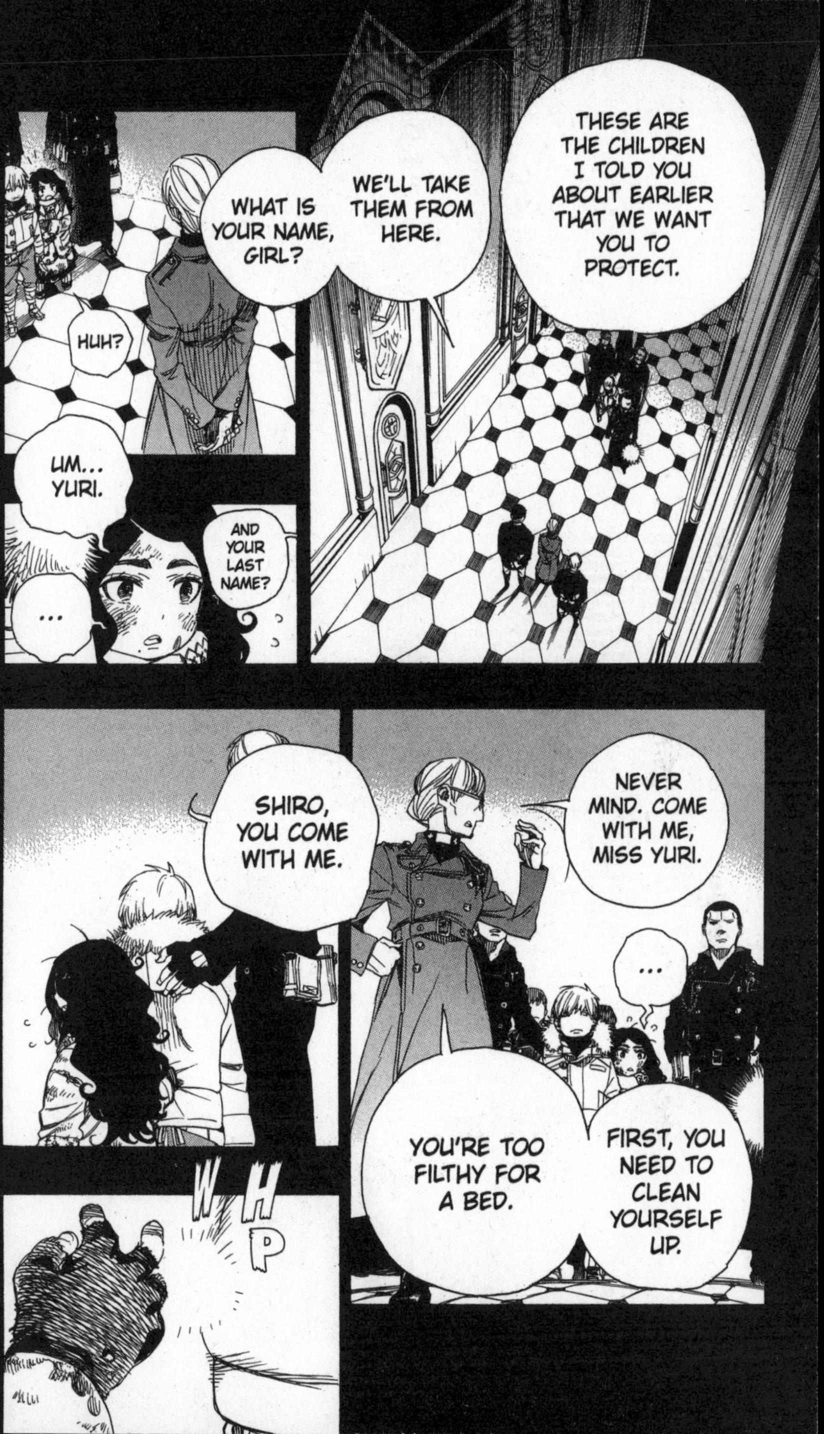
THESE ARE THE CHILDREN I TOLD YOU ABOUT EARLIER THAT WE WANT YOU TO PROTECT.
WE'LL TAKE THEM FROM HERE.
WHAT IS YOUR NAME, GIRL?
HUH?
UM... YURI.
AND YOUR LAST NAME?
...
NEVER MIND. COME WITH ME, MISS YURI.
...
FIRST, YOU NEED TO CLEAN YOURSELF UP.
YOU'RE TOO FILTHY FOR A BED.
SHIRO, YOU COME WITH ME.
WHP

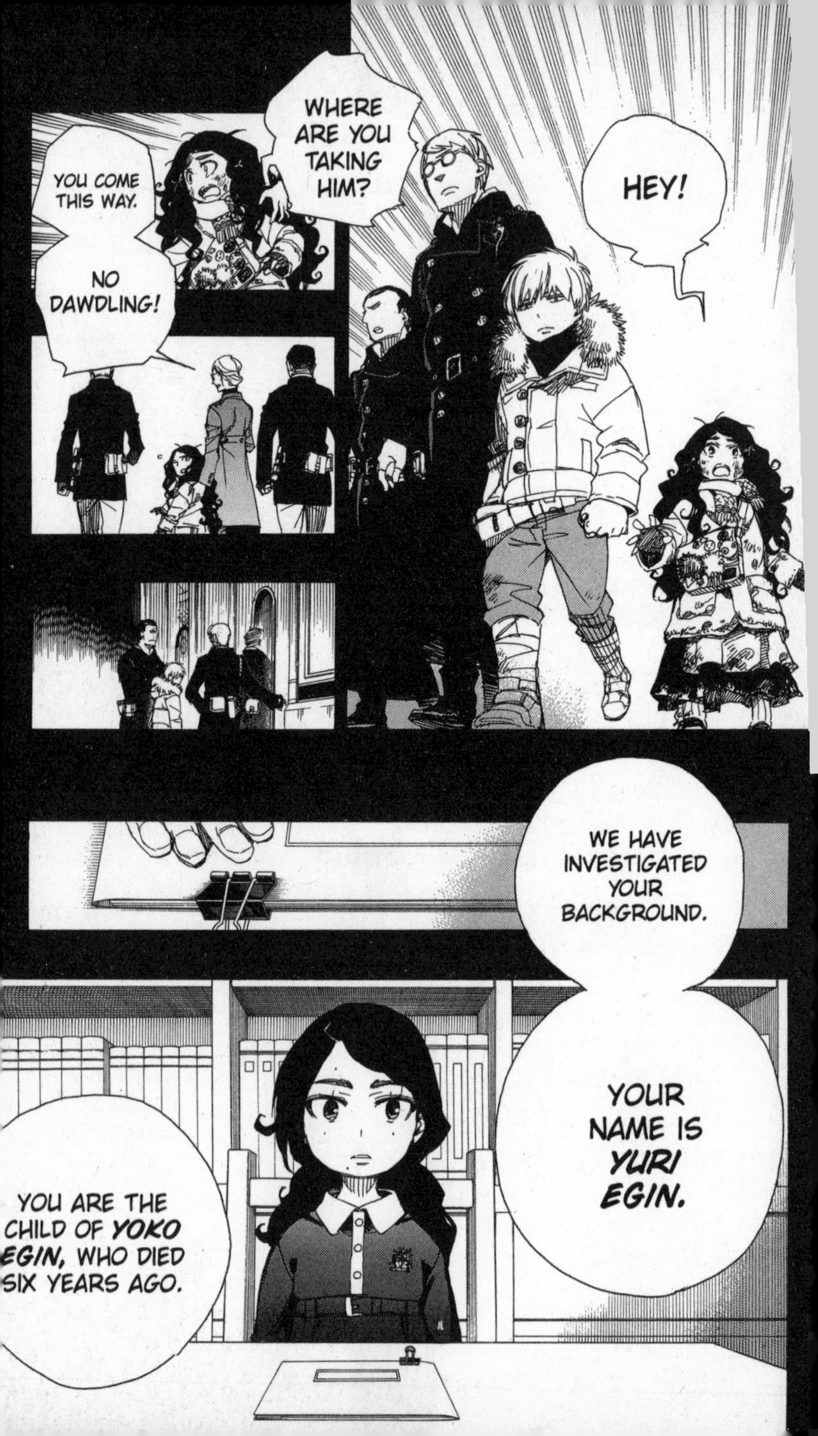
HEY!
WHERE ARE YOU TAKING HIM?
YOU COME THIS WAY.
NO DAWDLING!
WE HAVE INVESTIGATED YOUR BACKGROUND.
YOUR NAME IS *YURI EGIN.*
YOU ARE THE CHILD OF *YOKO EGIN,* WHO DIED SIX YEARS AGO.

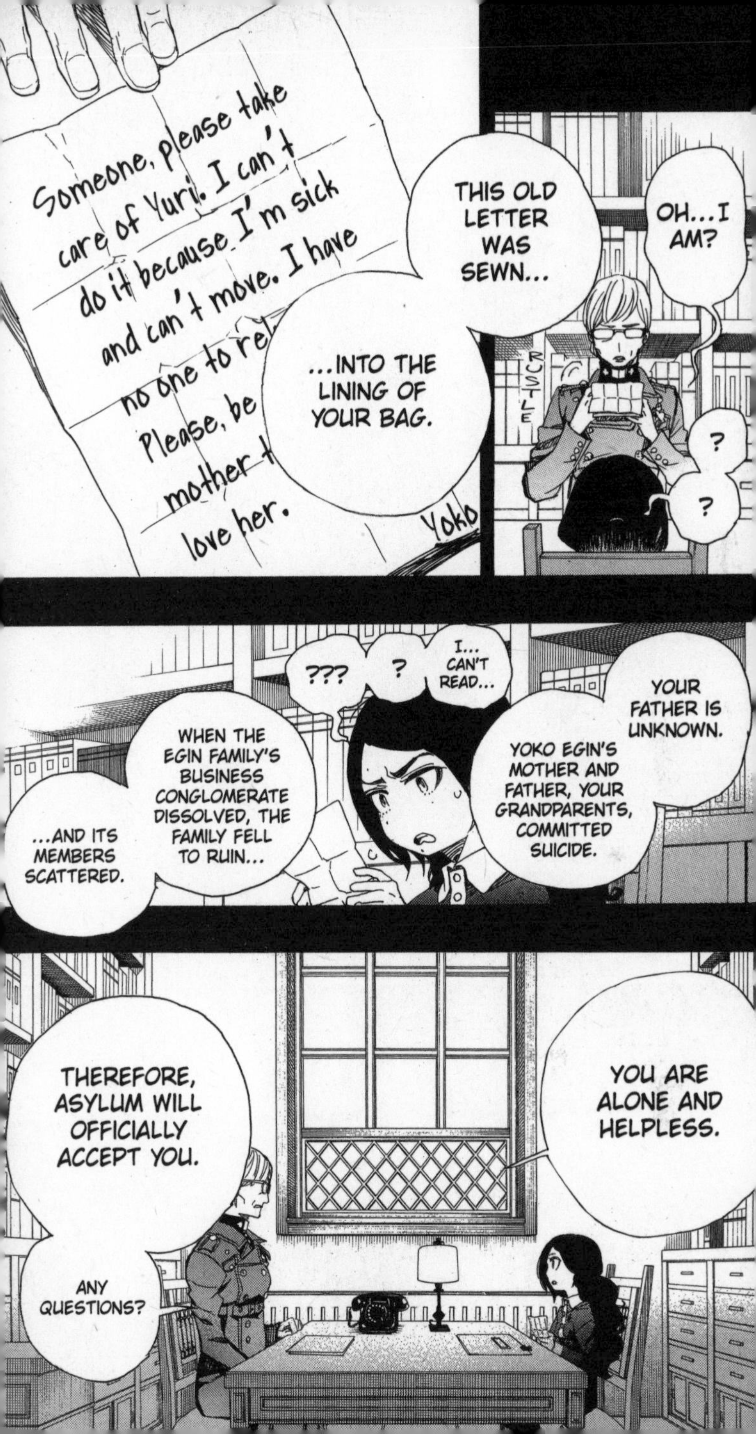
RUSTLE
OH...I AM?
?
?
Someone, please take care of Yuri. I can't do it because I'm sick and can't move. I have no one to rel
Please, be
mother t
love her.
Yoko
THIS OLD LETTER WAS SEWN...
...INTO THE LINING OF YOUR BAG.
YOUR FATHER IS UNKNOWN.
YOKO EGIN'S MOTHER AND FATHER, YOUR GRANDPARENTS, COMMITTED SUICIDE.
I... CAN'T READ...
?
???
WHEN THE EGIN FAMILY'S BUSINESS CONGLOMERATE DISSOLVED, THE FAMILY FELL TO RUIN...
...AND ITS MEMBERS SCATTERED.
YOU ARE ALONE AND HELPLESS.
THEREFORE, ASYLUM WILL OFFICIALLY ACCEPT YOU.
ANY QUESTIONS?

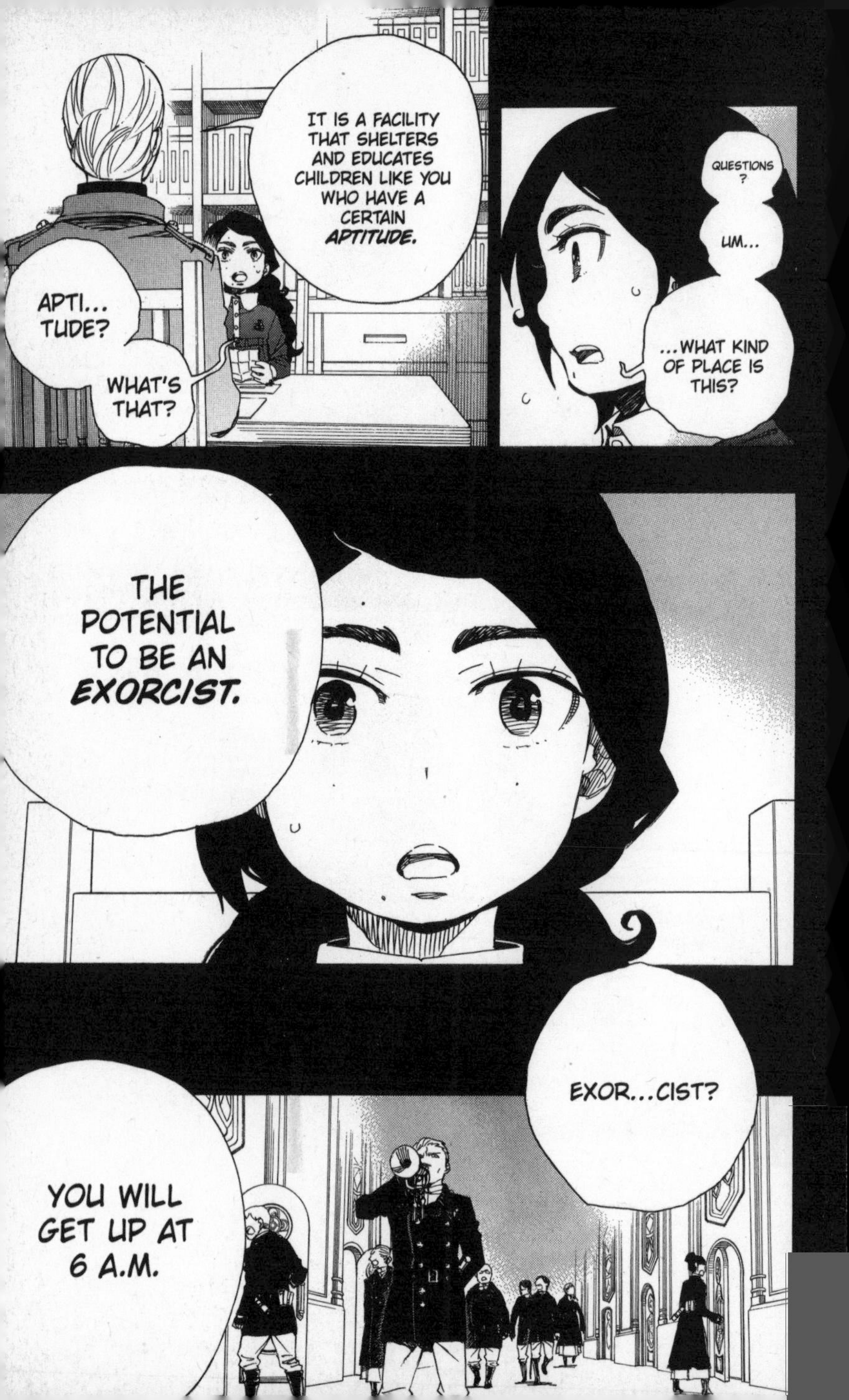
QUESTIONS?
UM...
...WHAT KIND OF PLACE IS THIS?
IT IS A FACILITY THAT SHELTERS AND EDUCATES CHILDREN LIKE YOU WHO HAVE A CERTAIN *APTITUDE.*
APTI... TUDE?
WHAT'S THAT?
THE POTENTIAL TO BE AN *EXORCIST.*
EXOR...CIST?
YOU WILL GET UP AT 6 A.M.

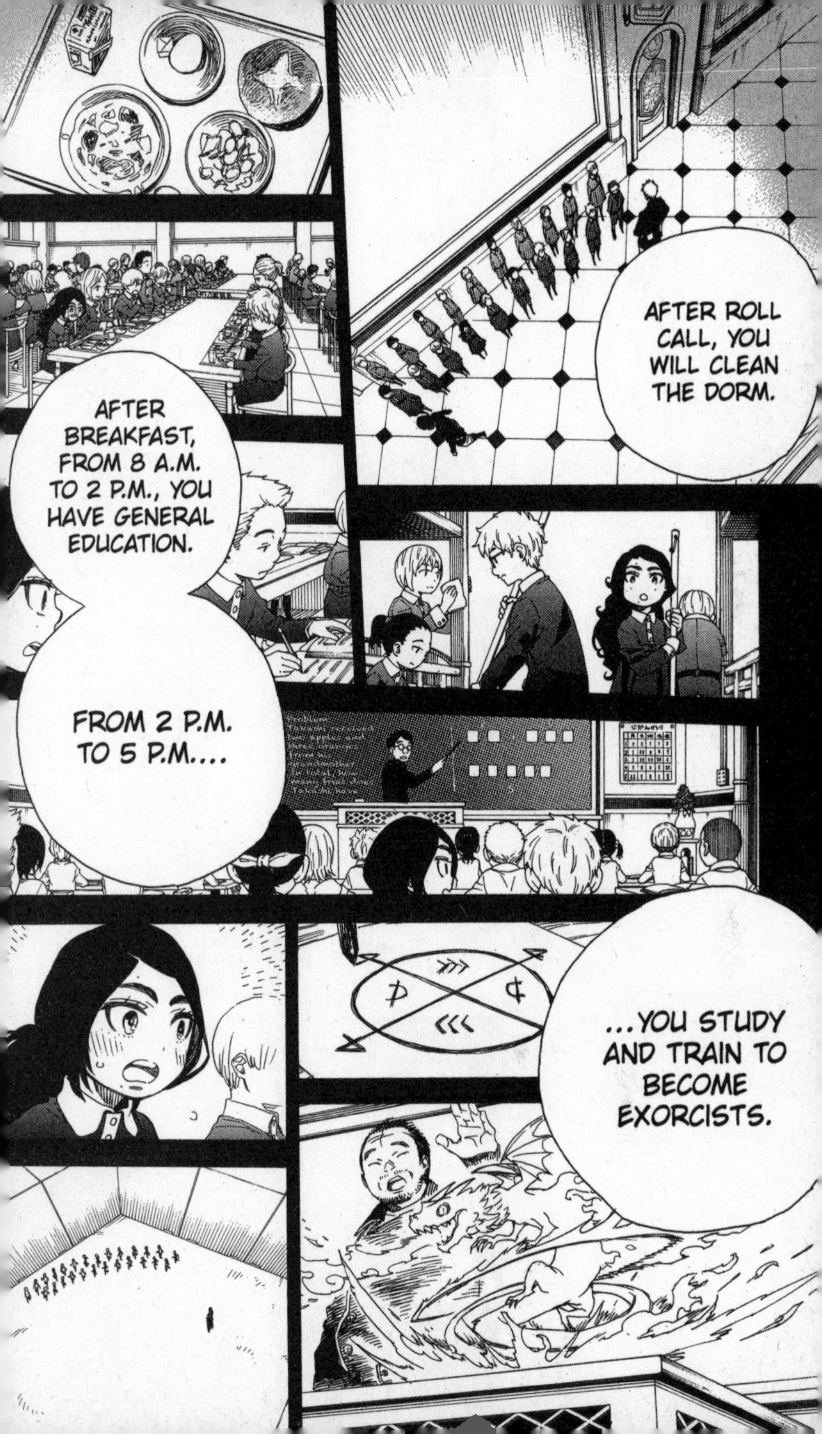
AFTER ROLL CALL, YOU WILL CLEAN THE DORM.
AFTER BREAKFAST, FROM 8 A.M. TO 2 P.M., YOU HAVE GENERAL EDUCATION.
FROM 2 P.M. TO 5 P.M....
...YOU STUDY AND TRAIN TO BECOME EXORCISTS.

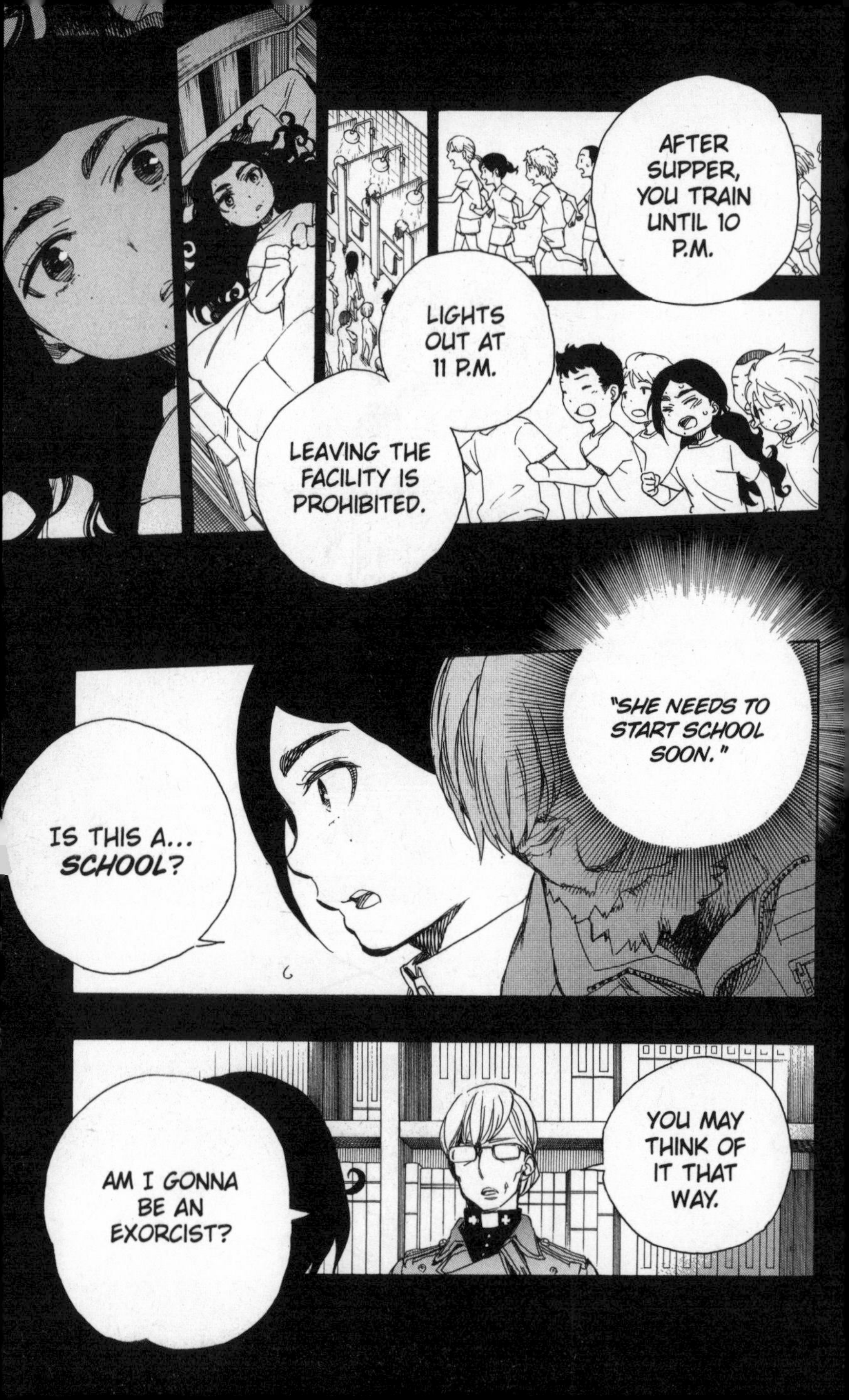

AFTER SUPPER, YOU TRAIN UNTIL 10 P.M.
LIGHTS OUT AT 11 P.M.
LEAVING THE FACILITY IS PROHIBITED.
"SHE NEEDS TO START SCHOOL SOON."
IS THIS A... *SCHOOL?*
AM I GONNA BE AN EXORCIST?
YOU MAY THINK OF IT THAT WAY.

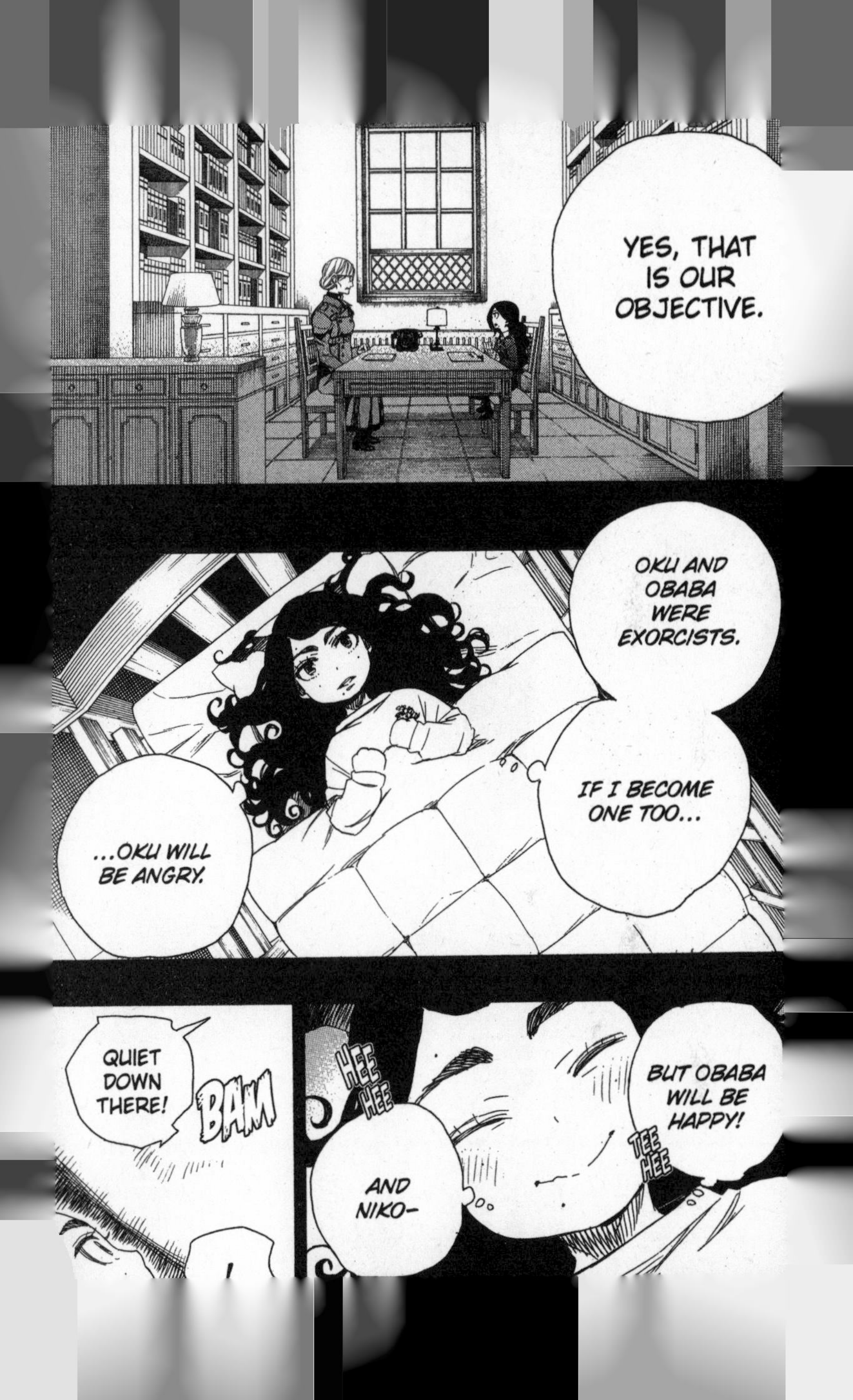
YES, THAT IS OUR OBJECTIVE.
OKU AND OBABA WERE EXORCISTS.
IF I BECOME ONE TOO...
...OKU WILL BE ANGRY.
BUT OBABA WILL BE HAPPY!
TEE HEE
HEE HEE
AND NIKO-
QUIET DOWN THERE!
BAM

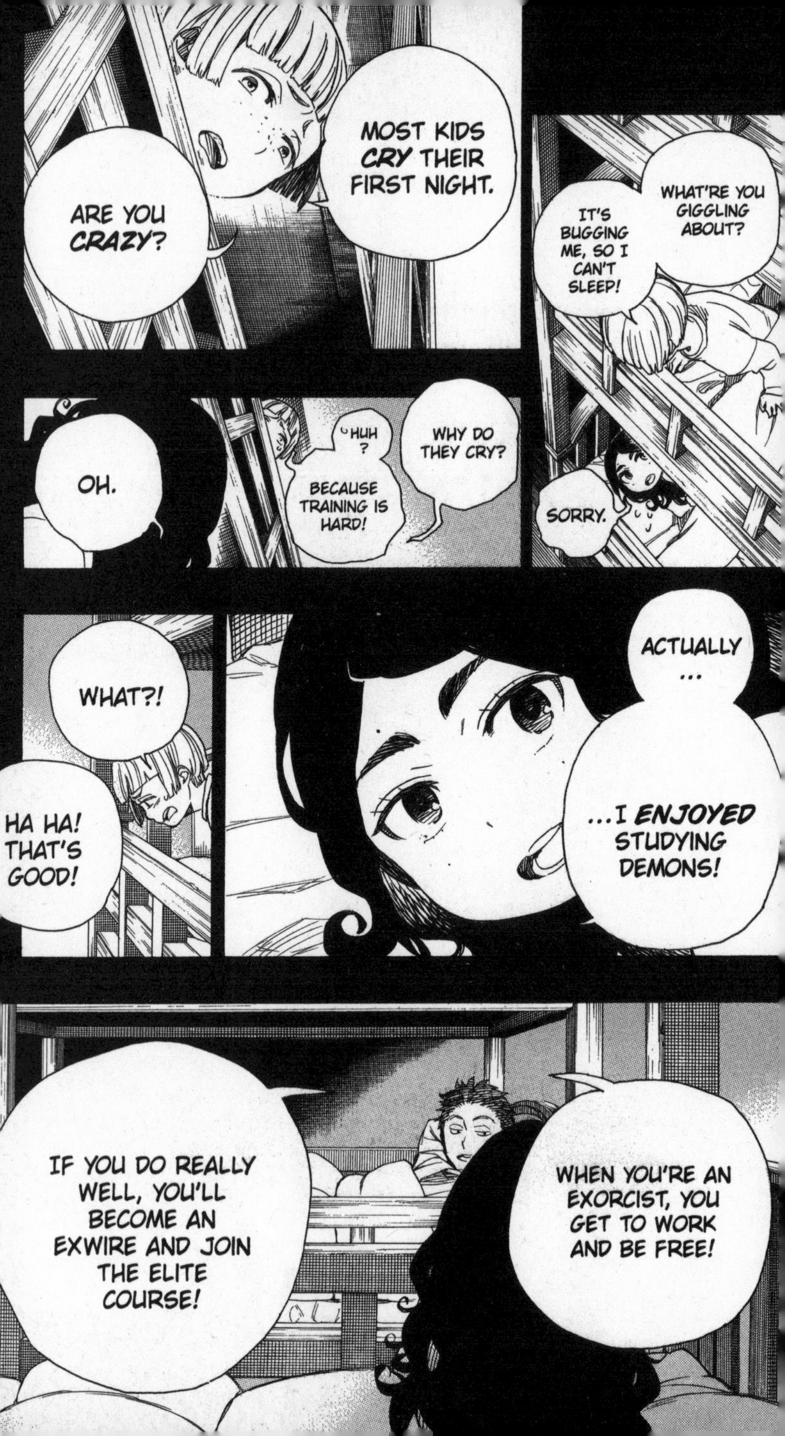
WHAT'RE YOU GIGGLING ABOUT?
IT'S BUGGING ME, SO I CAN'T SLEEP!
SORRY.
MOST KIDS *CRY* THEIR FIRST NIGHT.
ARE YOU *CRAZY*?
WHY DO THEY CRY?
HUH? BECAUSE TRAINING IS HARD!
OH.
ACTUALLY...
...I *ENJOYED* STUDYING DEMONS!
WHAT?!
HA HA! THAT'S GOOD!
WHEN YOU'RE AN EXORCIST, YOU GET TO WORK AND BE FREE!
IF YOU DO REALLY WELL, YOU'LL BECOME AN EXWIRE AND JOIN THE ELITE COURSE!

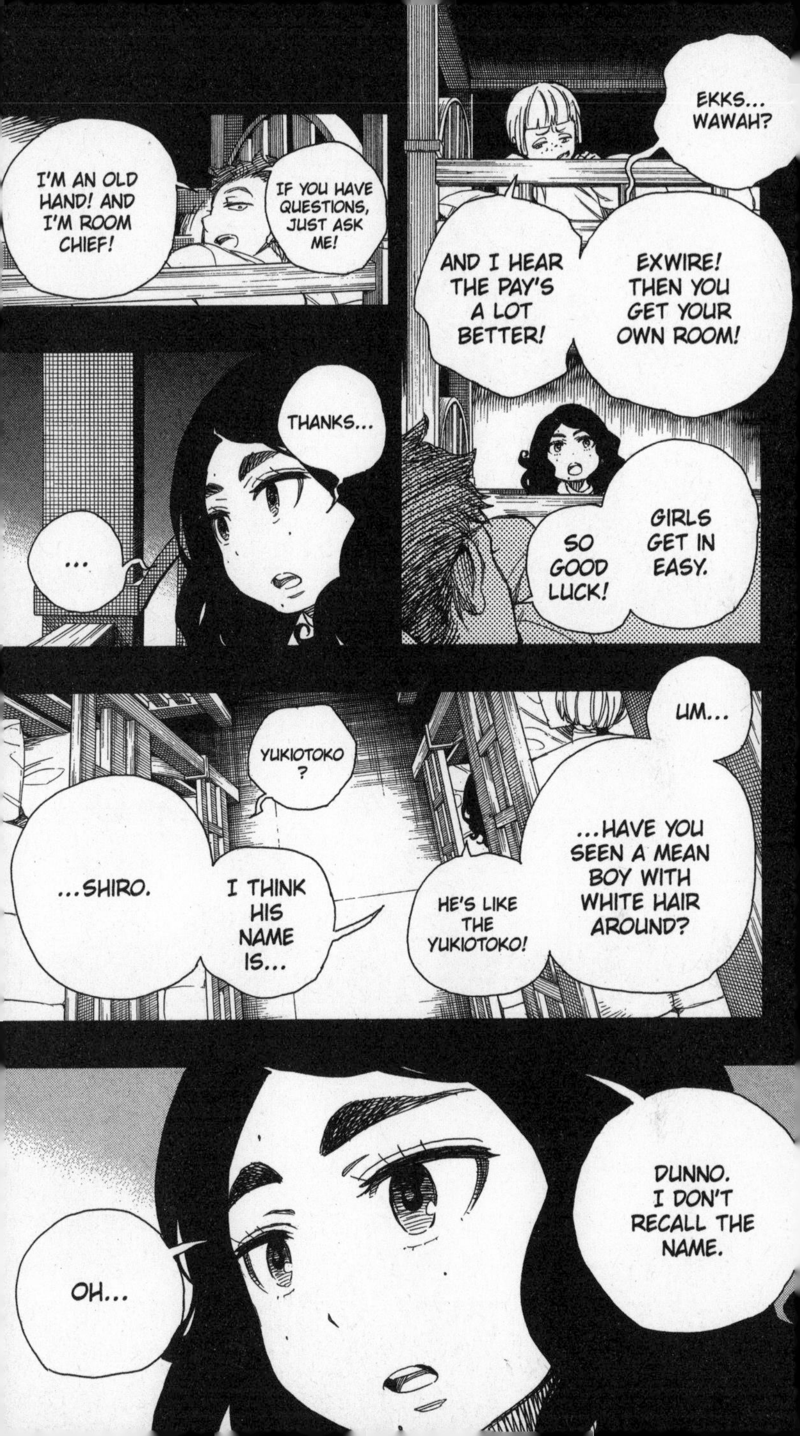
EKKS... WAWAH?
EXWIRE! THEN YOU GET YOUR OWN ROOM!
AND I HEAR THE PAY'S A LOT BETTER!
IF YOU HAVE QUESTIONS, JUST ASK ME!
I'M AN OLD HAND! AND I'M ROOM CHIEF!
GIRLS GET IN EASY.
SO GOOD LUCK!
THANKS...
...
UM...
...HAVE YOU SEEN A MEAN BOY WITH WHITE HAIR AROUND?
HE'S LIKE THE YUKIOTOKO!
YUKIOTOKO?
I THINK HIS NAME IS...
...SHIRO.
DUNNO. I DON'T RECALL THE NAME.
OH...

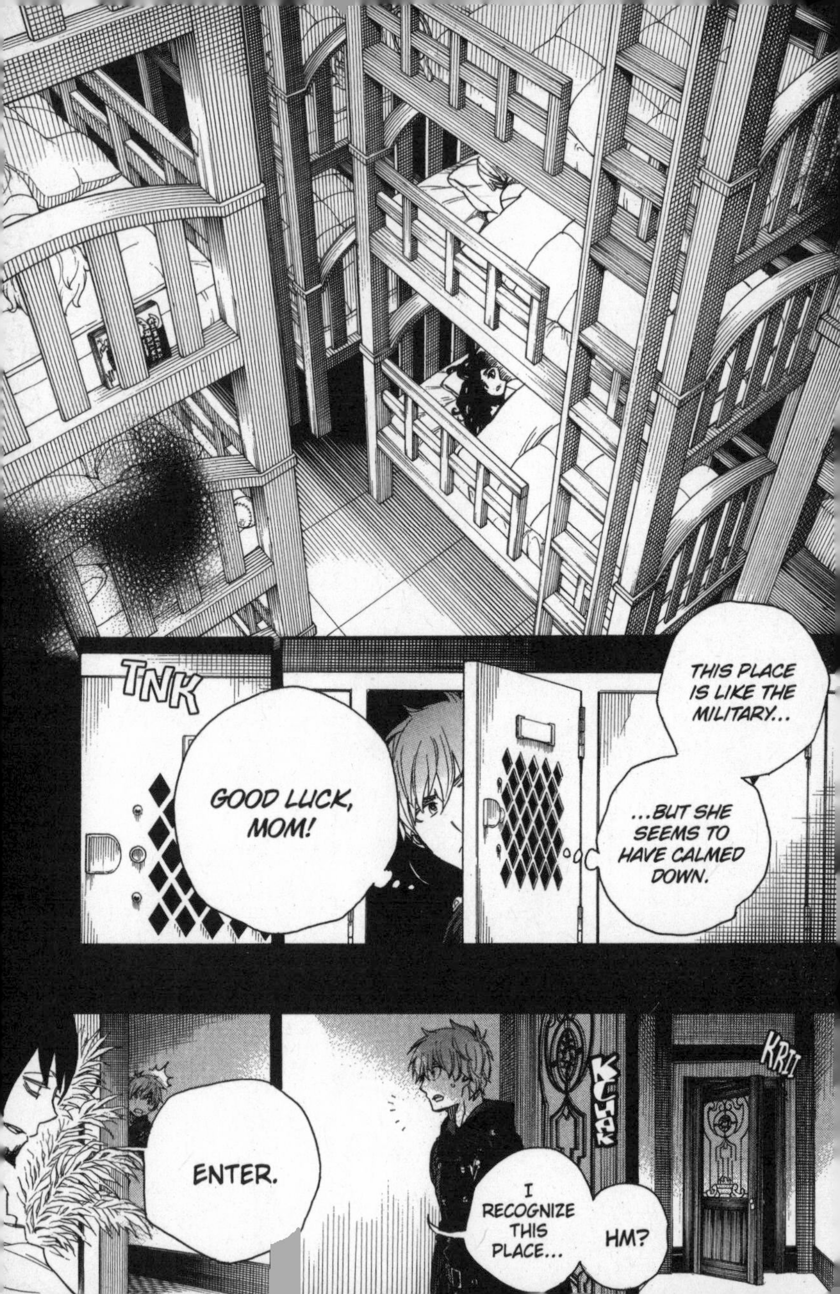
THIS PLACE IS LIKE THE MILITARY...
...BUT SHE SEEMS TO HAVE CALMED DOWN.
GOOD LUCK, MOM!
TNK
KRII
KCHAK
HM?
I RECOGNIZE THIS PLACE...
ENTER.

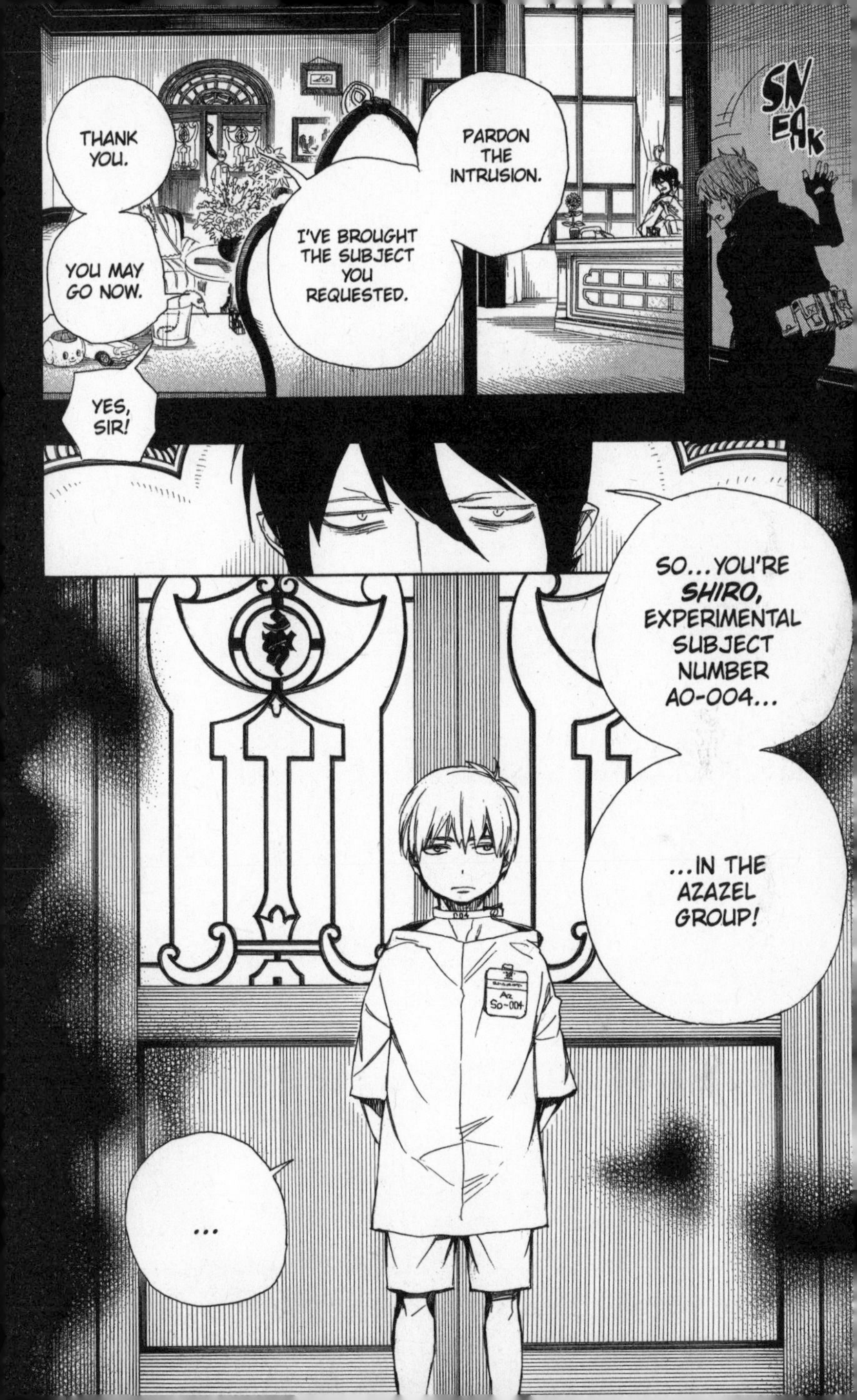
SNEAK
PARDON THE INTRUSION.
I'VE BROUGHT THE SUBJECT YOU REQUESTED.
THANK YOU.
YOU MAY GO NOW.
YES, SIR!
SO... YOU'RE SHIRO, EXPERIMENTAL SUBJECT NUMBER AO-004...
...IN THE AZAZEL GROUP!
...

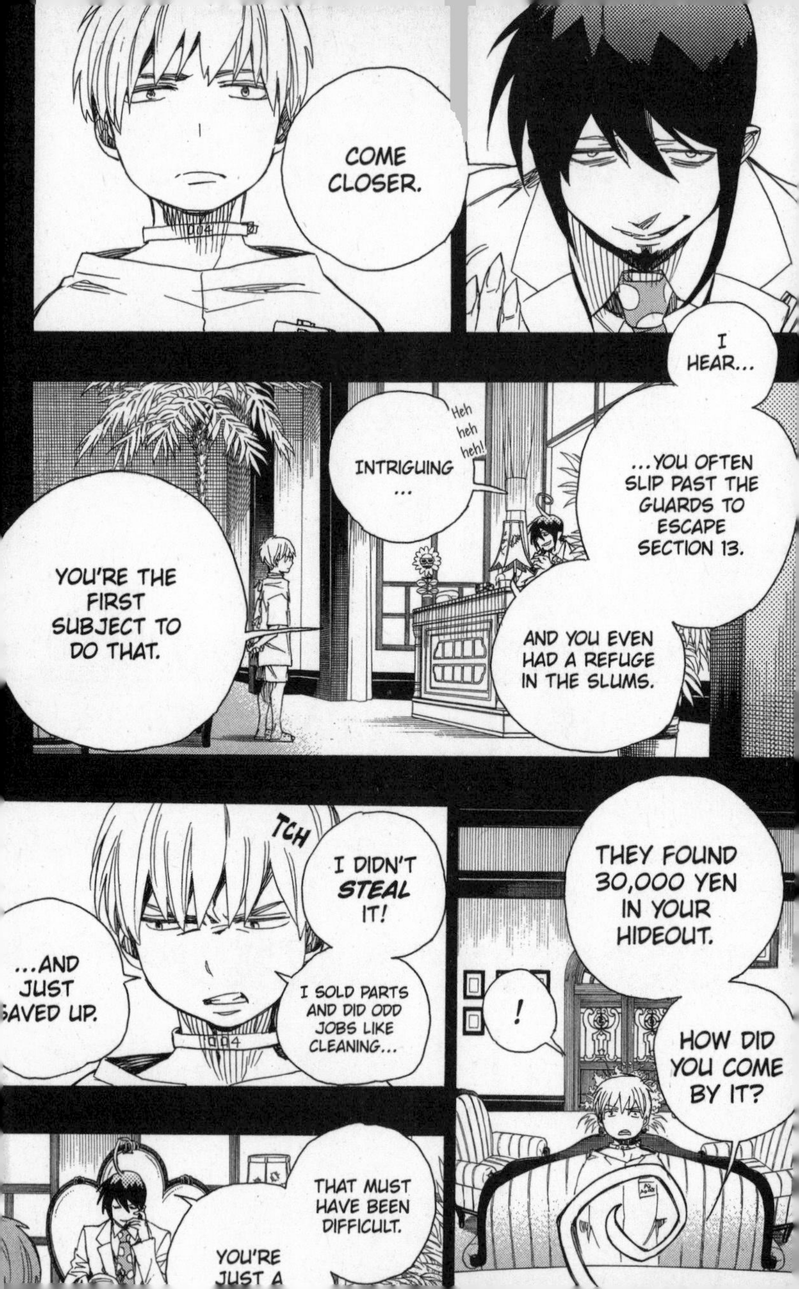

COME CLOSER.
I HEAR...
...YOU OFTEN SLIP PAST THE GUARDS TO ESCAPE SECTION 13.
AND YOU EVEN HAD A REFUGE IN THE SLUMS.
Heh heh heh!
INTRIGUING...
YOU'RE THE FIRST SUBJECT TO DO THAT.
THEY FOUND 30,000 YEN IN YOUR HIDEOUT.
!
HOW DID YOU COME BY IT?
TCH
I DIDN'T *STEAL* IT!
I SOLD PARTS AND DID ODD JOBS LIKE CLEANING...
...AND JUST SAVED UP.
THAT MUST HAVE BEEN DIFFICULT.
YOU'RE JUST A

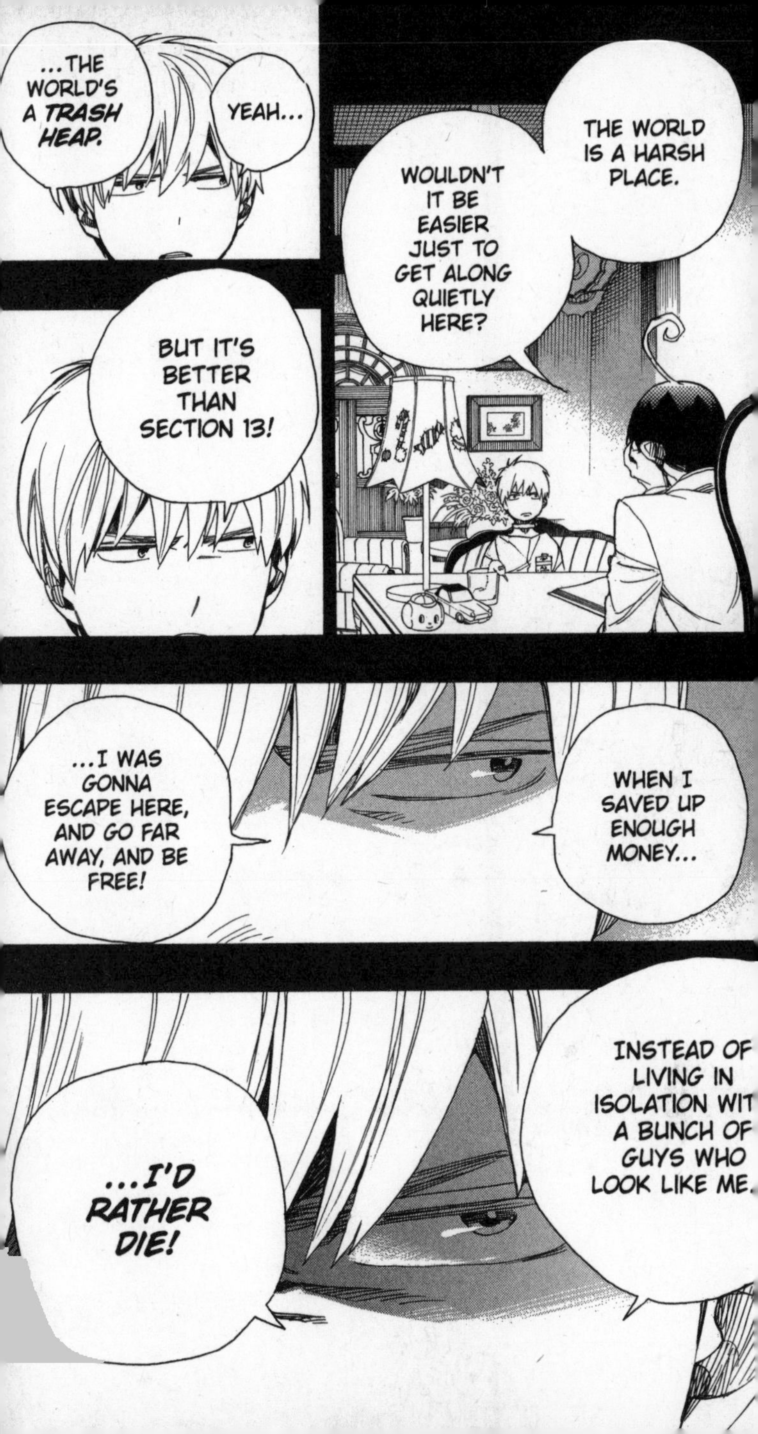
THE WORLD IS A HARSH PLACE.
WOULDN'T IT BE EASIER JUST TO GET ALONG QUIETLY HERE?
YEAH...
...THE WORLD'S A *TRASH HEAP.*
BUT IT'S BETTER THAN SECTION 13!
WHEN I SAVED UP ENOUGH MONEY...
...I WAS GONNA ESCAPE HERE, AND GO FAR AWAY, AND BE FREE!
INSTEAD OF LIVING IN ISOLATION WIT A BUNCH OF GUYS WHO LOOK LIKE ME.
...I'D RATHER DIE!

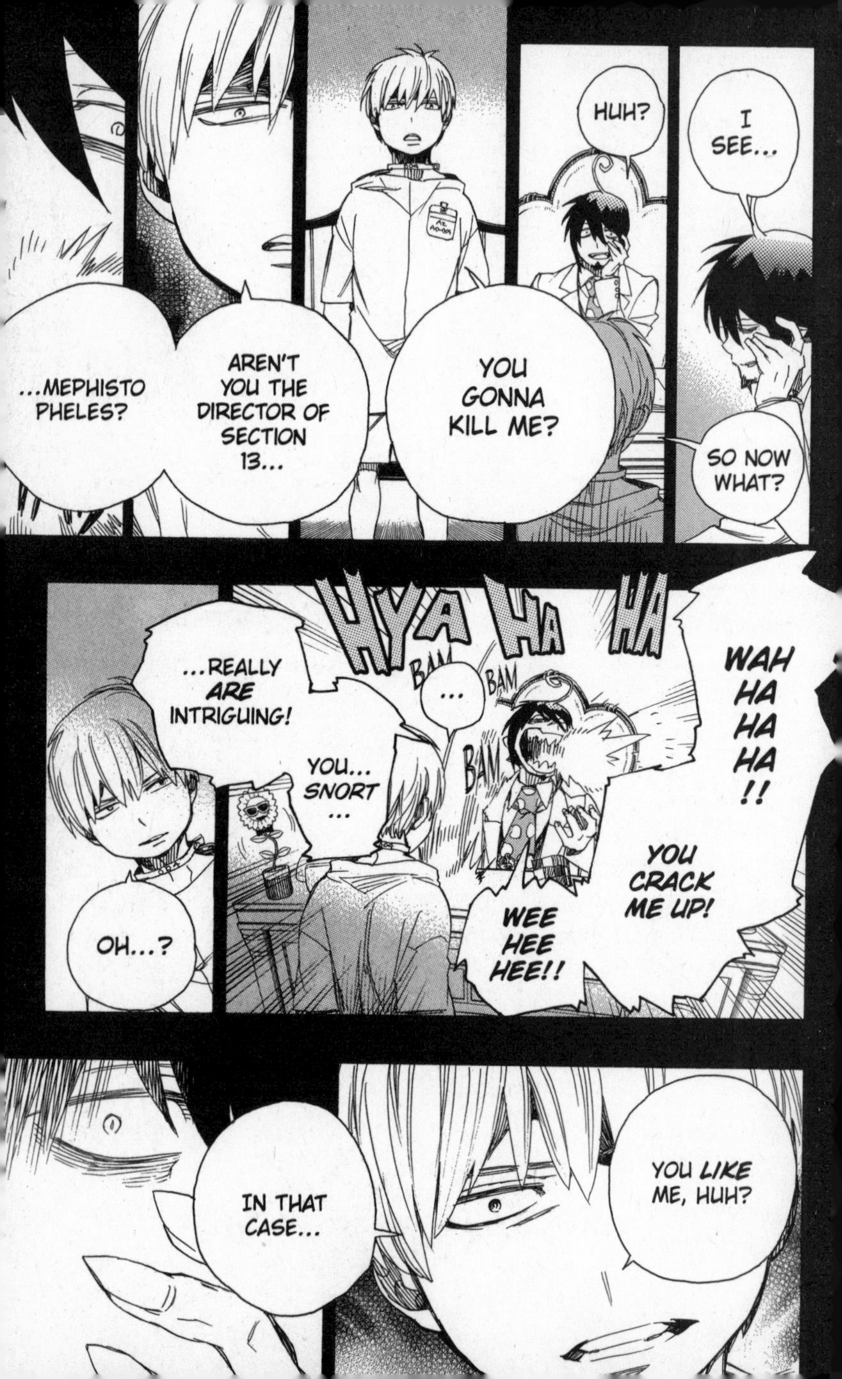
I SEE...
SO NOW WHAT?
HUH?
YOU GONNA KILL ME?
AREN'T YOU THE DIRECTOR OF SECTION 13...
...MEPHISTO PHELES?
HYA HA HA
WAH HA HA HA!!
YOU CRACK ME UP!
WEE HEE HEE!!
BAM
BAM
BAM
...
YOU... SNORT ...
...REALLY ARE INTRIGUING!
OH...?
YOU LIKE ME, HUH?
IN THAT CASE...

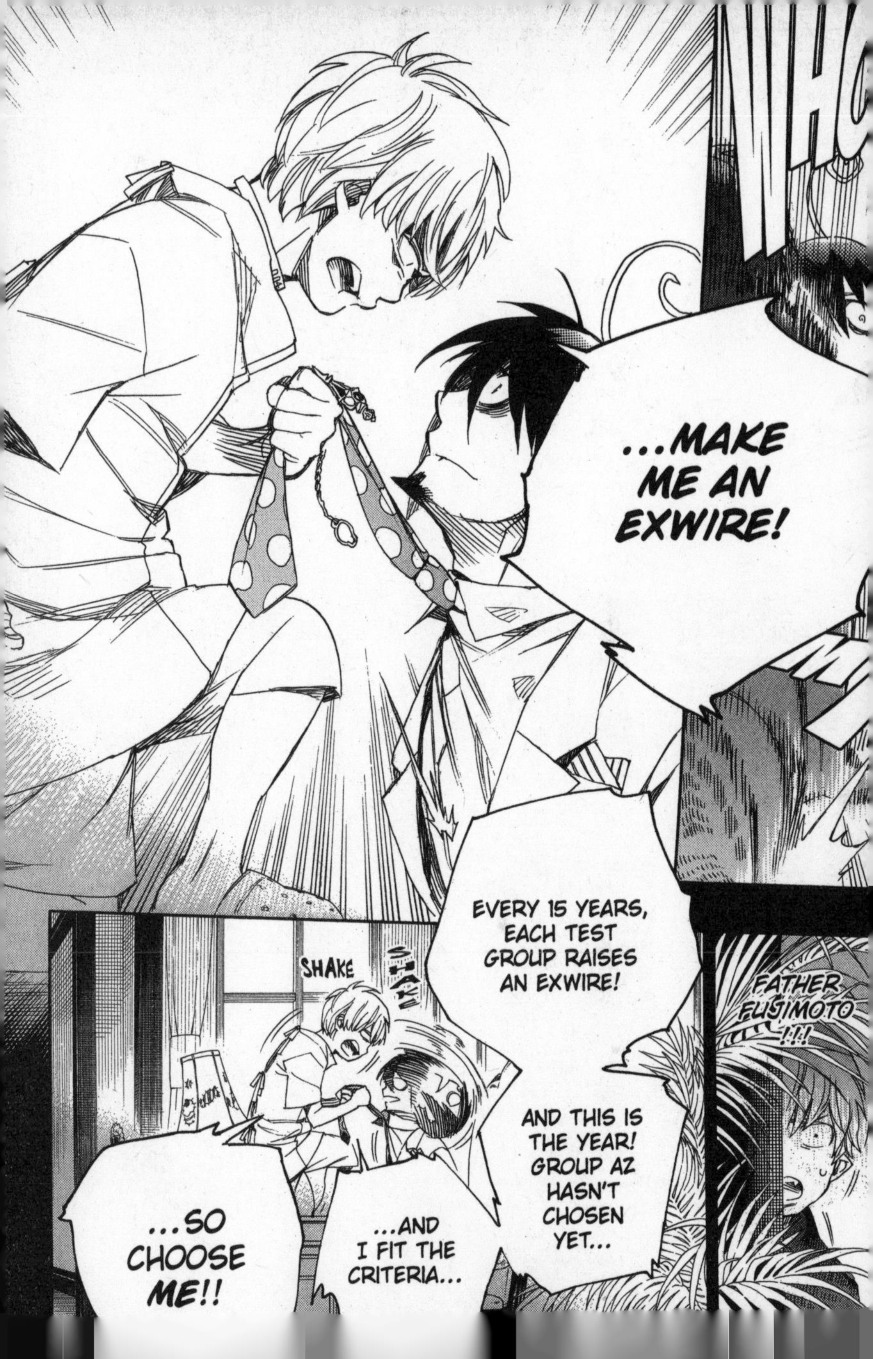
...MAKE ME AN EXWIRE!
FATHER FUJIMOTO!!!
EVERY 15 YEARS, EACH TEST GROUP RAISES AN EXWIRE!
SHAKE
AND THIS IS THE YEAR! GROUP AZ HASN'T CHOSEN YET...
...AND I FIT THE CRITERIA...
...SO CHOOSE ME!!

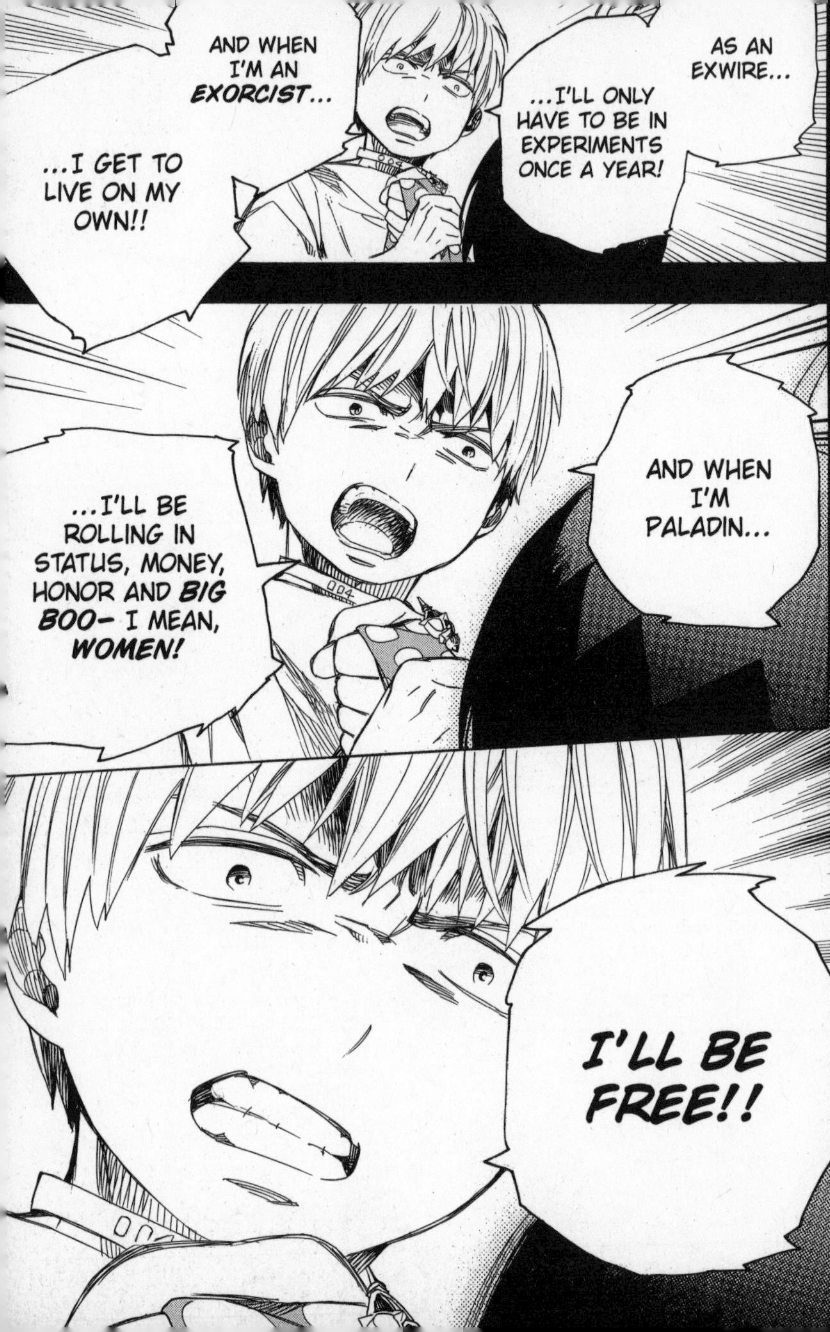
AS AN EXWIRE...
...I'LL ONLY HAVE TO BE IN EXPERIMENTS ONCE A YEAR!
AND WHEN I'M AN EXORCIST...
...I GET TO LIVE ON MY OWN!!
AND WHEN I'M PALADIN...
...I'LL BE ROLLING IN STATUS, MONEY, HONOR AND BIG BOO- I MEAN, WOMEN!
I'LL BE FREE!!

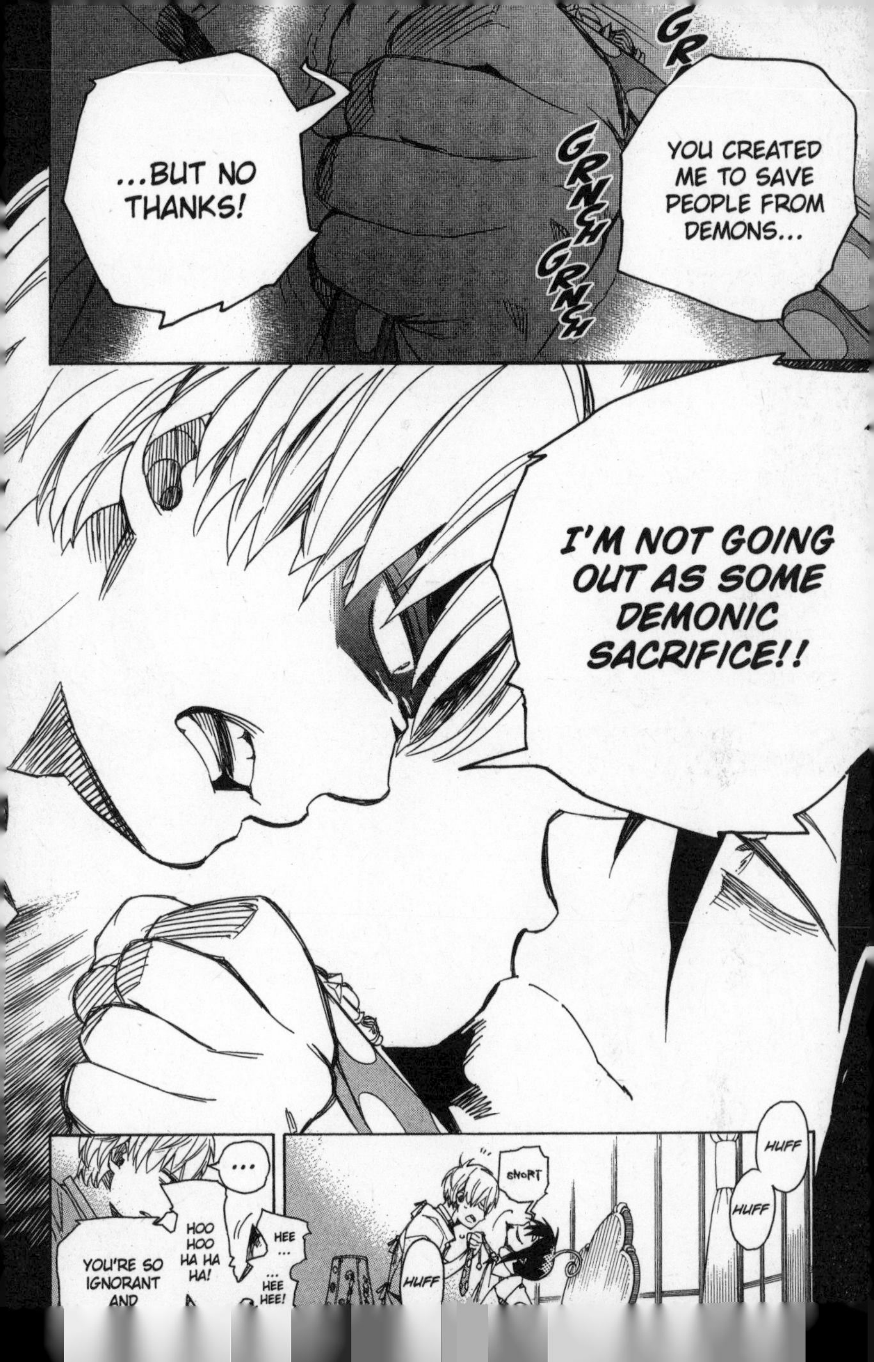
YOU CREATED ME TO SAVE PEOPLE FROM DEMONS...
GRNCH GRNCH
...BUT NO THANKS!
I'M NOT GOING OUT AS SOME DEMONIC SACRIFICE!!
HUFF
HUFF
SNORT
HUFF
...
HEE ... ... HEE HEE!
HOO HOO HA HA HA!
YOU'RE SO IGNORANT AND

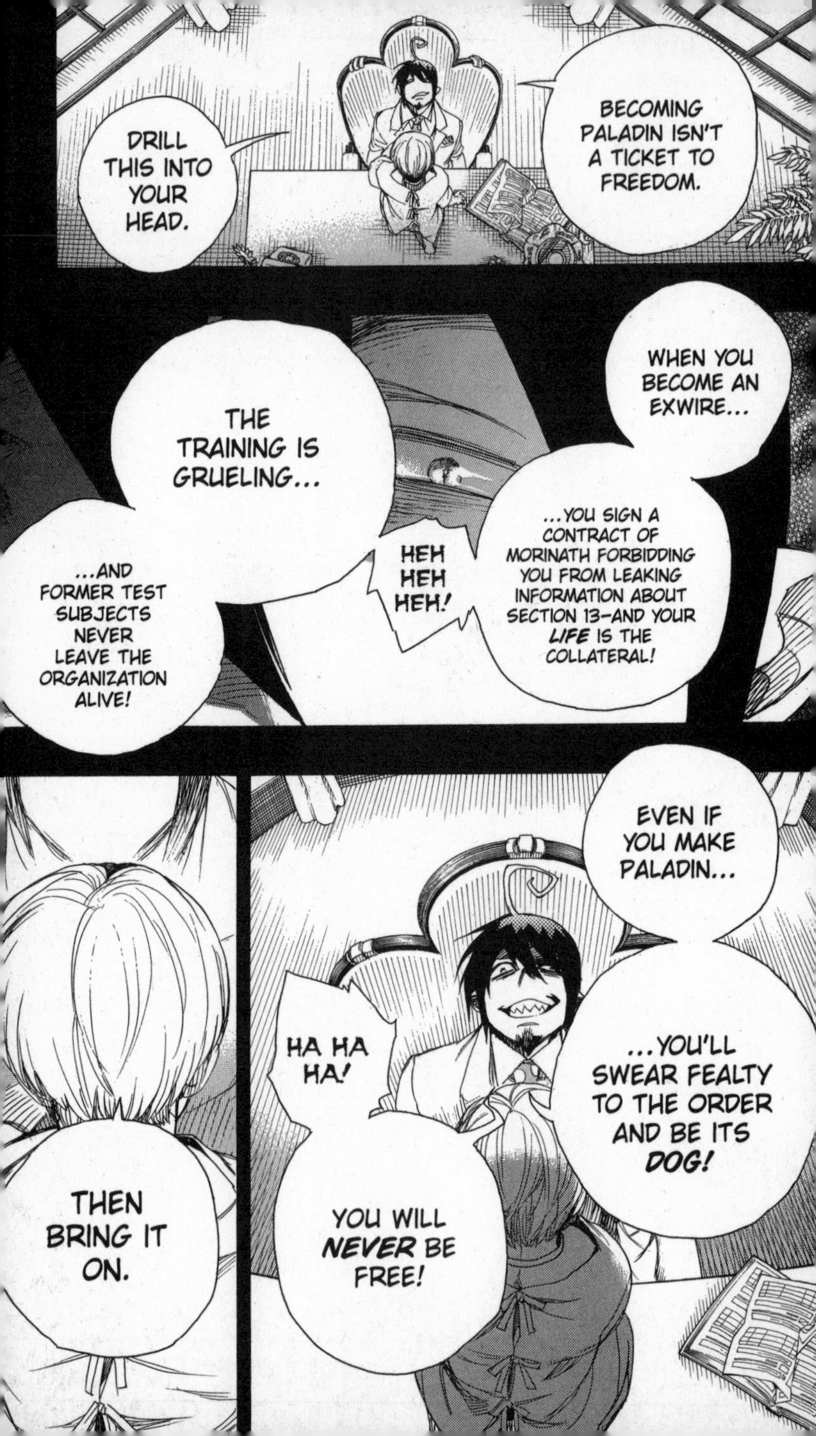
BECOMING PALADIN ISN'T A TICKET TO FREEDOM.
DRILL THIS INTO YOUR HEAD.
WHEN YOU BECOME AN EXWIRE...
...YOU SIGN A CONTRACT OF MORINATH FORBIDDING YOU FROM LEAKING INFORMATION ABOUT SECTION 13—AND YOUR *LIFE* IS THE COLLATERAL!
HEH HEH HEH!
THE TRAINING IS GRUELING...
...AND FORMER TEST SUBJECTS NEVER LEAVE THE ORGANIZATION ALIVE!
EVEN IF YOU MAKE PALADIN...
...YOU'LL SWEAR FEALTY TO THE ORDER AND BE ITS *DOG!*
HA HA HA!
YOU WILL *NEVER* BE FREE!
THEN BRING IT ON.

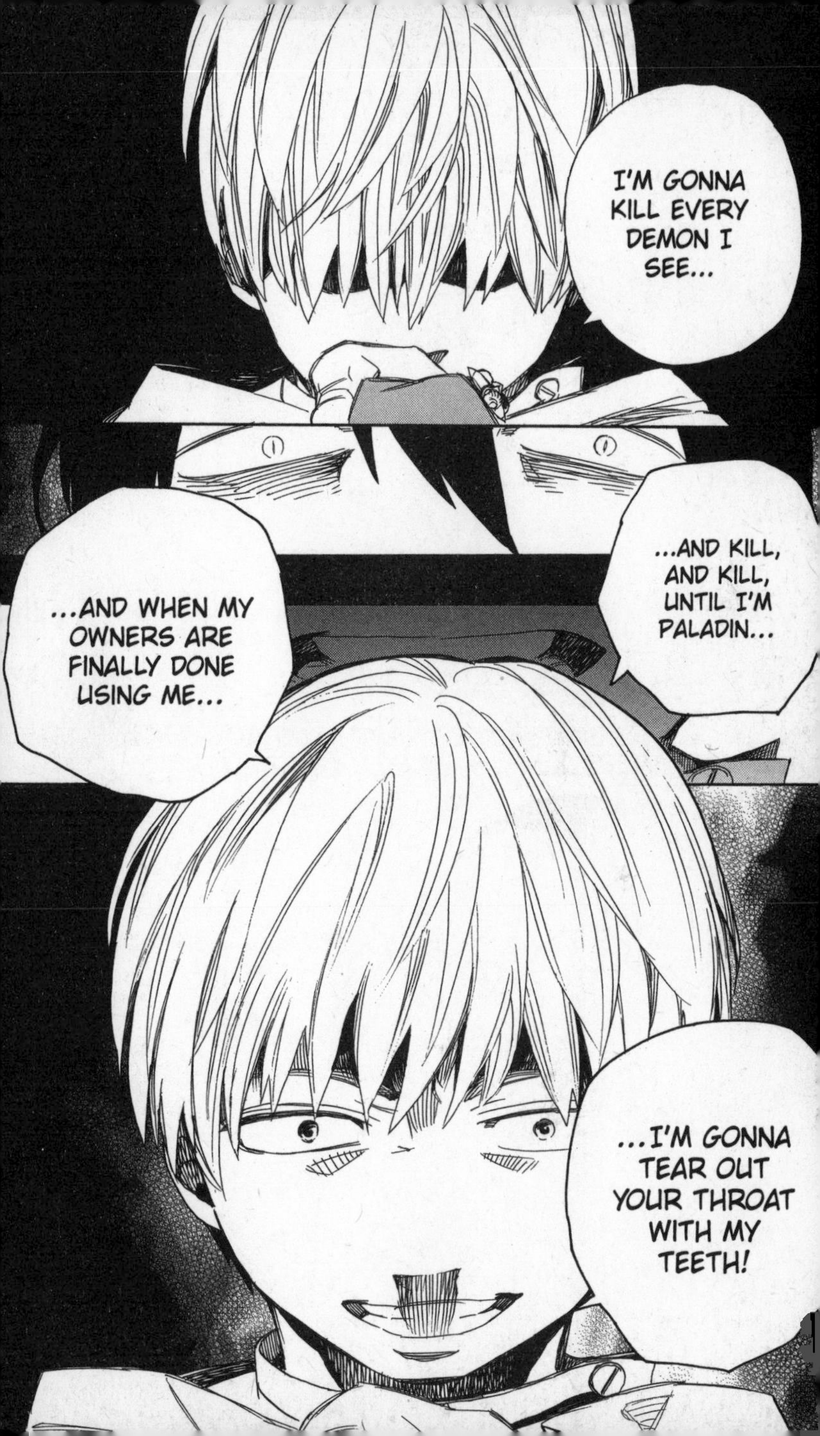
I'M GONNA KILL EVERY DEMON I SEE...
...AND KILL, AND KILL, UNTIL I'M PALADIN...
...AND WHEN MY OWNERS ARE FINALLY DONE USING ME...
...I'M GONNA TEAR OUT YOUR THROAT WITH MY TEETH!

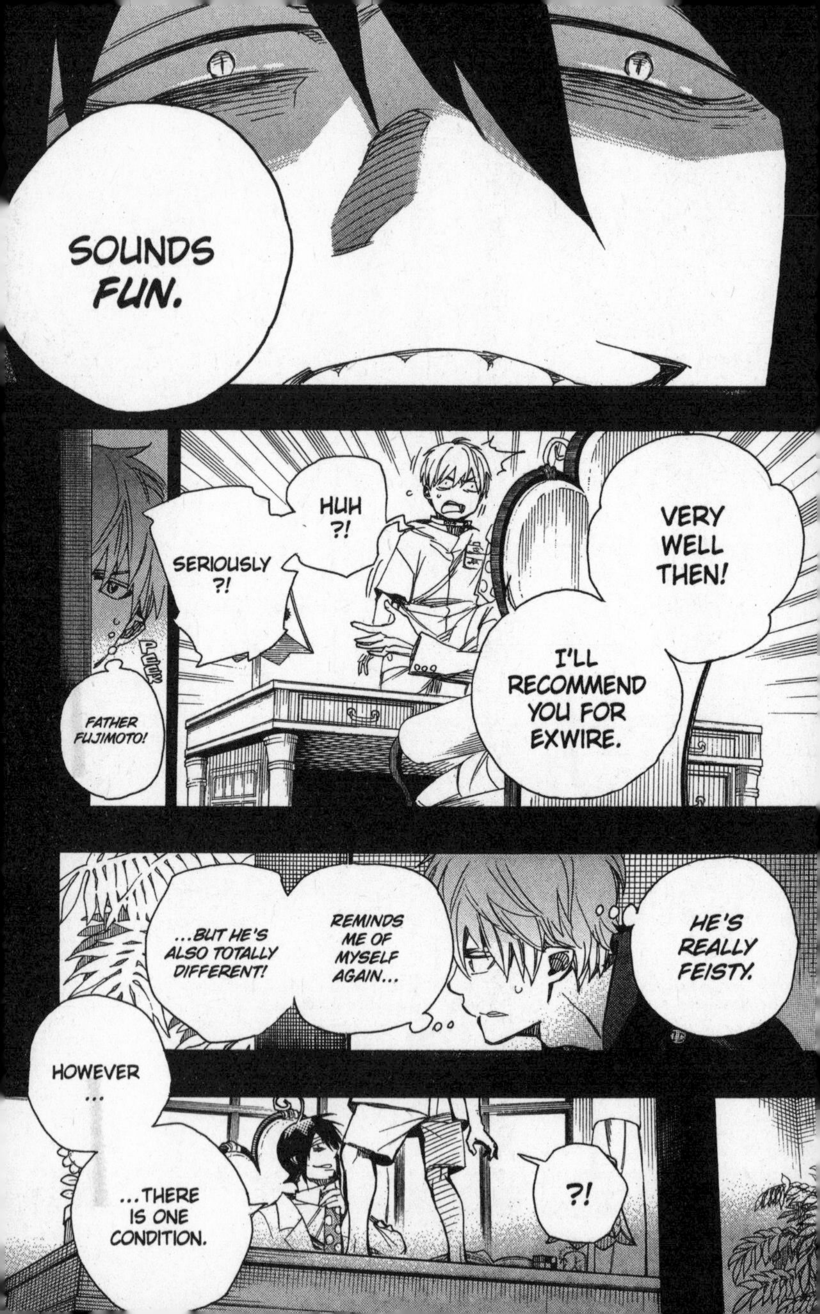
SOUNDS FUN.
VERY WELL THEN!
I'LL RECOMMEND YOU FOR EXWIRE.
HUH ?!
SERIOUSLY ?!
PEEK
FATHER FUJIMOTO!
HE'S REALLY FEISTY.
REMINDS ME OF MYSELF AGAIN...
...BUT HE'S ALSO TOTALLY DIFFERENT!
?!
HOWEVER ...
...THERE IS ONE CONDITION.

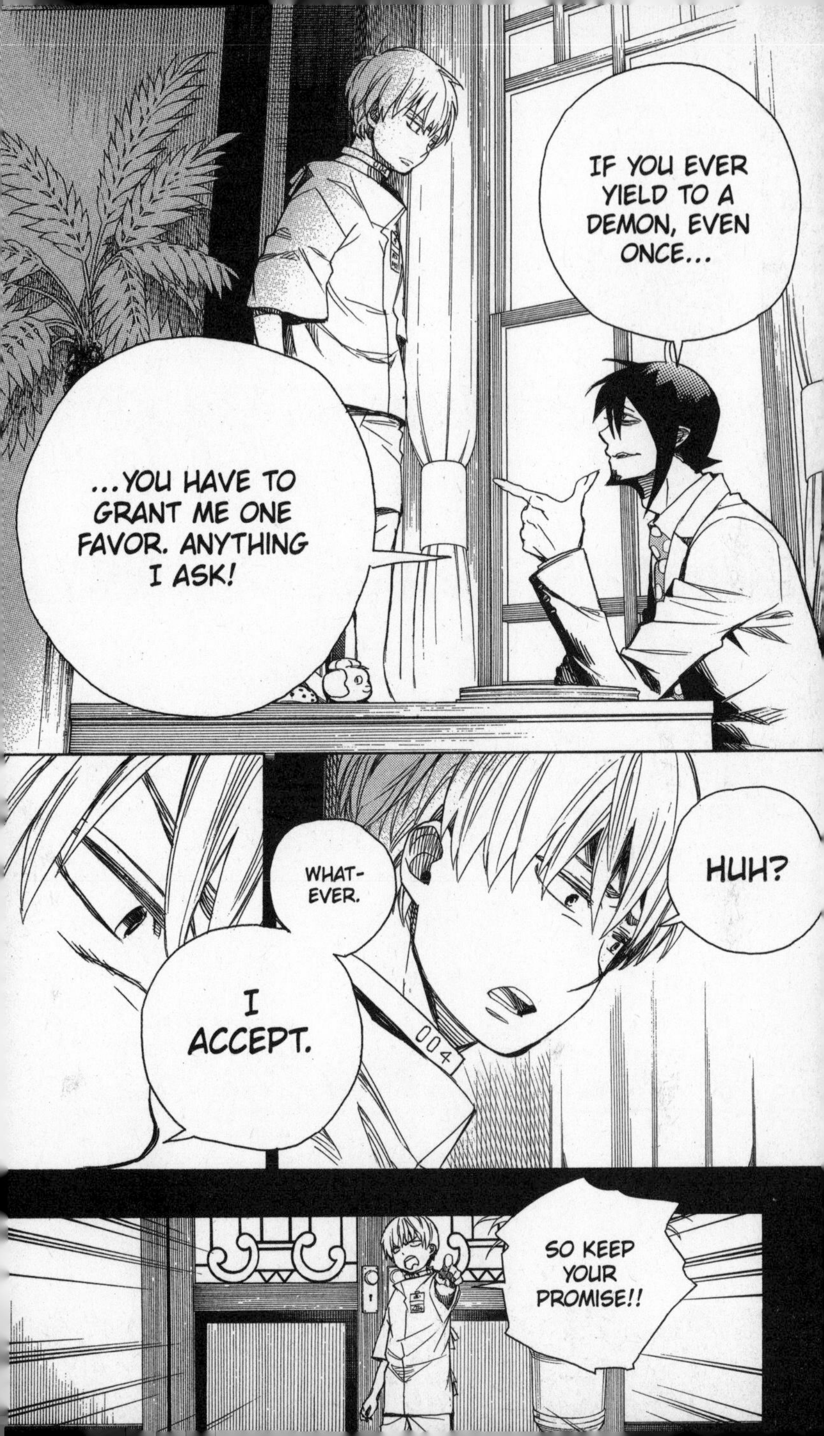
IF YOU EVER YIELD TO A DEMON, EVEN ONCE...
...YOU HAVE TO GRANT ME ONE FAVOR. ANYTHING I ASK!
HUH?
WHAT-EVER.
I ACCEPT.
SO KEEP YOUR PROMISE!!

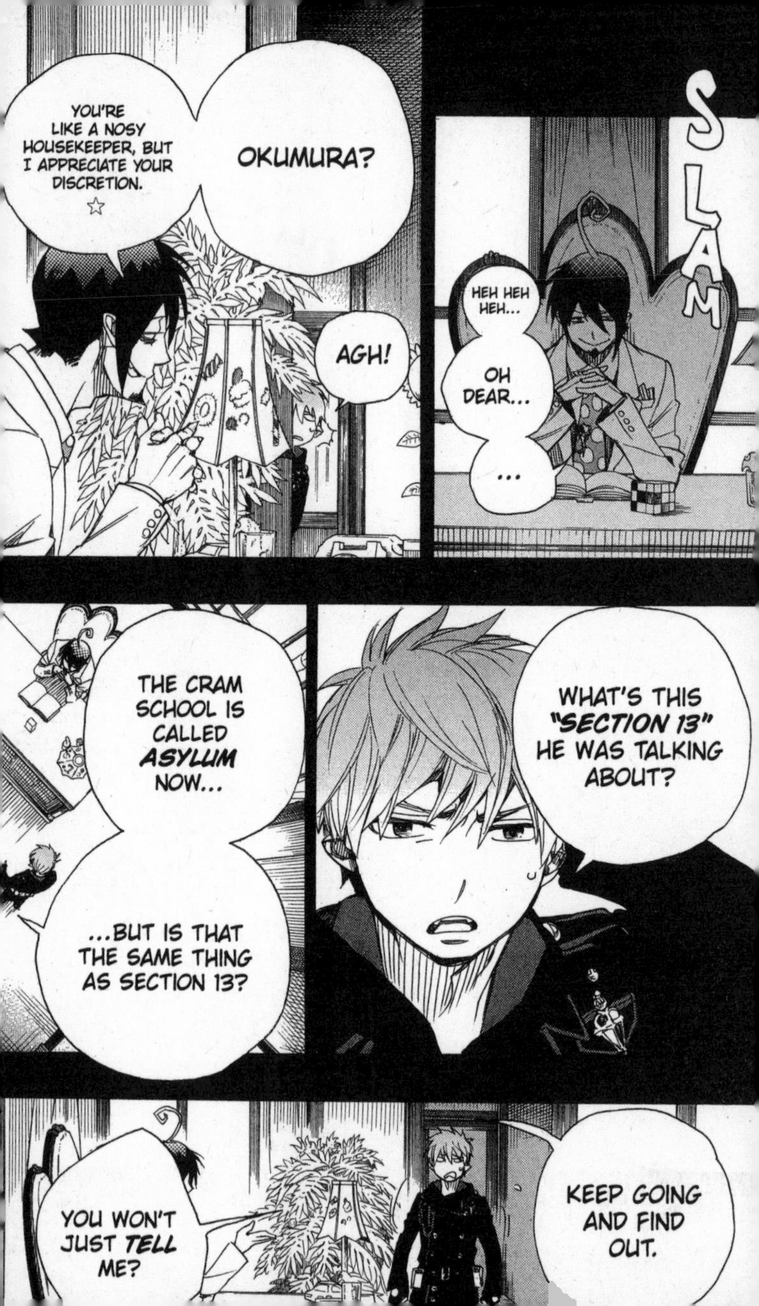
SLAM
HEH HEH HEH...
OH DEAR...
...
OKUMURA?
YOU'RE LIKE A NOSY HOUSEKEEPER, BUT I APPRECIATE YOUR DISCRETION. ☆
AGH!
WHAT'S THIS "SECTION 13" HE WAS TALKING ABOUT?
THE CRAM SCHOOL IS CALLED ASYLUM NOW...
...BUT IS THAT THE SAME THING AS SECTION 13?
KEEP GOING AND FIND OUT.
YOU WON'T JUST TELL ME?

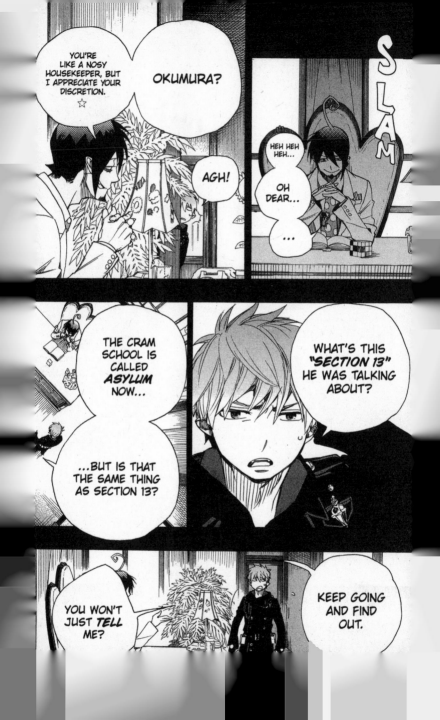

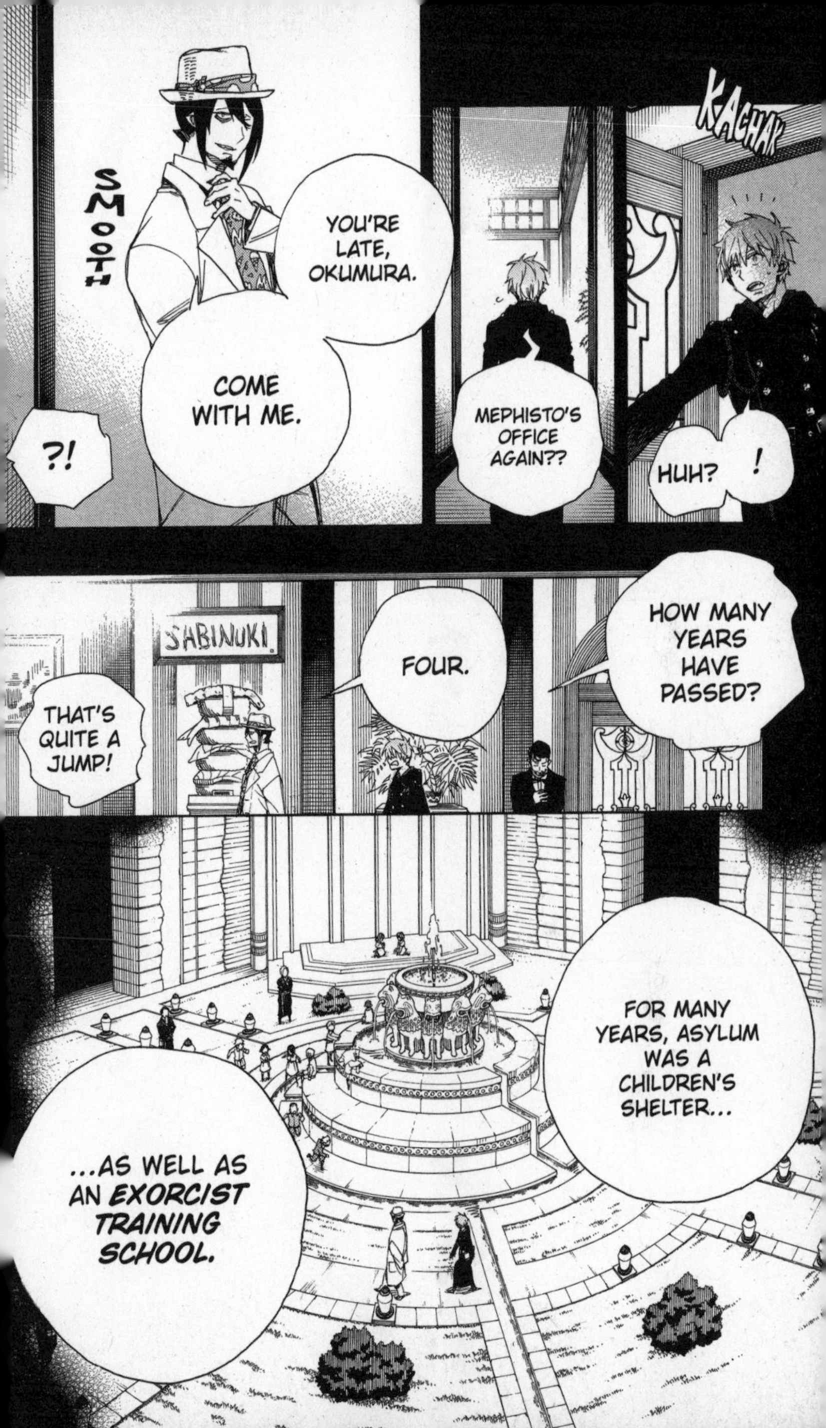
KACHAK
HUH?
!
MEPHISTO'S OFFICE AGAIN??
YOU'RE LATE, OKUMURA.
SMOOTH
COME WITH ME.
?!
HOW MANY YEARS HAVE PASSED?
FOUR.
SABINUKI
THAT'S QUITE A JUMP!
FOR MANY YEARS, ASYLUM WAS A CHILDREN'S SHELTER...
...AS WELL AS AN *EXORCIST TRAINING SCHOOL.*

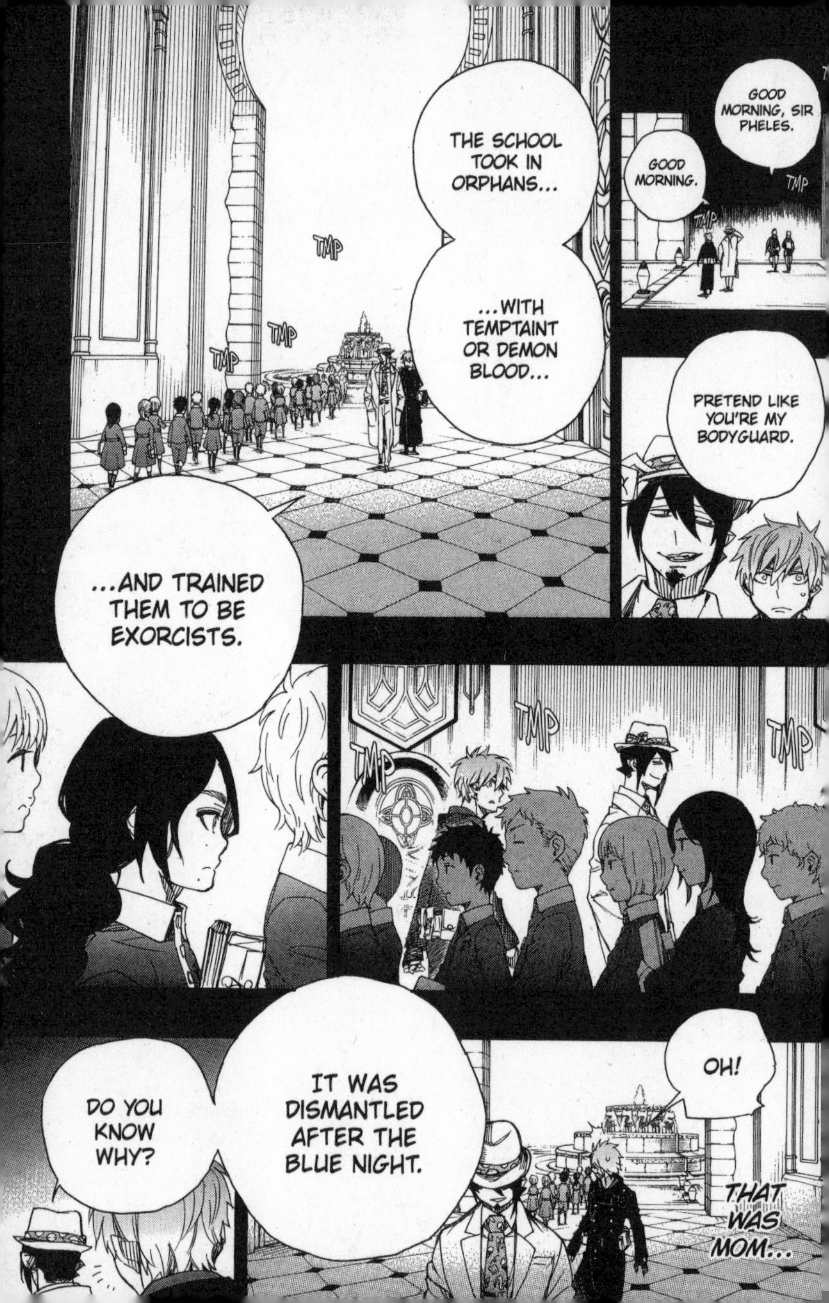
GOOD MORNING, SIR PHELES.
TMP
GOOD MORNING.
TMP
PRETEND LIKE YOU'RE MY BODYGUARD.
THE SCHOOL TOOK IN ORPHANS...
...WITH TEMPTAINT OR DEMON BLOOD...
TMP
TMP
TMP
...AND TRAINED THEM TO BE EXORCISTS.
TMP
TMP
TMP
OH!
THAT WAS MOM...
IT WAS DISMANTLED AFTER THE BLUE NIGHT.
DO YOU KNOW WHY?

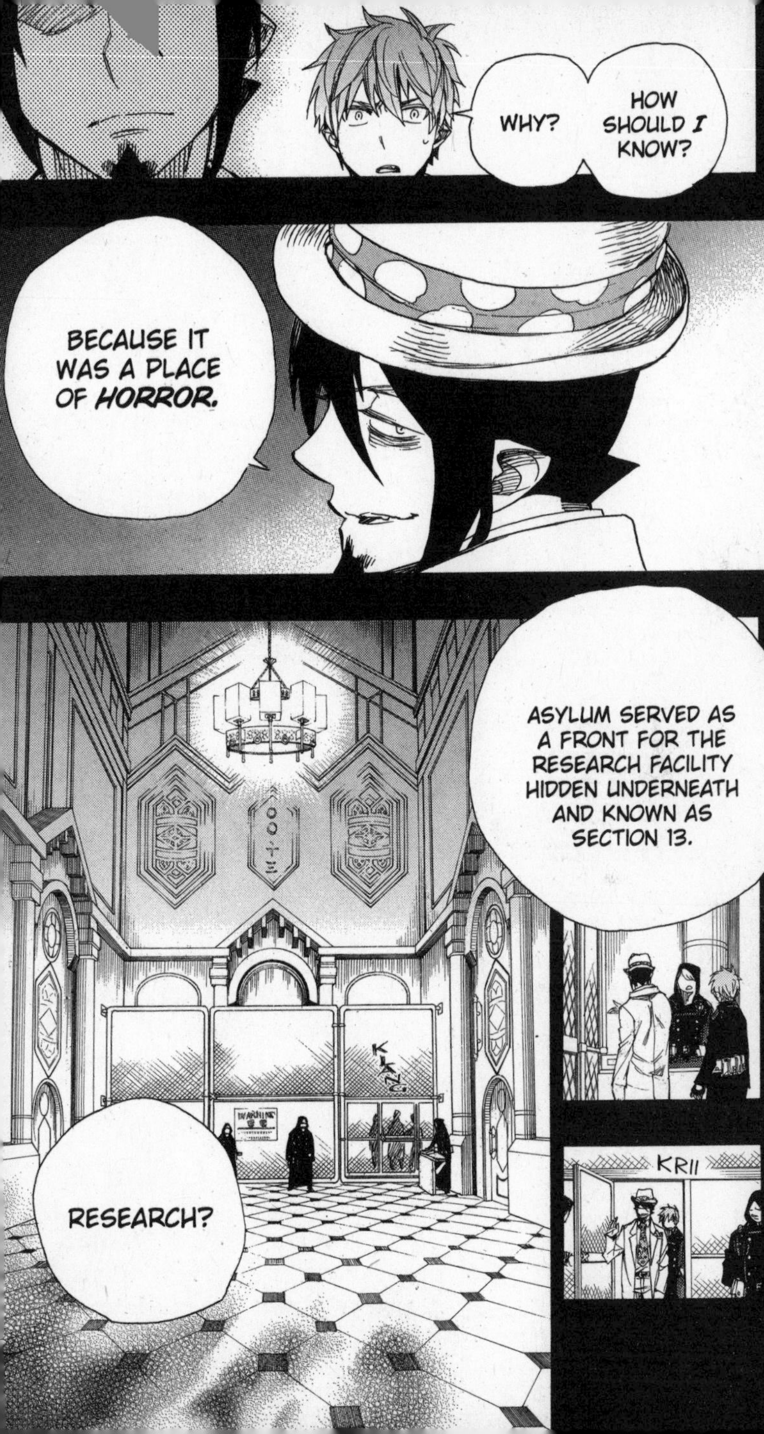
WHY?
HOW SHOULD I KNOW?
BECAUSE IT WAS A PLACE OF HORROR.
ASYLUM SERVED AS A FRONT FOR THE RESEARCH FACILITY HIDDEN UNDERNEATH AND KNOWN AS SECTION 13.
KRII
KLANG
WARNING
RESEARCH?

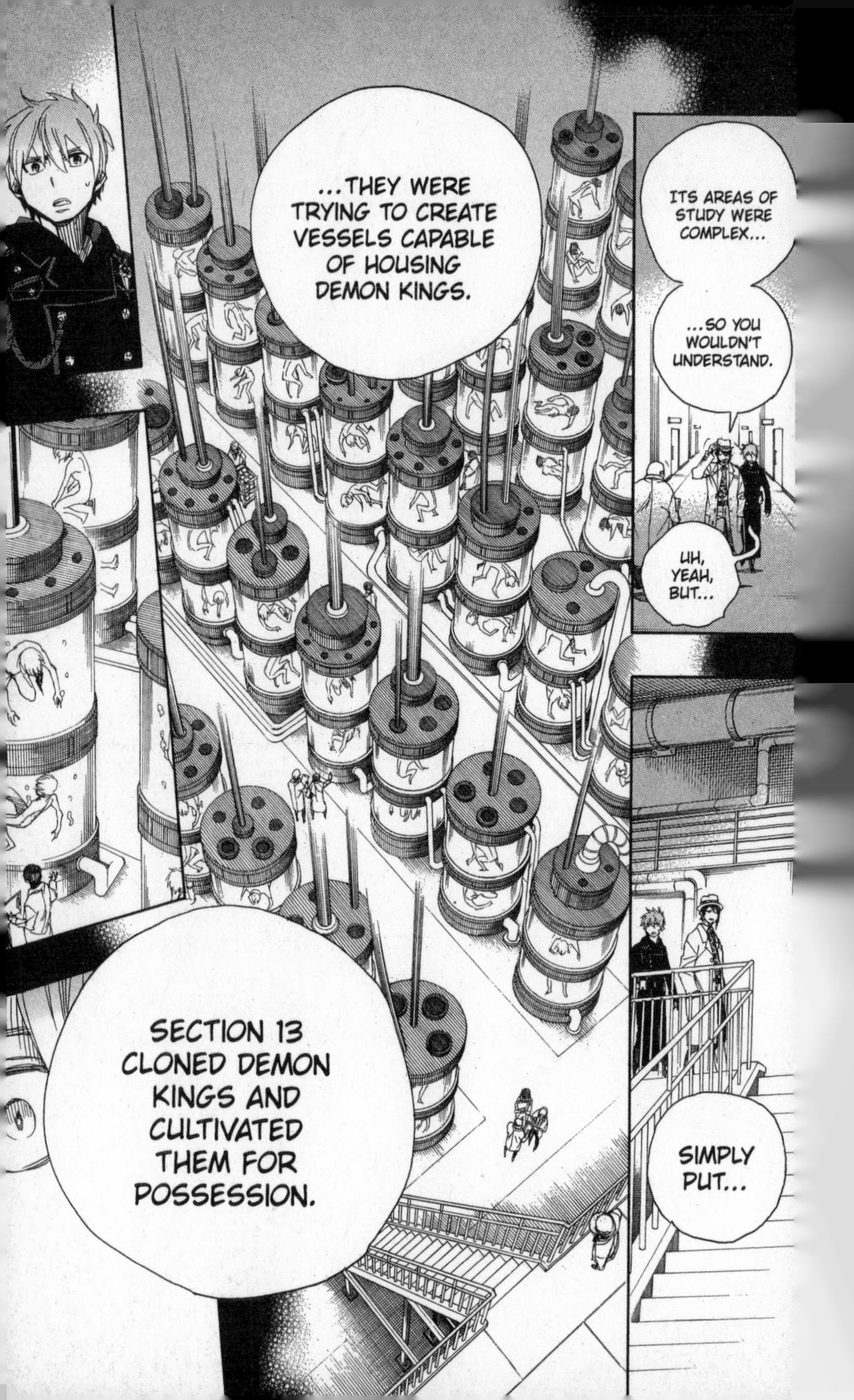
ITS AREAS OF STUDY WERE COMPLEX...
...SO YOU WOULDN'T UNDERSTAND.
UH, YEAH, BUT...
SIMPLY PUT...
...THEY WERE TRYING TO CREATE VESSELS CAPABLE OF HOUSING DEMON KINGS.
SECTION 13 CLONED DEMON KINGS AND CULTIVATED THEM FOR POSSESSION.

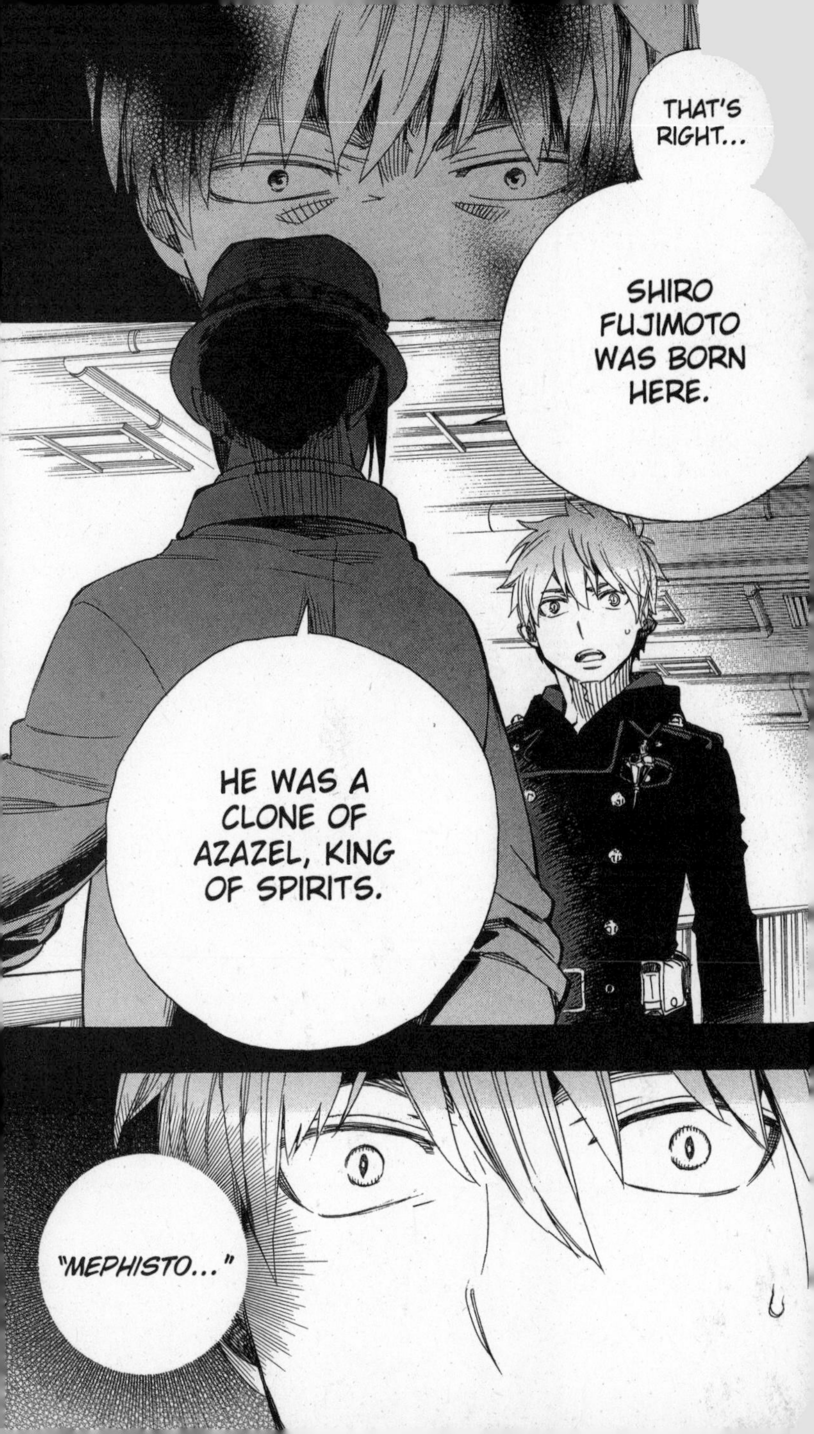
THAT'S RIGHT...
SHIRO FUJIMOTO WAS BORN HERE.
HE WAS A CLONE OF AZAZEL, KING OF SPIRITS.
"MEPHISTO..."

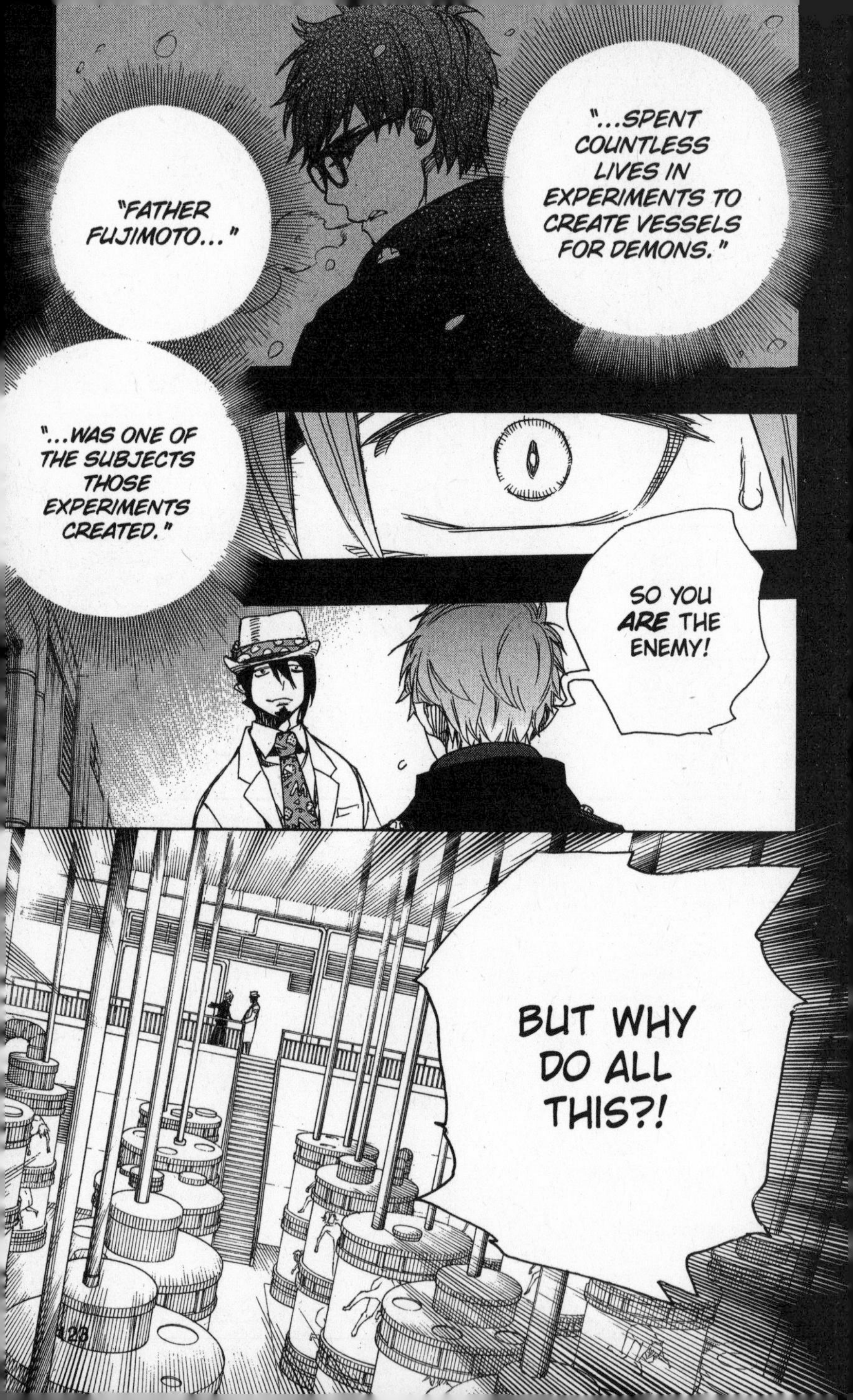
"FATHER FUJIMOTO..."
"...SPENT COUNTLESS LIVES IN EXPERIMENTS TO CREATE VESSELS FOR DEMONS."
"...WAS ONE OF THE SUBJECTS THOSE EXPERIMENTS CREATED."
SO YOU ARE THE ENEMY!
BUT WHY DO ALL THIS?!

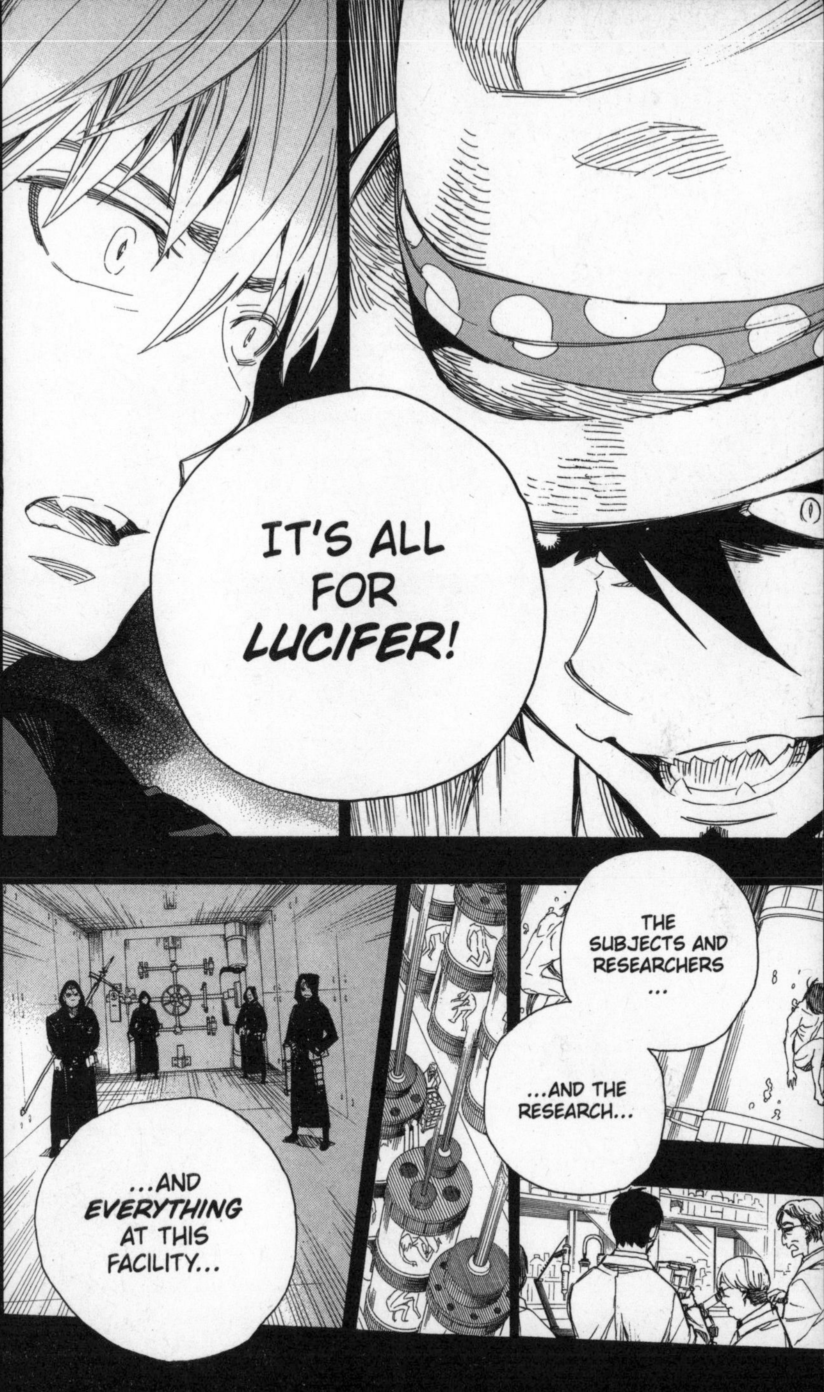
IT'S ALL FOR LUCIFER!
THE SUBJECTS AND RESEARCHERS ...
...AND THE RESEARCH...
...AND EVERYTHING AT THIS FACILITY...

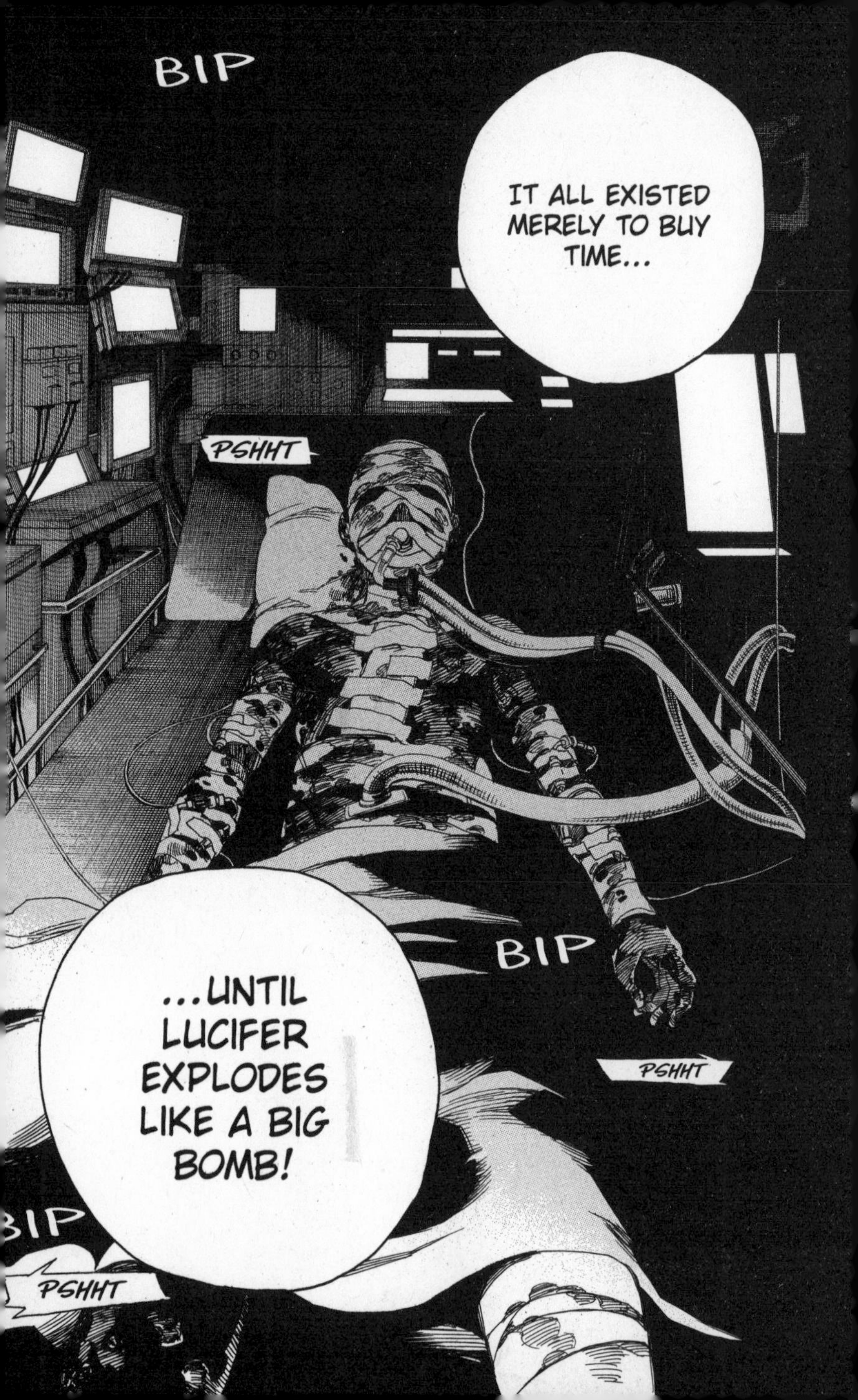
BIP
IT ALL EXISTED MERELY TO BUY TIME...
PSHHT
BIP
...UNTIL LUCIFER EXPLODES LIKE A BIG BOMB!
PSHHT
BIP
PSHHT

Blue Exorcist Chapter 101: SsC04:36

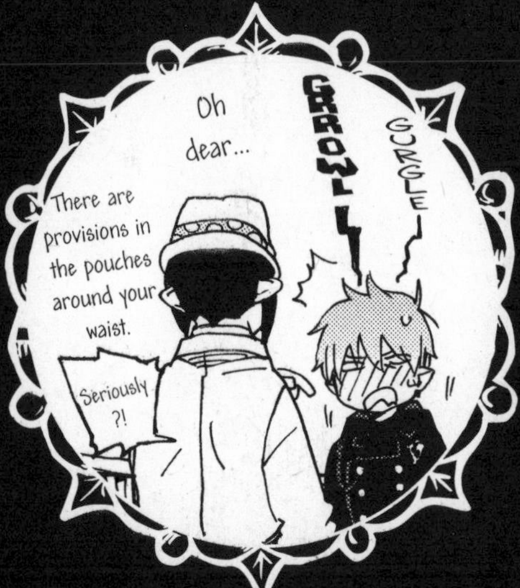
GURGLE
GRROWL
Oh dear...
There are provisions in the pouches around your waist.
Seriously ?!

CHAPTER 102: SsC05:35

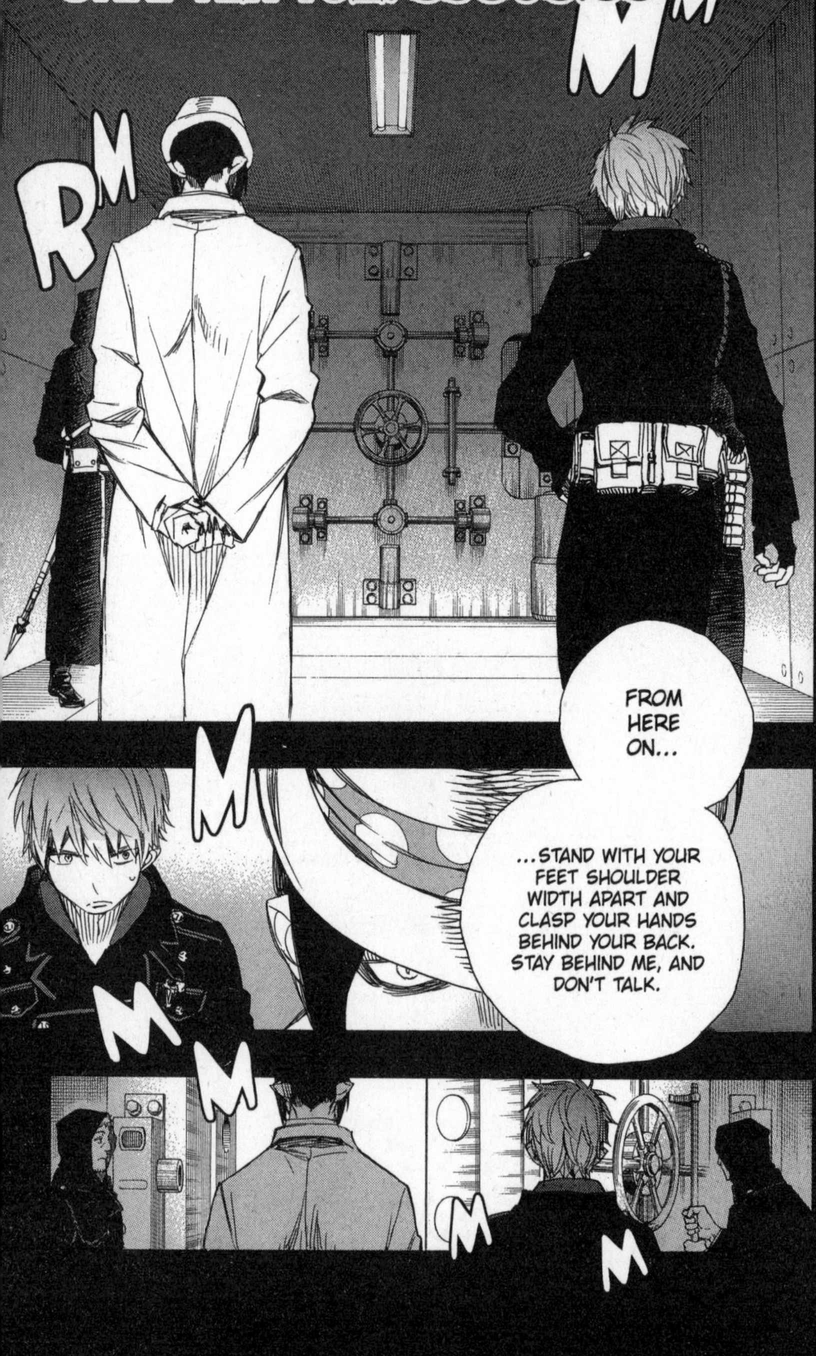
MMM
RM
FROM HERE ON...
...STAND WITH YOUR FEET SHOULDER WIDTH APART AND CLASP YOUR HANDS BEHIND YOUR BACK. STAY BEHIND ME, AND DON'T TALK.
MM
MM
MM
M

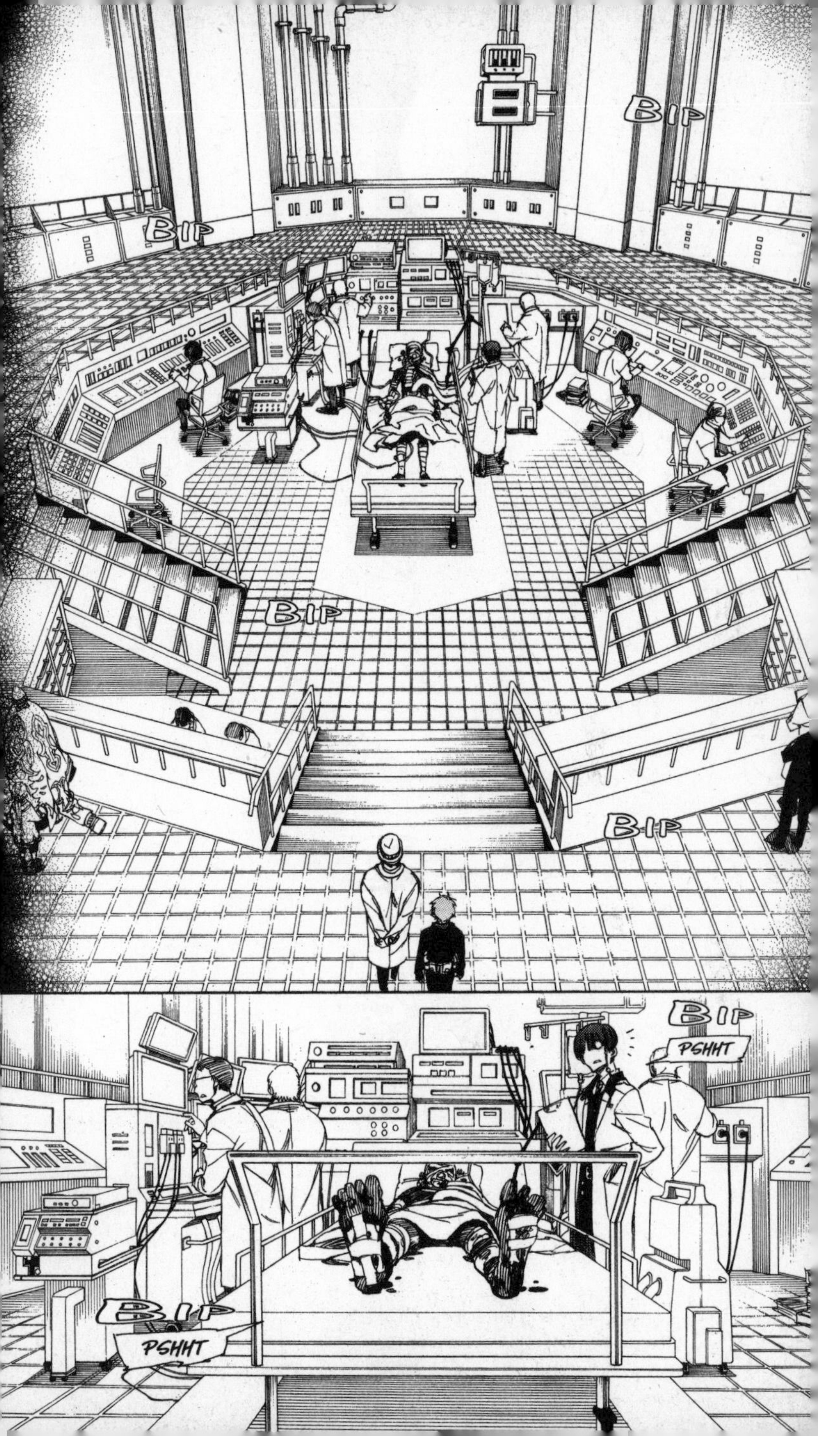
BIP
BIP
BIP
BIP
BIP
PSHHT
BIP
PSHHT

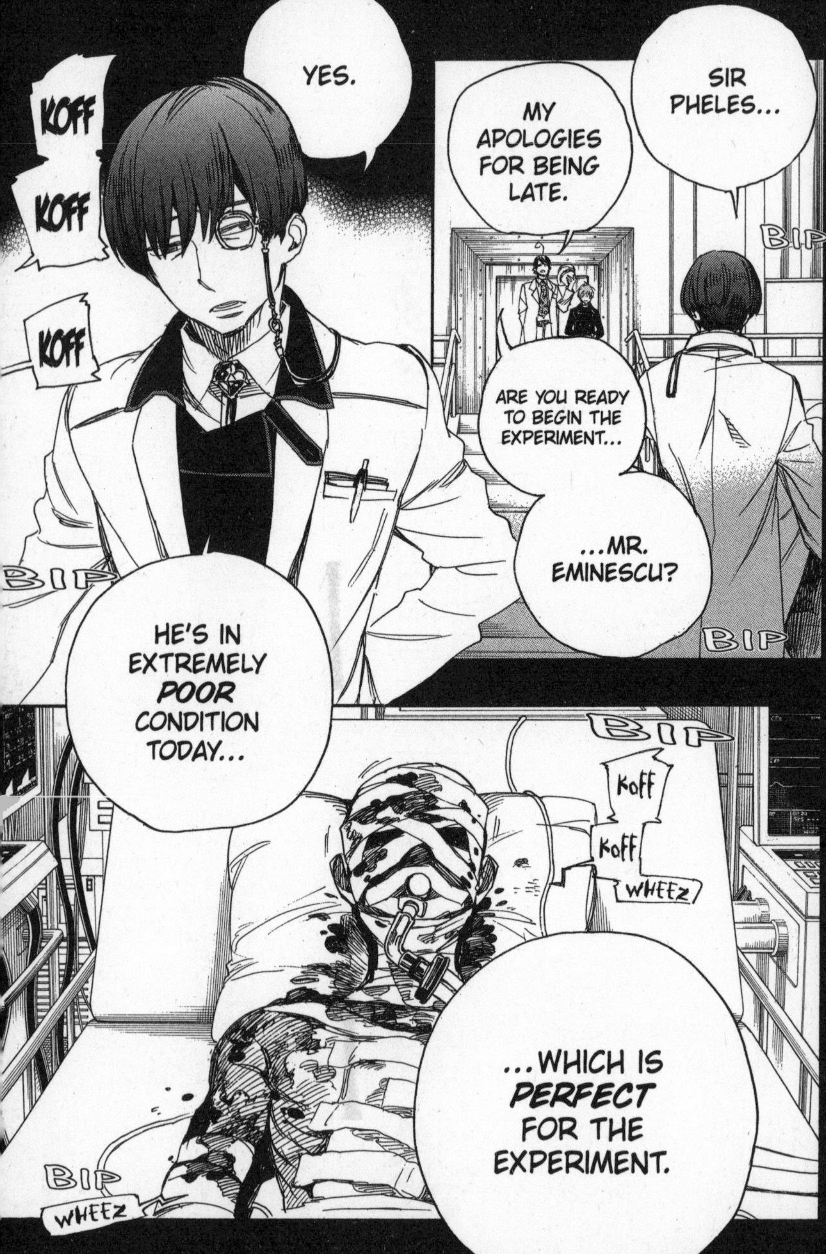
SIR PHELES...
MY APOLOGIES FOR BEING LATE.
BIP
ARE YOU READY TO BEGIN THE EXPERIMENT...
...MR. EMINESCU?
BIP
YES.
KOFF
KOFF
KOFF
BIP
HE'S IN EXTREMELY *POOR* CONDITION TODAY...
BIP
KOFF
KOFF
WHEEZ
...WHICH IS *PERFECT* FOR THE EXPERIMENT.
BIP
WHEEZ

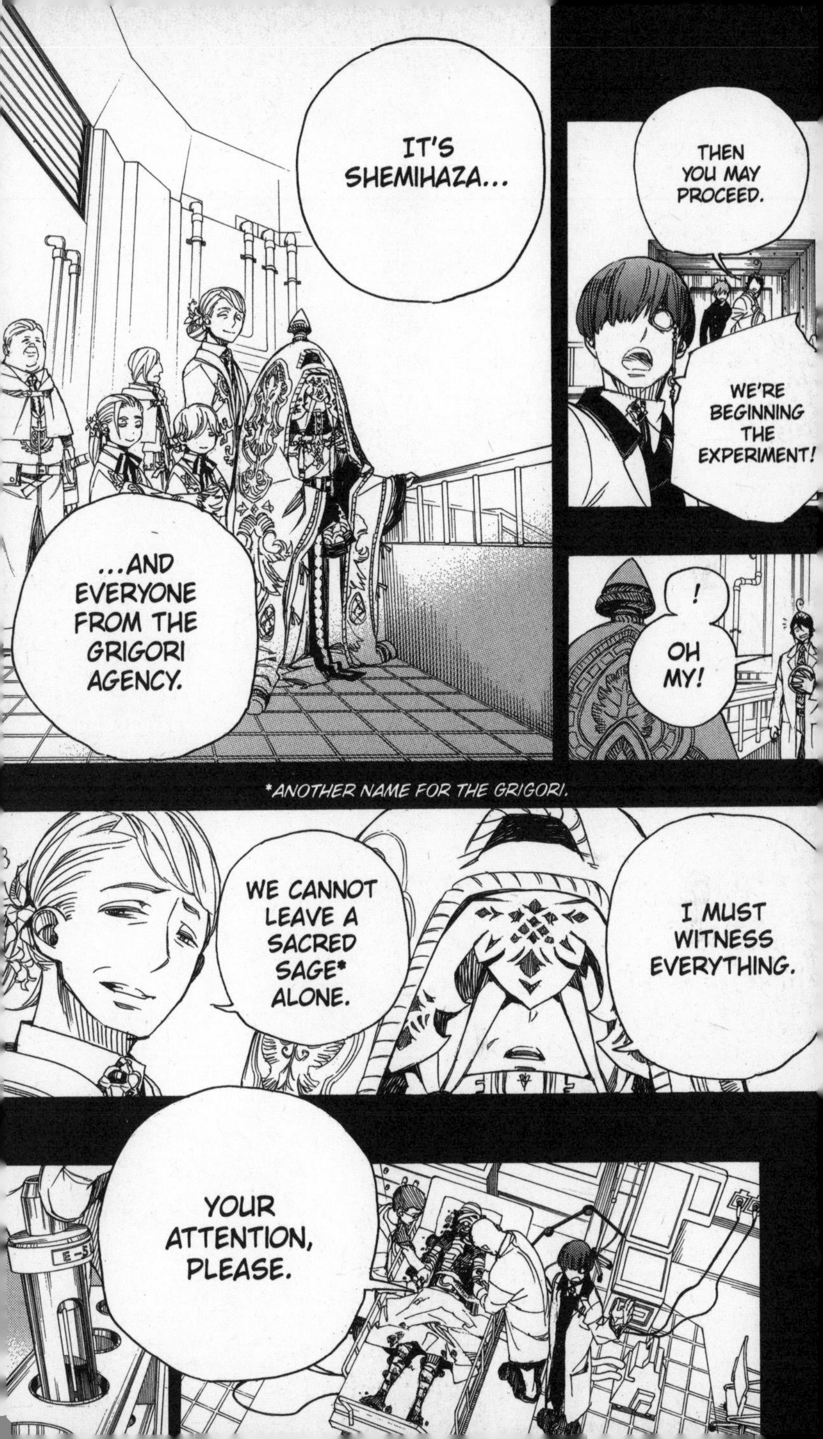
THEN YOU MAY PROCEED.
WE'RE BEGINNING THE EXPERIMENT!
!
OH MY!
IT'S SHEMIHAZA...
...AND EVERYONE FROM THE GRIGORI AGENCY.
I MUST WITNESS EVERYTHING.
WE CANNOT LEAVE A SACRED SAGE* ALONE.
YOUR ATTENTION, PLEASE.

*ANOTHER NAME FOR THE GRIGORI.

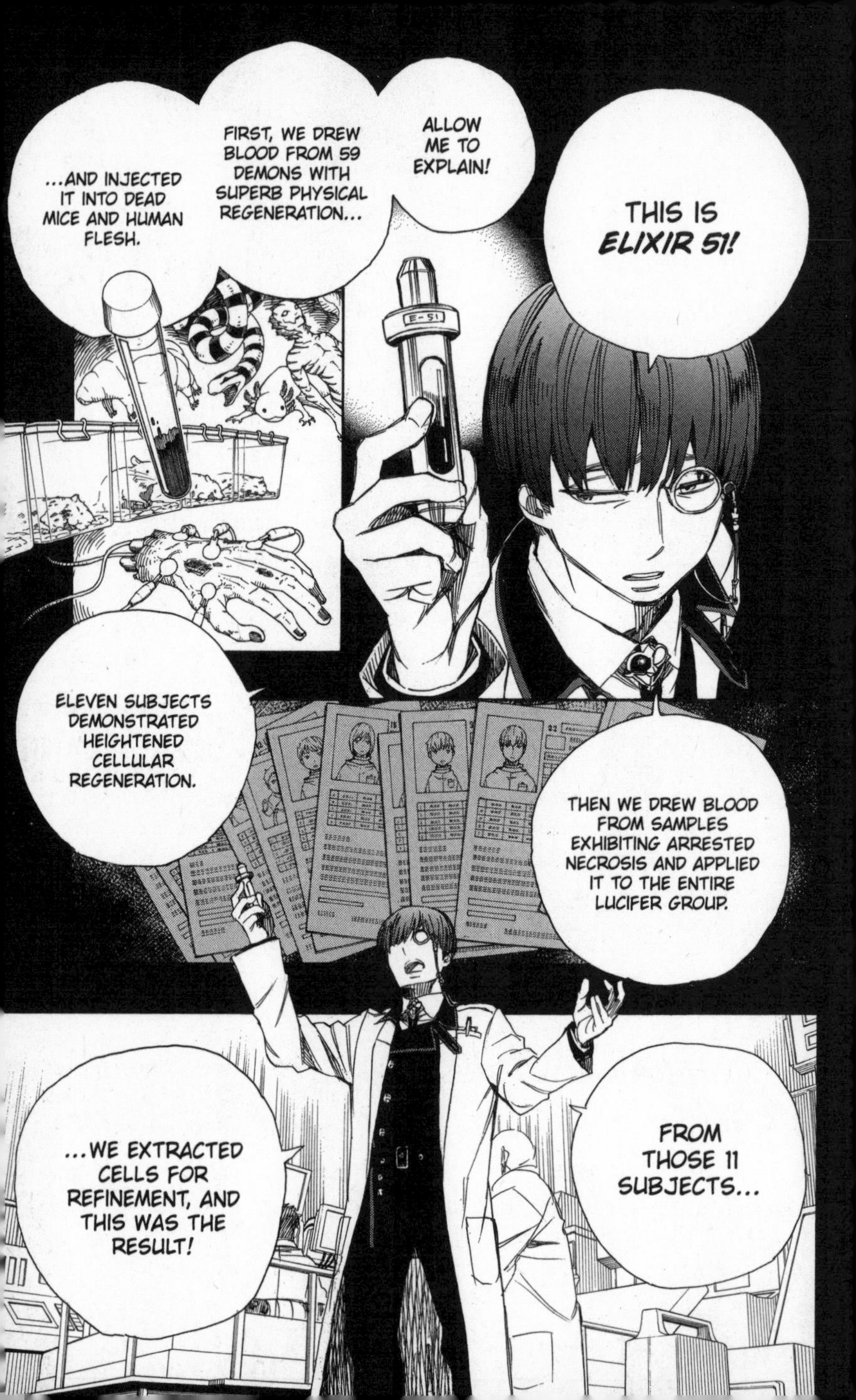
THIS IS *ELIXIR 51!*
ALLOW ME TO EXPLAIN!
FIRST, WE DREW BLOOD FROM 59 DEMONS WITH SUPERB PHYSICAL REGENERATION...
...AND INJECTED IT INTO DEAD MICE AND HUMAN FLESH.
E-51
ELEVEN SUBJECTS DEMONSTRATED HEIGHTENED CELLULAR REGENERATION.
THEN WE DREW BLOOD FROM SAMPLES EXHIBITING ARRESTED NECROSIS AND APPLIED IT TO THE ENTIRE LUCIFER GROUP.
FROM THOSE 11 SUBJECTS...
...WE EXTRACTED CELLS FOR REFINEMENT, AND THIS WAS THE RESULT!

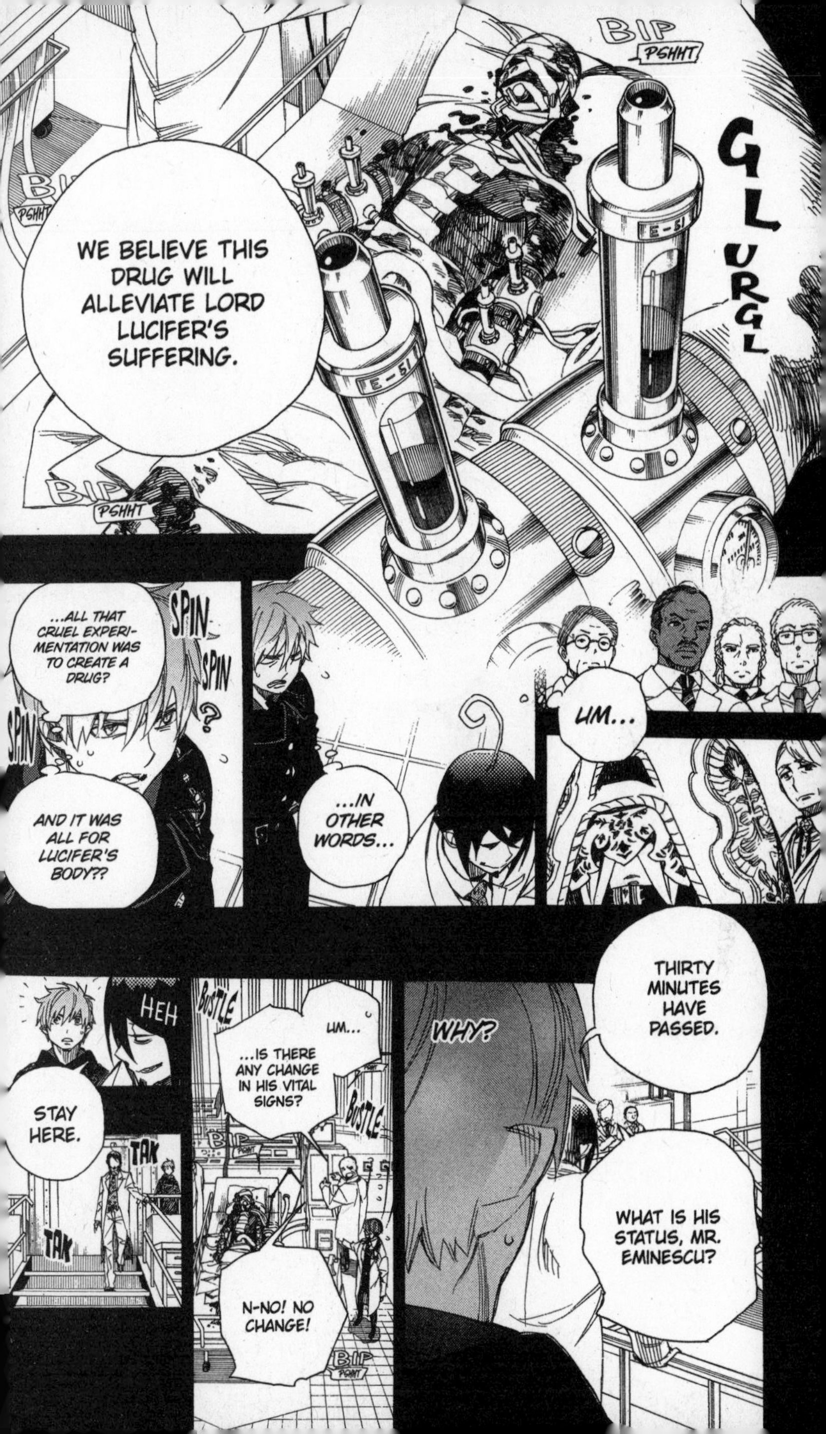
BIP
PSHHT
GL URGL
WE BELIEVE THIS DRUG WILL ALLEVIATE LORD LUCIFER'S SUFFERING.
BIP
PSHHT
BIP
PSHHT
UM...
...IN OTHER WORDS...
...ALL THAT CRUEL EXPERIMENTATION WAS TO CREATE A DRUG?
SPIN
SPIN
?
SPIN
AND IT WAS ALL FOR LUCIFER'S BODY??
THIRTY MINUTES HAVE PASSED.
WHY?
WHAT IS HIS STATUS, MR. EMINESCU?
BUSTLE
UM...
...IS THERE ANY CHANGE IN HIS VITAL SIGNS?
BUSTLE
BIP
PSHHT
N-NO! NO CHANGE!
BIP
PSHHT
HEH
STAY HERE.
TAK
TAK

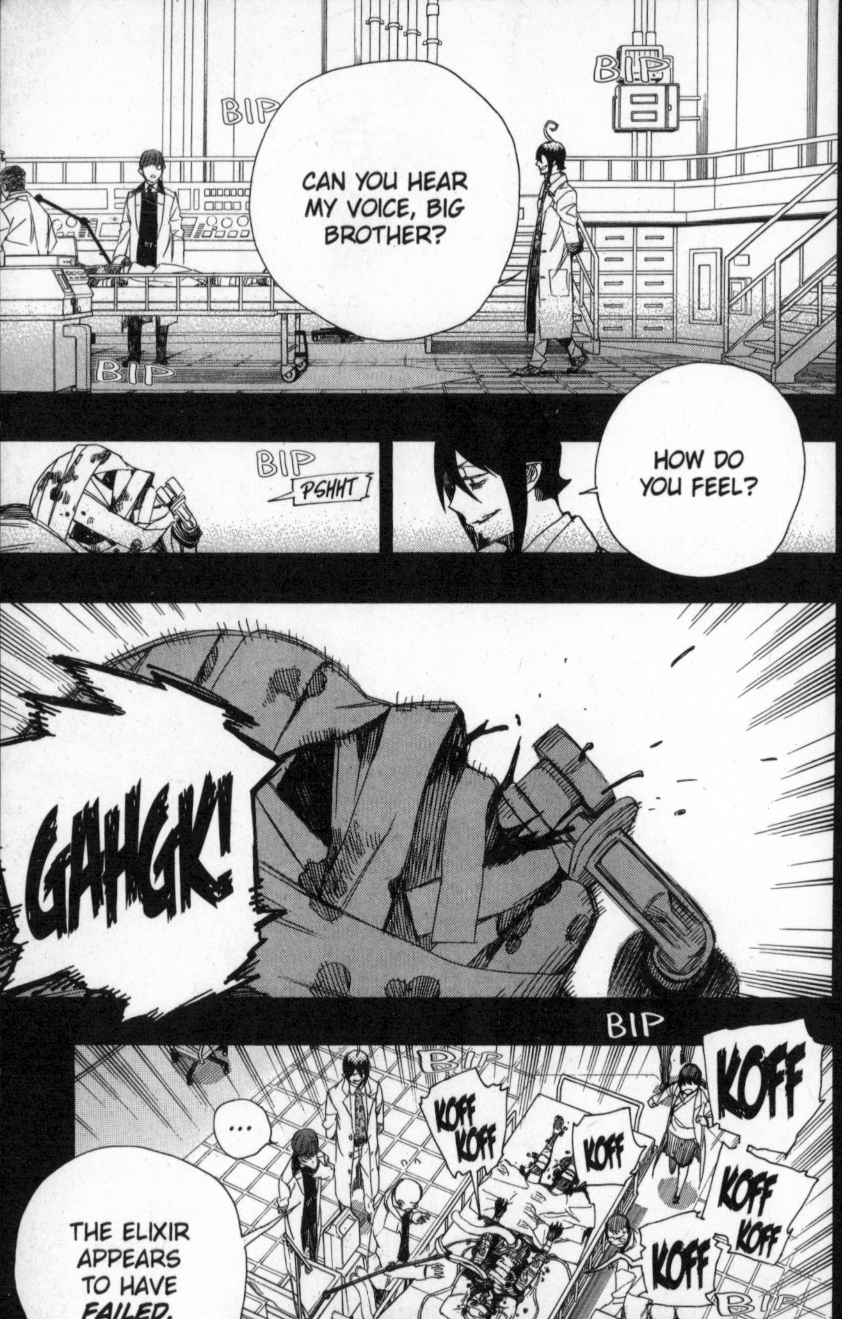
BIP
BIP
CAN YOU HEAR MY VOICE, BIG BROTHER?
BIP
HOW DO YOU FEEL?
BIP
PSHHT
GAHGK!
BIP
KOFF
BIP
KOFF KOFF
KOFF
KOFF KOFF
KOFF
BIP
...
THE ELIXIR APPEARS TO HAVE *FAILED.*

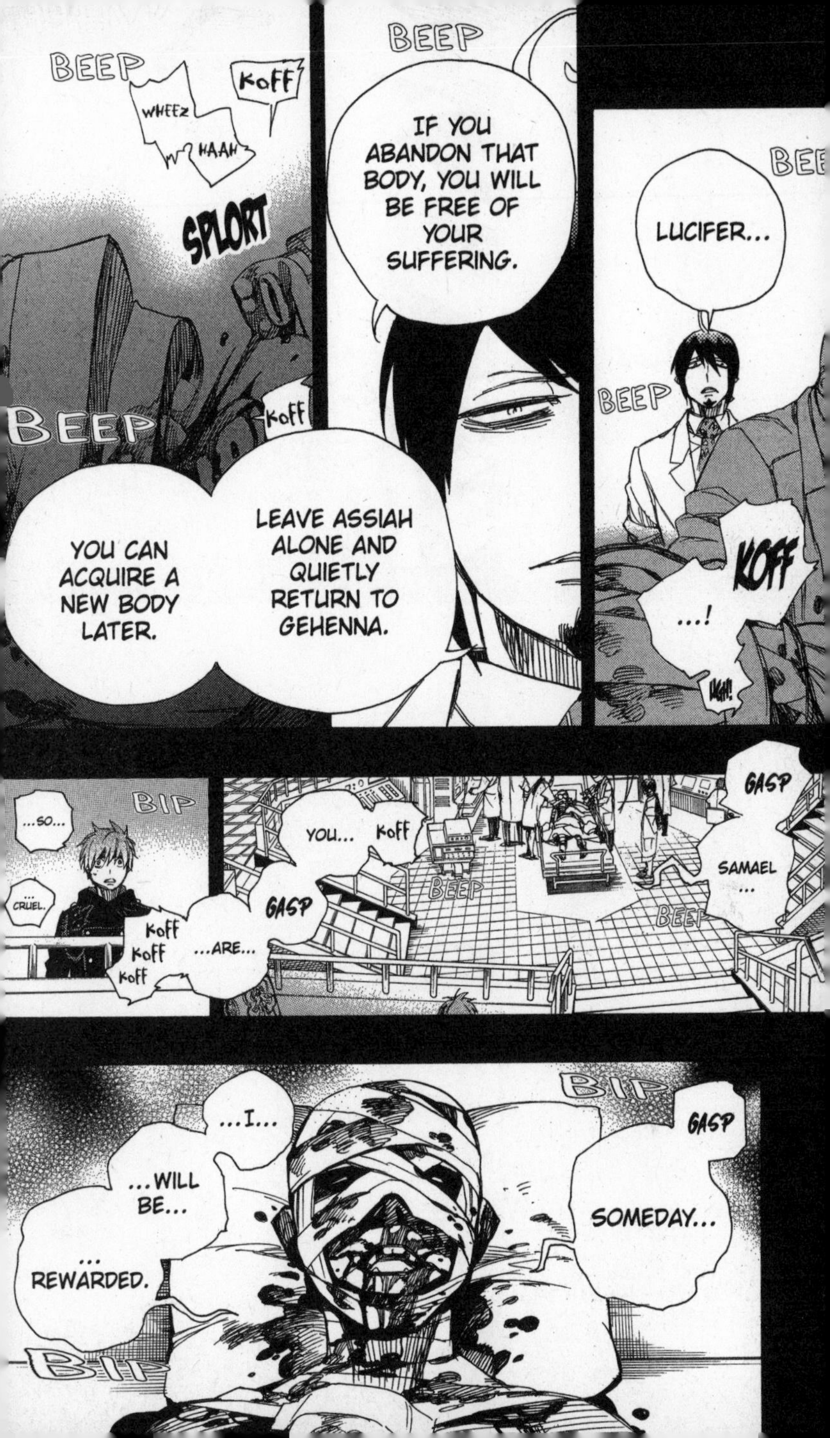
BEEP
LUCIFER...
BEEP
KOFF
...!
UGH!
BEEP
IF YOU ABANDON THAT BODY, YOU WILL BE FREE OF YOUR SUFFERING.
LEAVE ASSIAH ALONE AND QUIETLY RETURN TO GEHENNA.
YOU CAN ACQUIRE A NEW BODY LATER.
KOFF
BEEP
WHEEZ
HAAH
SPLORT
BEEP
KOFF
GASP
SAMAEL...
BEEP
YOU... KOFF
BEEP
GASP
...ARE...
KOFF KOFF KOFF
BIP
...SO...
...CRUEL.
GASP
BIP
SOMEDAY...
...I...
...WILL BE...
...REWARDED.
BIP

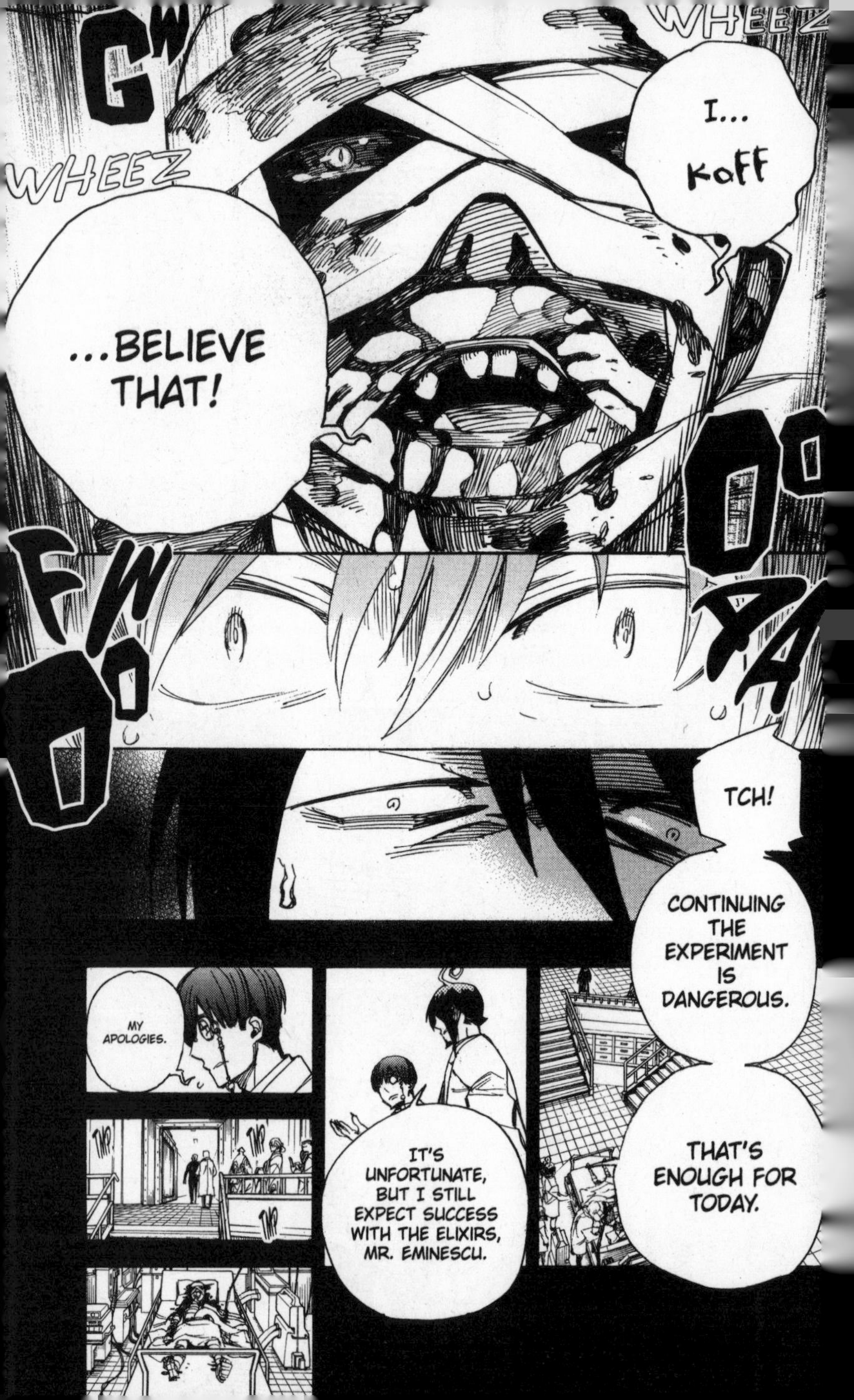
WHEEZ
I... KOFF
GW
WHEEZ
...BELIEVE THAT!
TCH!
CONTINUING THE EXPERIMENT IS DANGEROUS.
THAT'S ENOUGH FOR TODAY.
IT'S UNFORTUNATE, BUT I STILL EXPECT SUCCESS WITH THE ELIXIRS, MR. EMINESCU.
MY APOLOGIES.

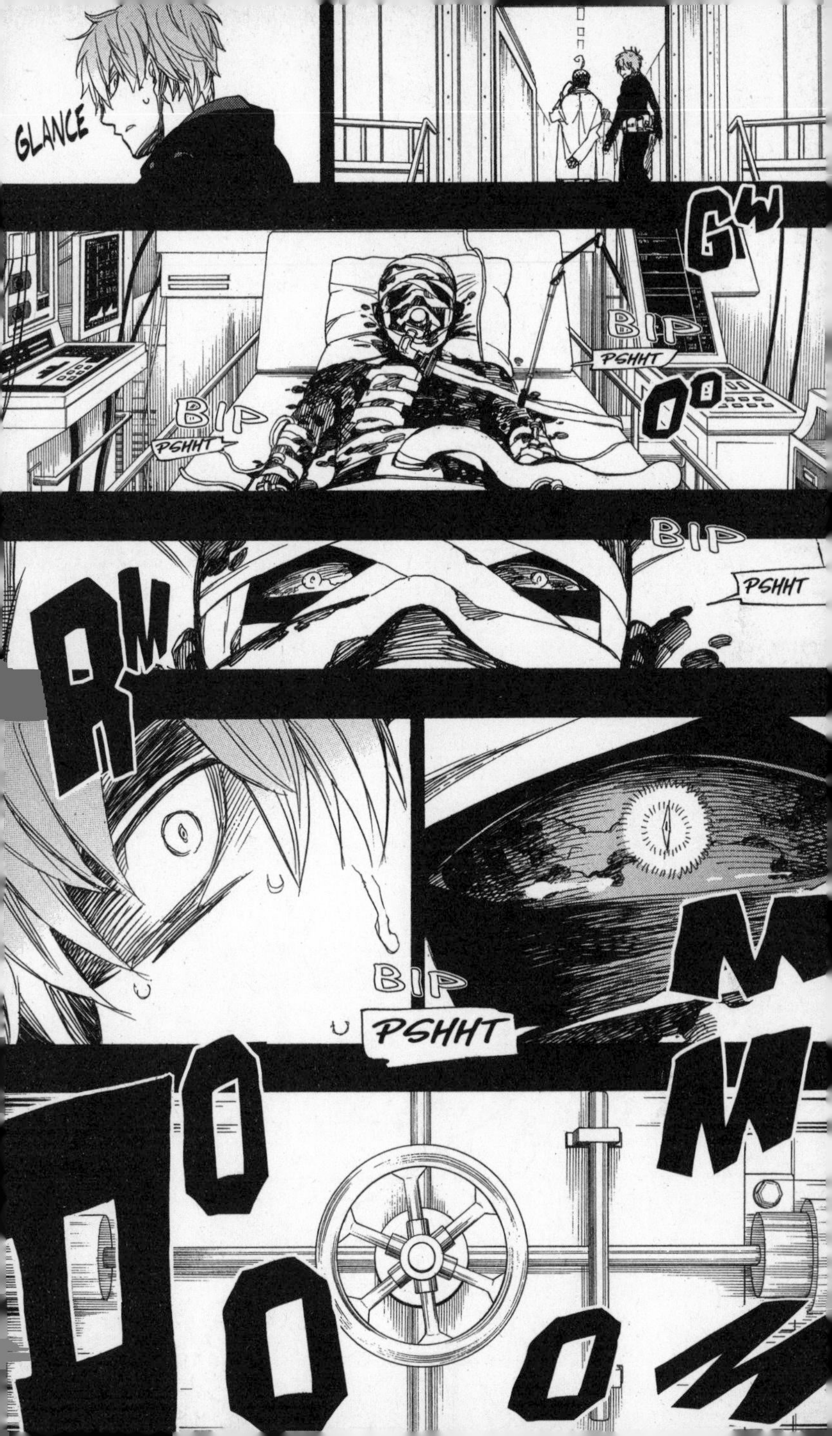
GLANCE
GW
BIP
PSHHT
OO
BIP
PSHHT
BIP
PSHHT
RM
M
BIP
PSHHT
M
DOOOM

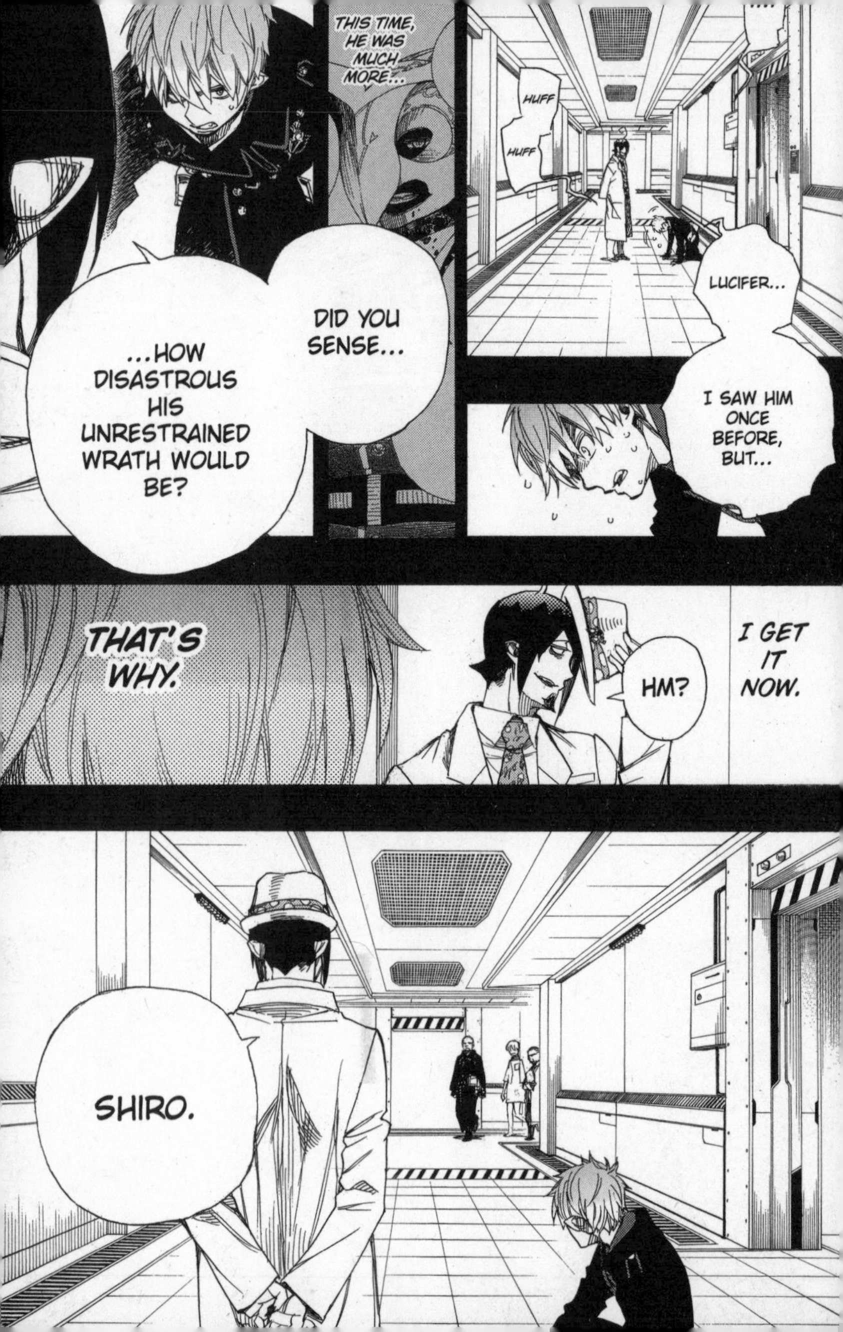

...
HUFF
HUFF
LUCIFER...
I SAW HIM ONCE BEFORE, BUT...
THIS TIME, HE WAS MUCH MORE...
DID YOU SENSE...
...HOW DISASTROUS HIS UNRESTRAINED WRATH WOULD BE?
I GET IT NOW.
HM?
THAT'S WHY.
SHIRO.

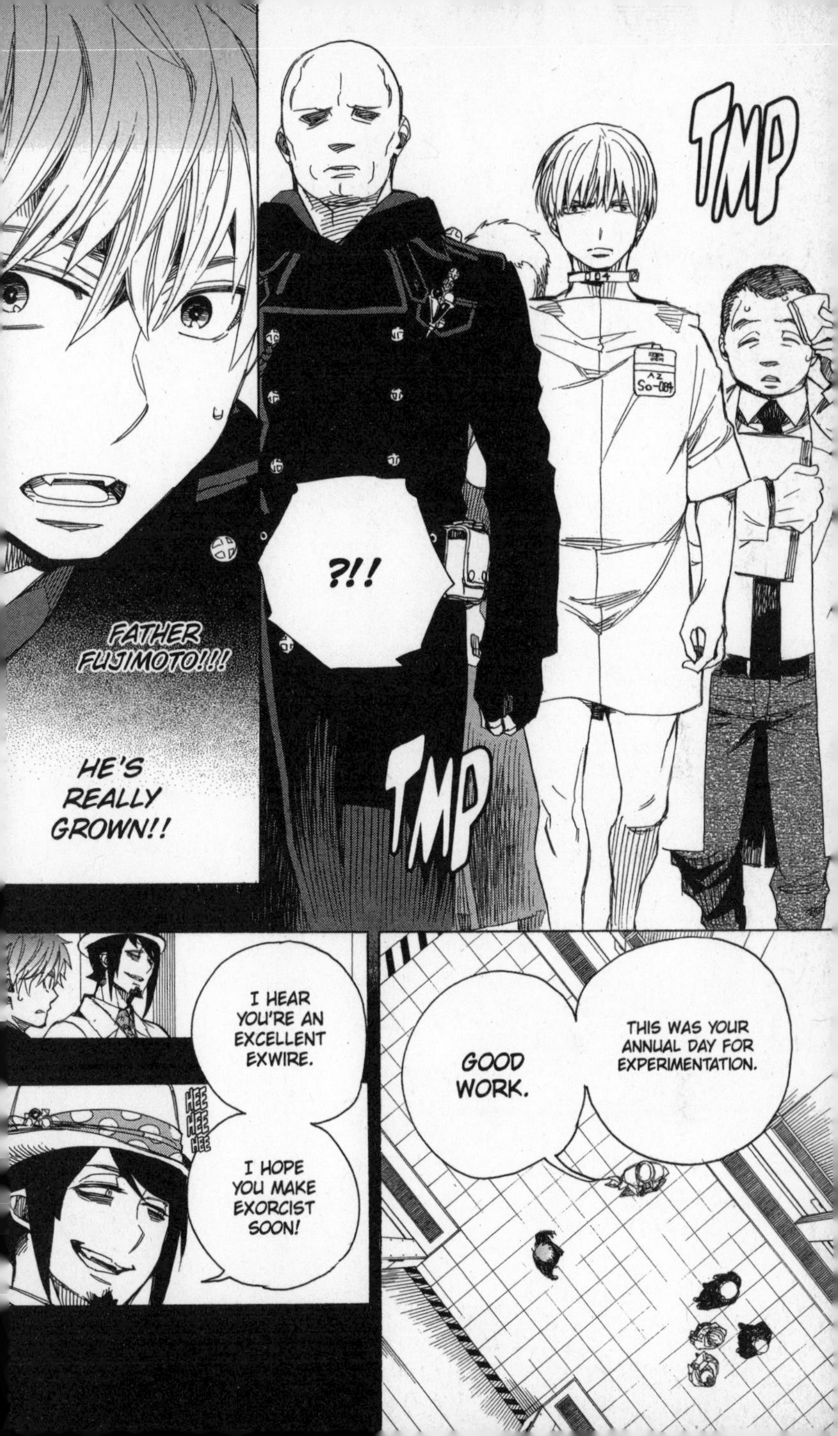
TMP
?!!
TMP
FATHER FUJIMOTO!!!
HE'S REALLY GROWN!!
THIS WAS YOUR ANNUAL DAY FOR EXPERIMENTATION.
GOOD WORK.
I HEAR YOU'RE AN EXCELLENT EXWIRE.
HEE HEE HEE
I HOPE YOU MAKE EXORCIST SOON!

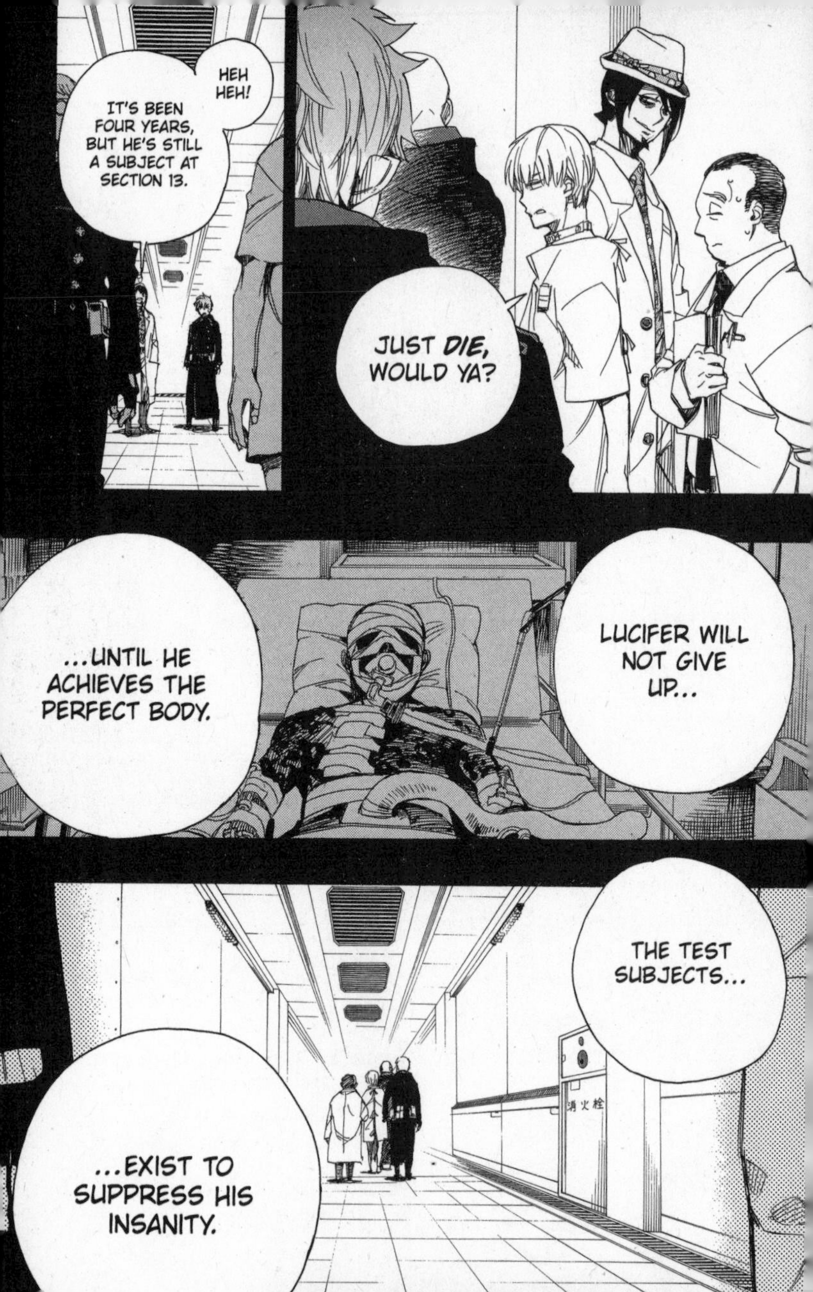
JUST *DIE*, WOULD YA?
HEH HEH!
IT'S BEEN FOUR YEARS, BUT HE'S STILL A SUBJECT AT SECTION 13.
LUCIFER WILL NOT GIVE UP...
...UNTIL HE ACHIEVES THE PERFECT BODY.
THE TEST SUBJECTS...
消火栓
...EXIST TO SUPPRESS HIS INSANITY.

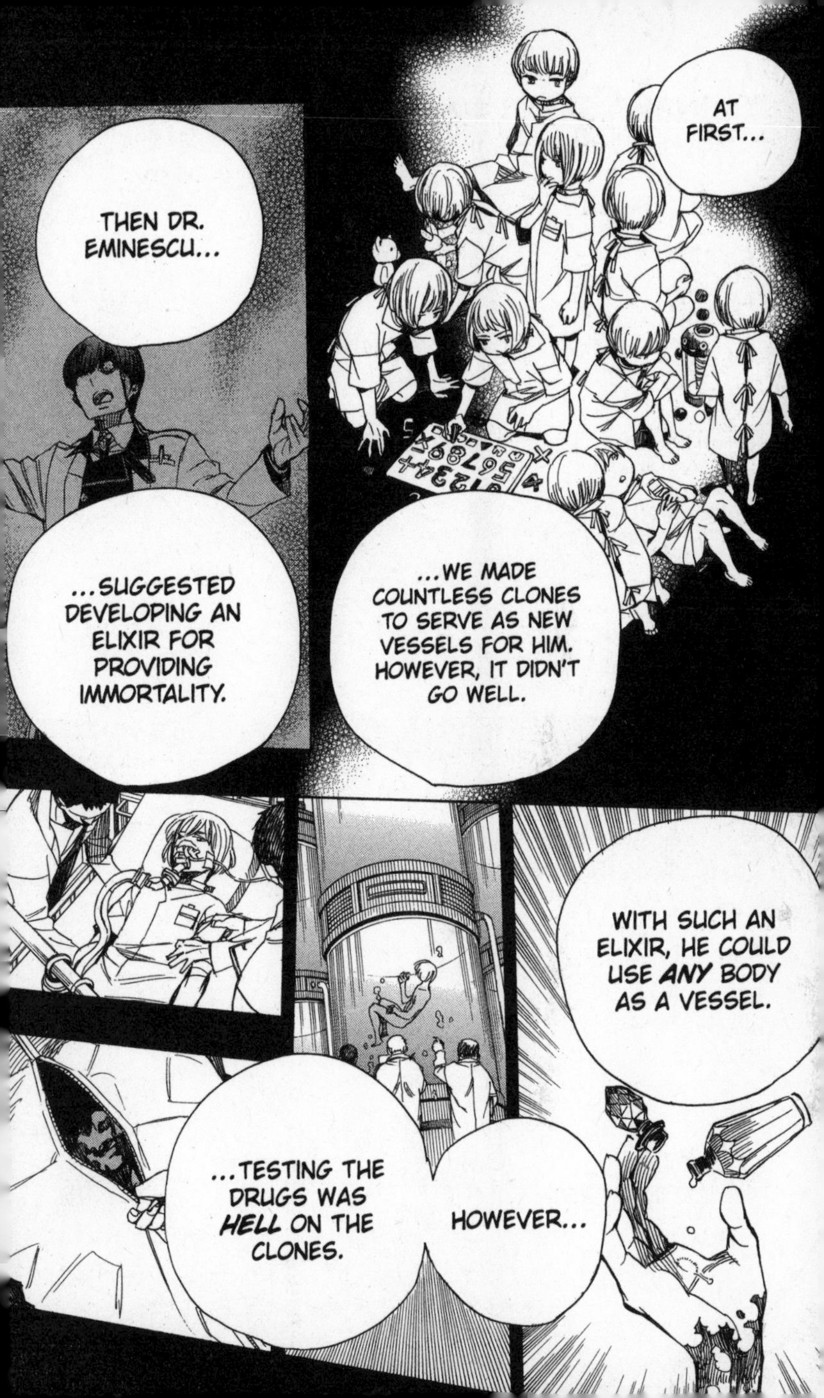
AT FIRST...
...WE MADE COUNTLESS CLONES TO SERVE AS NEW VESSELS FOR HIM. HOWEVER, IT DIDN'T GO WELL.
THEN DR. EMINESCU...
...SUGGESTED DEVELOPING AN ELIXIR FOR PROVIDING IMMORTALITY.
WITH SUCH AN ELIXIR, HE COULD USE *ANY* BODY AS A VESSEL.
HOWEVER...
...TESTING THE DRUGS WAS *HELL* ON THE CLONES.

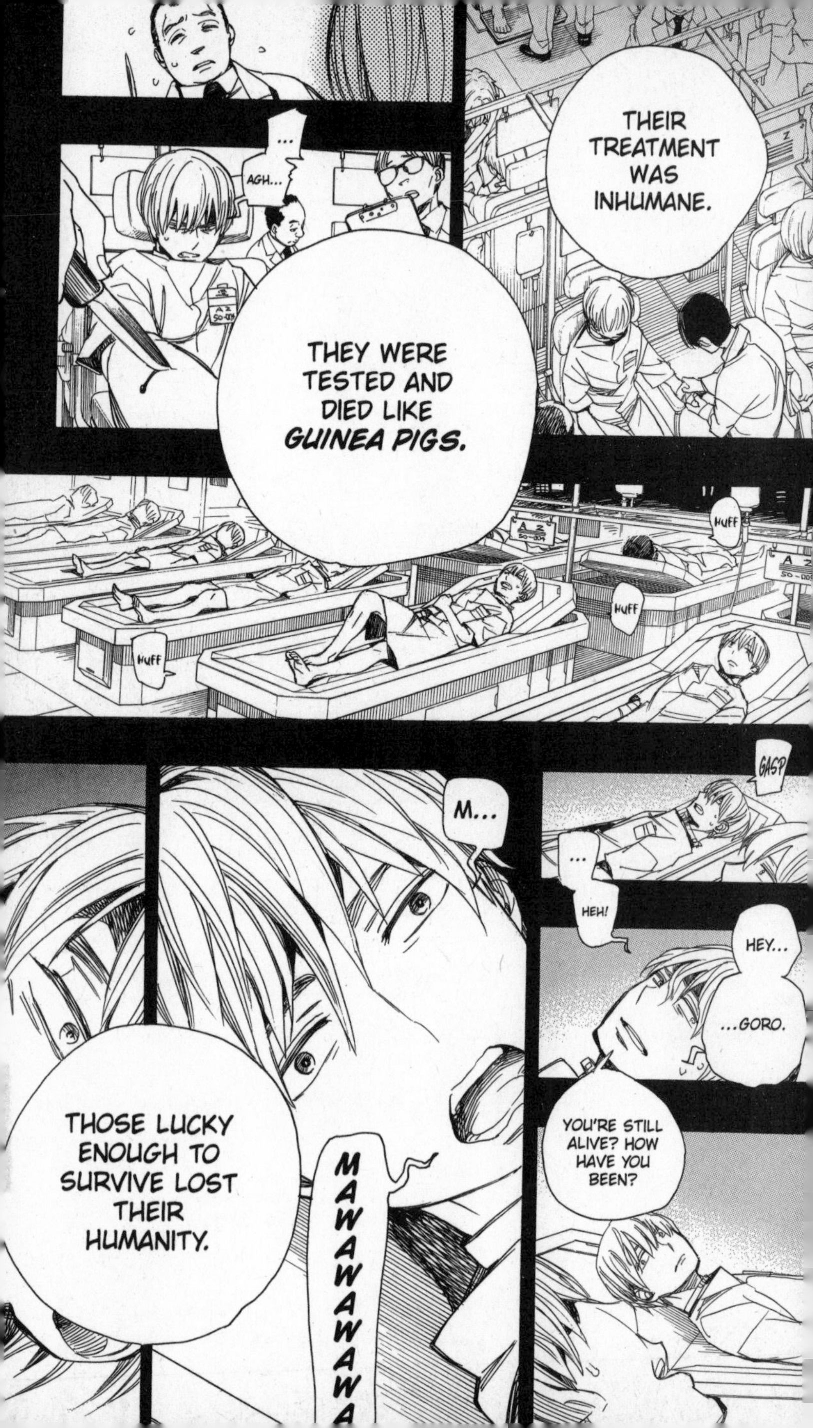
THEIR TREATMENT WAS INHUMANE.
...
AGH...
THEY WERE TESTED AND DIED LIKE GUINEA PIGS.
HUFF
HUFF
HUFF
GASP
...
HEH!
HEY...
...GORO.
YOU'RE STILL ALIVE? HOW HAVE YOU BEEN?
M...
MAWAWAWAWAWA
THOSE LUCKY ENOUGH TO SURVIVE LOST THEIR HUMANITY.

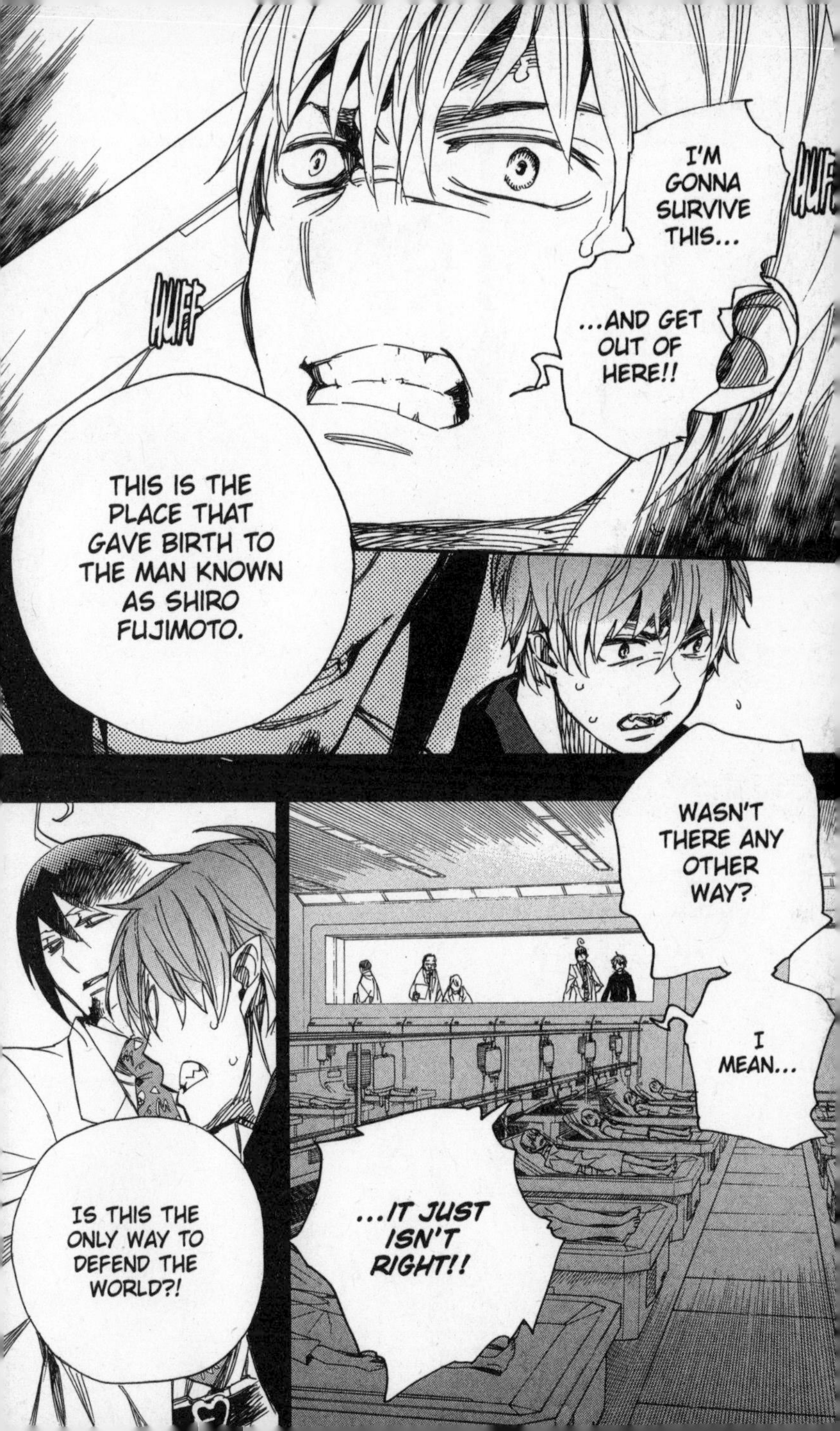
HUFF
I'M GONNA SURVIVE THIS...
...AND GET OUT OF HERE!!
HUFF
THIS IS THE PLACE THAT GAVE BIRTH TO THE MAN KNOWN AS SHIRO FUJIMOTO.
WASN'T THERE ANY OTHER WAY?
I MEAN...
...IT JUST ISN'T RIGHT!!
IS THIS THE ONLY WAY TO DEFEND THE WORLD?!

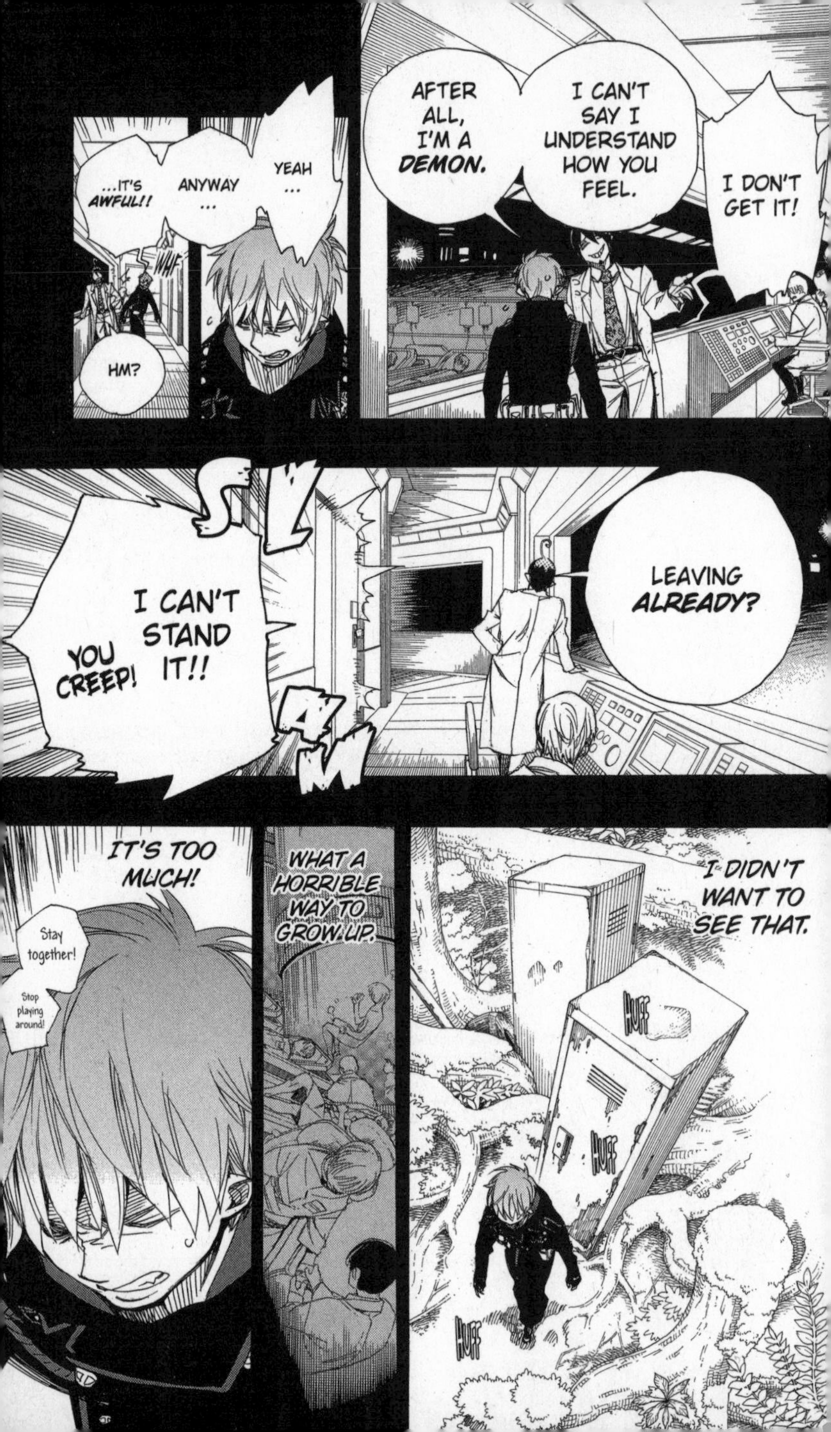
I DON'T GET IT!
I CAN'T SAY I UNDERSTAND HOW YOU FEEL.
AFTER ALL, I'M A DEMON.
YEAH...
ANYWAY...
...IT'S AWFUL!!
HM?
LEAVING ALREADY?
SLAM
I CAN'T STAND IT!!
YOU CREEP!
I DIDN'T WANT TO SEE THAT.
HUFF
HUFF
HUFF
WHAT A HORRIBLE WAY TO GROW UP.
IT'S TOO MUCH!
Stay together!
Stop playing around!

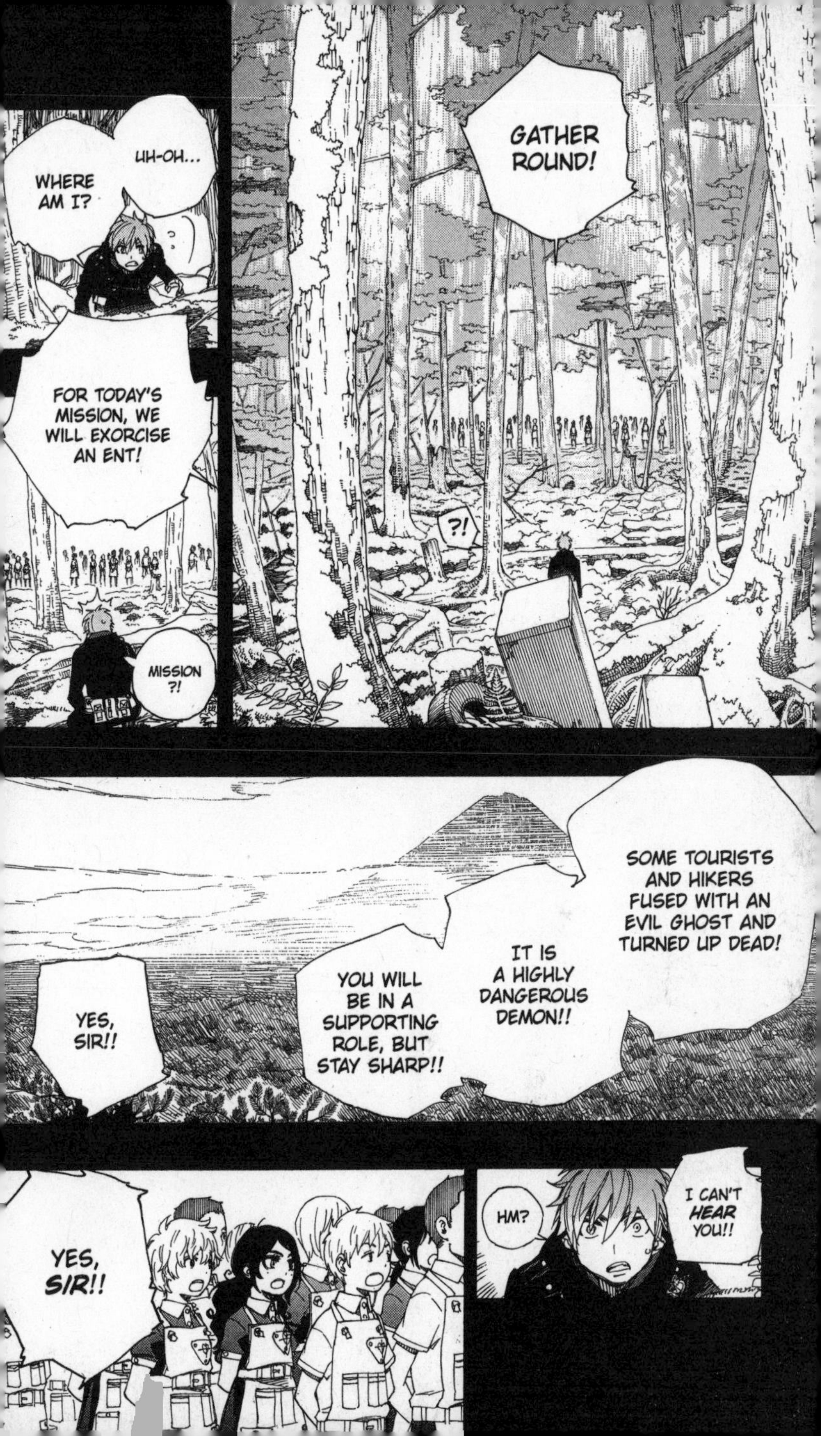
GATHER ROUND!
?!
UH-OH...
WHERE AM I?
FOR TODAY'S MISSION, WE WILL EXORCISE AN ENT!
MISSION?!
SOME TOURISTS AND HIKERS FUSED WITH AN EVIL GHOST AND TURNED UP DEAD!
IT IS A HIGHLY DANGEROUS DEMON!!
YOU WILL BE IN A SUPPORTING ROLE, BUT STAY SHARP!!
YES, SIR!!
I CAN'T HEAR YOU!!
HM?
YES, SIR!!

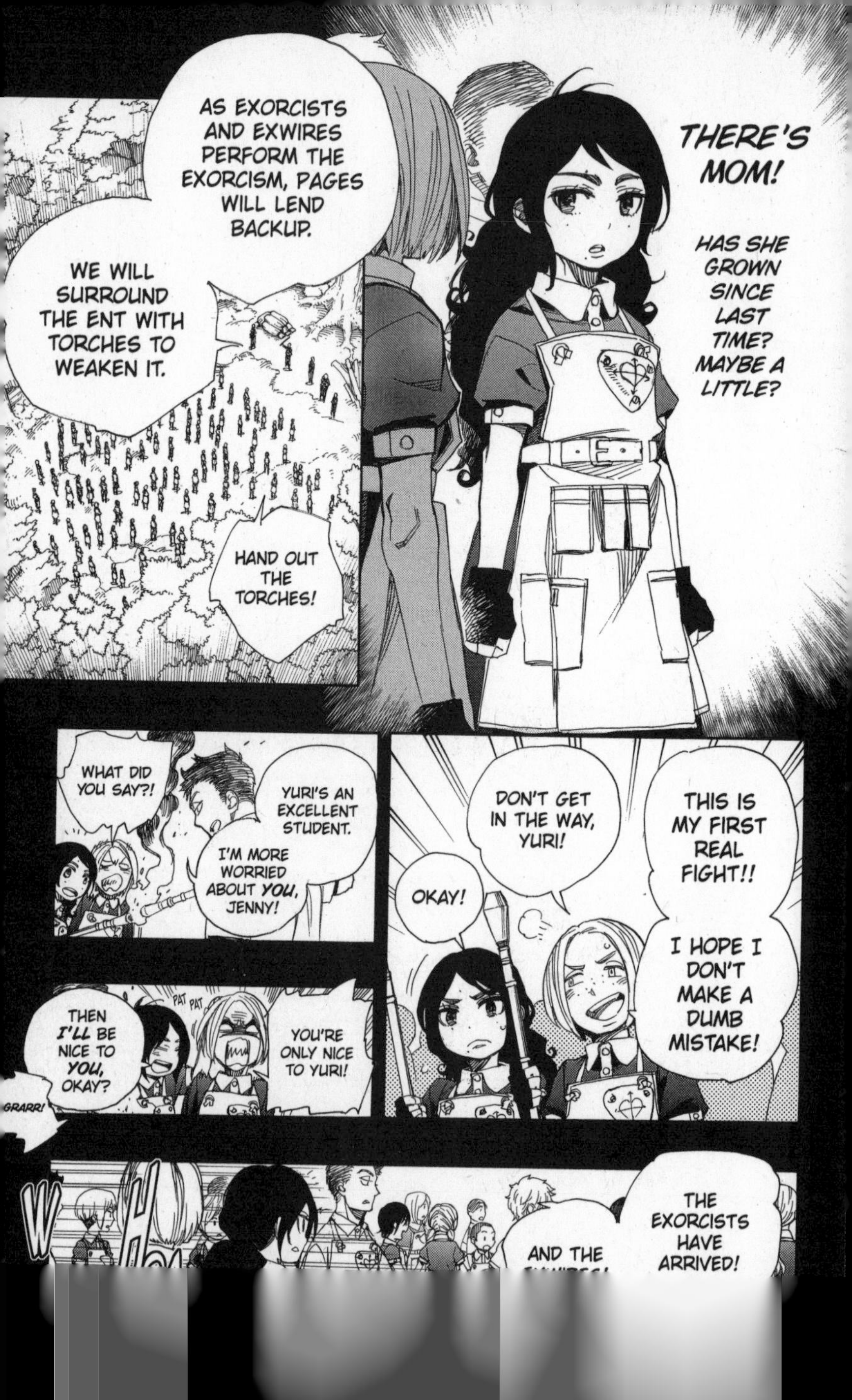

AS EXORCISTS AND EXWIRES PERFORM THE EXORCISM, PAGES WILL LEND BACKUP.
THERE'S MOM!
HAS SHE GROWN SINCE LAST TIME? MAYBE A LITTLE?
WE WILL SURROUND THE ENT WITH TORCHES TO WEAKEN IT.
HAND OUT THE TORCHES!
THIS IS MY FIRST REAL FIGHT!!
DON'T GET IN THE WAY, YURI!
OKAY!
I HOPE I DON'T MAKE A DUMB MISTAKE!
YURI'S AN EXCELLENT STUDENT.
I'M MORE WORRIED ABOUT YOU, JENNY!
WHAT DID YOU SAY?!
YOU'RE ONLY NICE TO YURI!
PAT PAT
THEN I'LL BE NICE TO YOU, OKAY?
GRARR!
THE EXORCISTS HAVE ARRIVED!
AND THE

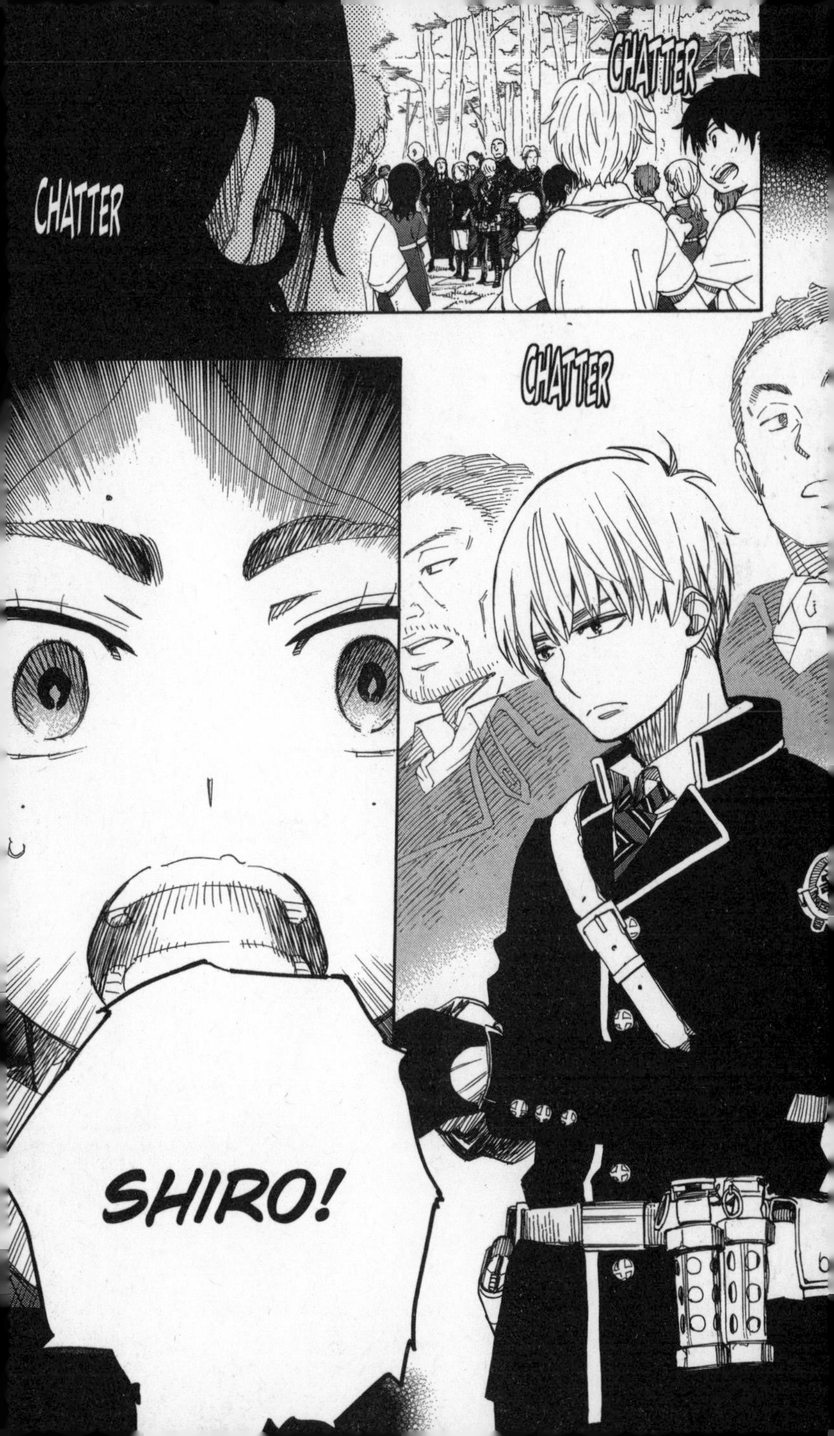
CHATTER
CHATTER
CHATTER
SHIRO!

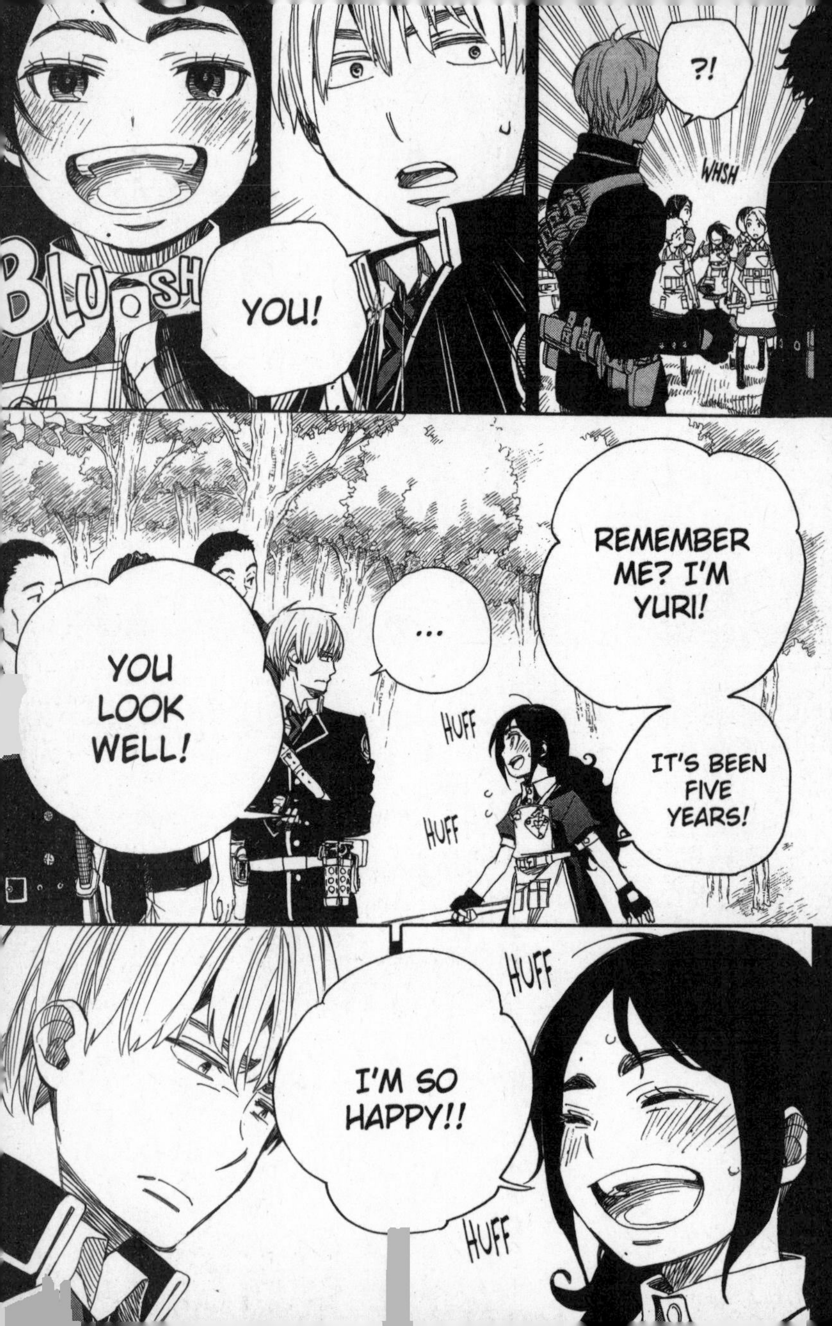
?!
WHSH
YOU!
BLUSH
REMEMBER ME? I'M YURI!
IT'S BEEN FIVE YEARS!
...
HUFF
HUFF
YOU LOOK WELL!
HUFF
I'M SO HAPPY!!
HUFF

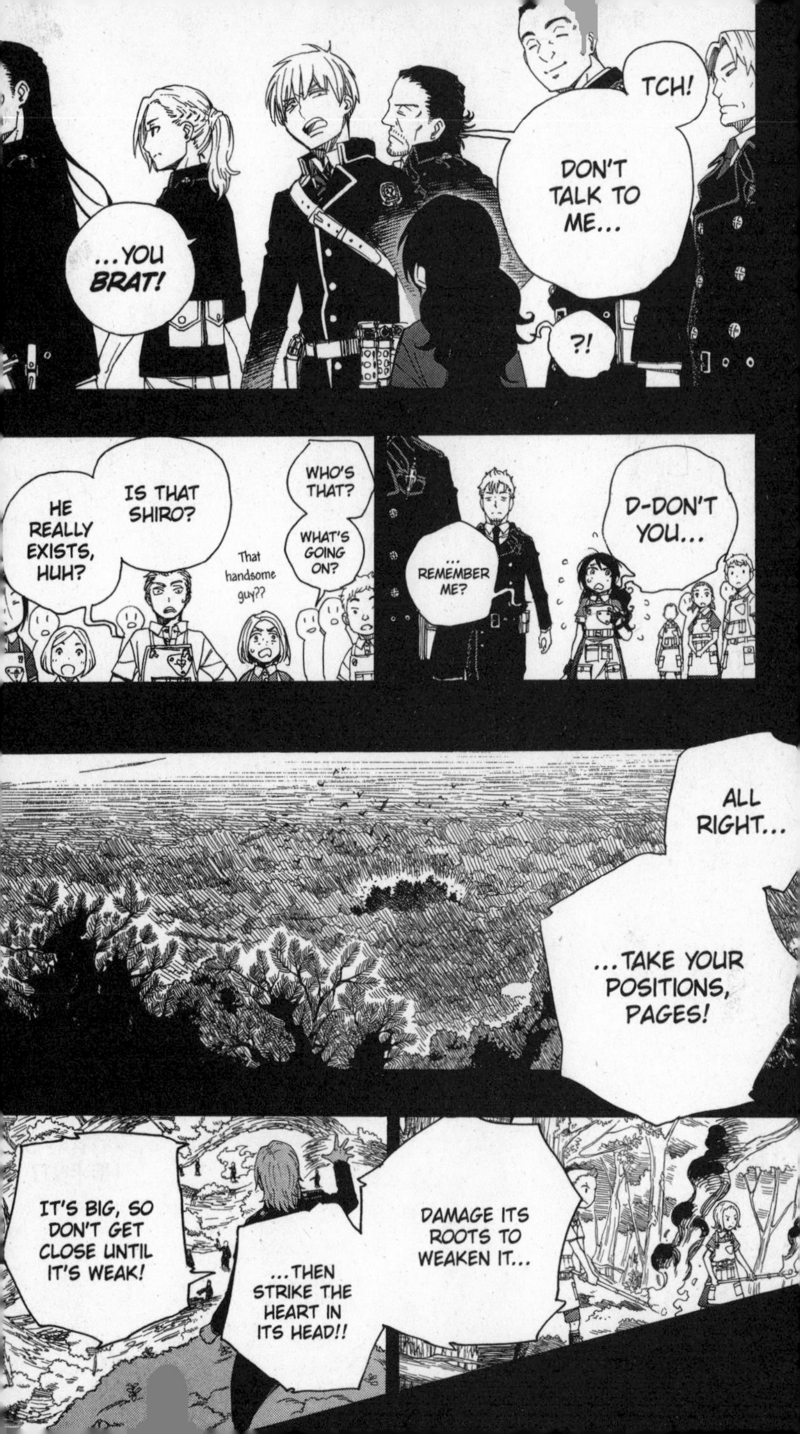
TCH!
DON'T TALK TO ME...
?!
...YOU BRAT!
D-DON'T YOU...
...REMEMBER ME?
WHO'S THAT?
WHAT'S GOING ON?
IS THAT SHIRO?
That handsome guy??
HE REALLY EXISTS, HUH?
ALL RIGHT...
...TAKE YOUR POSITIONS, PAGES!
DAMAGE ITS ROOTS TO WEAKEN IT...
...THEN STRIKE THE HEART IN ITS HEAD!!
IT'S BIG, SO DON'T GET CLOSE UNTIL IT'S WEAK!

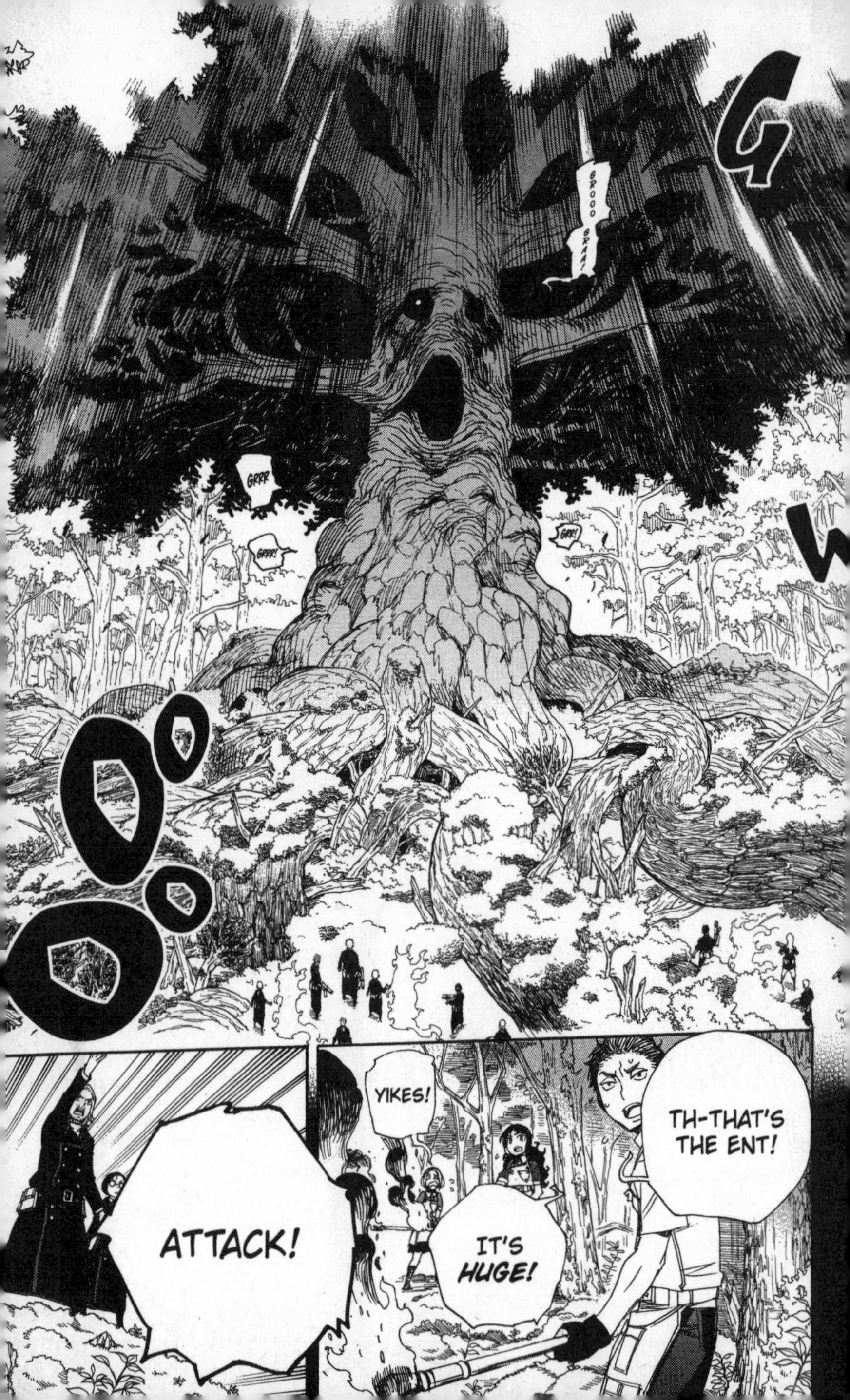

GROOO GRAA!
GWOOOO
GRRR
GRRR!
GRR!
TH-THAT'S THE ENT!
IT'S HUGE!
YIKES!
ATTACK!

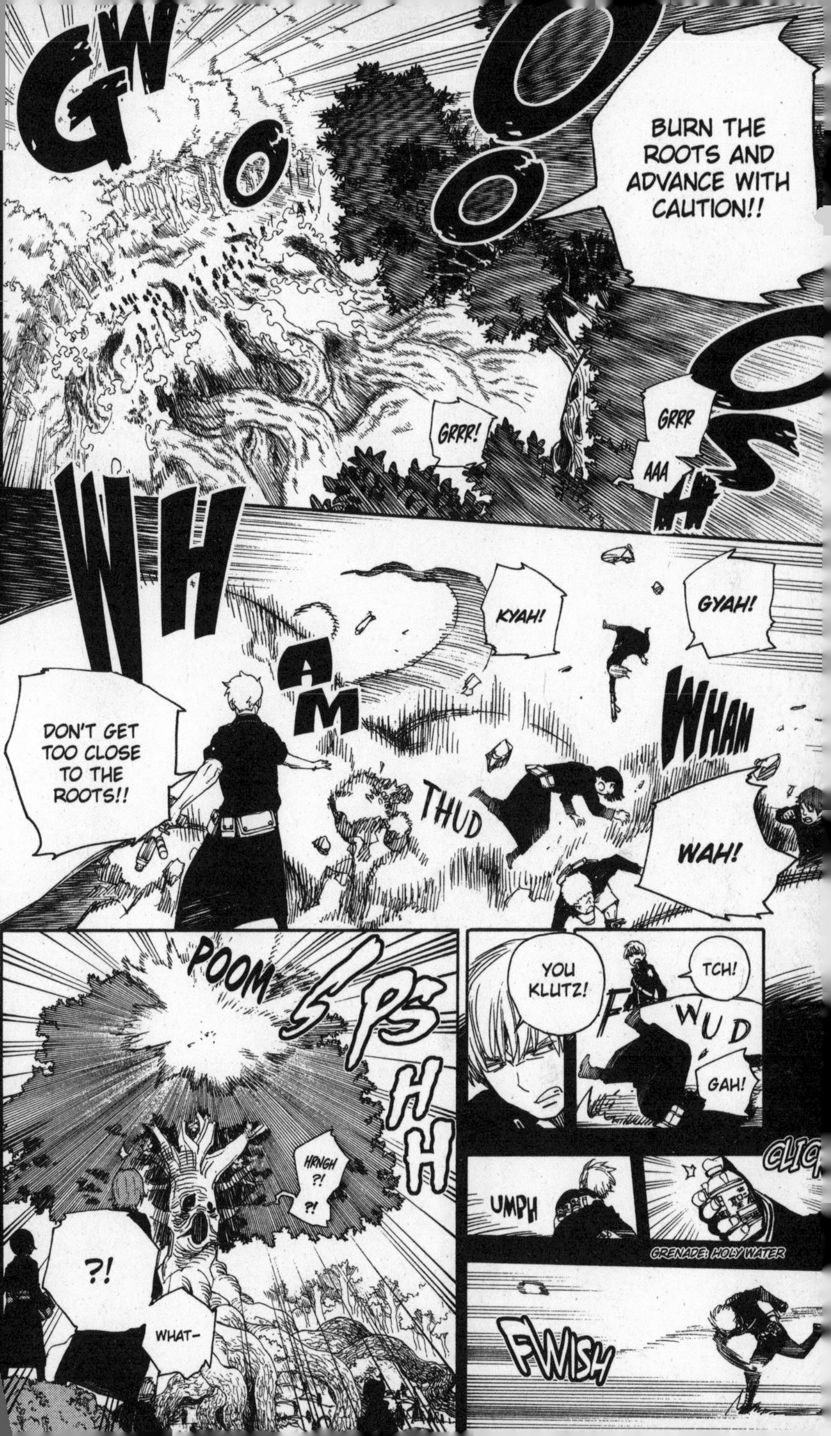
GWOOOOOSH
BURN THE ROOTS AND ADVANCE WITH CAUTION!!
GRRR AAA
GRRR!
WHAM
GYAH!
KYAH!
WHAM
WAH!
THUD
DON'T GET TOO CLOSE TO THE ROOTS!!
TCH!
YOU KLUTZ!
FWUD
GAH!
CLIC
GRENADE: HOLY WATER
UMPH
FWISH
POOM
SPSHHH
HRNGH ?! ?!
?!
WHAT-

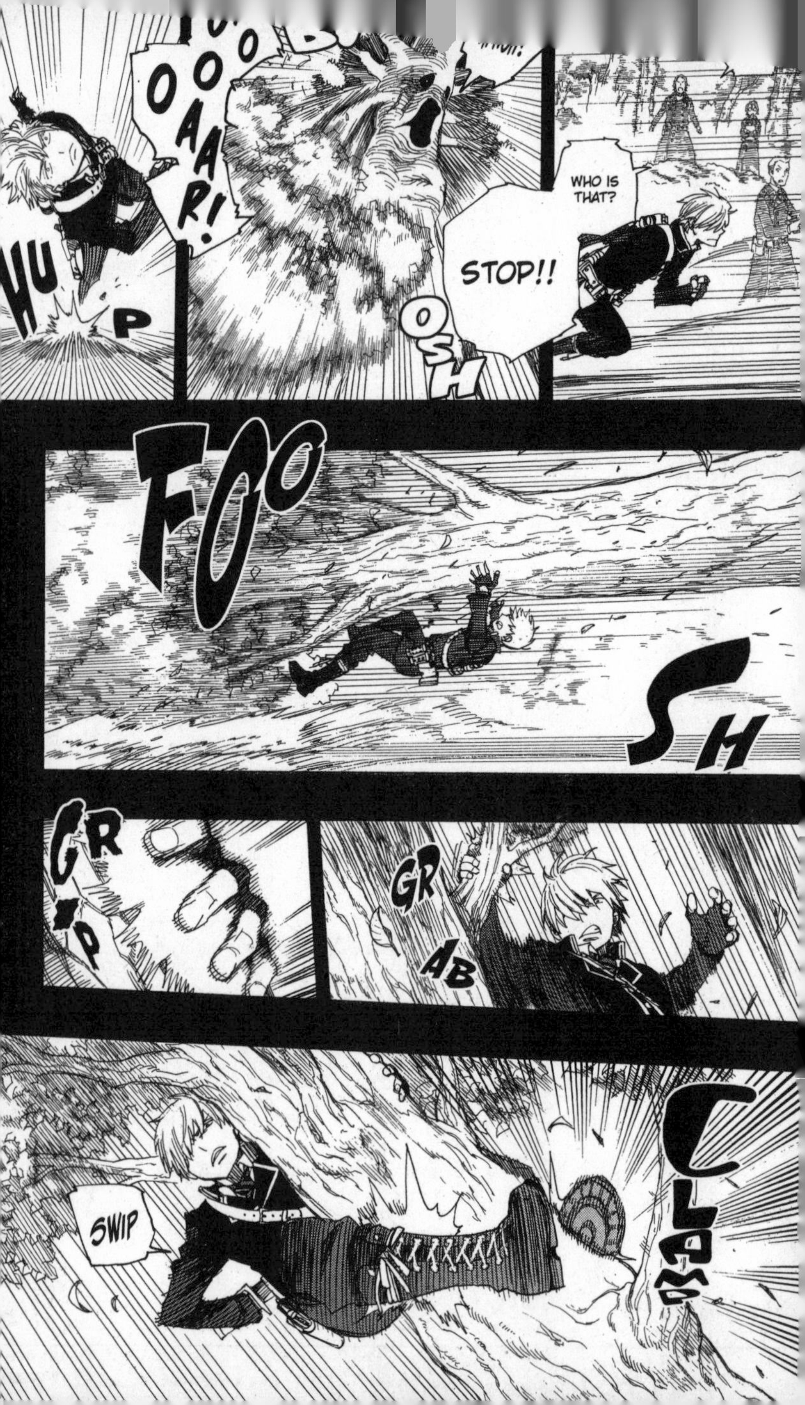
WHO IS THAT?
STOP!!
OSH
OOOOAAAR!
HUP
FOO
SH
GRAB
GRIP
CLAMP
SWIP

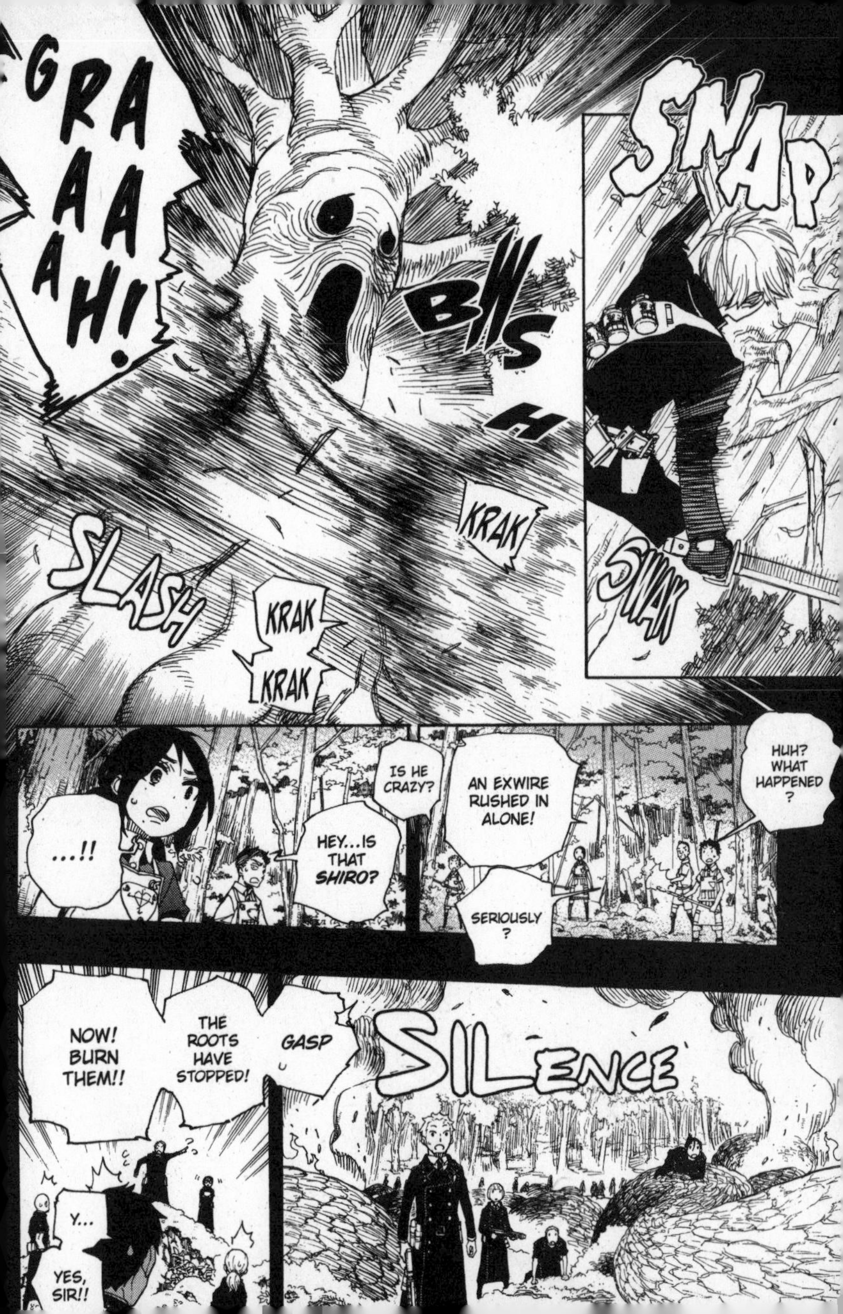
SNAP
SWAK
BWSH
GRAAAAH!
KRAK
SLASH
KRAK
KRAK
HUH? WHAT HAPPENED?
AN EXWIRE RUSHED IN ALONE!
SERIOUSLY?
IS HE CRAZY?
HEY...IS THAT *SHIRO*?
...!!
SILENCE
GASP
THE ROOTS HAVE STOPPED!
NOW! BURN THEM!!
Y...
YES, SIR!!

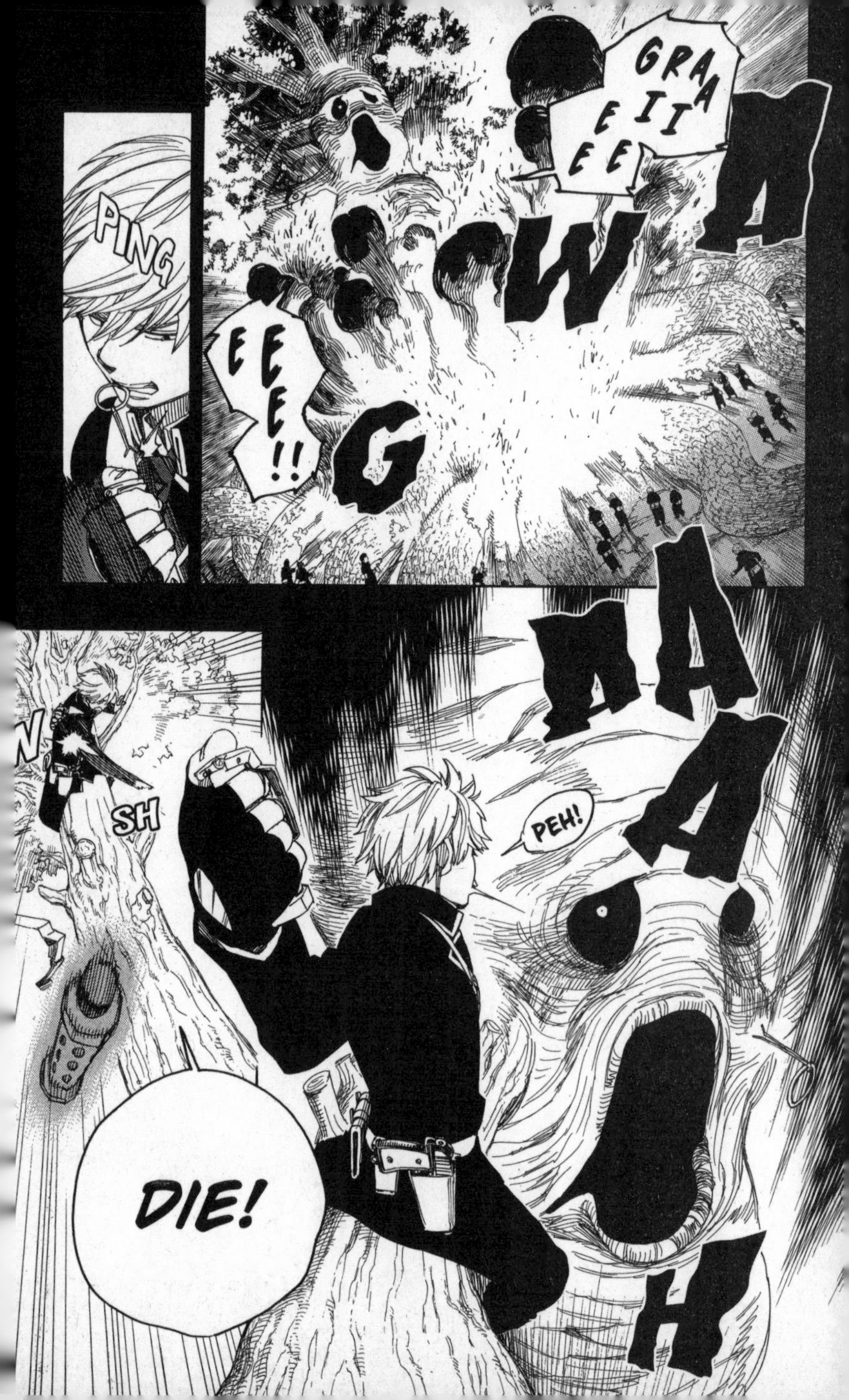

GRAAIIEEE
GWA
EEEE!!
PING
AAA!
PEH!
DIE!
H!
SH

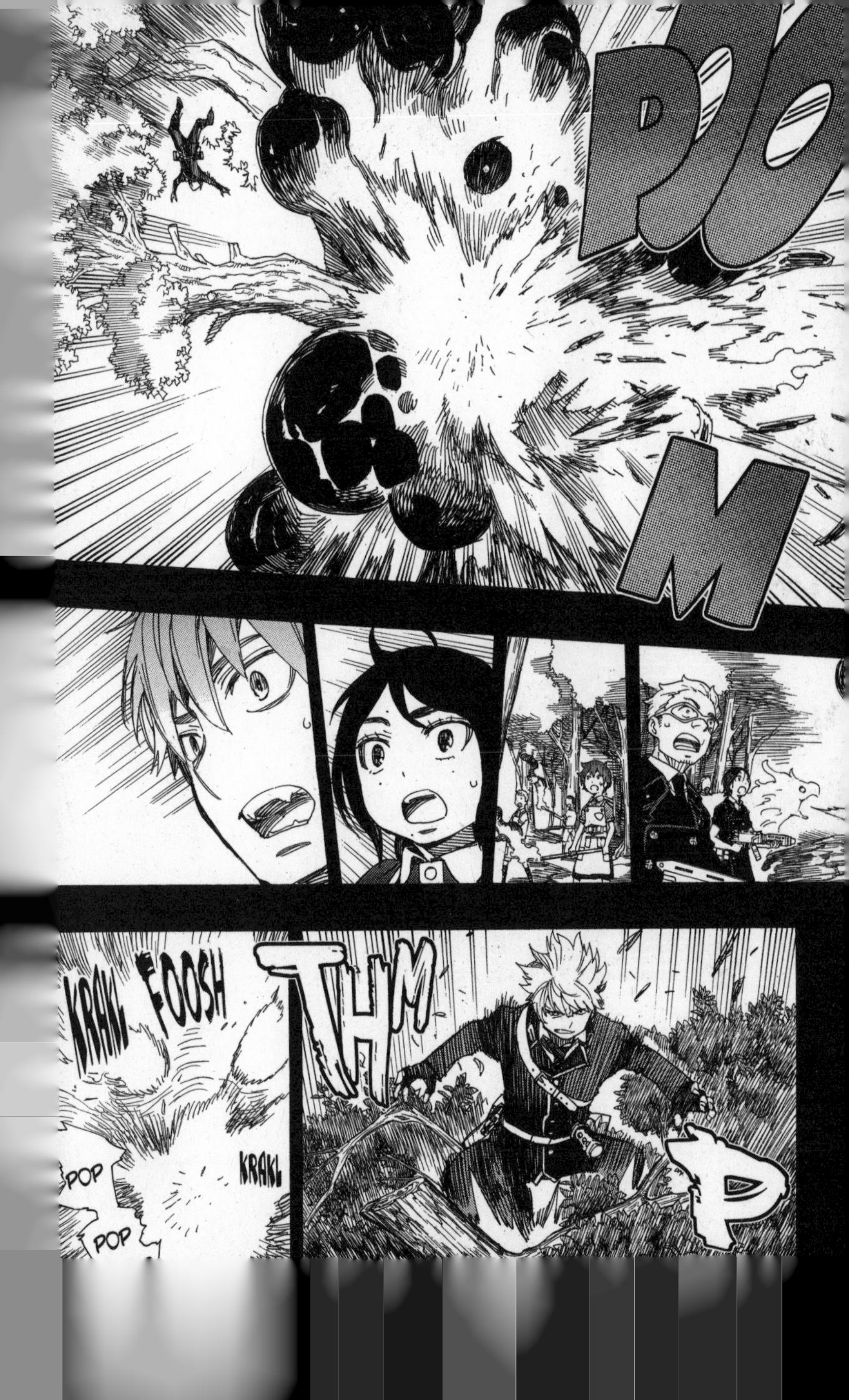
POM
THM
P
FOOSH
KRAKL
KRAKL
POP
POP

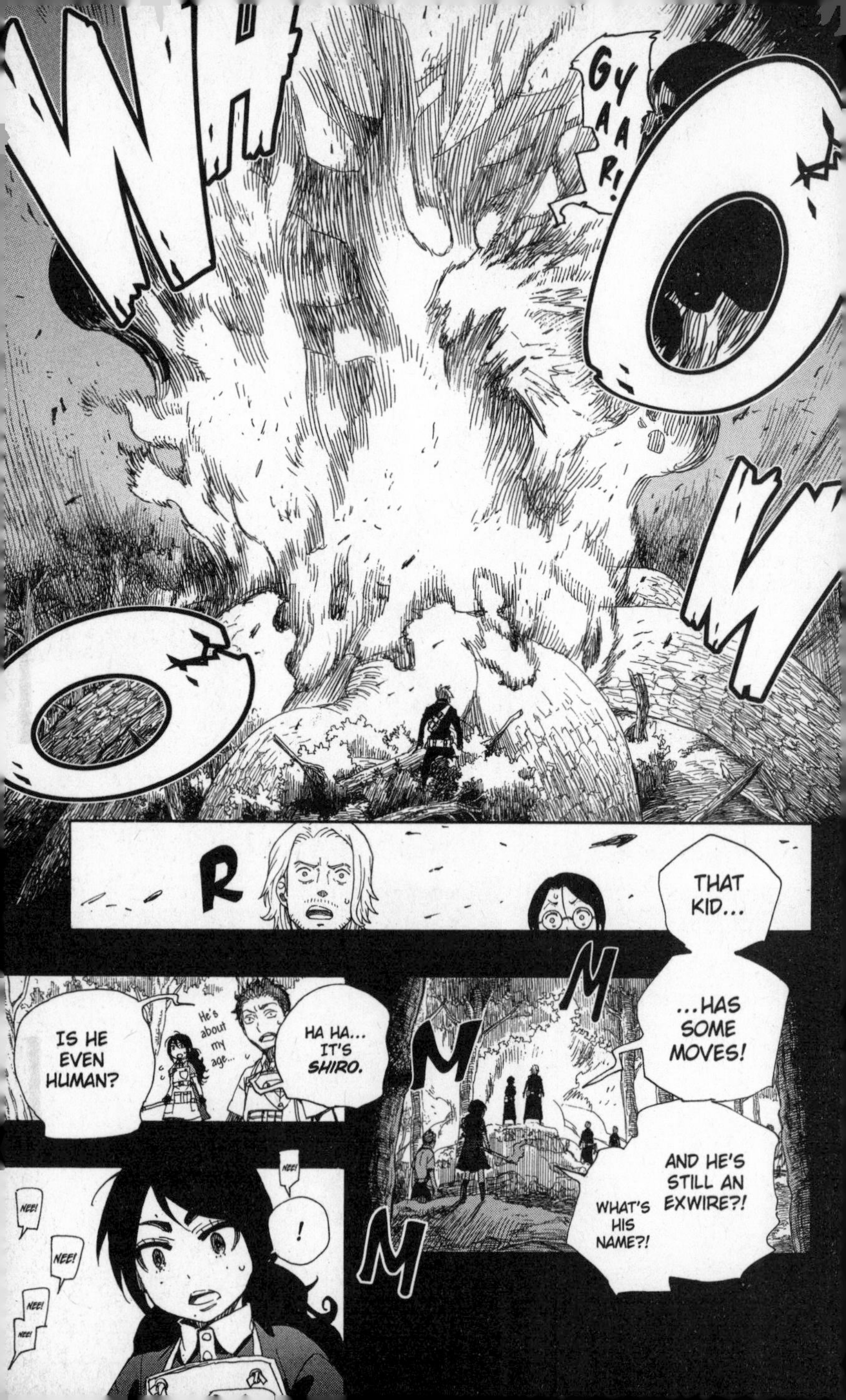

GYAAR!
WHOOM
R
THAT KID...
...HAS SOME MOVES!
AND HE'S STILL AN EXWIRE?!
WHAT'S HIS NAME?!
MMM
HA HA... IT'S SHIRO.
He's about my age...
IS HE EVEN HUMAN?
NEE!
!
NEE!
NEE!
NEE!
NEE!

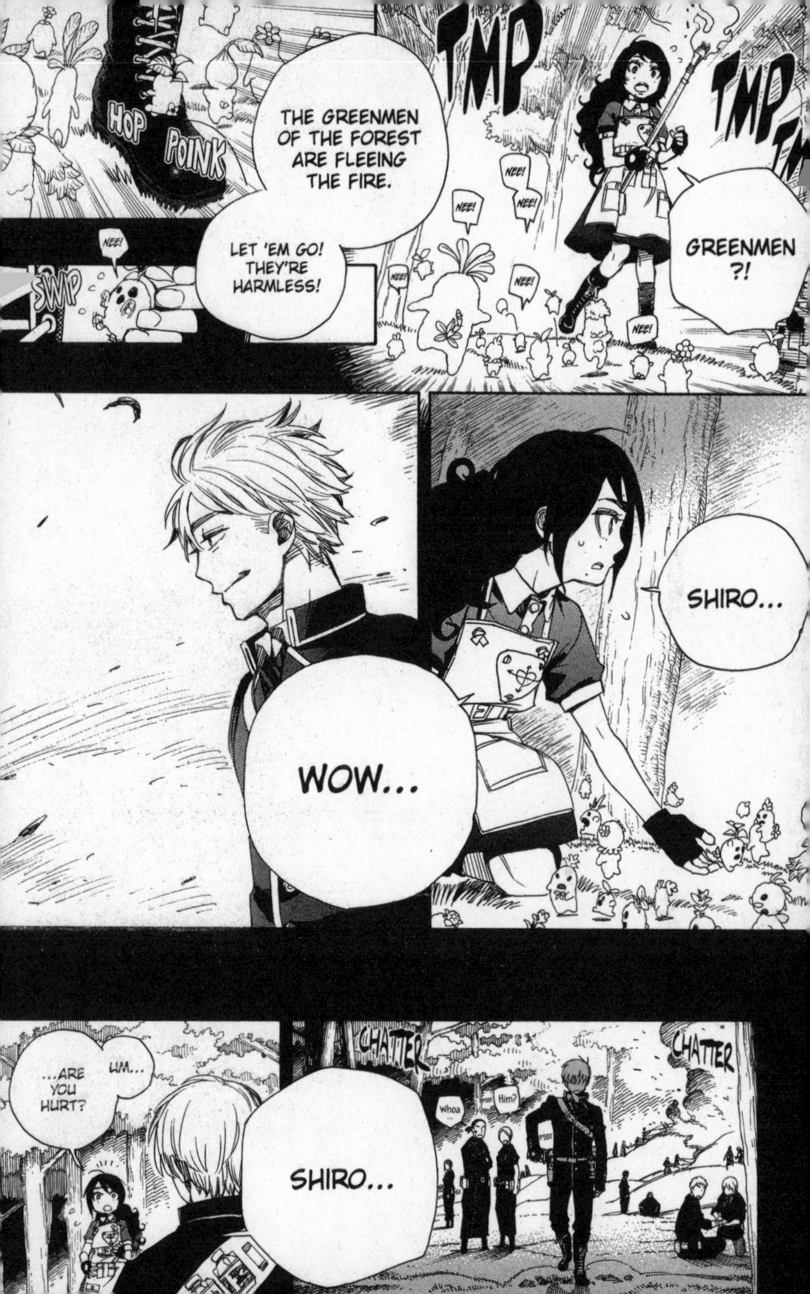
TMP
TMP
TM
GREENMEN ?!
NEE!
NEE!
NEE!
NEE!
NEE!
NEE!
THE GREENMEN OF THE FOREST ARE FLEEING THE FIRE.
LET 'EM GO! THEY'RE HARMLESS!
HOP
POINK
NEE!
SWIP
SHIRO...
WOW...
CHATTER
CHATTER
Him?
Whoa...
SHIRO...
UM...
...ARE YOU HURT?

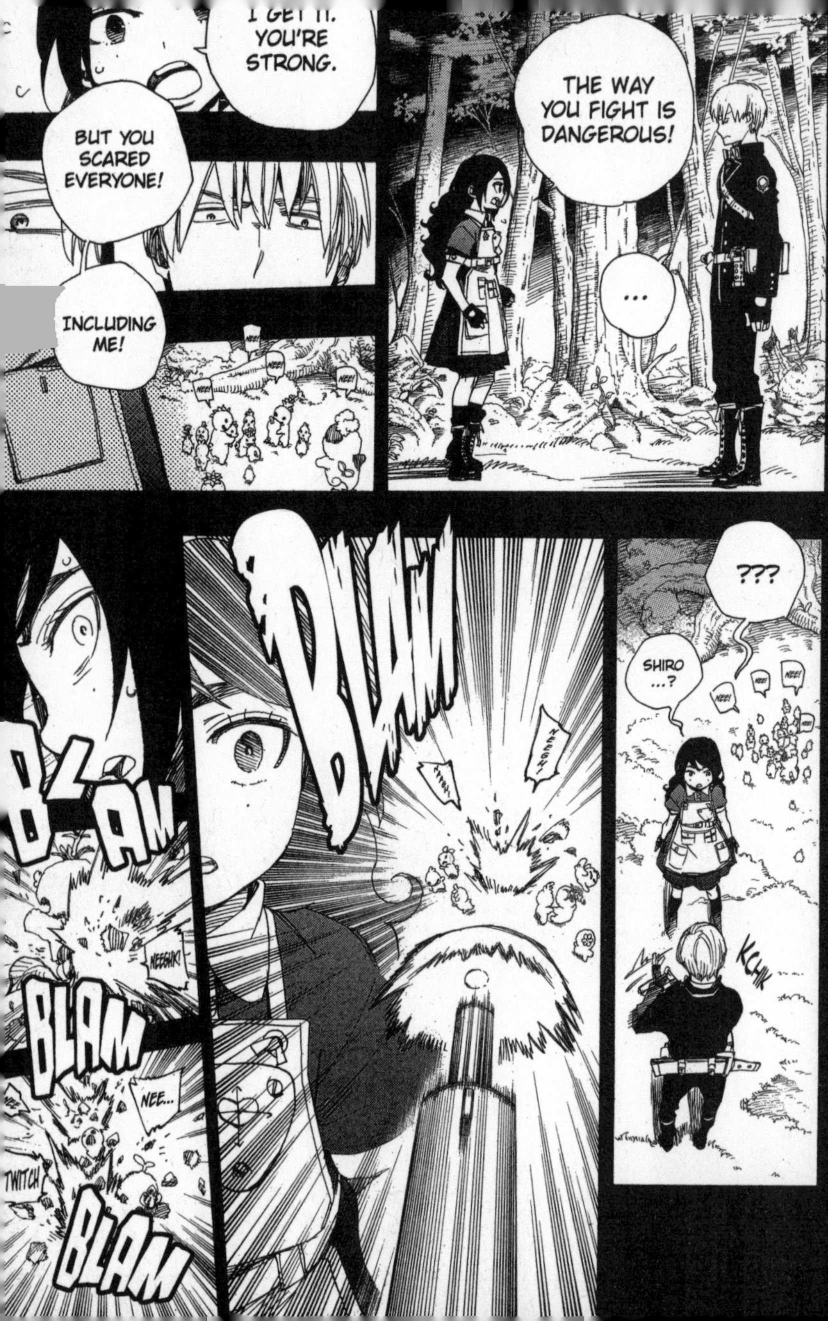
THE WAY YOU FIGHT IS DANGEROUS!
...
I GET IT. YOU'RE STRONG.
BUT YOU SCARED EVERYONE!
INCLUDING ME!
NEE!
NEE!
NEE!
NEE!
???
SHIRO ...?
NEE!
NEE!
NEE!
NEE!
KCHK
BLAM
NEEGH!
BLAM
NEEGH!
BLAM
NEE...
TWITCH
BLAM

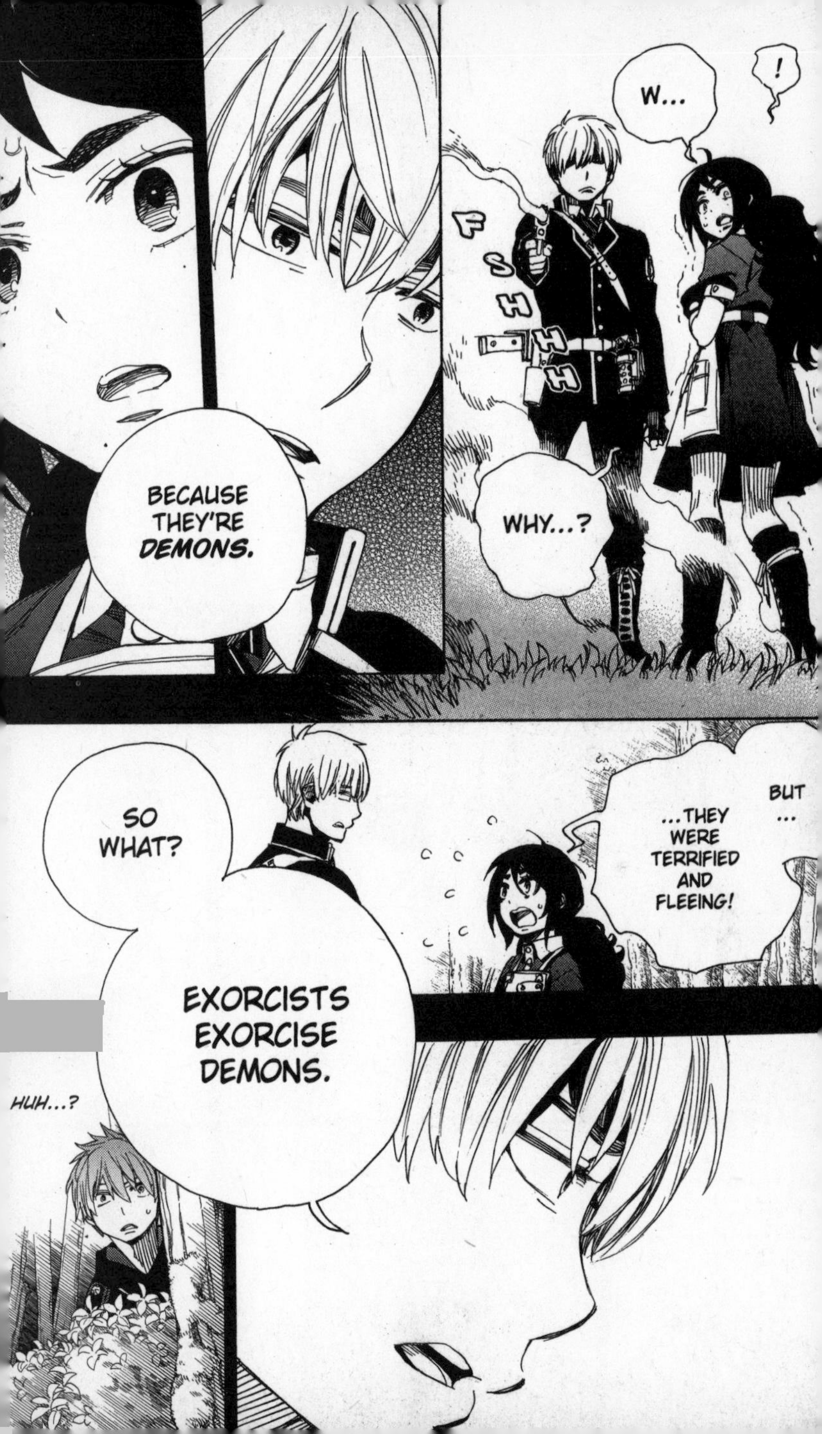
!
W...
FSHHHH
WHY...?
BECAUSE THEY'RE *DEMONS.*
BUT... ...THEY WERE TERRIFIED AND FLEEING!
SO WHAT?
EXORCISTS EXORCISE DEMONS.
HUH...?

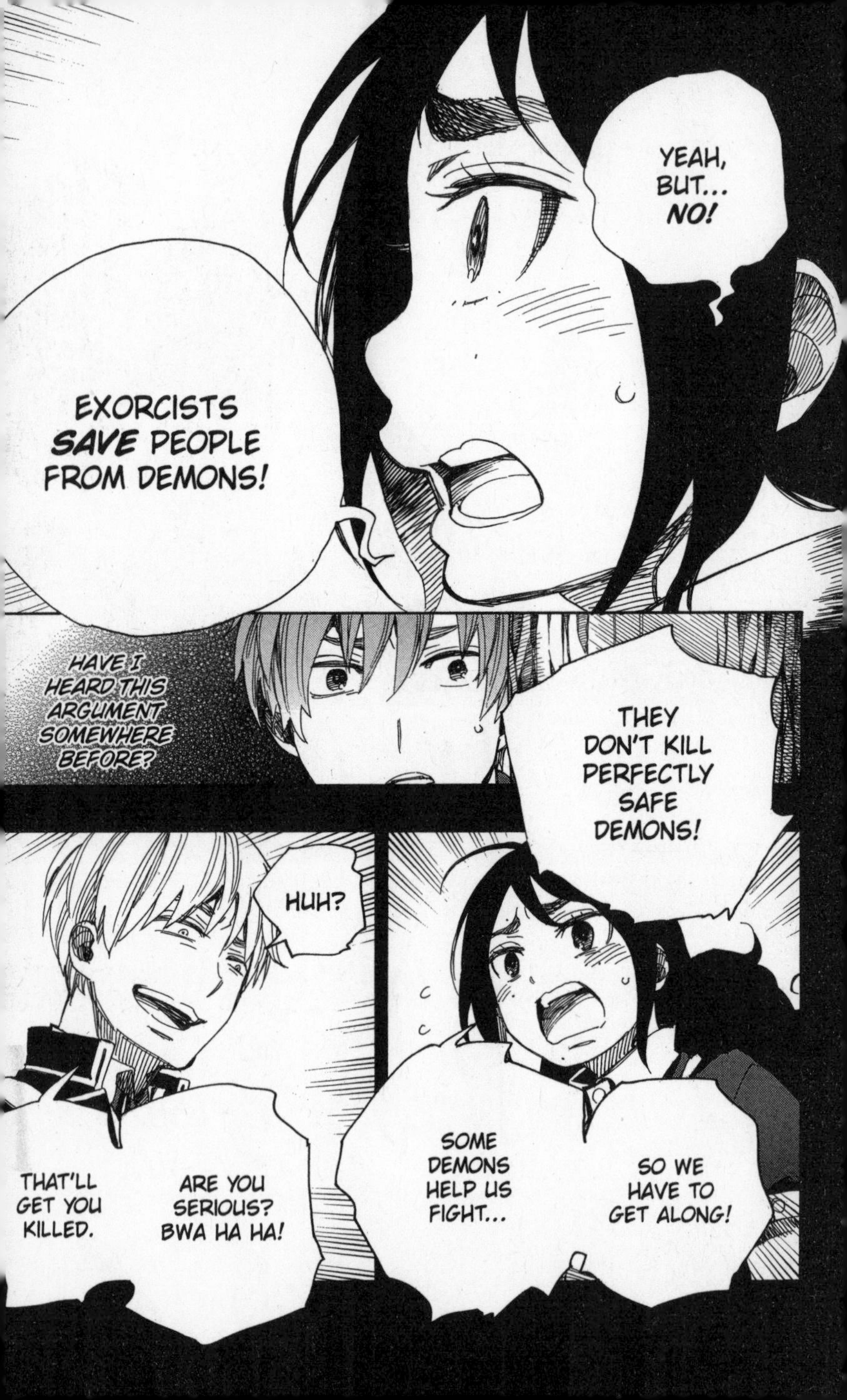
YEAH, BUT... NO!
EXORCISTS SAVE PEOPLE FROM DEMONS!
THEY DON'T KILL PERFECTLY SAFE DEMONS!
HAVE I HEARD THIS ARGUMENT SOMEWHERE BEFORE?
SOME DEMONS HELP US FIGHT...
SO WE HAVE TO GET ALONG!
HUH?
ARE YOU SERIOUS? BWA HA HA!
THAT'LL GET YOU KILLED.

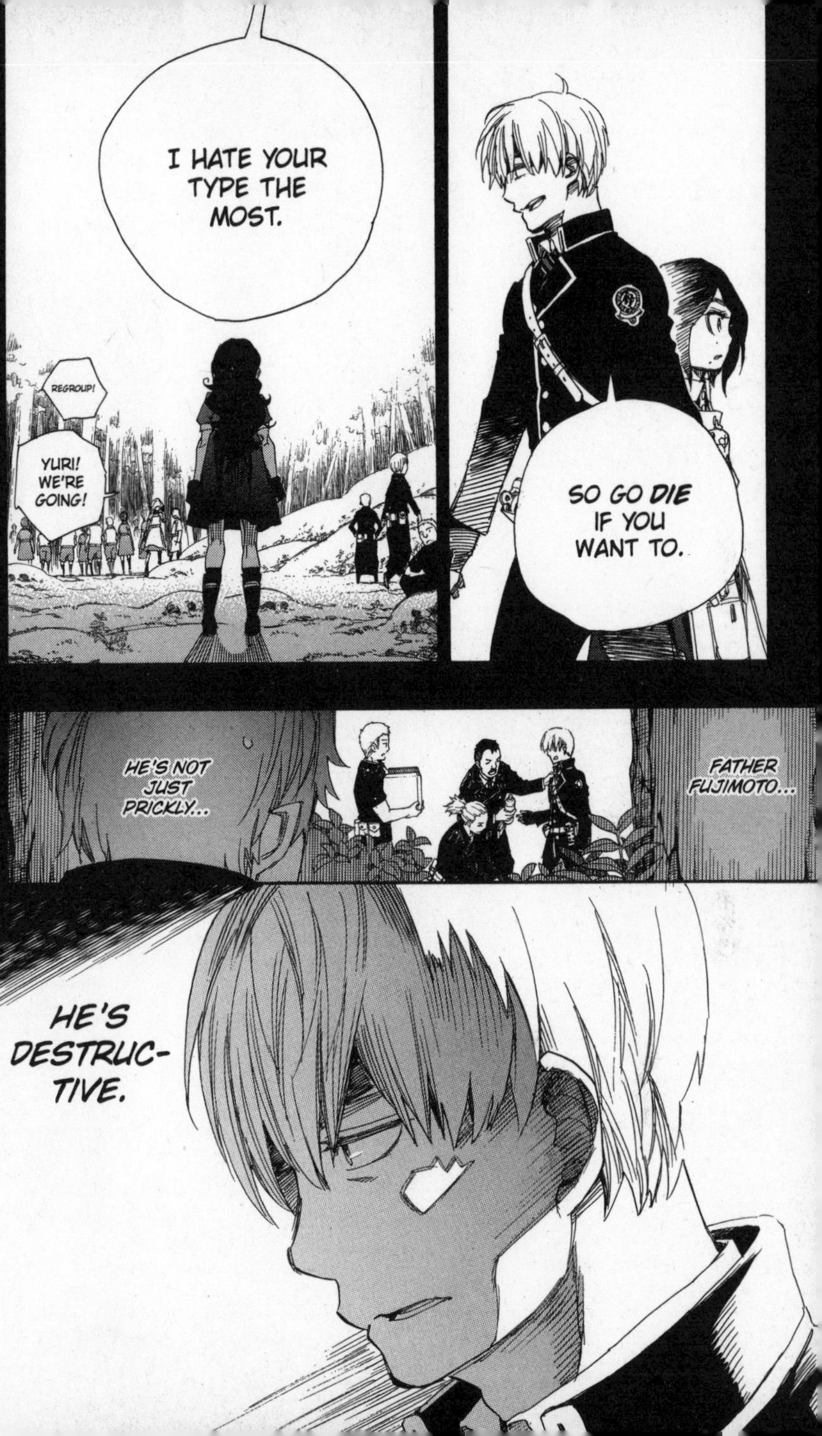
SO GO DIE IF YOU WANT TO.
I HATE YOUR TYPE THE MOST.
REGROUP!
YURI! WE'RE GOING!
FATHER FUJIMOTO...
HE'S NOT JUST PRICKLY...
HE'S DESTRUC-TIVE.

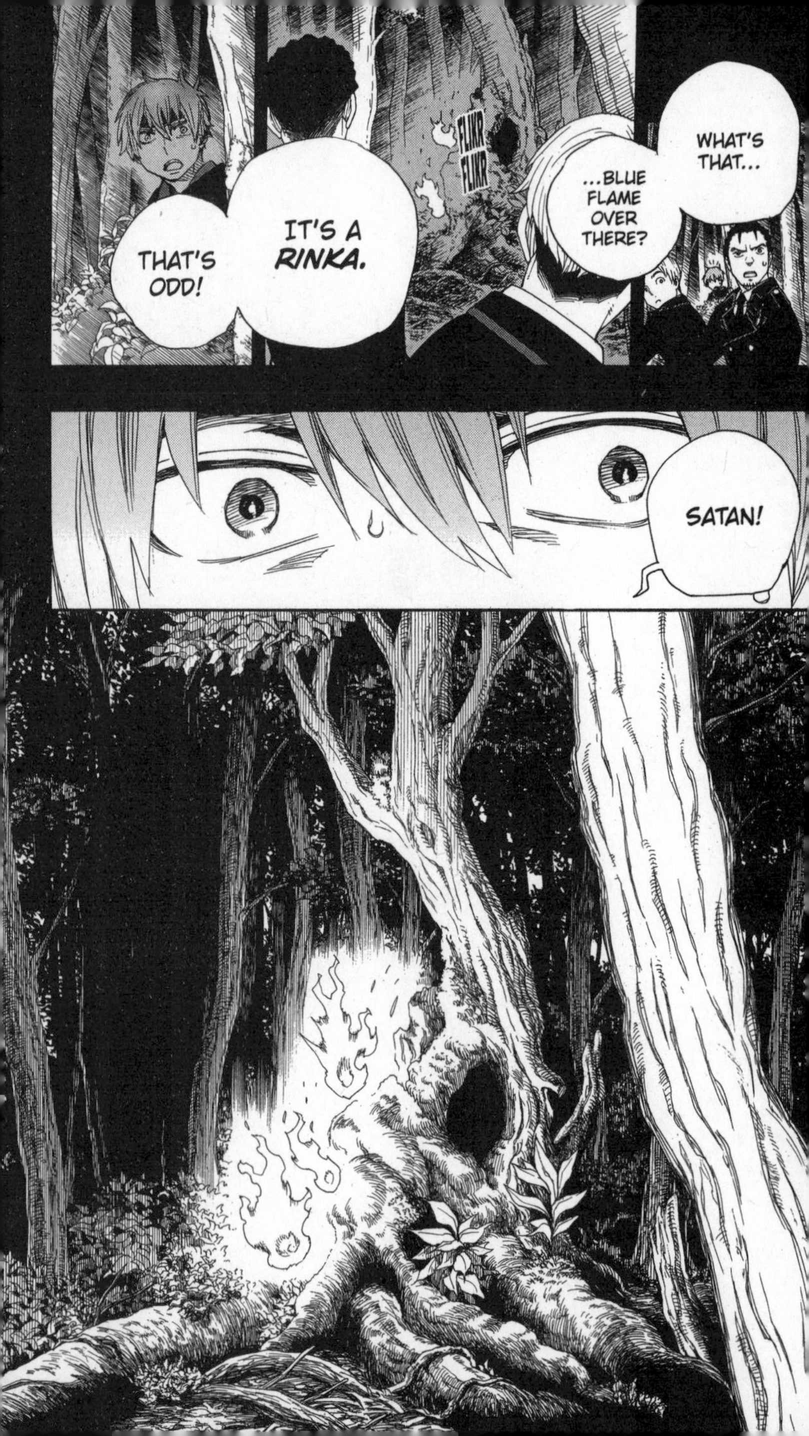
WHAT'S THAT...
...BLUE FLAME OVER THERE?
FLIKR FLIKR
IT'S A RINKA.
THAT'S ODD!
SATAN!

Blue Exorcist Chapter 102: SsC05:35

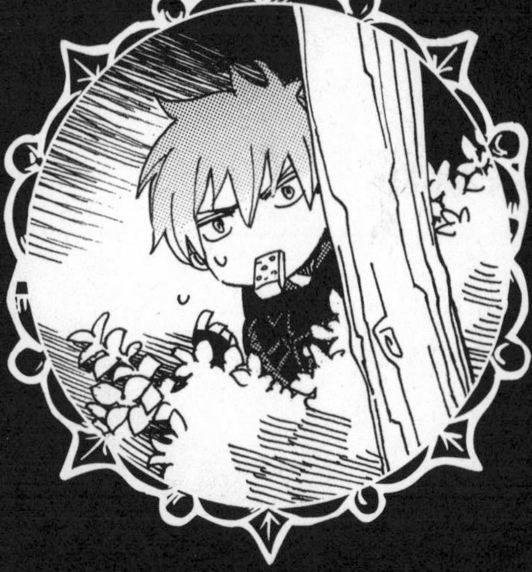

CHAPTER 103: SsC11:29

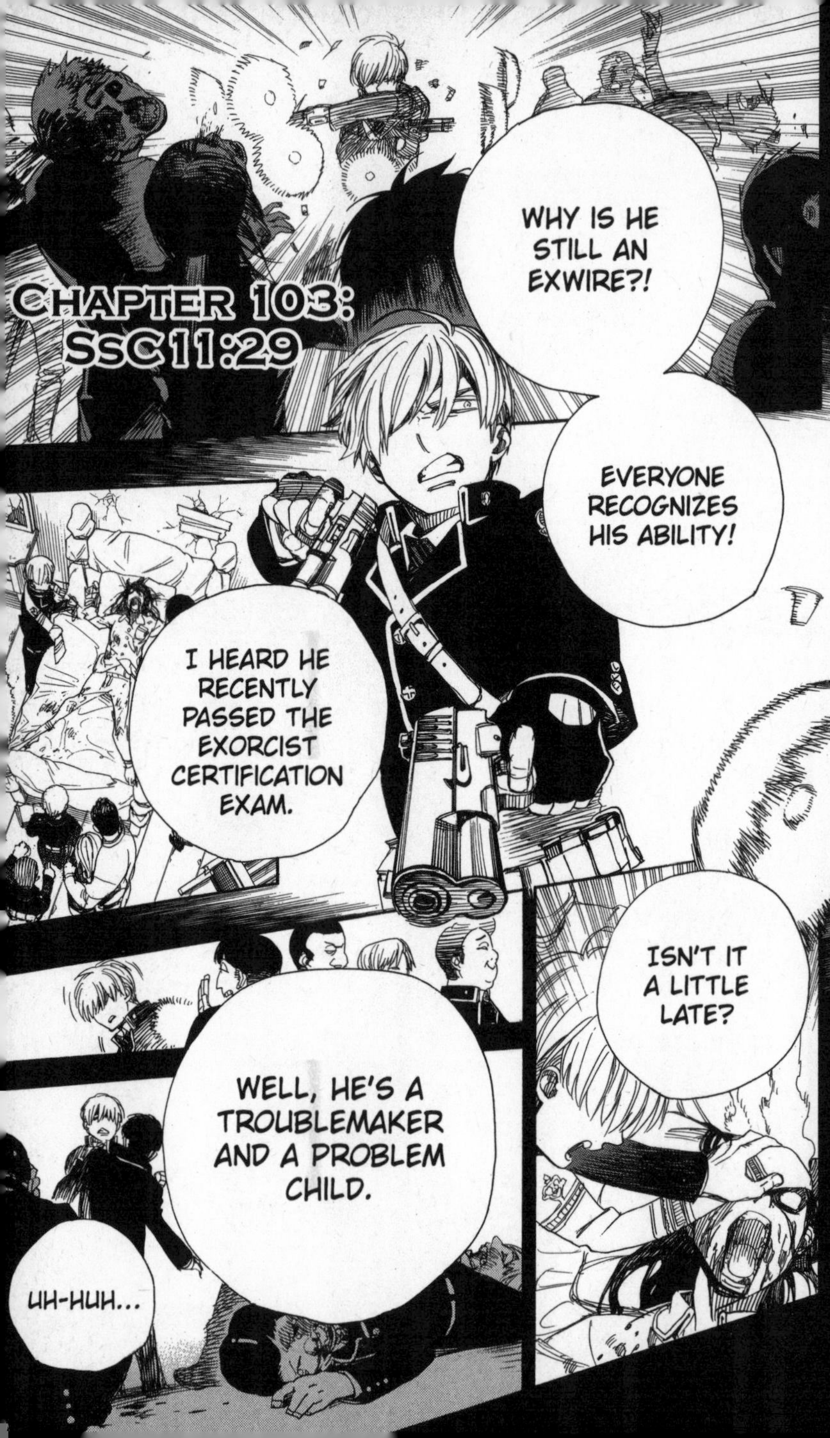
WHY IS HE STILL AN EXWIRE?!
EVERYONE RECOGNIZES HIS ABILITY!
I HEARD HE RECENTLY PASSED THE EXORCIST CERTIFICATION EXAM.
ISN'T IT A LITTLE LATE?
WELL, HE'S A TROUBLEMAKER AND A PROBLEM CHILD.
UH-HUH...

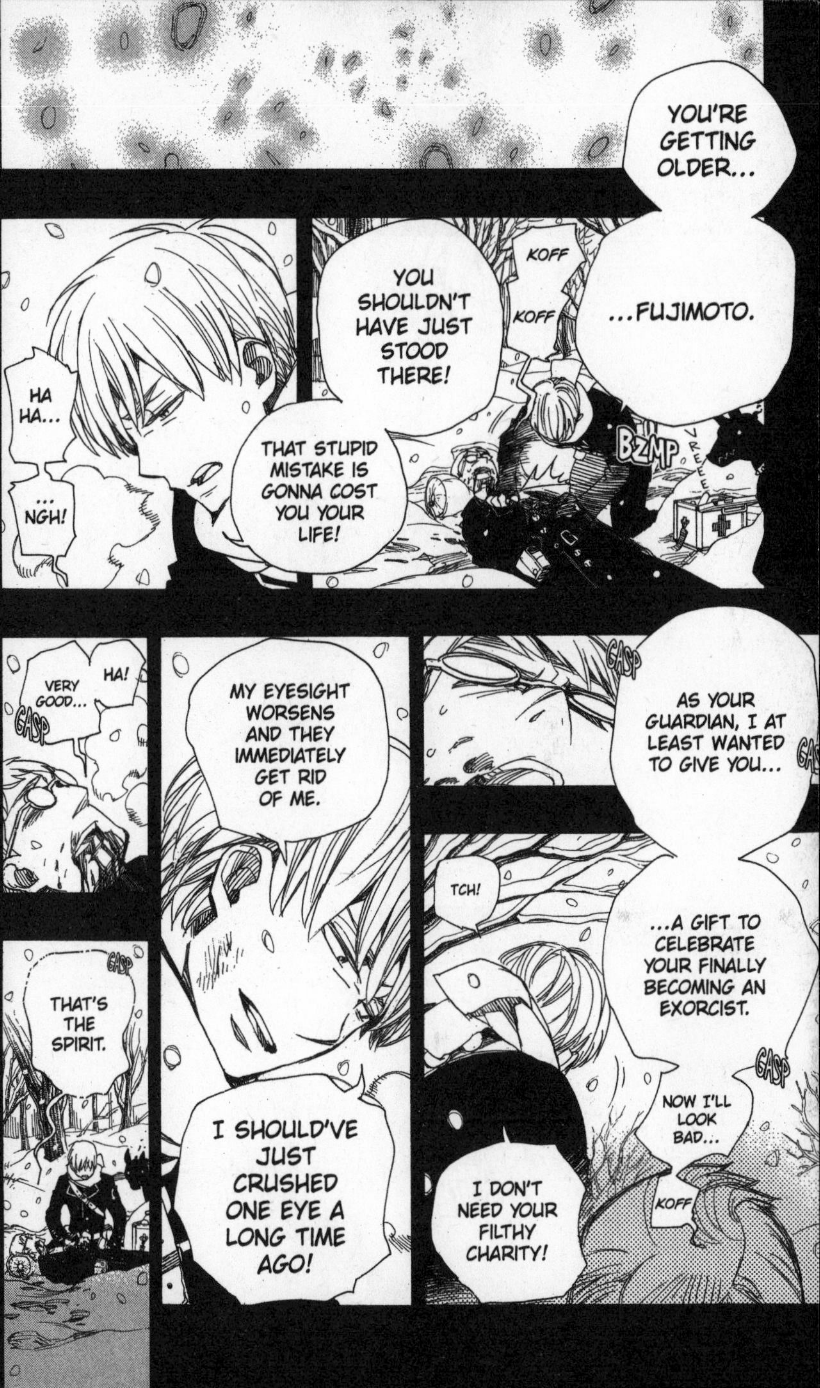
YOU'RE GETTING OLDER...
KOFF
KOFF
...FUJIMOTO.
YOU SHOULDN'T HAVE JUST STOOD THERE!
BZMP
VREEE
THAT STUPID MISTAKE IS GONNA COST YOU YOUR LIFE!
HA HA...
... NGH!
GASP
AS YOUR GUARDIAN, I AT LEAST WANTED TO GIVE YOU...
...A GIFT TO CELEBRATE YOUR FINALLY BECOMING AN EXORCIST.
TCH!
GASP
NOW I'LL LOOK BAD...
KOFF
I DON'T NEED YOUR FILTHY CHARITY!
MY EYESIGHT WORSENS AND THEY IMMEDIATELY GET RID OF ME.
I SHOULD'VE JUST CRUSHED ONE EYE A LONG TIME AGO!
HA!
VERY GOOD...
GASP
GASP
THAT'S THE SPIRIT.

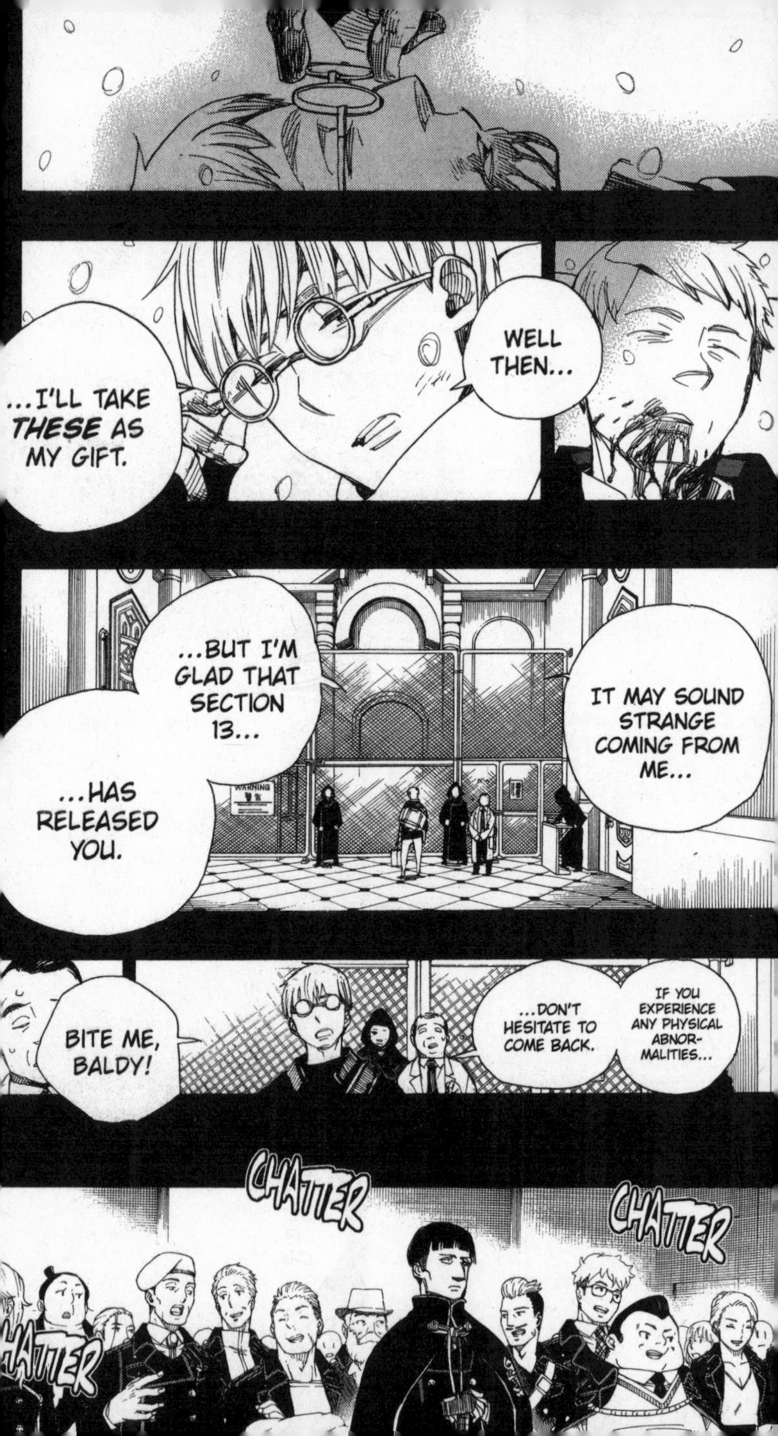
WELL THEN...
...I'LL TAKE *THESE* AS MY GIFT.
IT MAY SOUND STRANGE COMING FROM ME...
...BUT I'M GLAD THAT SECTION 13...
...HAS RELEASED YOU.
IF YOU EXPERIENCE ANY PHYSICAL ABNOR-MALITIES...
...DON'T HESITATE TO COME BACK.
BITE ME, BALDY!
CHATTER
CHATTER
CHATTER

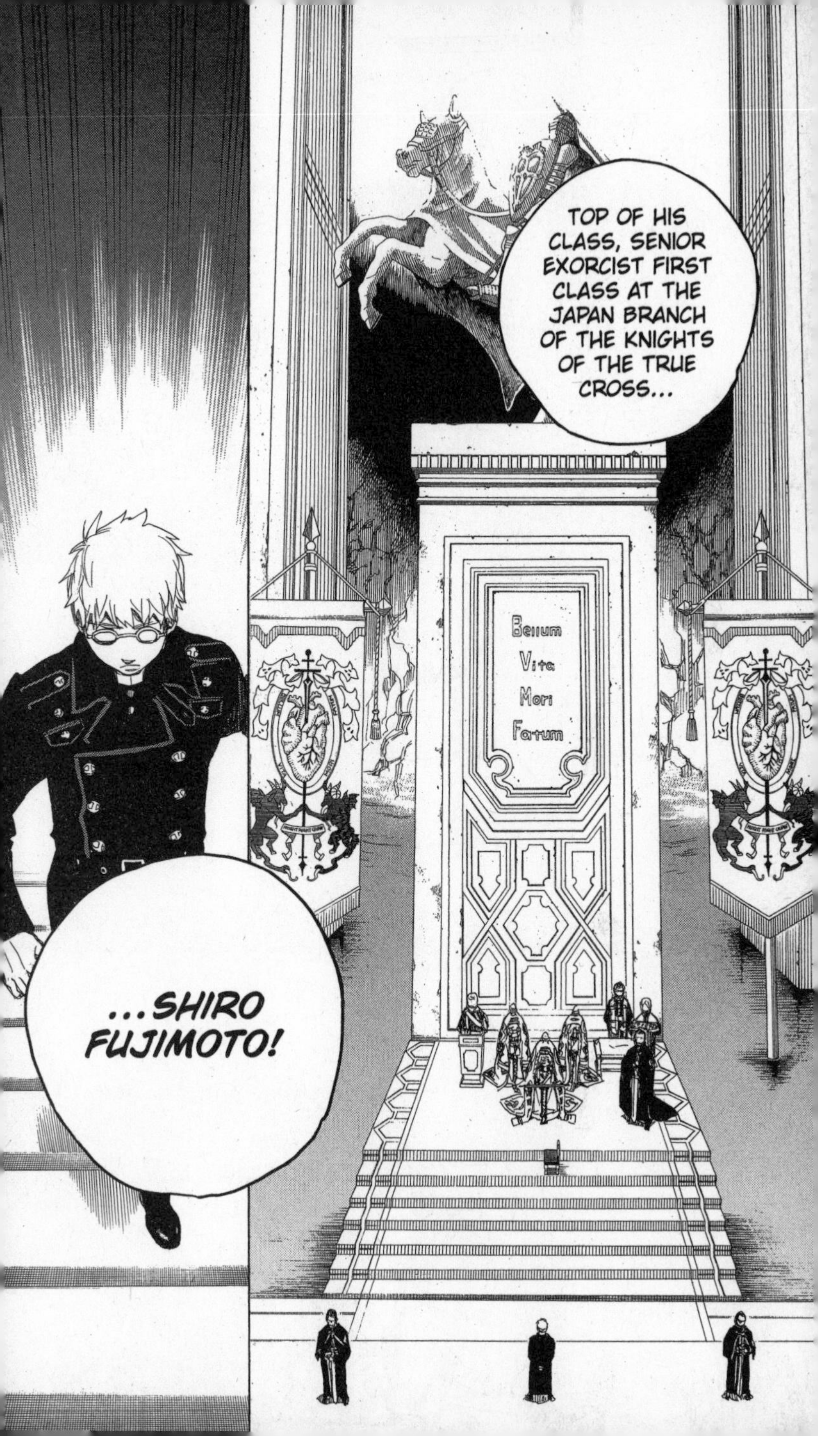
TOP OF HIS CLASS, SENIOR EXORCIST FIRST CLASS AT THE JAPAN BRANCH OF THE KNIGHTS OF THE TRUE CROSS...
Bellum Vita Mori Fatum
...SHIRO FUJIMOTO!

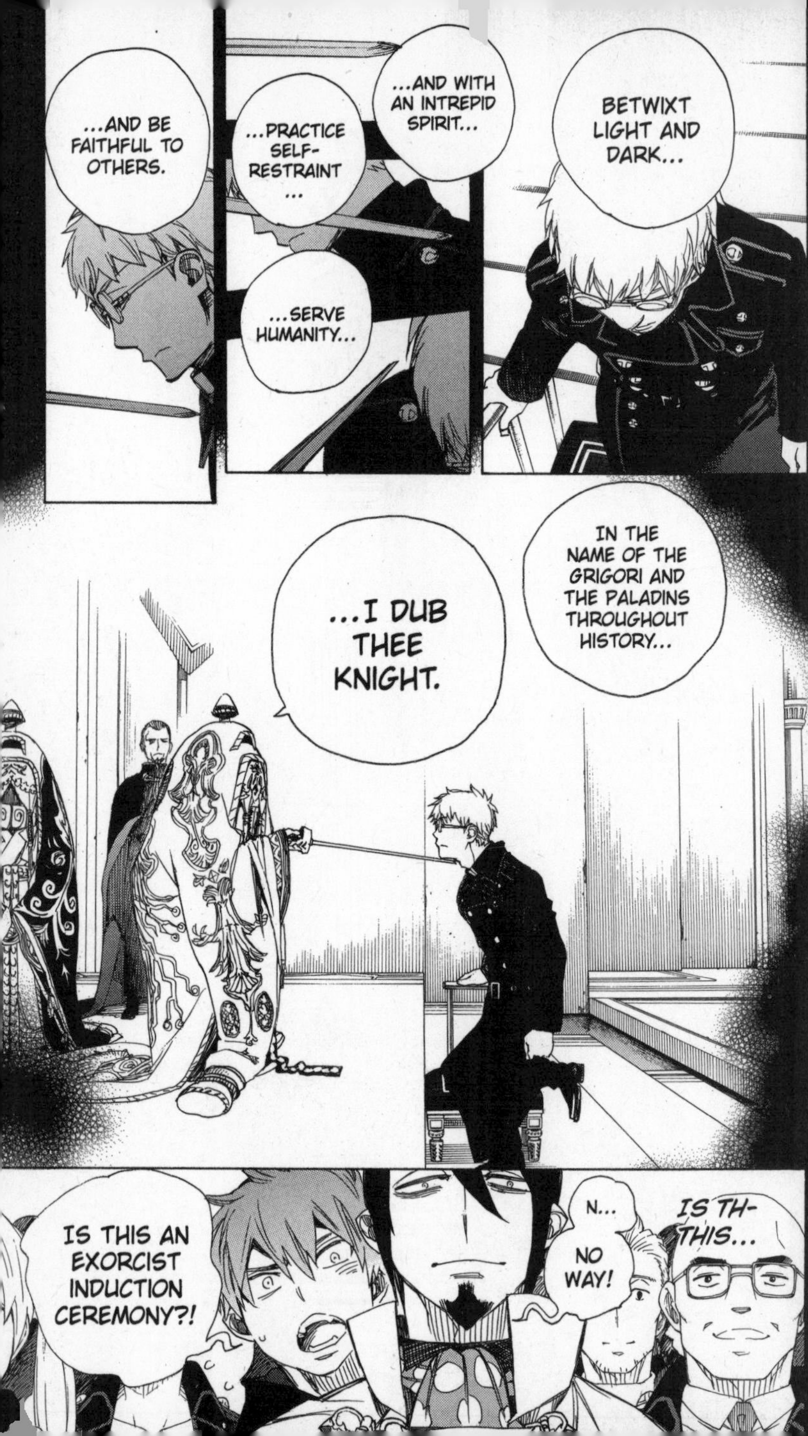
BETWIXT LIGHT AND DARK...
...AND WITH AN INTREPID SPIRIT...
...PRACTICE SELF-RESTRAINT...
...SERVE HUMANITY...
...AND BE FAITHFUL TO OTHERS.
IN THE NAME OF THE GRIGORI AND THE PALADINS THROUGHOUT HISTORY...
...I DUB THEE KNIGHT.
IS TH-THIS...
N...
NO WAY!
IS THIS AN EXORCIST INDUCTION CEREMONY?!

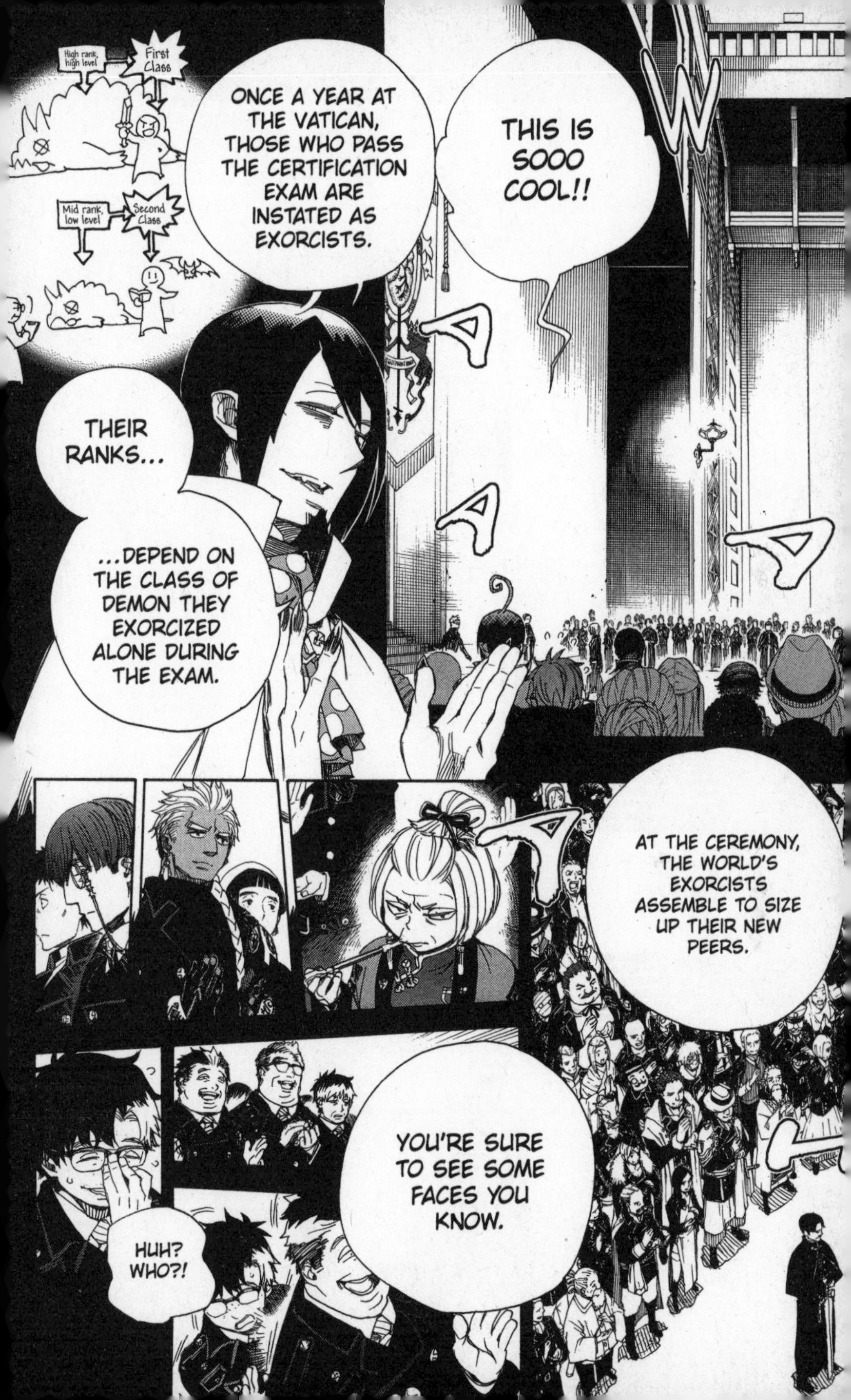
THIS IS SOOO COOL!!
ONCE A YEAR AT THE VATICAN, THOSE WHO PASS THE CERTIFICATION EXAM ARE INSTATED AS EXORCISTS.
First Class
High rank, high level
Second Class
Mid rank, low level
THEIR RANKS...
...DEPEND ON THE CLASS OF DEMON THEY EXORCIZED ALONE DURING THE EXAM.
AT THE CEREMONY, THE WORLD'S EXORCISTS ASSEMBLE TO SIZE UP THEIR NEW PEERS.
YOU'RE SURE TO SEE SOME FACES YOU KNOW.
HUH? WHO?!

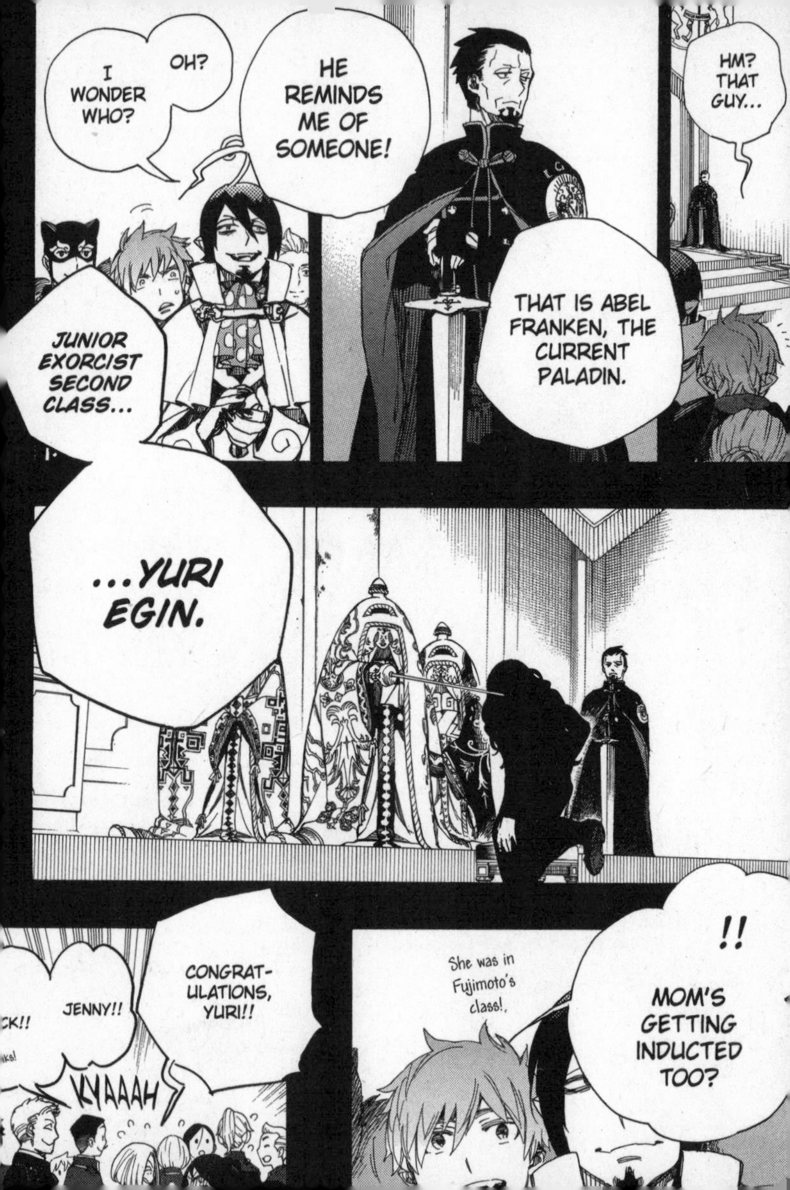
HM? THAT GUY...
THAT IS ABEL FRANKEN, THE CURRENT PALADIN.
HE REMINDS ME OF SOMEONE!
OH? I WONDER WHO?
JUNIOR EXORCIST SECOND CLASS...
...YURI EGIN.
!!
MOM'S GETTING INDUCTED TOO?
She was in Fujimoto's class!
CONGRAT-ULATIONS, YURI!!
JENNY!!
KYAAAH

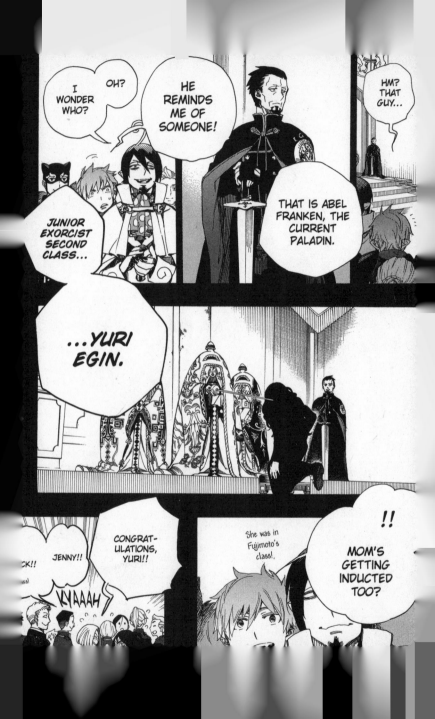

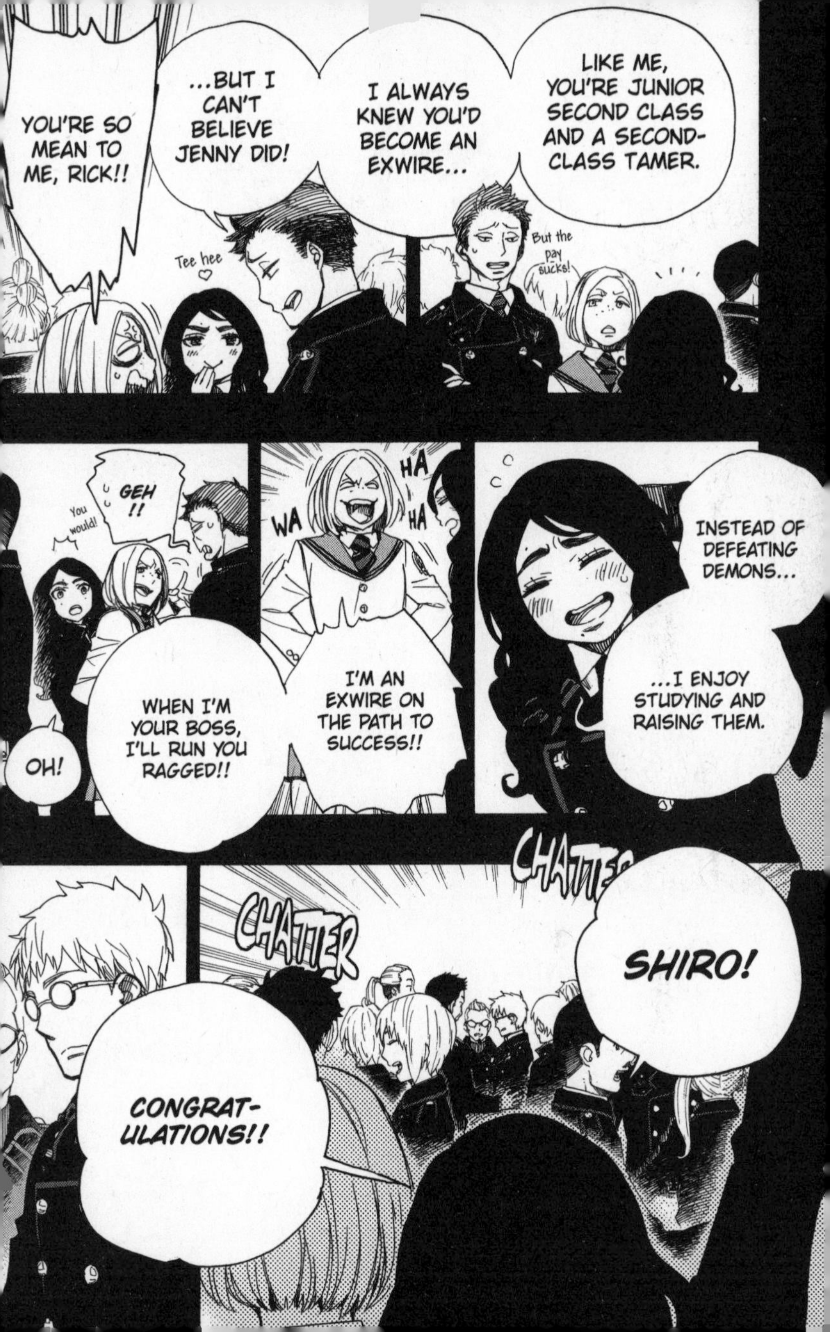
LIKE ME, YOU'RE JUNIOR SECOND CLASS AND A SECOND-CLASS TAMER.
But the pay sucks!
I ALWAYS KNEW YOU'D BECOME AN EXWIRE...
...BUT I CAN'T BELIEVE JENNY DID!
YOU'RE SO MEAN TO ME, RICK!!
Tee hee
INSTEAD OF DEFEATING DEMONS...
...I ENJOY STUDYING AND RAISING THEM.
HA
HA
WA
I'M AN EXWIRE ON THE PATH TO SUCCESS!!
GEH !!
You would!
WHEN I'M YOUR BOSS, I'LL RUN YOU RAGGED!!
OH!
SHIRO!
CHATTER
CONGRAT-ULATIONS!!

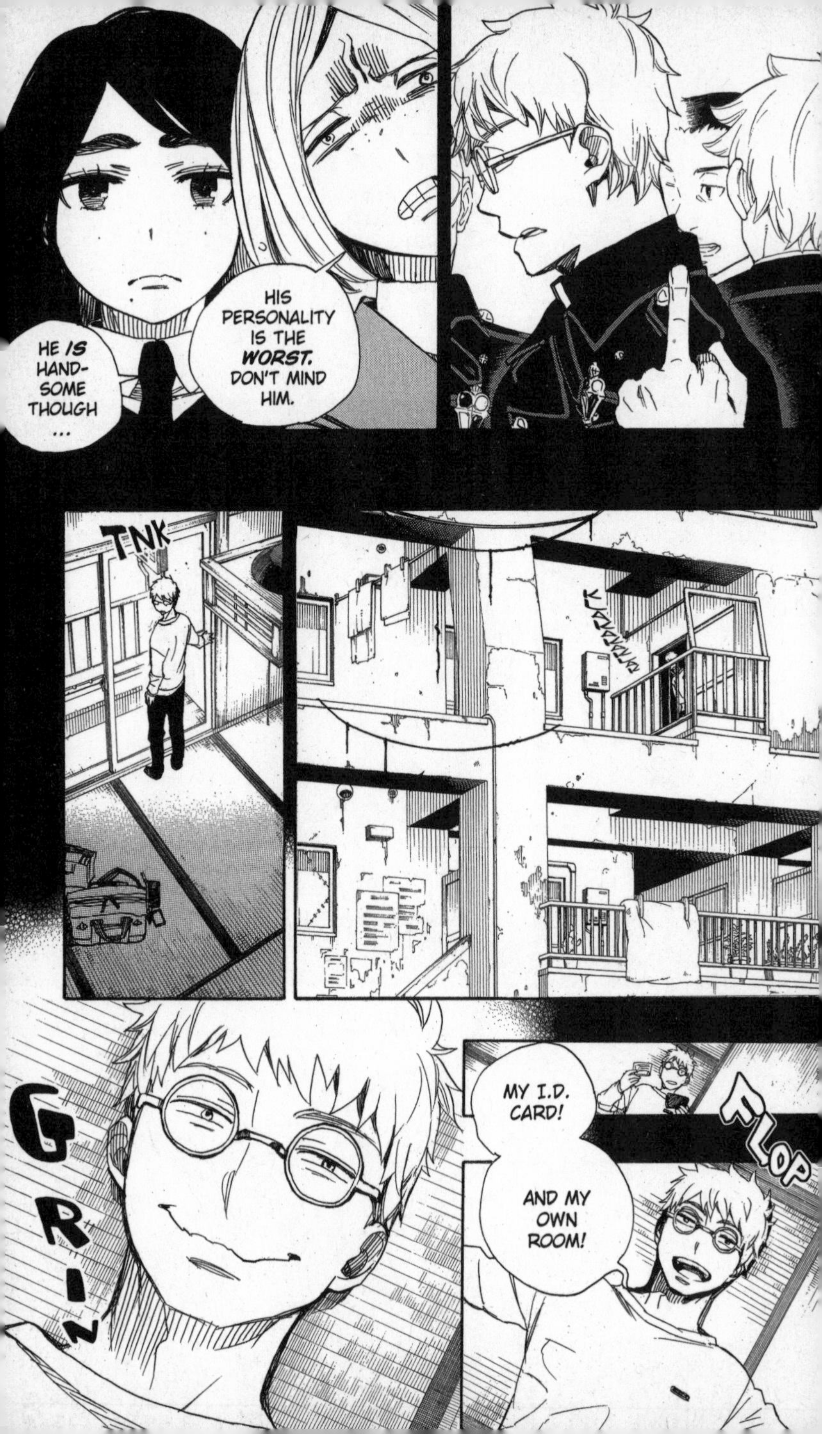
HIS PERSONALITY IS THE WORST. DON'T MIND HIM.
HE IS HANDSOME THOUGH...
TNK
MY I.D. CARD!
AND MY OWN ROOM!
FLOP
GRIN

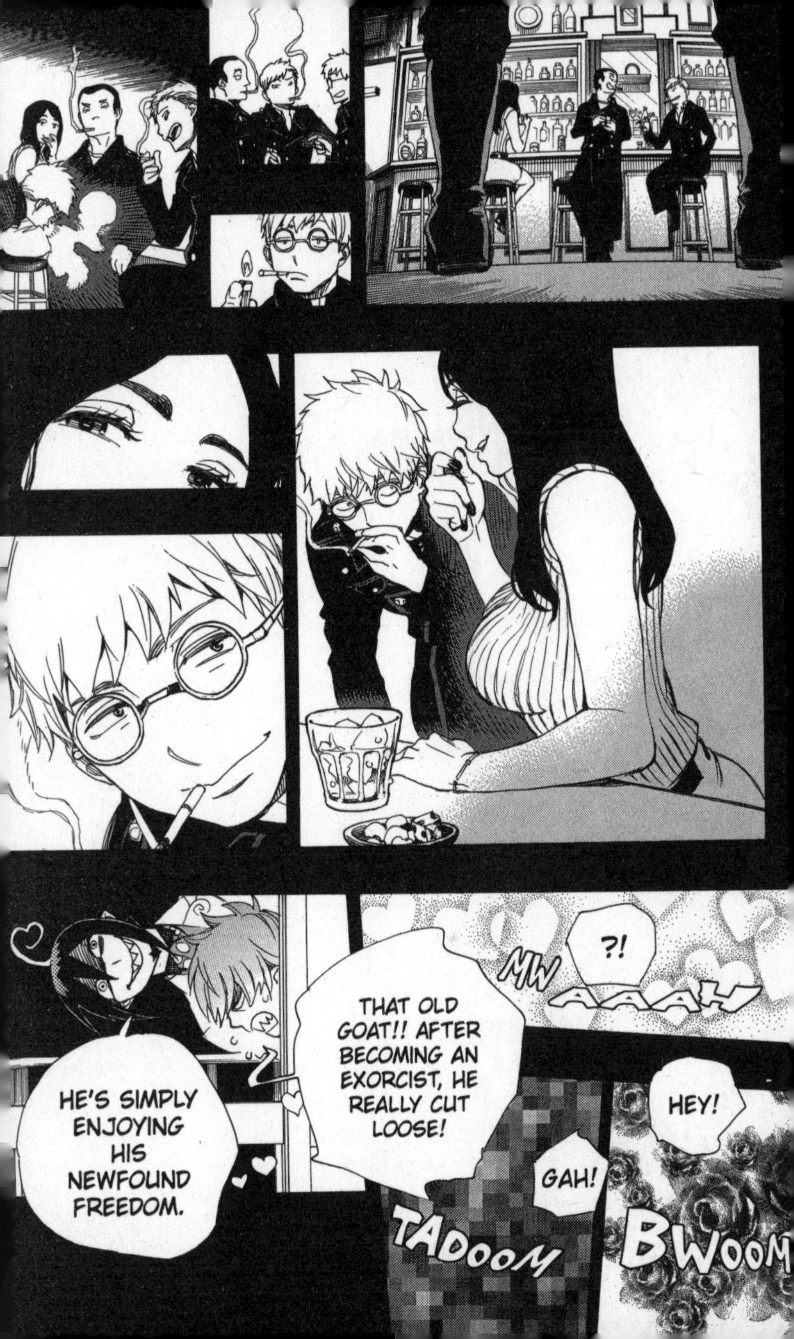
?!
MWAAAH
HEY!
BWOOM
GAH!
TADOOM
THAT OLD GOAT!! AFTER BECOMING AN EXORCIST, HE REALLY CUT LOOSE!
HE'S SIMPLY ENJOYING HIS NEWFOUND FREEDOM.

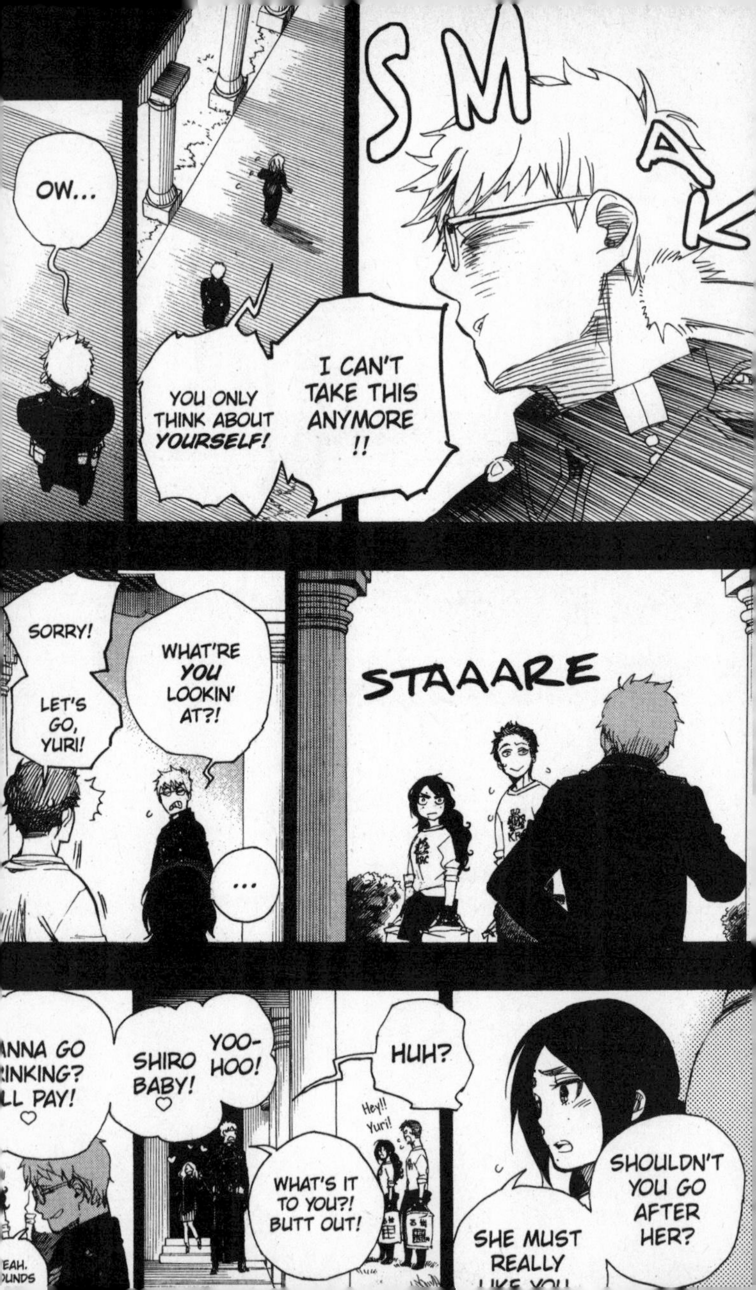
SMAK
I CAN'T TAKE THIS ANYMORE!!
YOU ONLY THINK ABOUT *YOURSELF!*
OW...
STAAARE
WHAT'RE *YOU* LOOKIN' AT?!
SORRY!
LET'S GO, YURI!
...
SHOULDN'T YOU GO AFTER HER?
SHE MUST REALLY LIKE YOU
HUH?
Hey!! Yuri!
WHAT'S IT TO YOU?! BUTT OUT!
YOO-HOO!
SHIRO BABY! ♡
ANNA GO
RINKING?
LL PAY! ♡
EAH.
OUNDS

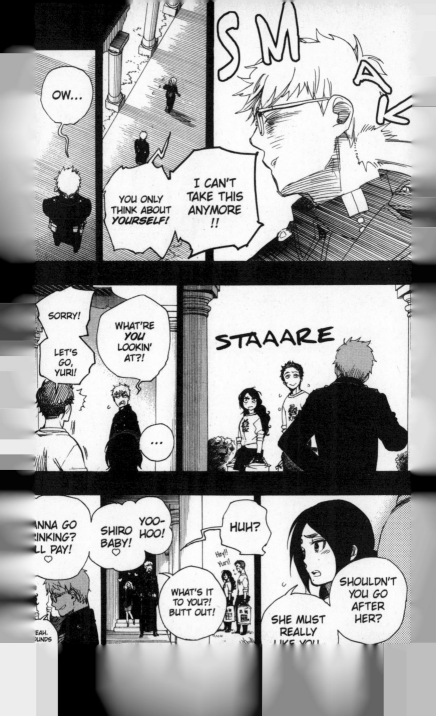

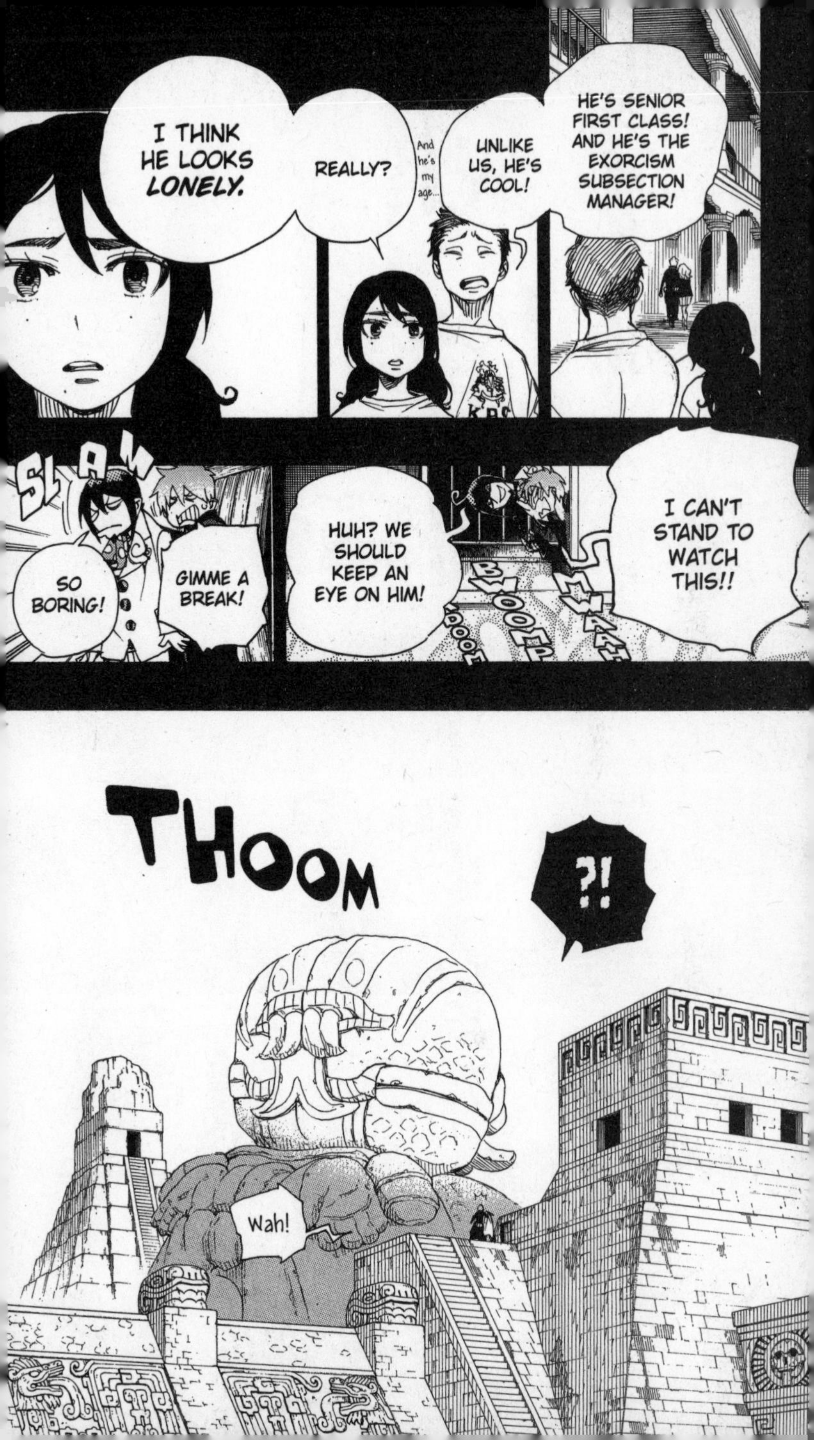
HE'S SENIOR FIRST CLASS! AND HE'S THE EXORCISM SUBSECTION MANAGER!
UNLIKE US, HE'S COOL!
And he's my age...
REALLY?
I THINK HE LOOKS *LONELY.*
I CAN'T STAND TO WATCH THIS!!
BWOOMP
HUH? WE SHOULD KEEP AN EYE ON HIM!
SLAM
GIMME A BREAK!
SO BORING!
THOOM
?!
Wah!

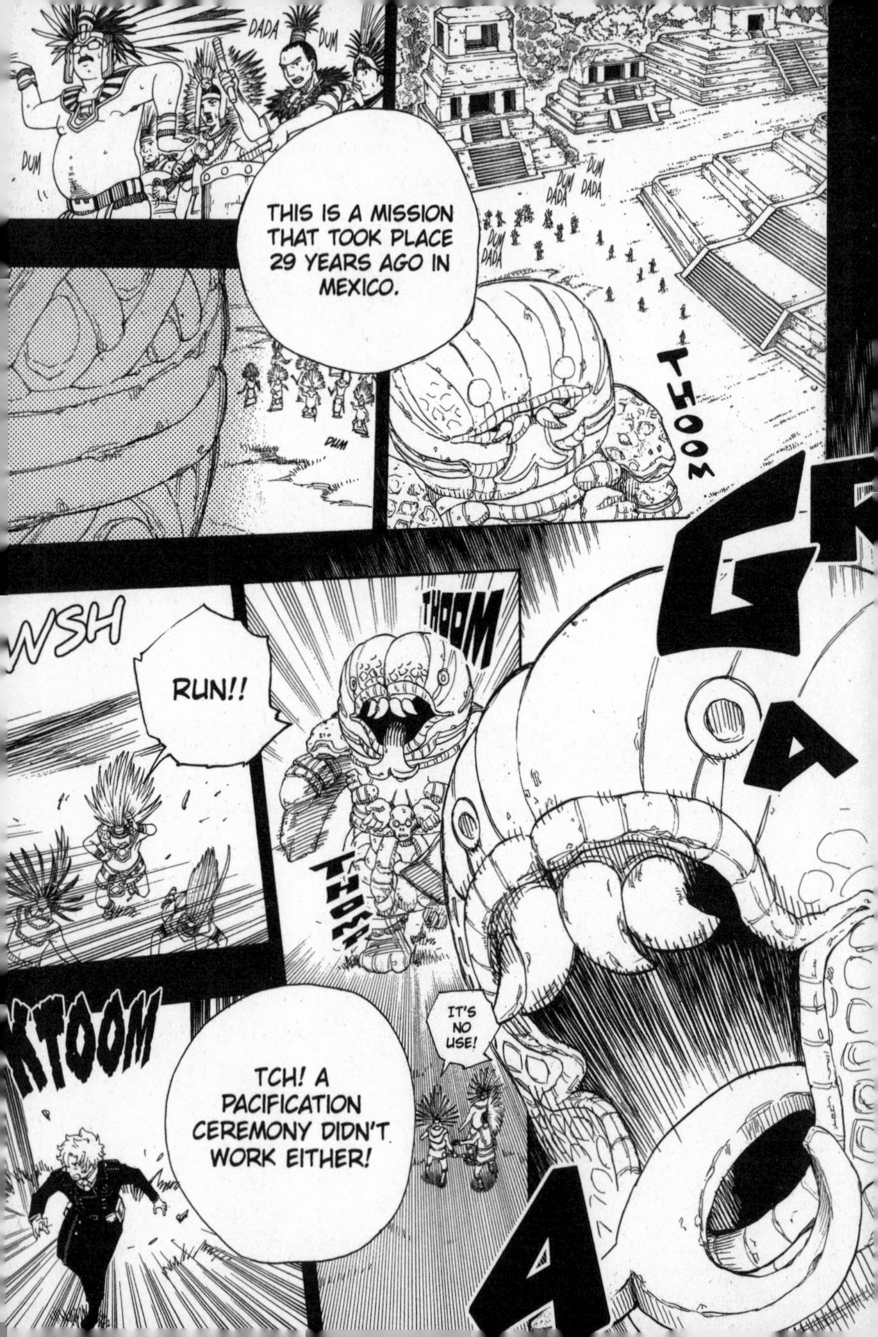
THIS IS A MISSION THAT TOOK PLACE 29 YEARS AGO IN MEXICO.
DUM DADA DUM DADA
DUM DADA
THOOM
DADA DUM
DUM
DUM
GR
A
A
THOOM
THOOM
RUN!!
WSH
IT'S NO USE!
KTOOM
TCH! A PACIFICATION CEREMONY DIDN'T WORK EITHER!

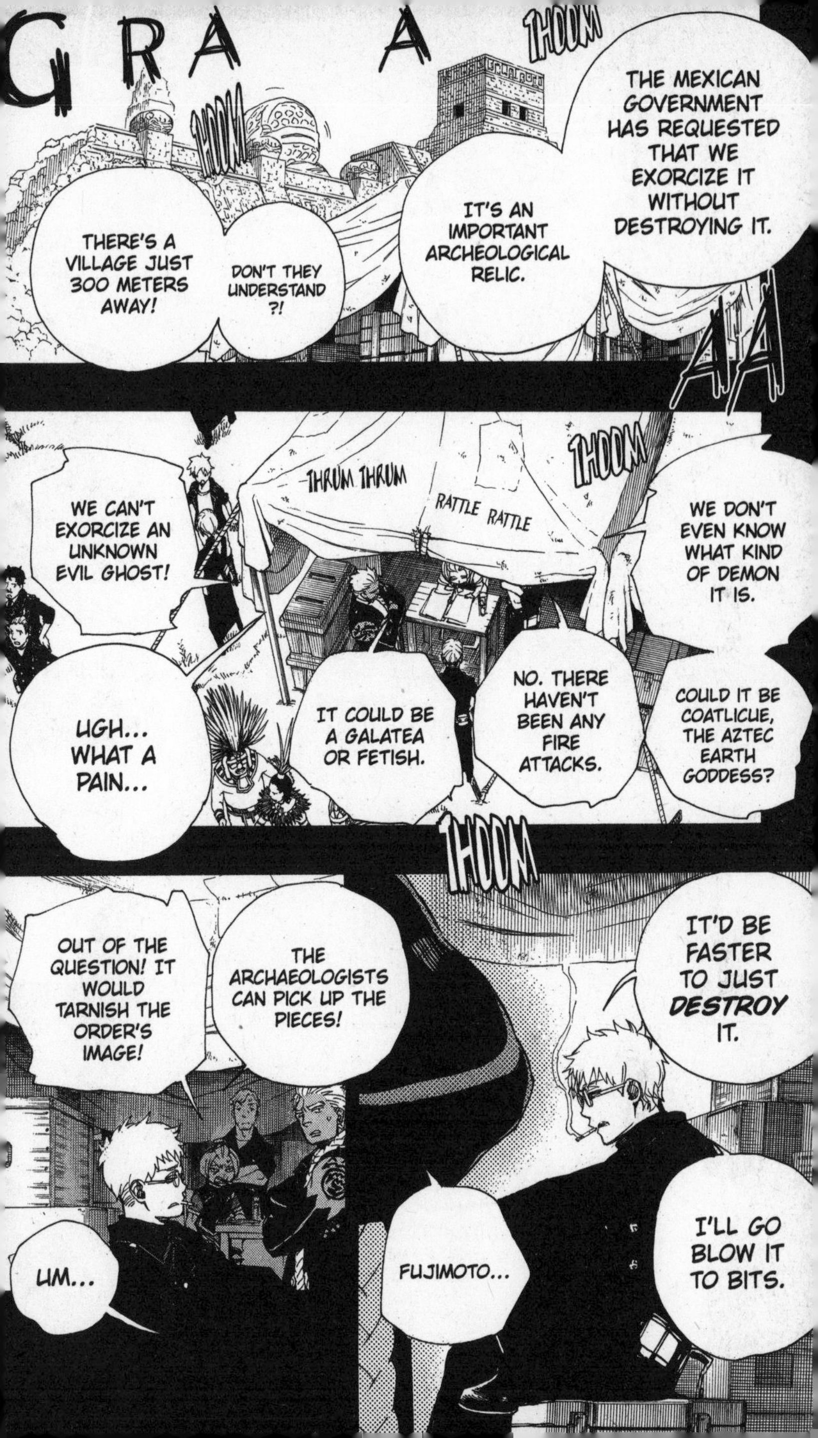
GRAAAA
THOOM
THOOM
THE MEXICAN GOVERNMENT HAS REQUESTED THAT WE EXORCIZE IT WITHOUT DESTROYING IT.
IT'S AN IMPORTANT ARCHEOLOGICAL RELIC.
DON'T THEY UNDERSTAND ?!
THERE'S A VILLAGE JUST 300 METERS AWAY!
THOOM
WE DON'T EVEN KNOW WHAT KIND OF DEMON IT IS.
RATTLE RATTLE
THRUM THRUM
WE CAN'T EXORCIZE AN UNKNOWN EVIL GHOST!
COULD IT BE COATLICUE, THE AZTEC EARTH GODDESS?
NO. THERE HAVEN'T BEEN ANY FIRE ATTACKS.
IT COULD BE A GALATEA OR FETISH.
UGH... WHAT A PAIN...
THOOM
IT'D BE FASTER TO JUST *DESTROY* IT.
I'LL GO BLOW IT TO BITS.
FUJIMOTO...
THE ARCHAEOLOGISTS CAN PICK UP THE PIECES!
OUT OF THE QUESTION! IT WOULD TARNISH THE ORDER'S IMAGE!
UM...

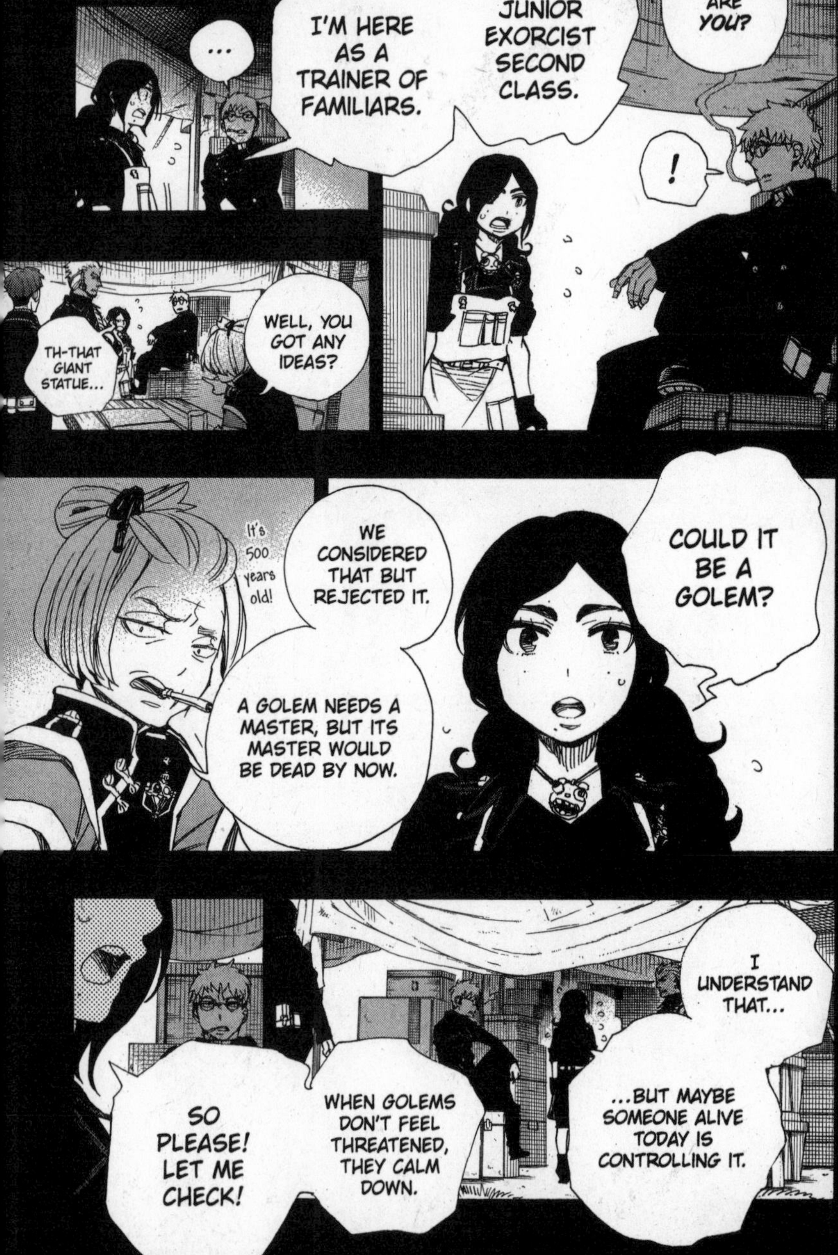
WHO ARE YOU?
YURI EGIN, JUNIOR EXORCIST SECOND CLASS.
I'M HERE AS A TRAINER OF FAMILIARS.
!
...
WELL, YOU GOT ANY IDEAS?
TH-THAT GIANT STATUE...
COULD IT BE A GOLEM?
WE CONSIDERED THAT BUT REJECTED IT.
It's 500 years old!
A GOLEM NEEDS A MASTER, BUT ITS MASTER WOULD BE DEAD BY NOW.
I UNDERSTAND THAT...
...BUT MAYBE SOMEONE ALIVE TODAY IS CONTROLLING IT.
WHEN GOLEMS DON'T FEEL THREATENED, THEY CALM DOWN.
SO PLEASE! LET ME CHECK!

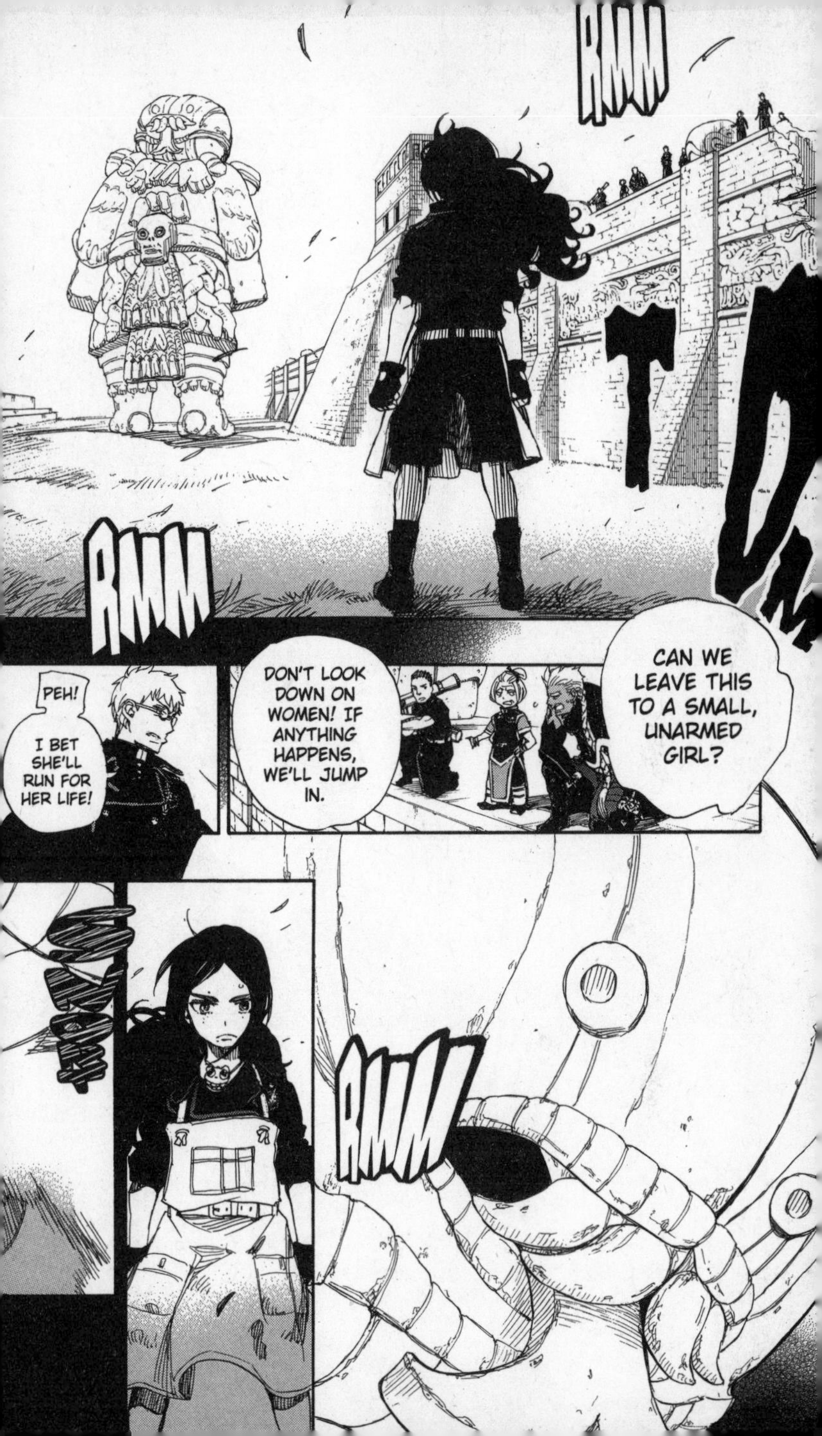
RMM
RMM
CAN WE LEAVE THIS TO A SMALL, UNARMED GIRL?
DON'T LOOK DOWN ON WOMEN! IF ANYTHING HAPPENS, WE'LL JUMP IN.
PEH!
I BET SHE'LL RUN FOR HER LIFE!
RMM

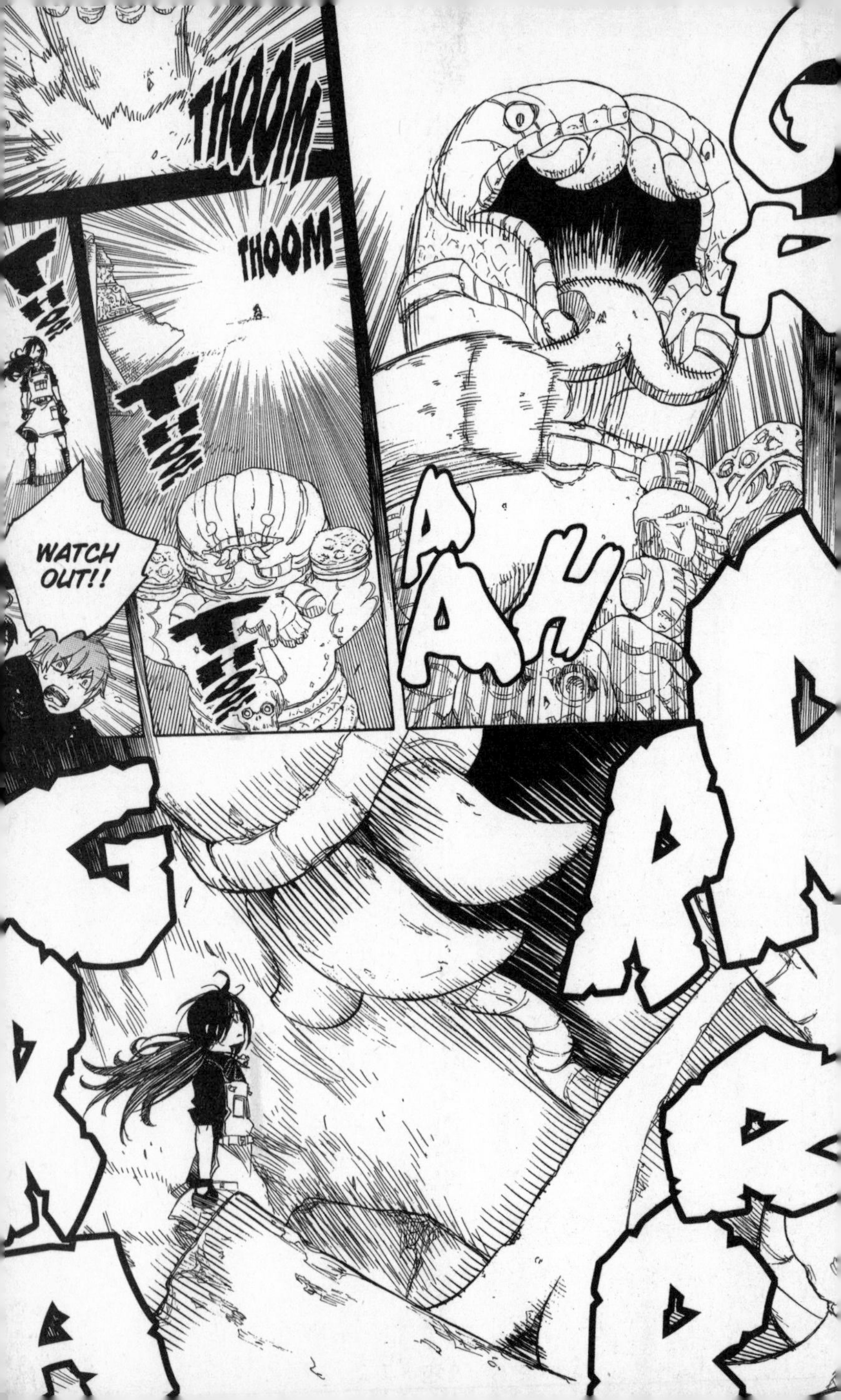
THOOM
THOOM
THOOM
THOOM
WATCH OUT!!
THOOM

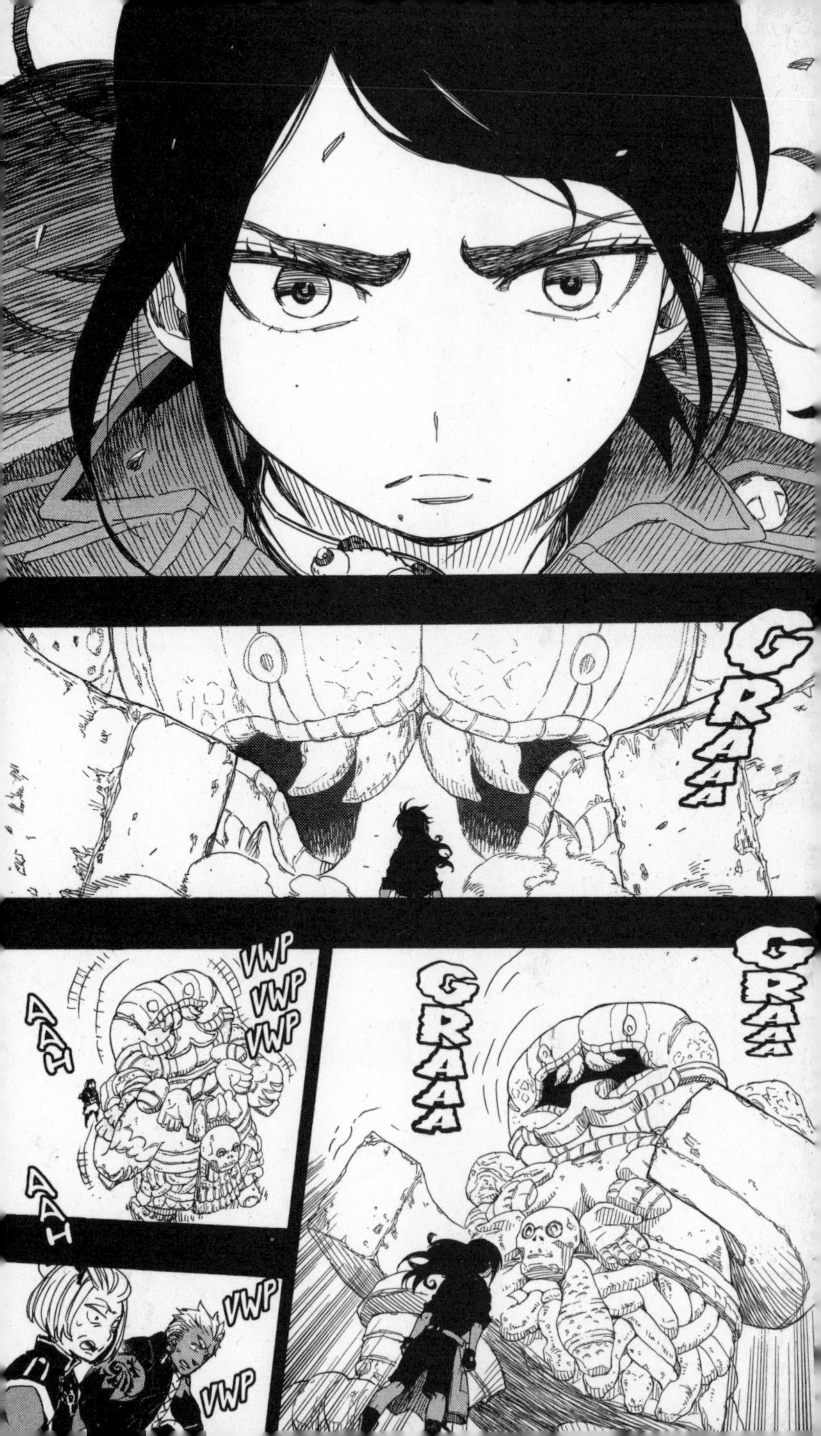
GRAAAA
GRAAA
GRAAAA
VWP
VWP
VWP
AAH
AAH
VWP
VWP

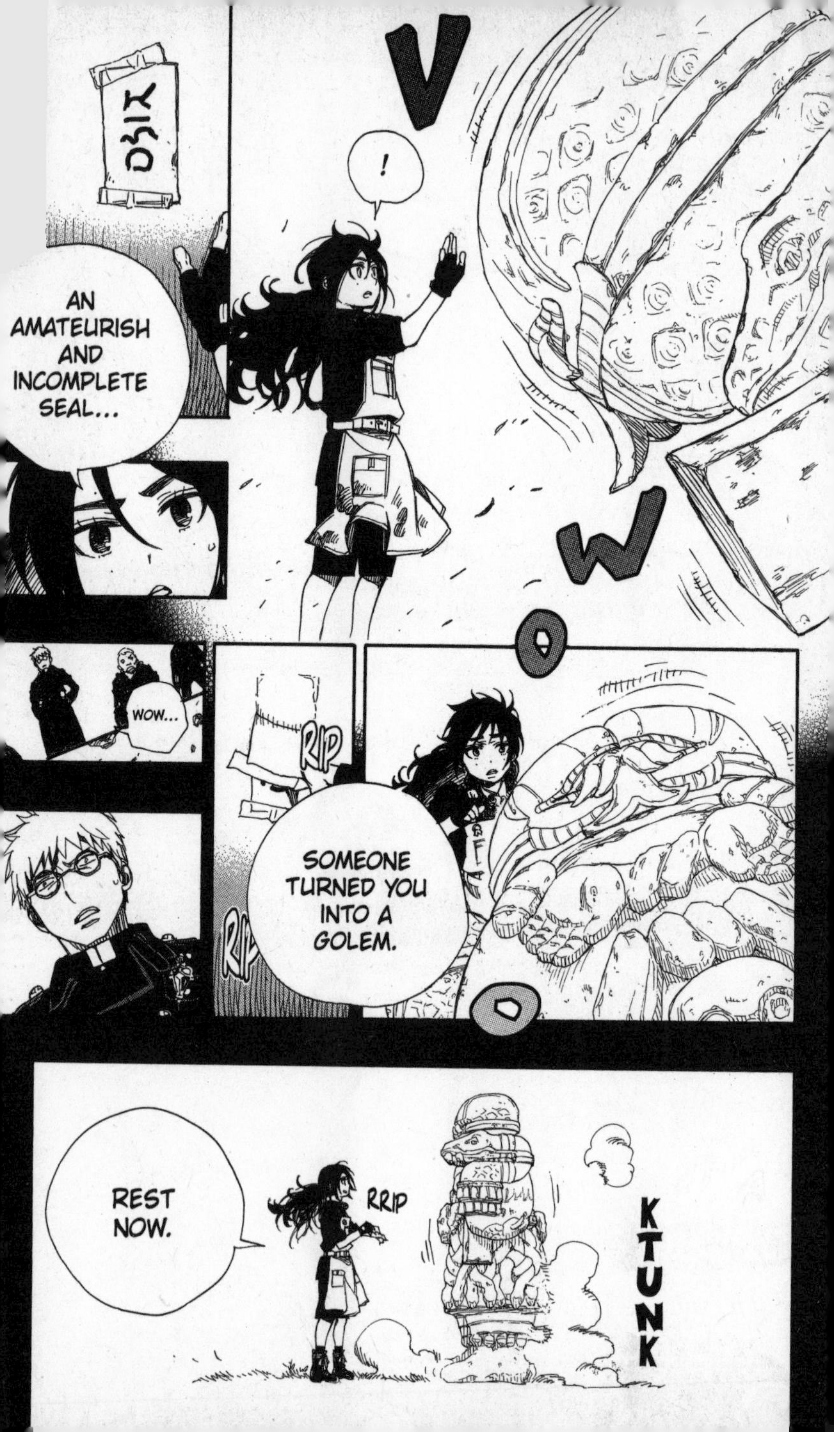

V
!
W
O
AN AMATEURISH AND INCOMPLETE SEAL...
O
SOMEONE TURNED YOU INTO A GOLEM.
RIP
RIP
WOW...
KTUNK
RRIP
REST NOW.

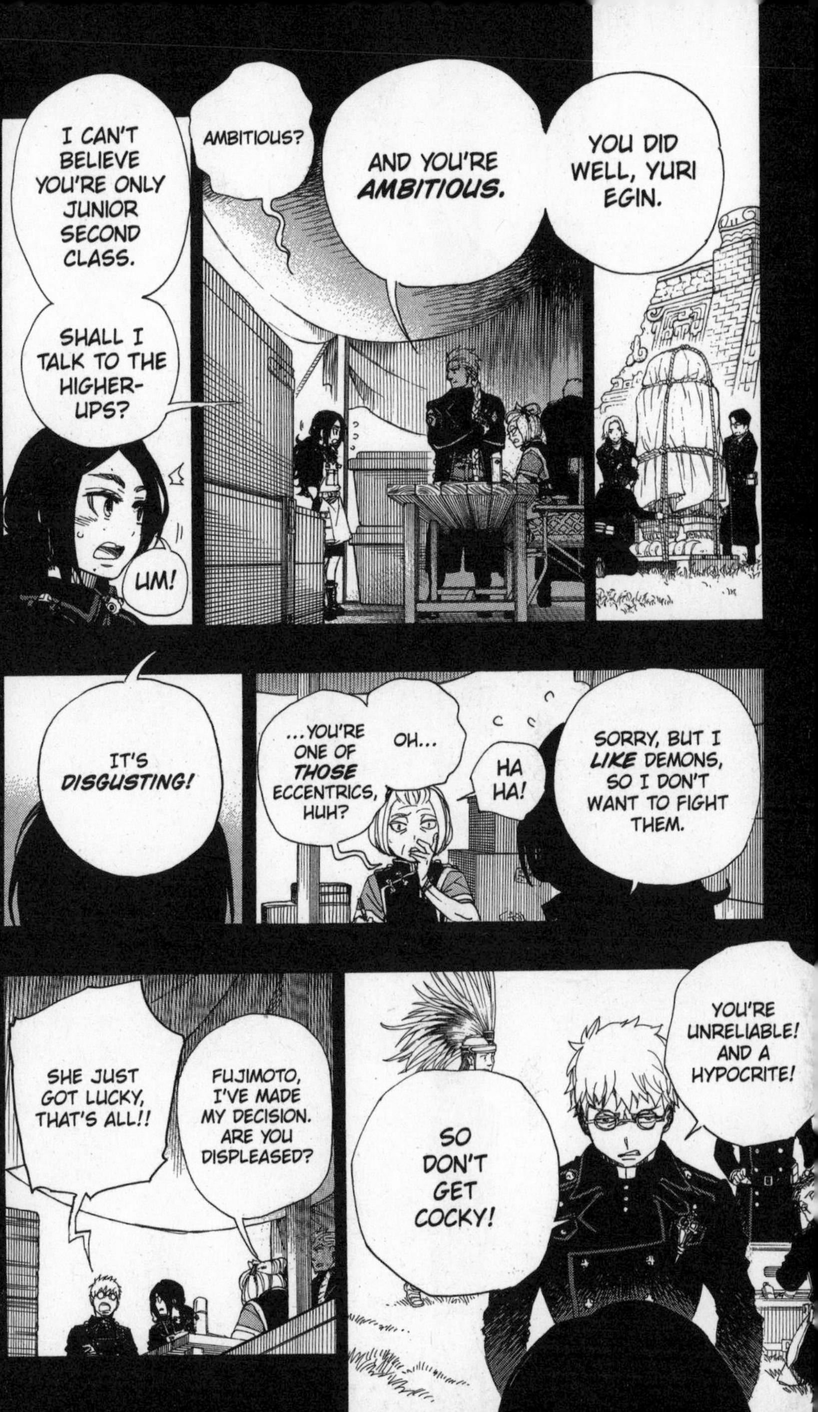
YOU DID WELL, YURI EGIN.
AND YOU'RE *AMBITIOUS.*
AMBITIOUS?
I CAN'T BELIEVE YOU'RE ONLY JUNIOR SECOND CLASS.
SHALL I TALK TO THE HIGHER-UPS?
UM!
SORRY, BUT I *LIKE* DEMONS, SO I DON'T WANT TO FIGHT THEM.
HA HA!
OH...
...YOU'RE ONE OF *THOSE* ECCENTRICS, HUH?
IT'S *DISGUSTING!*
YOU'RE UNRELIABLE! AND A HYPOCRITE!
SO DON'T GET COCKY!
FUJIMOTO, I'VE MADE MY DECISION. ARE YOU DISPLEASED?
SHE JUST GOT LUCKY, THAT'S ALL!!

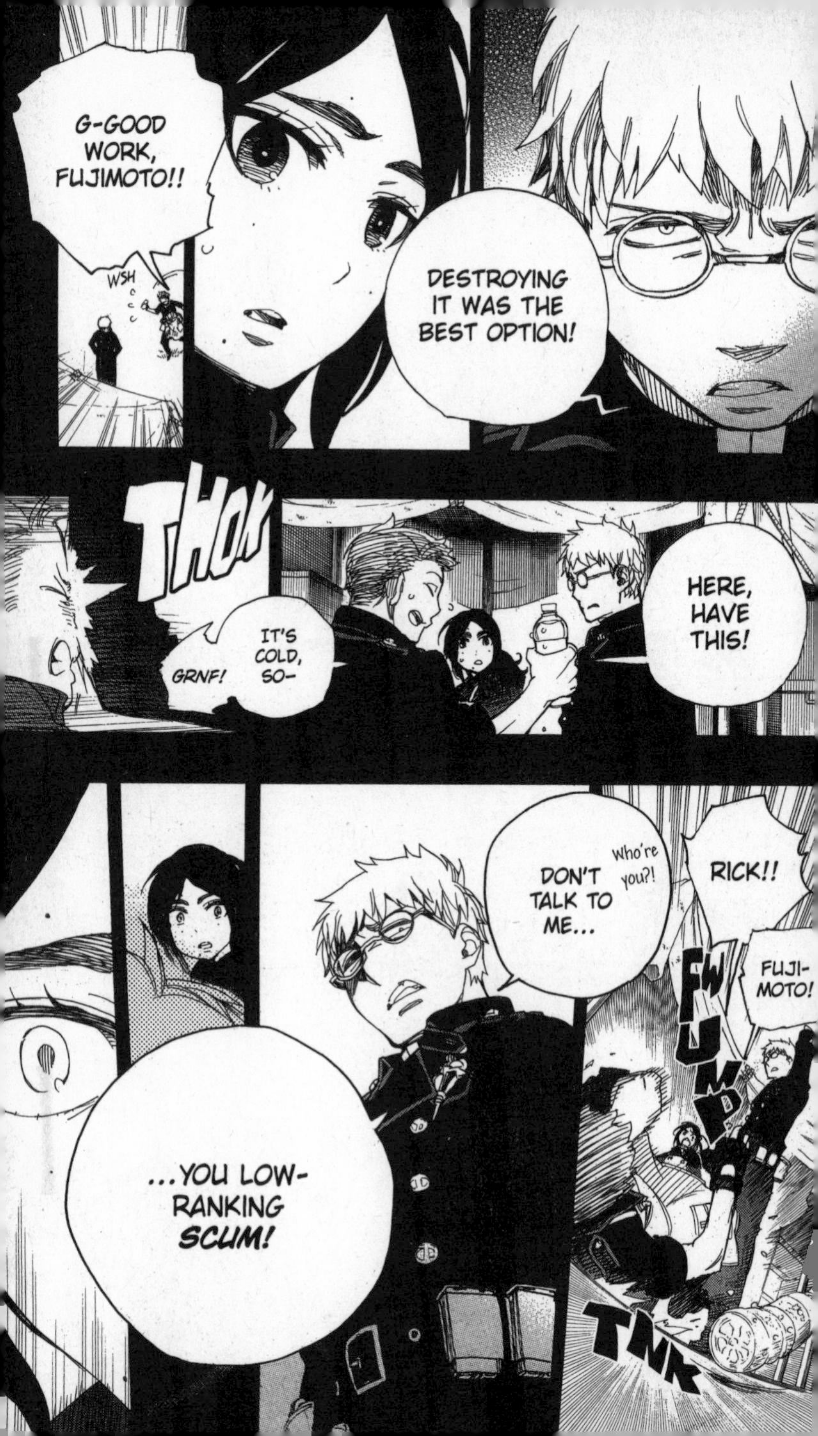
DESTROYING IT WAS THE BEST OPTION!
G-GOOD WORK, FUJIMOTO!!
WSH
HERE, HAVE THIS!
IT'S COLD, SO-
THOK
GRNF!
RICK!!
FUJI-MOTO!
FWUMP
TNK
Who're you?!
DON'T TALK TO ME...
...YOU LOW-RANKING SCUM!

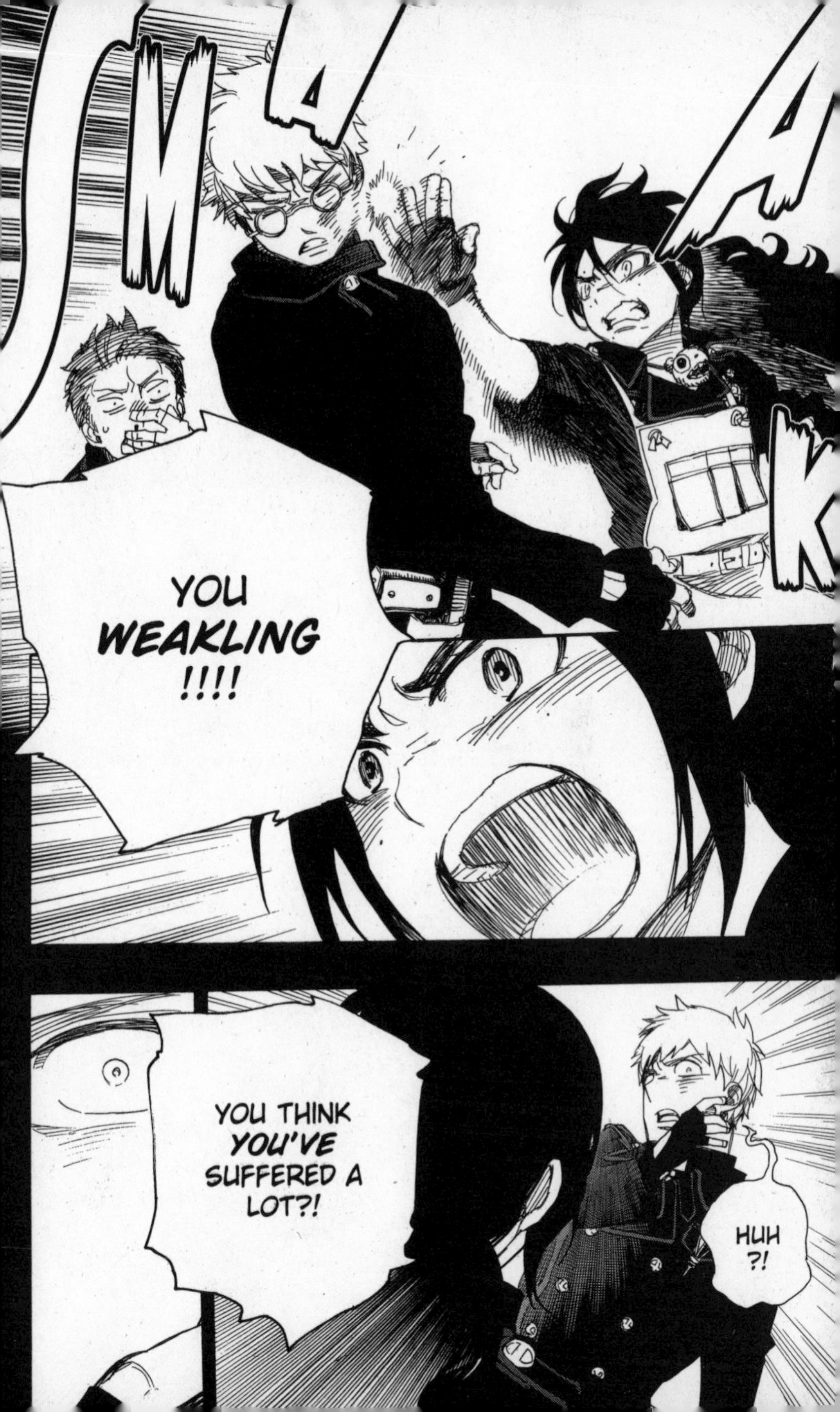
YOU WEAKLING !!!!
YOU THINK YOU'VE SUFFERED A LOT?!
HUH ?!

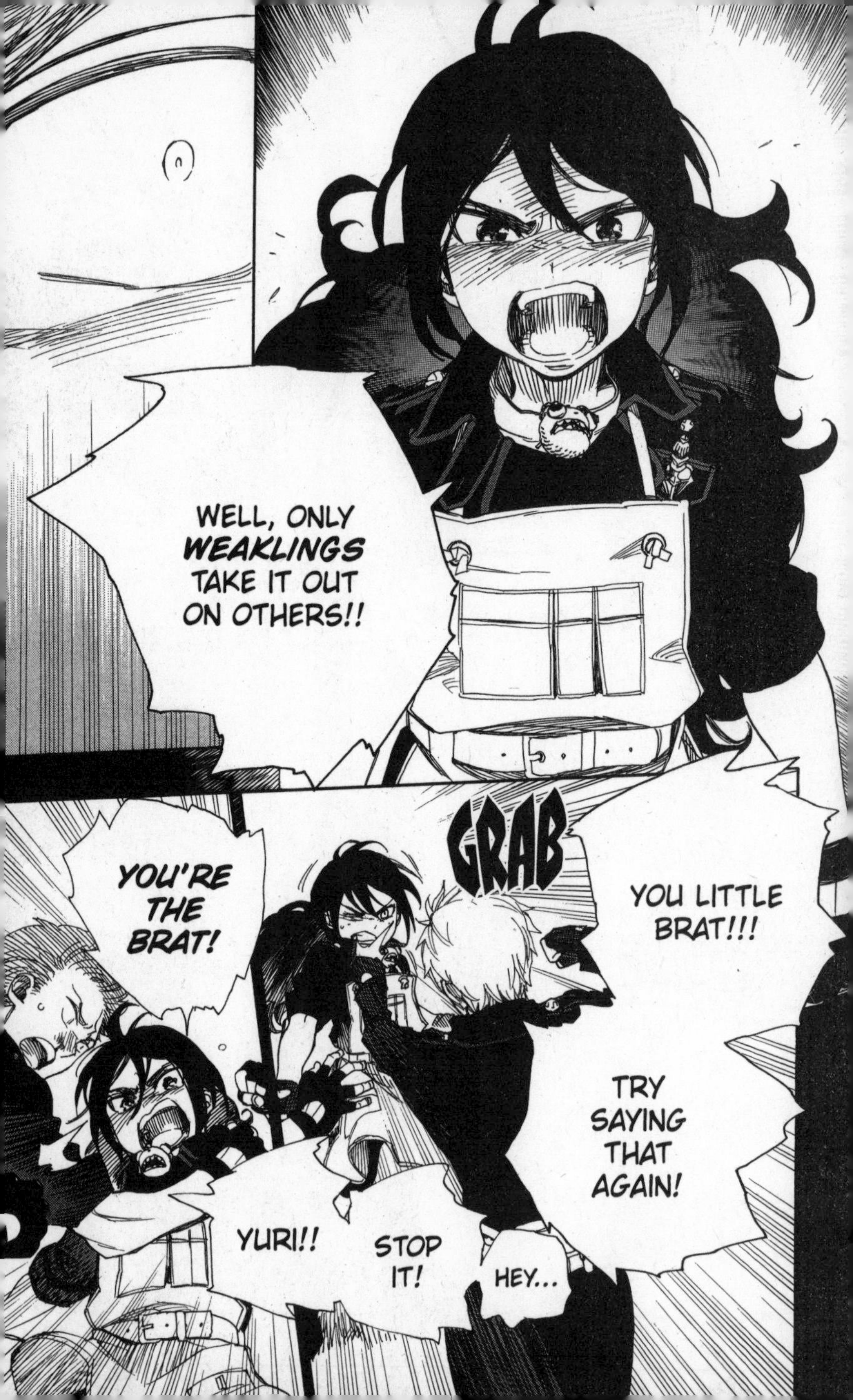
WELL, ONLY WEAKLINGS TAKE IT OUT ON OTHERS!!
YOU LITTLE BRAT!!!
GRAB
TRY SAYING THAT AGAIN!
YOU'RE THE BRAT!
HEY...
STOP IT!
YURI!!

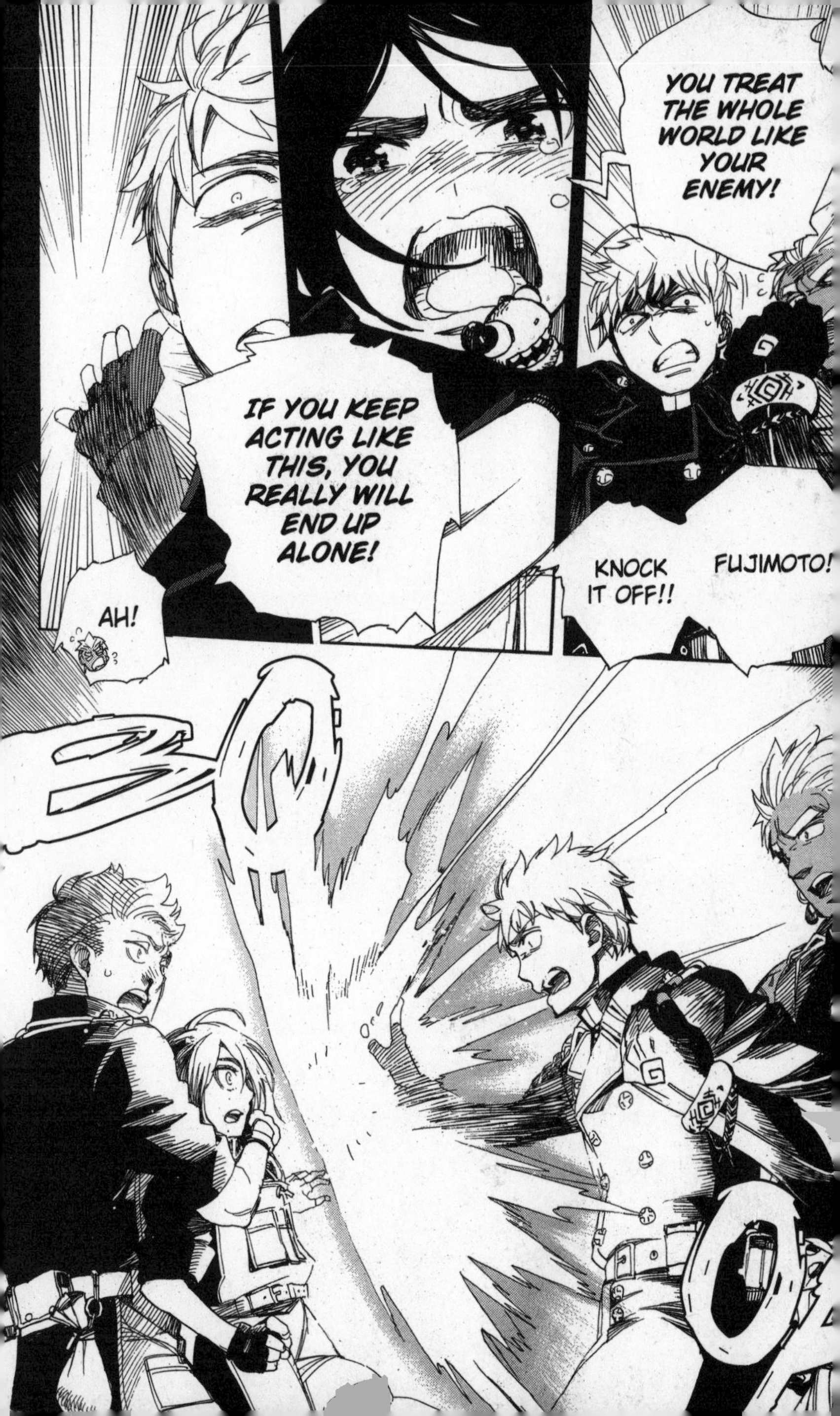
YOU TREAT THE WHOLE WORLD LIKE YOUR ENEMY!
IF YOU KEEP ACTING LIKE THIS, YOU REALLY WILL END UP ALONE!
FUJIMOTO!
KNOCK IT OFF!!
AH!

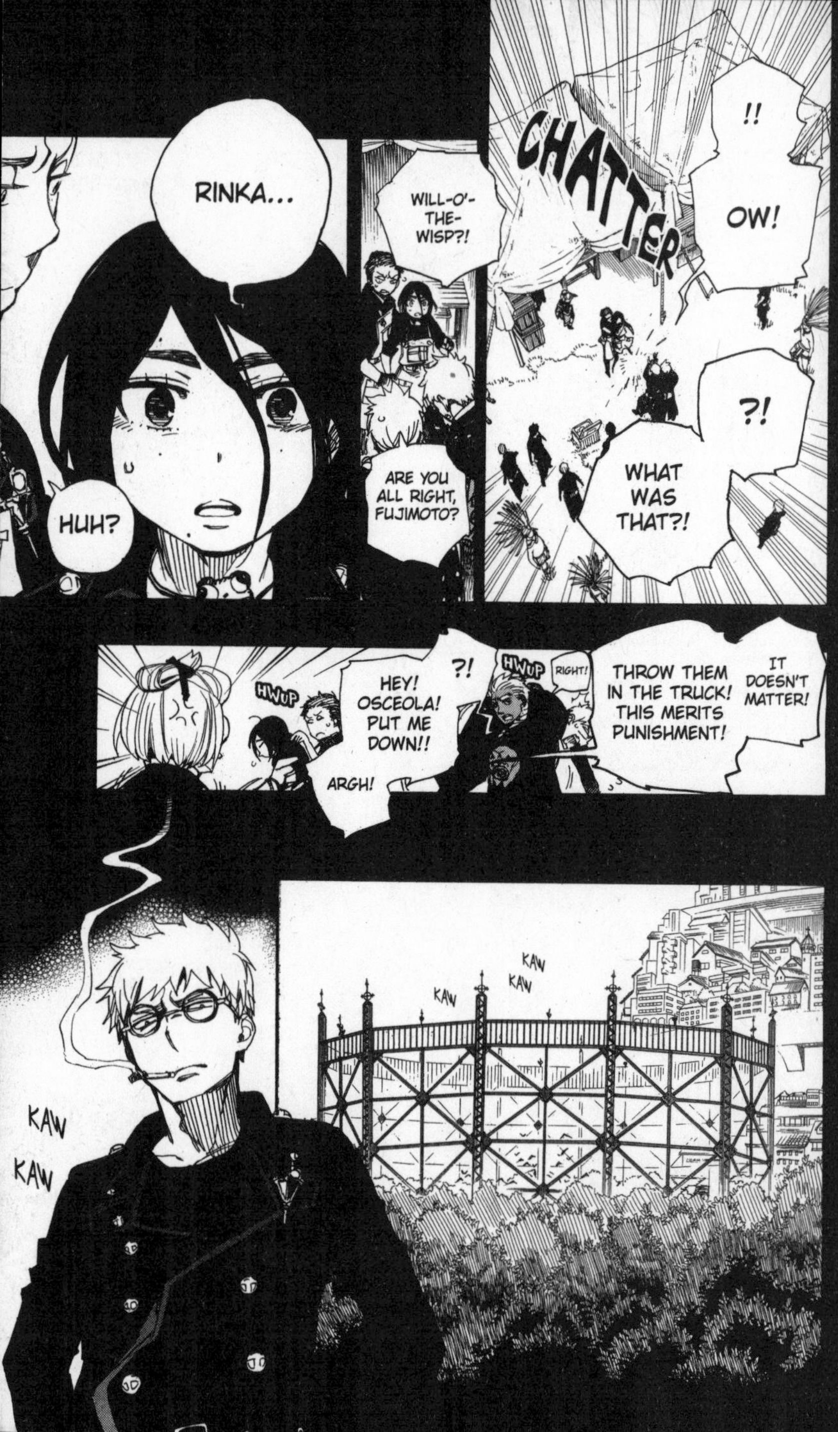
!!
OW!
CHATTER
?!
WHAT WAS THAT?!
WILL-O'-THE-WISP?!
ARE YOU ALL RIGHT, FUJIMOTO?
RINKA...
HUH?
IT DOESN'T MATTER!
THROW THEM IN THE TRUCK! THIS MERITS PUNISHMENT!
RIGHT!
HWUP
?!
HEY! OSCEOLA! PUT ME DOWN!!
HWUP
ARGH!
KAW
KAW
KAW
KAW
KAW

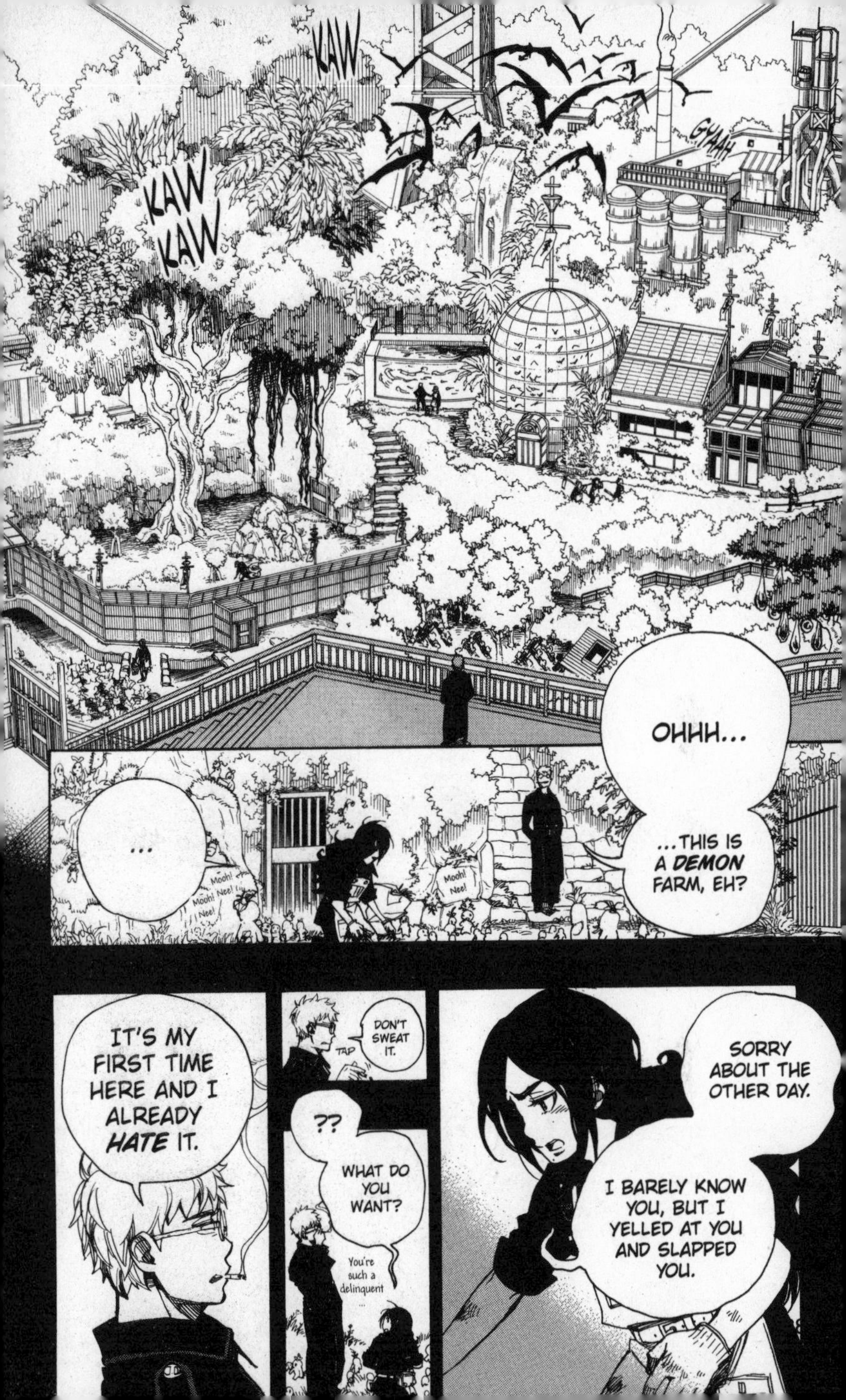
GYAAH
KAW
KAW KAW
OHHH...
...THIS IS A *DEMON* FARM, EH?
Mooh! Nee!
Mooh! Nee! Mooh! Nee!
...
SORRY ABOUT THE OTHER DAY.
I BARELY KNOW YOU, BUT I YELLED AT YOU AND SLAPPED YOU.
DON'T SWEAT IT.
TAP
??
WHAT DO YOU WANT?
You're such a delinquent ...
IT'S MY FIRST TIME HERE AND I ALREADY *HATE* IT.

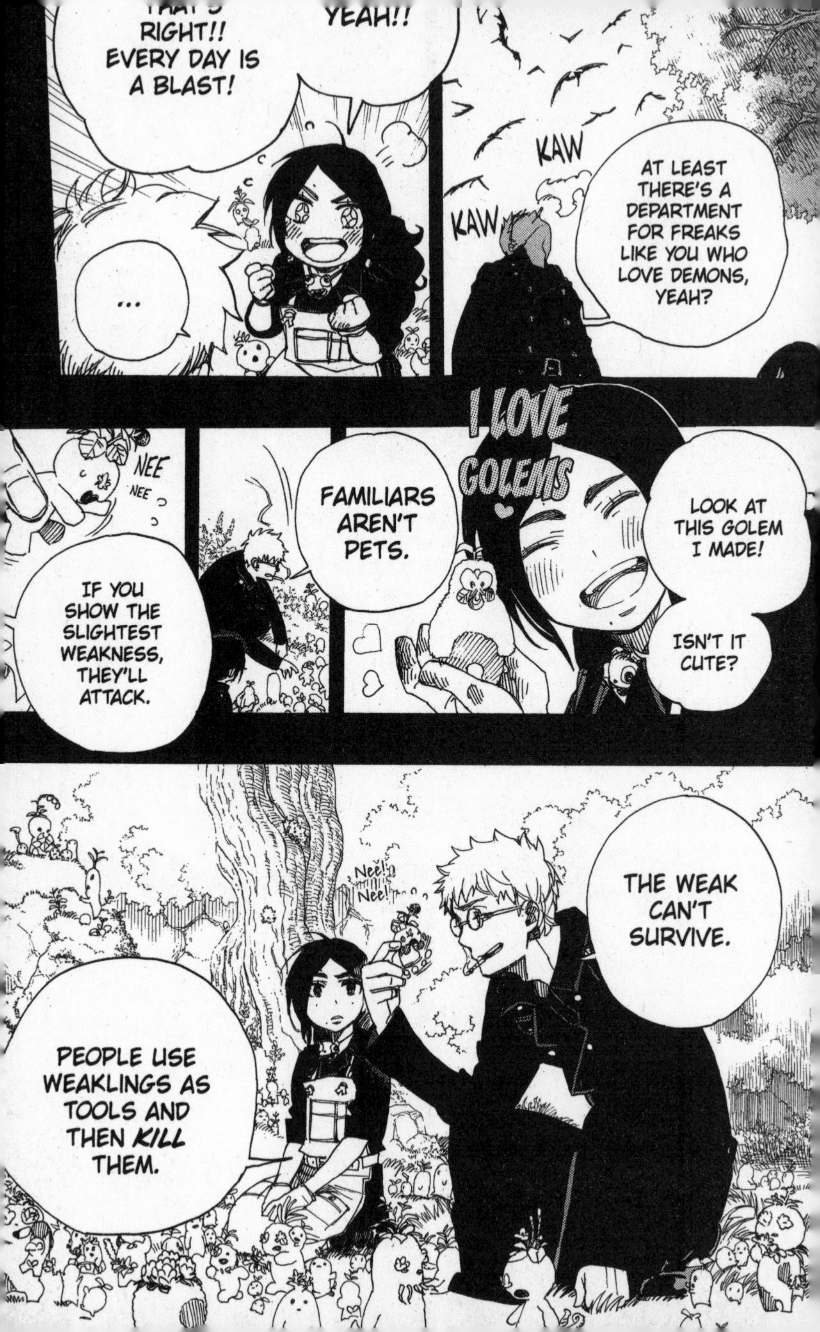
KAW
KAW
AT LEAST THERE'S A DEPARTMENT FOR FREAKS LIKE YOU WHO LOVE DEMONS, YEAH?
RIGHT!! EVERY DAY IS A BLAST!
YEAH!!
...
I LOVE GOLEMS
LOOK AT THIS GOLEM I MADE!
ISN'T IT CUTE?
FAMILIARS AREN'T PETS.
NEE NEE
IF YOU SHOW THE SLIGHTEST WEAKNESS, THEY'LL ATTACK.
THE WEAK CAN'T SURVIVE.
Nee! Nee!
PEOPLE USE WEAKLINGS AS TOOLS AND THEN KILL THEM.

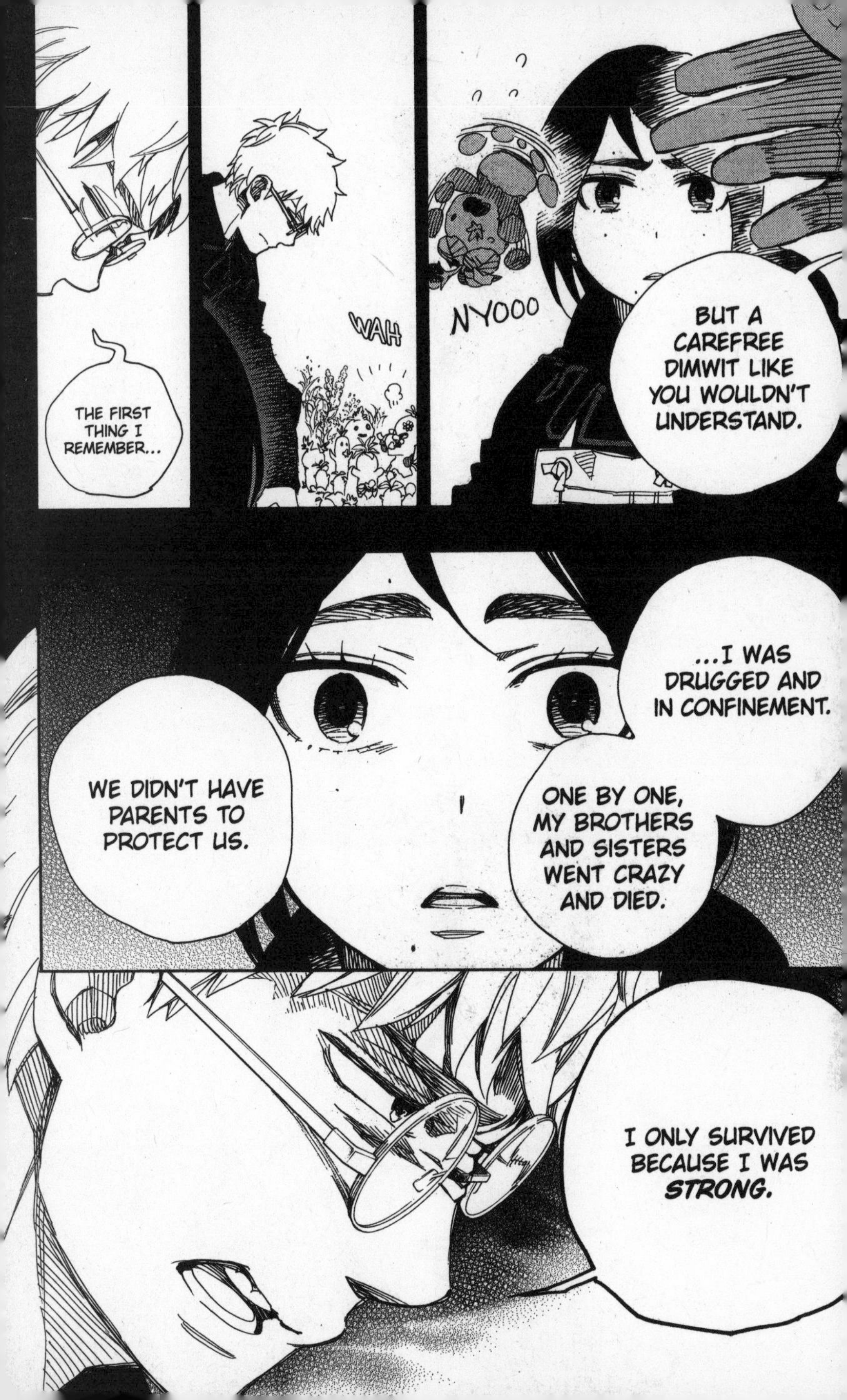
NYOOO
BUT A CAREFREE DIMWIT LIKE YOU WOULDN'T UNDERSTAND.
WAH
THE FIRST THING I REMEMBER...
...I WAS DRUGGED AND IN CONFINEMENT.
ONE BY ONE, MY BROTHERS AND SISTERS WENT CRAZY AND DIED.
WE DIDN'T HAVE PARENTS TO PROTECT US.
I ONLY SURVIVED BECAUSE I WAS *STRONG.*

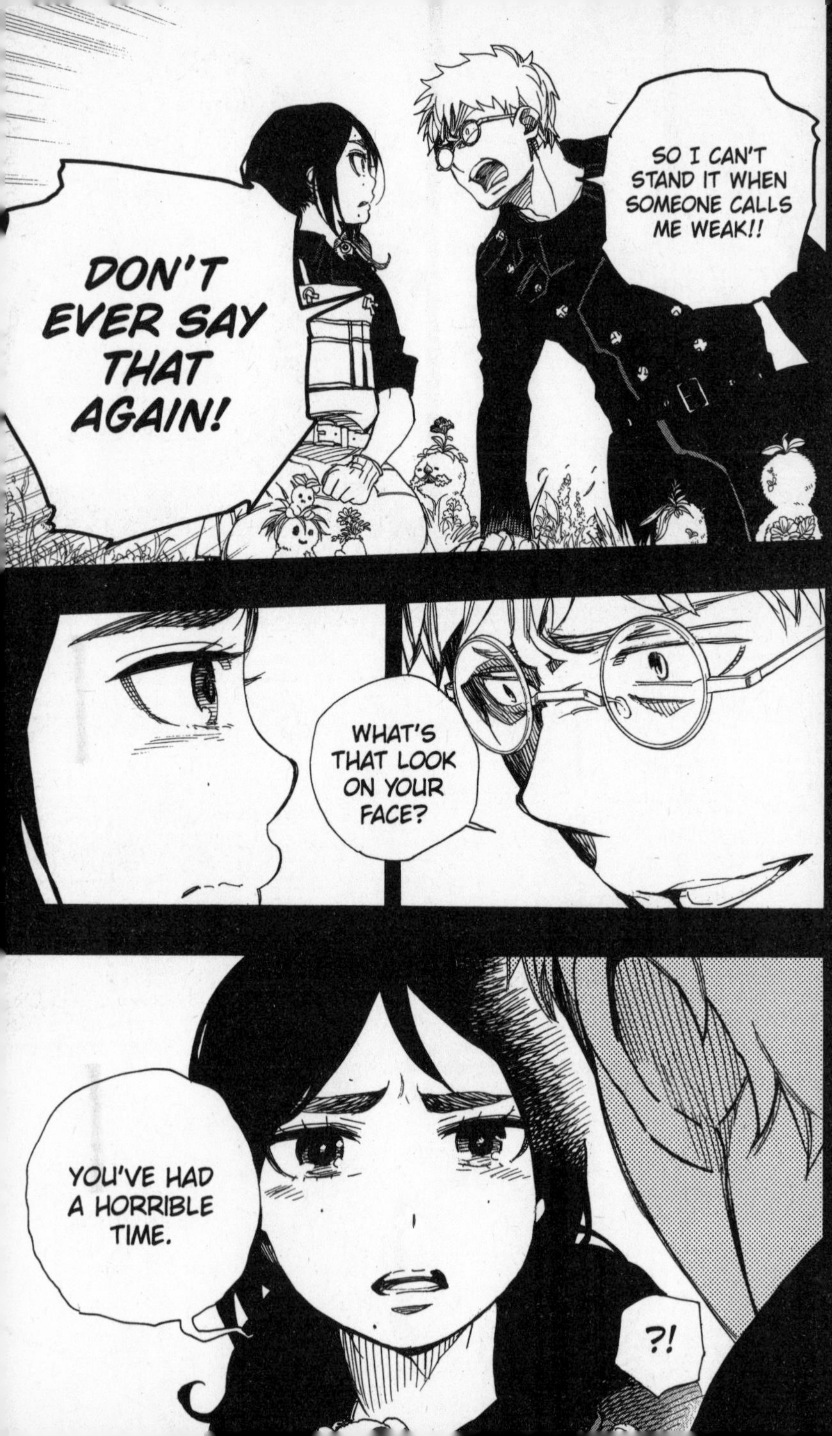
SO I CAN'T STAND IT WHEN SOMEONE CALLS ME WEAK!!
DON'T EVER SAY THAT AGAIN!
WHAT'S THAT LOOK ON YOUR FACE?
YOU'VE HAD A HORRIBLE TIME.
?!

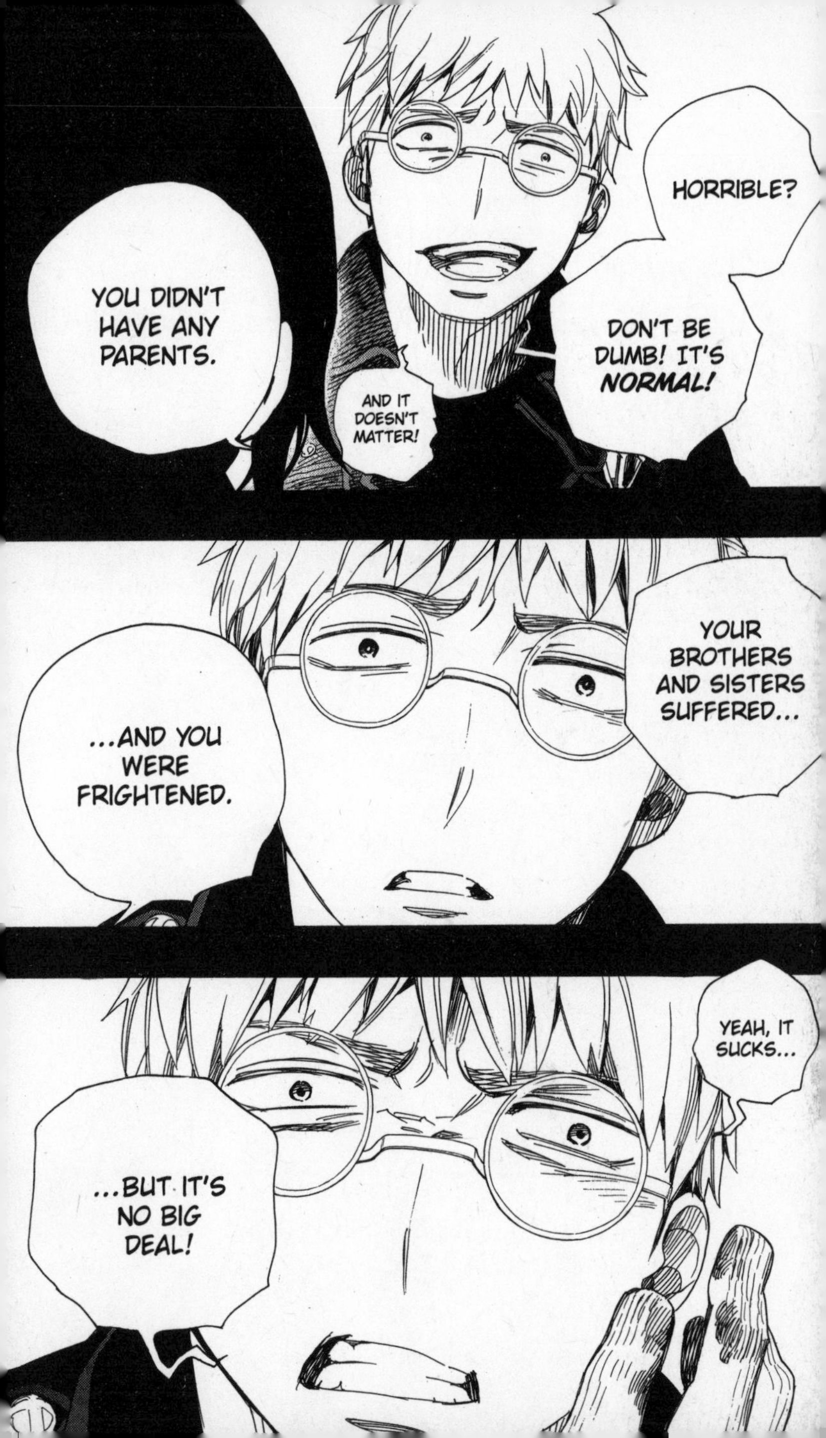
HORRIBLE?
DON'T BE DUMB! IT'S *NORMAL!*
AND IT DOESN'T MATTER!
YOU DIDN'T HAVE ANY PARENTS.
YOUR BROTHERS AND SISTERS SUFFERED...
...AND YOU WERE FRIGHTENED.
YEAH, IT SUCKS...
...BUT IT'S NO BIG DEAL!

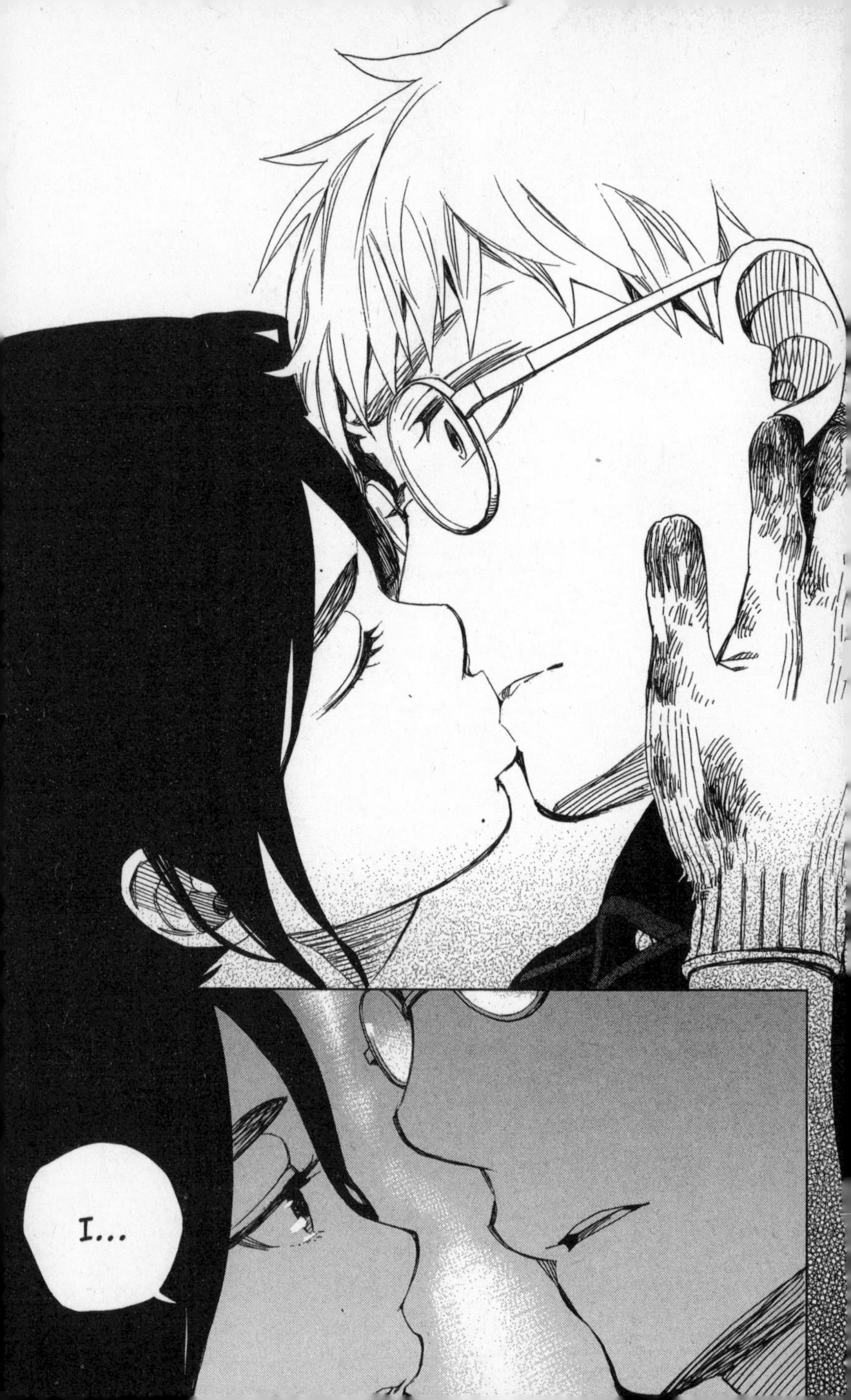
I...

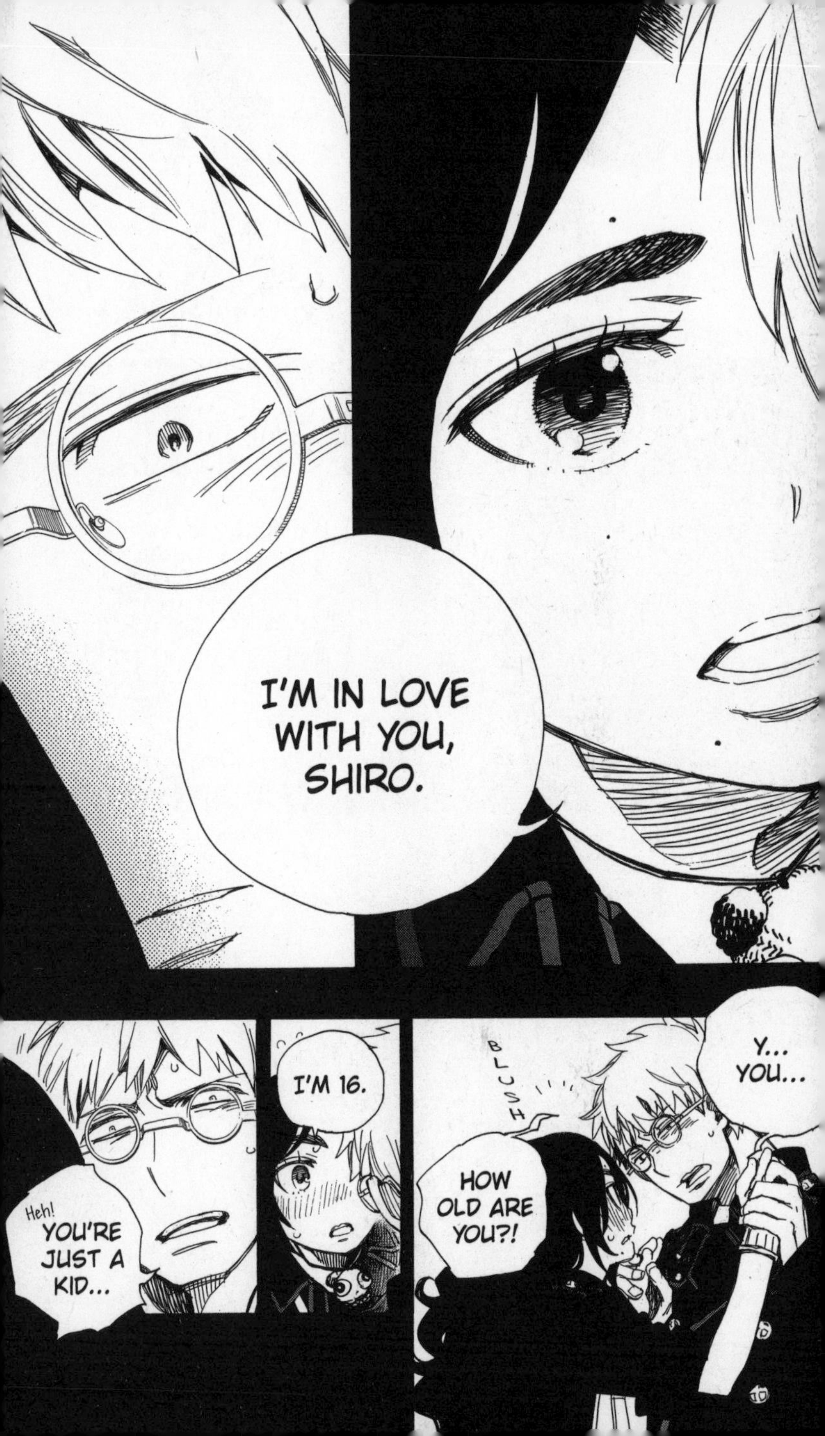
I'M IN LOVE WITH YOU, SHIRO.
Y... YOU...
BLUSH
HOW OLD ARE YOU?!
I'M 16.
Heh!
YOU'RE JUST A KID...

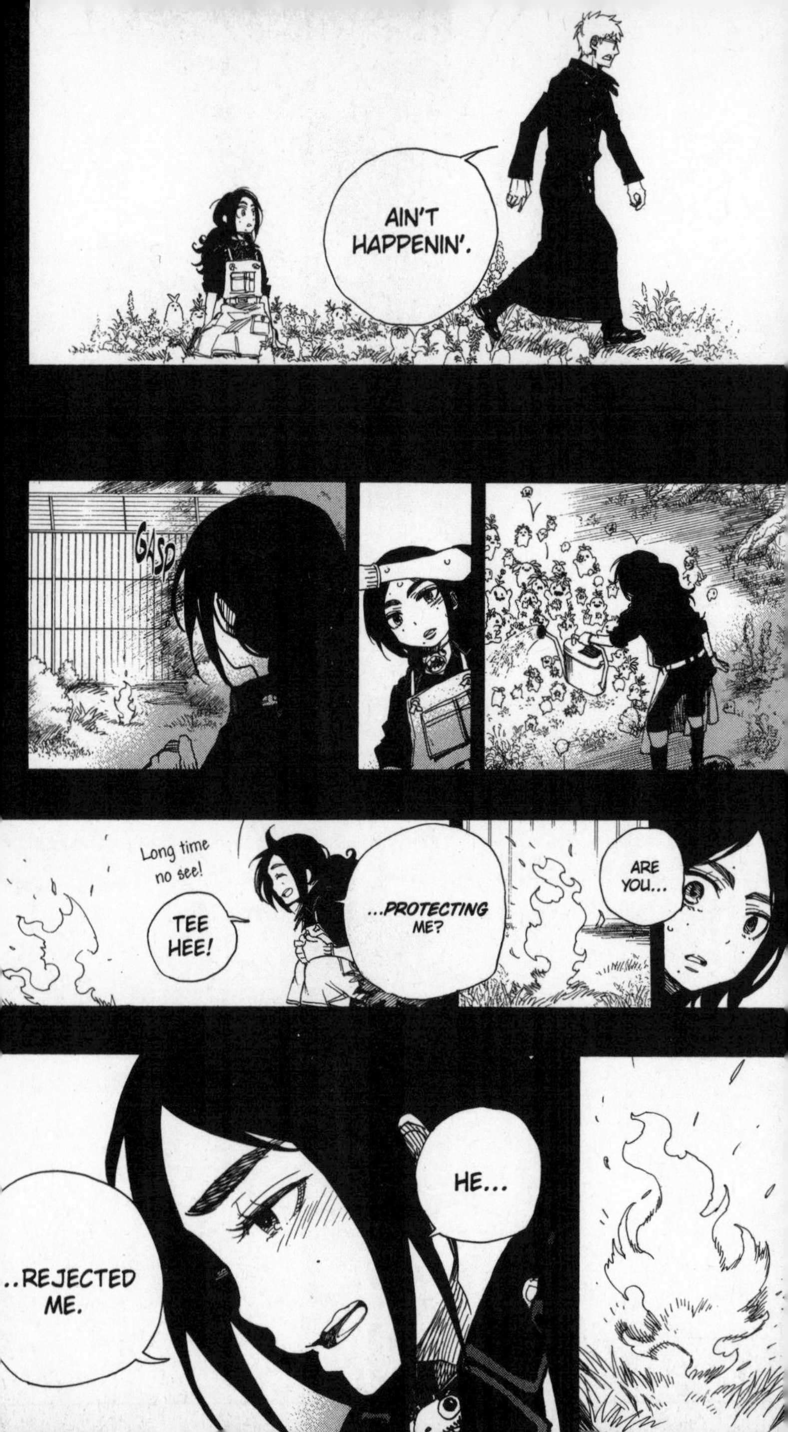
AIN'T HAPPENIN'.
GASP
ARE YOU...
...PROTECTING ME?
Long time no see!
TEE HEE!
HE...
..REJECTED ME.

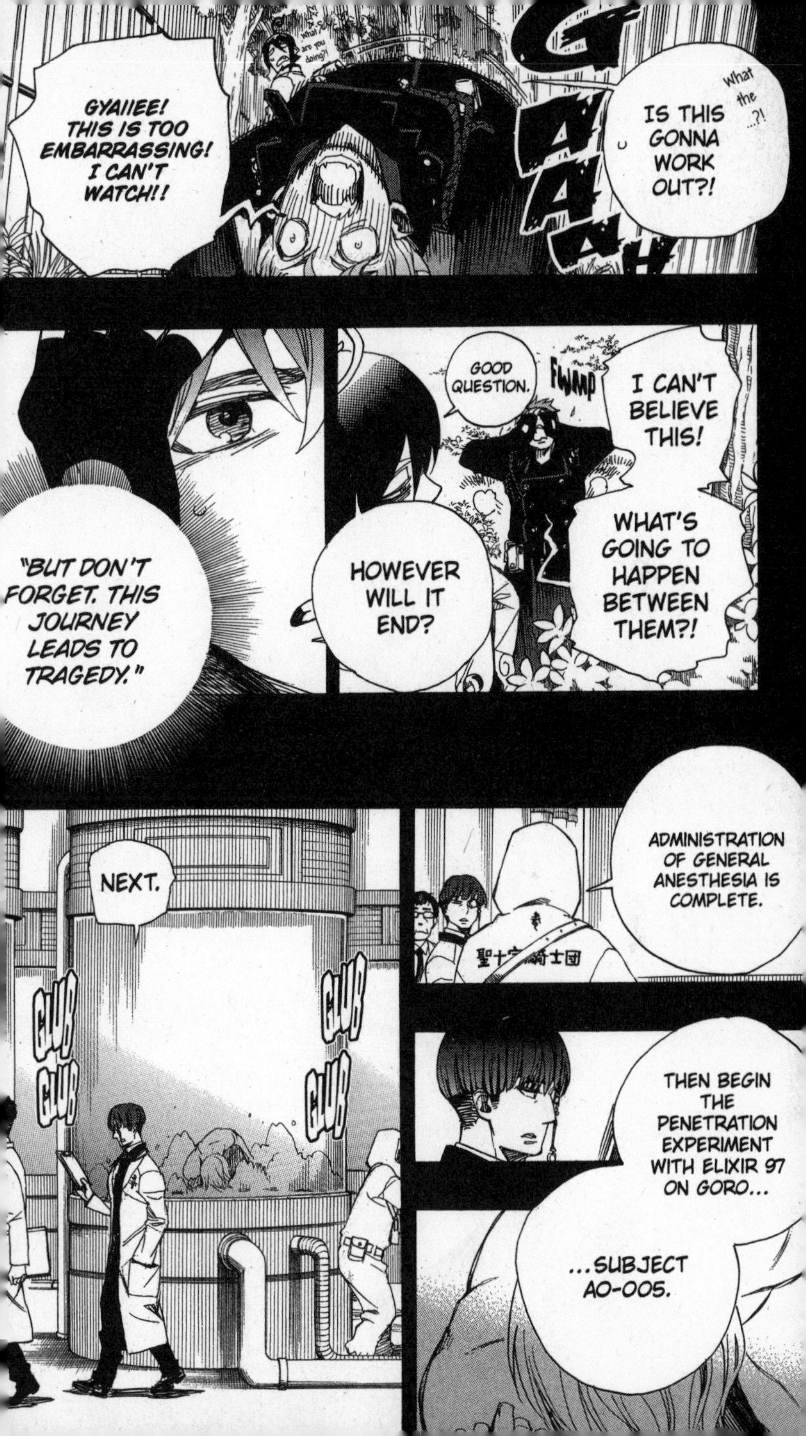
GAAAH
What the ...?!
IS THIS GONNA WORK OUT?!
What are you doing?!
GYAIIEE! THIS IS TOO EMBARRASSING! I CAN'T WATCH!!
I CAN'T BELIEVE THIS!
GOOD QUESTION.
FWMP
WHAT'S GOING TO HAPPEN BETWEEN THEM?!
HOWEVER WILL IT END?
"BUT DON'T FORGET. THIS JOURNEY LEADS TO TRAGEDY."
ADMINISTRATION OF GENERAL ANESTHESIA IS COMPLETE.
THEN BEGIN THE PENETRATION EXPERIMENT WITH ELIXIR 97 ON GORO...
...SUBJECT AO-005.
NEXT.
CLUB CLUB
CLUB CLUB

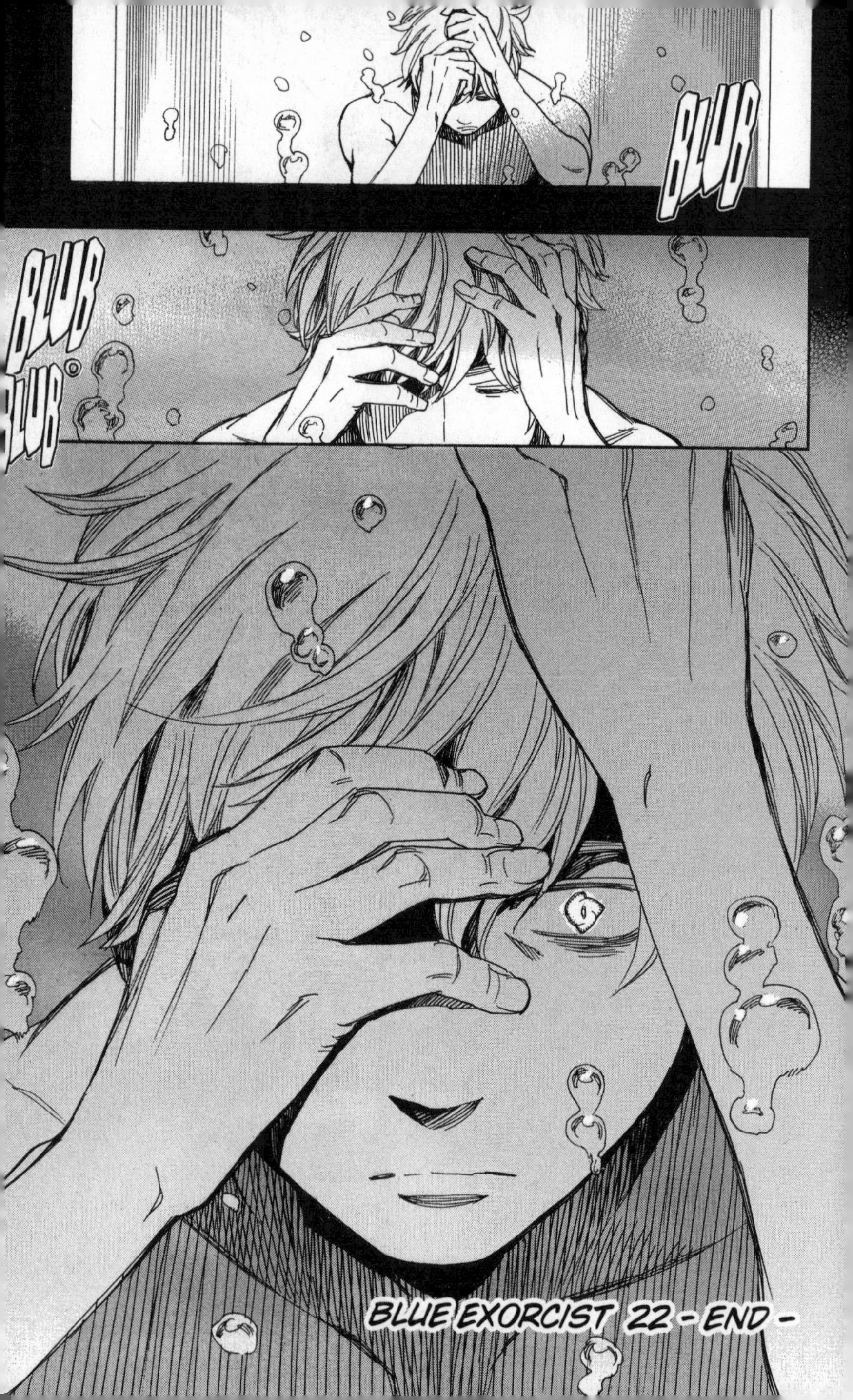
BLUB
BLUB BLUB
BLUE EXORCIST 22 - END -

BLUE EXORCIST CHAPTER 103: SsC11:29

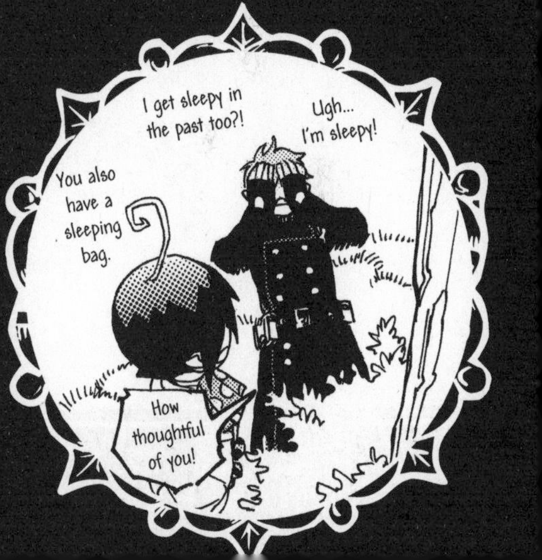
Ugh... I'm sleepy!
I get sleepy in the past too?!
You also have a sleeping bag.
How thoughtful of you!

BONUS

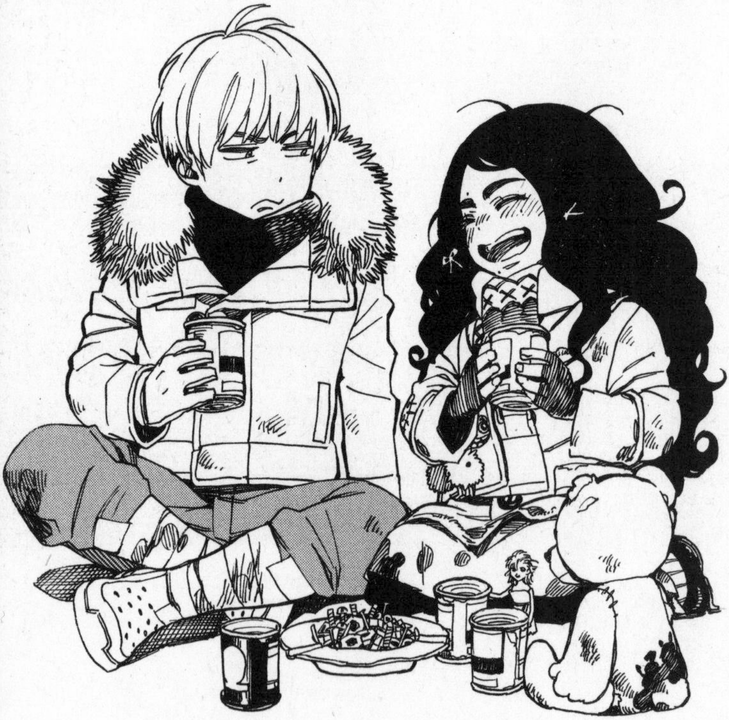

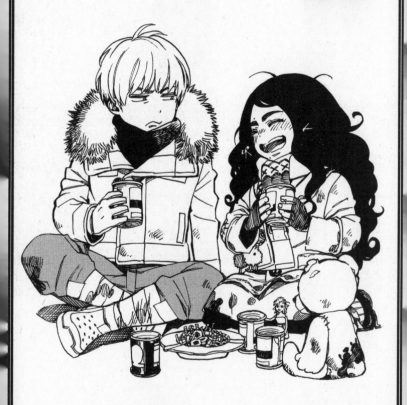

BLUE EXORCIST BONUS

BLUE QUESTORCIST

ALL RIGHT, LET'S KICK OFF VOLUME 22'S *QUESTORCIST!*

HOW MUCH DOES RIN EAT?

YUMI-RIINA (18), NIIGATA PREFECTURE

HOW MUCH? ME? UM...A NORMAL AMOUNT? I HAVE BREAKFAST AND EAT ABOUT THREE BREAD THINGIES BEFORE LUNCH. AFTER SCHOOL, I STOP BY THE DORM TO MAKE ABOUT FIVE RICE BALLS FOR TAKING TO CRAM SCHOOL. CLASSES FINISH ABOUT EIGHT OR NINE AT NIGHT, AND MY STOMACH IS KILLING ME BY THEN. SO WHEN I GET HOME, I EAT A LATE SUPPER. THAT'S NORMAL, RIGHT?

YES, THAT'S A NORMAL AMOUNT FOR A HIGH SCHOOL BOY.

OH...BUT AFTER I'VE EXERCISED A LOT, I'M SUPER HUNGRY, SO I EAT A TON OF MEAT AND RICE. I CAN GOBBLE UP FIVE SERVINGS IN NO TIME!

BUT THAT'S AN ***ABNORMAL*** AMOUNT.

DEMONS LIVE A LONG TIME, SO DO HUMANS WHO HAVE INHERITED DEMON BLOOD ALSO LIVE A LONG TIME?

FULL-POWER SO-SO (14), FUKUOKA PREFECTURE

I HEAR THEY DO. MY FAMILY HAS FOX-GOD BLOOD, AND I'VE HEARD THE FIRST GENERATION LIVED A LONG TIME. BUT MY GRANDMOTHER WAS THE 63RD GENERATION, AND SHE PASSED AWAY AT AGE 77, SO I DOUBT I'LL LIVE VERY LONG.

PEOPLE WHO ARE HALF DEMON AND HALF HUMAN ARE CALLED NEPHILIM, AND THE FIRST GENERATION INHERITS THE MOST POWER. BUT IF THE SECOND AND THIRD GENERATIONS' PARTNERS ARE HUMAN, THEIR CHILDREN'S DEMONIC ABILITIES WILL BE WEAKER.

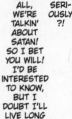

RIN OKUMURA IS A FIRST-GENERATION NEPHILIM BORN OF SATAN AND A HUMAN BEING, SO I BET HE'LL LIVE A LONG TIME.

HUH? SERIOUSLY?!

AFTER ALL, WE'RE TALKIN' ABOUT SATAN! SO I BET YOU WILL! I'D BE INTERESTED TO KNOW, BUT I DOUBT I'LL LIVE LONG ENOUGH TO FIND OUT. TOO BAD.

HUH? AM I REALLY GONNA LIVE THAT LONG?! I DON'T WANNA LIVE ON AFTER EVERYONE ELSE DIES! THAT'D SUCK!

YEAH. I DOUBT LIVING FOREVER WOULD BE A VERY HAPPY LIFE.

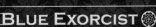

WELL, I DON'T THINK "FOREVER" IS POSSIBLE. I'VE HEARD THAT EVEN A LONG-LIVED NEPHILIM CAN ONLY LIVE ABOUT 200 YEARS. WHETHER A DEMON OR SOME OTHER LIFE-FORM, ALL MATTER CRUMBLES TO DUST. HOWEVER, YOU'RE THE FIRST NEPHILIM OF SATAN, SO I HAVE NO IDEA WHAT WILL HAPPEN. YOU MIGHT LIVE ON FOR ETERNITY OR YOUR BODY MIGHT GIVE OUT SOON.

THAT COULD HAPPEN ?!

MOST FIRST-GENERATION NEPHILIM LIVE A LONG TIME. DEPENDING ON THEIR CHARACTERISTICS, HOWEVER, THERE ARE CASES OF THEIR BODIES NOT LASTING. THEN THEY DIE, SORT OF LIKE HOW BODIES POSSESSED BY DEMONS RAPIDLY WEAKEN.

SO, UM... ANYWAY, YOU DON'T KNOW WHICH I'LL BE, RIGHT? I HOPE I DIE NATURALLY.

WELL, AT LEAST YOU'RE MATTER-OF-FACT ABOUT IT.

ACTUALLY, THOUGH, I DIDN'T REALLY GET MUCH OF THAT!

IN VOLUME 16, IT SEEMS LIKE THE THREE WISE MONKEYS ARE SERVING MEPHISTO. DOES THAT MEAN THEY'RE KIN OF THE KING OF TIME? OR IF YOU BECOME ONE OF THE BAAL, CAN YOU MAKE DEMONS WITH OTHER ATTRIBUTES OBEY YOU?

MOITOI (17), SHIGA PREFECTURE

FOR THE MOST PART, WE KINGS CAN ONLY USE OUR OWN KIN AS SUBORDINATES. BUT WE CAN USE DEMONS WITH OTHER ATTRIBUTES IF WE ASK THE KING OF THAT ELEMENT. SO IT'S IMPOSSIBLE FOR A KING TO BORROW DEMONS FROM A KING HE DOESN'T GET ALONG WELL WITH, BUT A KING CAN OFTEN BORROW FROM KINGS HE DOES GET ALONG WITH. IN MY CASE, I CAN BORROW DEMONS OF EARTH, INSECTS AND SPIRIT, BUT I CAN'T BORROW FROM LIGHT, FIRE, WATER AND ROT. THE THREE WISE MONKEYS DON'T BELONG TO ANY ELEMENT, SO I CAN REQUEST THEIR AID WHENEVER I WANT. I ACTUALLY GET ALONG WITH LOTS OF UNAFFILIATED DEMONS. THERE AREN'T MANY TIME DEMONS, SO THEY AREN'T VERY CONVENIENT.

HOW MANY TIMES HAS YUKIO RECEIVED A LOVE LETTER?

THE GREEN KNIGHT (12), OSAKA PREFECTURE

HUH?! A QUESTION FOR ME?! IN SEARCH OF POWER, I TURNED MY BACK ON TRUE CROSS ACADEMY AND MY OLDER BROTHER AND WENT TO THE ILLUMINATI. BUT YOU WANT TO KNOW HOW MANY LOVE LETTERS I GET? WHAT'S THE BIG IDEA?!

I UNDERSTAND YOUR CHAGRIN. I WAS GOING THROUGH A LOT AROUND THAT TIME TOO. BUT THE QUESTION CORNER HAS DEALT YOU THIS QUESTION, SO DON'T BE EMBARRASSED AND JUST TELL US.

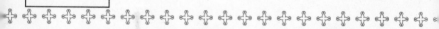

SORRY. TO BE HONEST, I HAVEN'T COUNTED. BUT I DOUBT IT'S UNDER 50.

WHAAAAAH?!

WHEN DID YUKIO START CALLING RIN HIS "BIG BROTHER"?

INDIGO EXORCIST (26), IWATE PREFECTURE

COME ON... ANOTHER ONE?!

HMM, I WONDER...

I DO OFTEN SPEAK TO YOU.

THESE ARE THE BONUS PAGES. AS A RULE, WE DON'T BRING IN STUFF FROM THE ACTUAL MANGA.

OH WELL. I'VE HEARD THAT THE TWINS OFTEN CALL EACH OTHER BY THEIR FIRST NAMES. IN THE ENGLISH TRANSLATION, I ACTUALLY USUALLY CALL YOU "RIN."

HUH? REALLY?!

I SEEM TO REMEMBER THAT I STARTED TO CALL YOU "BIG BROTHER" WHEN I WAS LITTLE BECAUSE I HEARD FATHER FUJIMOTO AND THE PEOPLE AT THE MONASTERY SAY THINGS LIKE, "RIN, YOU'RE HIS BIG BROTHER, RIGHT?" AND "YOU'RE HIS BIG BROTHER, SO DO YOUR BEST," WHEN THEY CHIDED OR COMFORTED YOU.

OH...COME TO THINK OF IT, WHEN I WAS LITTLE, THEY DID SAY STUFF LIKE THAT TO ME A LOT. IF THEY SAID, "TRY HARDER, BECAUSE YOU'RE YUKIO'S BIG BROTHER," THEN I WOULD TRY HARDER, SO THEY SAID IT TO ME ALL THE TIME. THAT SURE BRINGS BACK MEMORIES!

YEAH...

HEY, ISN'T IT ABOUT TIME WE STOPPED FIGHTING AND GOT ALONG? FIGHTING IS A PAIN.

WELL, THESE ARE THE BONUS PAGES. AS A RULE, WE DON'T BRING IN STUFF FROM THE ACTUAL MANGA.

TCH! OKAY... AS A TEST, CALL ME RIN!

WHY?! I DON'T WANT TO!

C'MON, DON'T BE EMBARRASSED.

I'M NOT EMBARRASSED!!

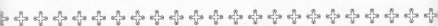

ON PAGES 62 AND 63 OF VOLUME 15, THERE'S A SCENE WHERE LUCIFER MAKES MICHAEL GEDOIN DISAPPEAR. WHY DID ONLY HIS HAIR REMAIN? SURELY IT WASN'T A WIG! OR WOULD HAIR JUST FALL IN ONE PIECE LIKE THAT? AND NOT FALL APART?

I LOVE EXERCISE ♡ (12), NAGASAKI PREFECTURE

GEDOIN ISN'T IN THE MAIN MANGA ANYMORE, BUT I REGULARLY HEAR FROM PEOPLE WHO WONDER ABOUT HIM—WHICH MAKES ME HAPPY! BUT HAVING HIM SHOW UP HERE WOULD BE A HASSLE, SO I'LL HAVE THE THREE OTHERS WHO WERE THERE PROVIDE ACCOUNTS.

IT'S A TOUPEE.

YEP.

GASP... KOFF CHOKE GAG KOFF KOFFFF!!

LORD LUCIFER-RRRR!!

HEY, YOU!!

GYAAAAAAH!!

NEXT QUESTION!!

I LOVE THE WAY THE MALE CHARACTERS HAVE INCREDIBLY REALISTIC PERSONALITIES. DID YOU BASE THEM ON YOUR OWN SIBLINGS OR OTHER REAL BOYS?

DANDELION (?), TOKYO PREFECTURE

THANK YOU FOR THIS QUESTION! FOR THE MOST PART, I DON'T MODEL THE CHARACTERS, WHETHER BOYS OR GIRLS, ON REAL PEOPLE.

BUT I DO WANT TO CREATE CHARACTERS THAT RESONATE WITH READERS AND MAKE THEM SAY, "I TOTALLY UNDERSTAND!" OR "I KNOW PEOPLE LIKE THAT!" SO I'M HAPPY IF THEY COME ACROSS AS EVEN A LITTLE REALISTIC. AND I DO HAVE A BROTHER!

WHAT ARE THOSE THINGS LIKE HORNS ON RIN'S FOREHEAD?

TM OF TIME (12), FUKUOKA PREFECTURE

HM? (PAT PAT) WHOA! YOU'RE RIGHT! THEY'RE HARD! IS THAT BONE? ARE THEY GOOSE EGGS? SCARY!

I SUPPOSE FULLY AWAKENING AS SATAN'S NEPHILIM IS HAVING AN EFFECT ON YOUR BODY. I SUSPECT IT'S LIKE HOW YOUR HAIR COLOR CHANGED, BUT WHAT ARE THEY REALLY?

HORNS.

HORNS??! BUT THEY LOOK LIKE GOOSE EGGS! IF YOU WERE GONNA GIVE ME HORNS, YOU SHOULD'VE MADE THEM LOOK COOLER!

OKAY! GRAH!

YIIIKES!!!

WELL, THAT'S ALL FOR NOW!!

THE LEGEND OF BLUE EXORCIST 22

Art Staff

 NO, I'M NOT THAT FAR YET! — Erika Uemura

 OH... UNDERSTOOD. — Ryoji Hayashi

 THERE'S BEEN A BARRIER SINCE HIGH SCHOOL, SO IT WON'T GET OUT! — Mari Oda

 THANK YOU VERY MUCH! — Sai Yamagishi

 THIS IS MY HUSBAND'S ROOM! — Aki Shiina

Art Assistants

 I HEAR LIN IS LEAVING! — Yamanaka-san

 I COULDN'T SELL THE HAIR... — Obata-san

 IT'S YEAR 1 FOR THE GALAXY! — Yoshiyama-kun

 SPIN I'LL TREASURE IT! — Sasaki-kun

Editors

 EDITORIAL WILL GET ANGRY... — Tadahiro Fukushima

 I'LL DO MY BEST AT JUMP+! — Shihei Lin (in charge of media)

Graphic Novel Editor

 PLEASE! — Ryusuke Kuroki

Graphic Novel Design

THEY'RE DESIGNING A 2019 CALENDAR FOR ME! — Shimada Hideaki

 Daiju Asami (L.S.D.)

Manga

 I'LL MAKE A NICE WORKPLACE!! — Kazue Kato

(In no particular order)
(Note: The caricatures and statements are from memory!)

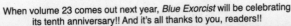 When volume 23 comes out next year, *Blue Exorcist* will be celebrating its tenth anniversary!! And it's all thanks to you, readers!!

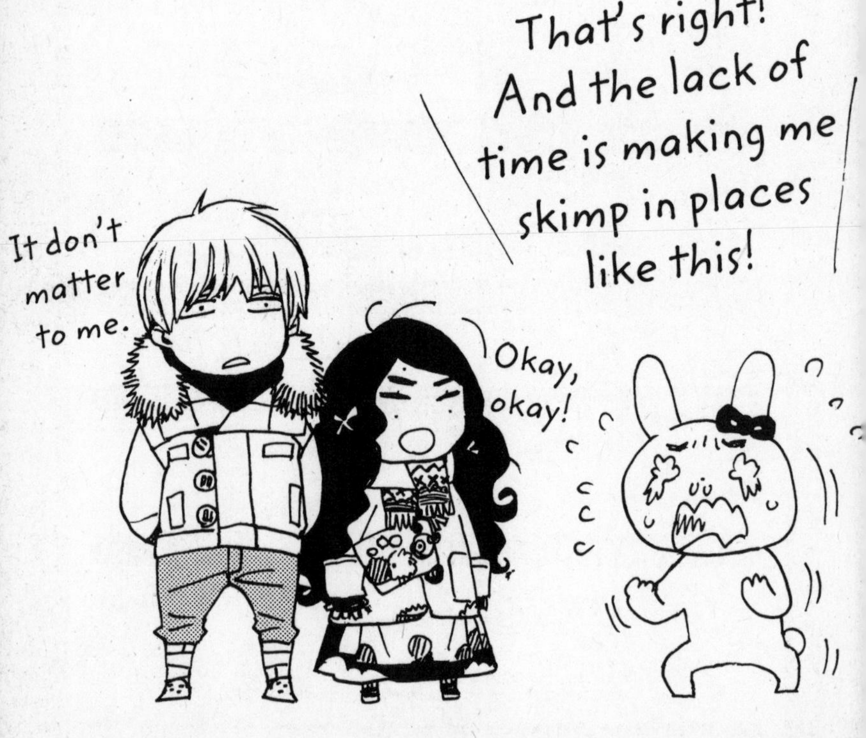
That's right! And the lack of time is making me skimp in places like this!
Okay, okay!
It don't matter to me.

Dark History

I'm Yuri.
What's your name?
Oh right...
... Guilty Silver-wolf.
I'm...
GAH
Guilty Silver-wolf?!
Wow...
That's kinda cool!!
Shiro!

4-panel comics are back!

I'm slowly building a house. (Status Update!)

It's so interesting...

KAZUE KATO

THIS VOLUME BEGINS TO EXPLORE SHIRO'S AND YURI'S PASTS AS THEY RELATE TO THE BLUE NIGHT. EVEN IF I PUSH THE STORY ALONG AT A FAST PACE, IT LOOKS LIKE IT COULD GET LONG. BUT I HAVE TO PAY SUFFICIENT ATTENTION TO CERTAIN EVENTS, SO I'M GOING TO PACE MYSELF LIKE I'M IN A RACE.

ENJOY THE MANGA!

BLUE EXORCIST

BLUE EXORCIST VOL. 22
SHONEN JUMP Manga Edition

STORY & ART BY KAZUE KATO

Translation & English Adaptation/John Werry
Touch-up Art & Lettering/John Hunt, Primary Graphix
Cover & Interior Design/Julian [JR] Robinson
Editor/Mike Montesa

Printed in the U.S.A.

Published by VIZ Media, LLC
P.O. Box 77010
San Francisco, CA 94107

10 9 8 7 6 5 4 3 2 1
First printing, September 2019

VIZ MEDIA
viz.com

SHONEN JUMP
shonenjump.com

ratings.viz.com
RATED T+ OLDER TEEN

PARENTAL ADVISORY
BLUE EXORCIST is rated T+ for Older Teen and is recommended for ages 16 and up. It contains violence, suggestive situations and some adult themes.

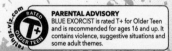

In the next volume...

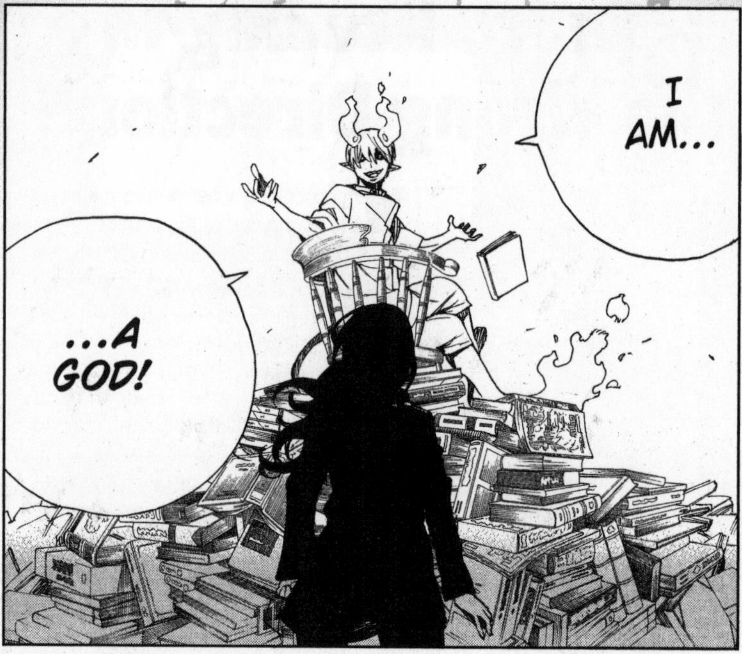
I AM...
...A GOD!

The tragic story of what happened to Rin and Yukio's mother, Yuri Egin, continues to unfold. Yuri and Father Fujimoto were once up-and-coming young Exorcists involved in Section 13's extensive operation to research elixirs of immortality and develop clones to house the spirits of demons. The project seemed to be moving ahead until the unexpected manifestation of a demonic spirt into one of the clone bodies. And this wasn't just any demon—the entity seemed to be the most powerful demon of all: Satan!

Coming February 2020!

You're Reading in the Wrong Direction!!

...arting at

...ing end of the comic!

...It's true! In keeping with the original Japanese format, **Blue Exorcist** is meant to be read from right to left, starting in the upper-right corner.

Unlike English, which is read from left to right, Japanese is read from right to left, meaning that action, sound effects and word-balloon order are completely reversed... something which can make readers unfamiliar with Japanese feel pretty backwards themselves. For this reason, manga or Japanese comics published in the U.S. in English have sometimes been published "flopped"—that is, printed in exact reverse order, as though seen from the other side of a mirror.

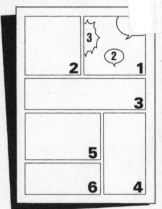

By flopping pages, U.S. publishers can avoid confusing readers, but the compromise is not without its downside. For one thing, a character in a flopped manga series who once wore in the original Japanese version a T-shirt emblazoned with "M A Y" (as in "the merry month of") now wears one which reads "Y A M"! Additionally, many manga creators in Japan are themselves unhappy with the process, as some feel the mirror-imaging of their art skews their original intentions.

We are proud to bring you Kazue Kato's **Blue Exorcist** in the original unflopped format. For now, though, turn to the other side of the book and let the adventure begin...!

—Editor